Oliver Ayer Roberts

The California Pilgrimage of Boston Commandery Knights Templars

August 4-September 4, 1883

Oliver Ayer Roberts

The California Pilgrimage of Boston Commandery Knights Templars
August 4-September 4, 1883

ISBN/EAN: 9783337297770

Printed in Europe, USA, Canada, Australia, Japan

Cover: Foto ©ninafisch / pixelio.de

More available books at **www.hansebooks.com**

THE
CALIFORNIA PILGRIMAGE
OF
BOSTON COMMANDERY
KNIGHTS TEMPLARS,

AUGUST 4 – SEPTEMBER 4, 1883.

BY SIR THE REV. OLIVER AYER ROBERTS,
PRELATE OF THE PILGRIMAGE.

PUBLISHED BY THE COMMITTEE IN CHARGE OF THE PILGRIMAGE.

BOSTON:
ALFRED MUDGE & SON, PRINTERS.
1884.

PREFACE.

"Attempt the end, and never stand to doubt;
Nothing's so hard but search will find it out."

UNAWARE, until subsequent to the return of the "pilgrims" to Boston, Sept. 4, 1883, that a compilation of the history of the pilgrimage would devolve upon me, I was unprepared for an immediate discharge of the duty with which the committee in charge of the California pilgrimage honored me. The work, however, was cheerfully undertaken. A vigorous gleaning from sources public and private has resulted in this volume, which, it is hoped, will prove a fitting memorial of an unprecedented pilgrimage. No thought or expense has been omitted that a volume cordially acceptable to the pilgrims might be produced.

The correspondence of "Ayer," published in the Boston *Journal*, was utilized as a beginning, from which this history has resulted. The search for the published experiences of different members of the party has been patient and diligent, and such correspondence has been freely woven into the story of the pilgrimage. The author would acknowledge his obligations to Geo. A. Crofutts, Esq., for aid received from his excellent overland guide in regard to distances, elevations, etc.; to Sir Charles E. Pierce, Captain General of St. Omer Commandery, for valued favors; to Messrs. Cummings,

Bean, Manning, Stephenson, and Dennis, general passenger agents of the railroads over which the pilgrimage was made, for kindnesses received, especially in procuring illustrations desired; to the San Francisco *Chronicle*, *Bulletin*, and *Call*, for copies of public addresses delivered during the Conclave, and for extracts, most of which are acknowledged in the body of the work; to Sir Tristam Burges, Grand Senior Warden of the Grand Commandery Knights Templars of California, for valuable assistance; and to W. W. Clapp, Esq., of the Boston *Journal*, for permission to utilize its correspondence relating to the pilgrimage.

The author has attempted only a compilation of the prominent facts connected with the pilgrimage, with such comments and explanations as seemed proper, and he hopes that the result of his labors will meet the approbation of the pilgrims.

Fraternally,
OLIVER AYER ROBERTS,
Prelate of the California Pilgrimage of Boston Commandery.

JULY 4, 1884.

CONTENTS.

CHAPTER I.
PAGE
INTRODUCTION 1

CHAPTER II.
SUGGESTION OF A PILGRIMAGE. APPOINTMENT OF COMMITTEES. REPORT OF COMMITTEE. PILGRIMAGE DECIDED UPON. GRAND TEMPLAR BALL. ITINERARY 8

CHAPTER III.
PRELIMINARY ORDER. PREPARATION FOR DEPARTURE. COMMANDERY OF KNIGHTS TEMPLARS OPENED. RECEPTION OF GRAND MASTER. COLLATION. MARCH TO DEPOT. LADIES RECEIVED. ROSTER OF THE COMMANDERY FOR THE PILGRIMAGE 39

CHAPTER IV.
DEPARTURE FROM BOSTON. NIGHT RIDE THROUGH VERMONT. MONTREAL AND FREDERICKSBURG, CANADA. PORT HURON, BATTLE CREEK, MICH. THORNTON, IND. CHICAGO AND QUINCY, ILL. KANSAS CITY, MO. 53

CHAPTER V.

Departure from Kansas City. Lawrence, Topeka, and Kinsley, Kansas. Colorado. La Junta. Raton Pass. Dick Wootton. New Mexico. Raton. Las Vegas Hot Springs. A Day's Tarry. Roster of the Pilgrims by Cars . 65

CHAPTER VI.

Las Vegas. Starvation Peak. Glorietta Pass. Rio Pecos. Santa Fé. "The Tertio." Extracts from the "New Mexicana." Wallace. Indian Dances. Eagle. Rincon. Good By 91

CHAPTER VII.

Deming. Bowie. Tucson. Great American Desert. Yuma. Southern California. Colton. Los Angeles. Reception, Visit, and Departure. Extracts from Los Angeles Papers. Merced. Oakland. Arrival at San Francisco. Reception. Palace Hotel. Dismissal . 109

CHAPTER VIII.

California's Greeting. Palace Hotel. Headquarters and their Decorations. Welcome of Grand Master. Serenades . 133

CHAPTER IX.

Grand Conclave Ball. Description of the Pavilion. Sir Sol. Smith Russell at Bush Street Theatre. Chinatown. Chinese Theatre, etc. 146

CHAPTER X.

Triennial Committee. Ladies' Triennial Union. Decorations. Masonic Temple. Arches. Hospitalities 164

CONTENTS. xi

CHAPTER XI.
PROGRAMME FOR CONCLAVE WEEK. SUNDAY SERVICES AT THE PAVILION. SERMON OF V. E. SIR THE REV. CLINTON LOCKE, D. D., GRAND PRELATE . 173

CHAPTER XII.
GRAND PARADE. TENTH DIVISION. STREETS AND THE PROCESSION. GRAND MASTER'S RECEPTION AT THE PAVILION. ADDRESSES. CONCLUSION 194

CHAPTER XIII.
BOSTON COMMANDERY ESCORTS THE GRAND MASTER TO MASONIC TEMPLE. OPENING OF THE CONCLAVE. EXTRACTS FROM ADDRESS OF GRAND MASTER. ELECTION OF OFFICERS. ORDER OF THANKS 221

CHAPTER XIV.
EXCURSIONS: NAPA VALLEY, MENLO PARK, HARBOR, SANTA CRUZ, SANTA ROSA, ETC. GRAND BANQUET. BREAKFAST GIVEN BY MARYSVILLE COMMANDERY. GRAND RECEPTION GIVEN BY BOSTON COMMANDERY . 228

CHAPTER XV.
LAYING CORNER-STONE OF GARFIELD MONUMENT. PAGEANT. COMPETITIVE DRILL, AND AWARDING PRIZES. FAREWELL ADDRESS TO THE TEMPLARS. PREPARATIONS OF BOSTON COMMANDERY FOR LEAVING. ITS FINAL VISIT. DEPARTURE FROM SAN FRANCISCO 261

CHAPTER XVI.
HOMEWARD. CROSSING THE MOUNTAINS. CAPE HORN SNOW-SHEDS. DONNER LAKE. TRUCKEE. RENO. NEVADA DESERT. OGDEN. SALT LAKE CITY 275

CHAPTER XVII.
SALT LAKE CITY. SIGHT-SEEING. IMPRESSIONS. VISIT TO GARFIELD. BATHING. EXTRACTS FROM NEWSPAPERS OF SALT LAKE CITY 291

CHAPTER XVIII.

DEPARTURE FROM OGDEN. GREEN RIVER. RAWLINGS. LARAMIE. SHERMAN. NORTH PLATTE. GRAND ISLAND AND COUNCIL BLUFFS. BURLINGTON. CHICAGO. BATTLE CREEK. PORT HURON. TORONTO AND MONTREAL . 305

CHAPTER XIX.

SUNDAY-EVENING SERVICE AT WINDSOR HOTEL, MONTREAL. SERMON BY REV. OLIVER AYER ROBERTS . . . 323

CHAPTER XX.

MONTREAL. EXTRACTS FROM MONTREAL PAPERS. LACHINE RAPIDS. DEPARTURE. KEENE. ARRIVAL IN BOSTON. RECEPTION. DE MOLAY COMMANDERY. BANQUET. ADDRESSES. CONCLAVE CLOSED . . . 336

CHAPTER XXI.

THE OFFICERS OF THE PILGRIMAGE, THEIR DUTIES AND EFFICIENCY . 351

CHAPTER XXII.

CONCLAVE OF BOSTON COMMANDERY, SEPT. 12, 1883. CORRESPONDENCE AND TESTIMONIALS . . 357

CHAPTER XXIII.

RECEPTION AT THE VENDÔME. ADDRESSES, PRESENTATIONS, ETC. 377

ILLUSTRATIONS.

		PAGE
1.	Portrait of Sir John L. Stevenson, P.·. E.·. Commander	*Frontispiece.*
2.	Windsor Hotel, Montreal	55
3.	Map of the Chicago, Burlington and Quincy Railroad	61
4.	Map of the Atchison, Topeka and Santa Fé Railroad	64
5.	Dogs on Guard	65
6.	Topeka, Kansas	66
7.	A Frontier Town	68
8.	Arkansas Valley.—Hutchinson in the Distance	70
9.	The New Settlement	72
10.	Wealth on Foot	73
11.	Stampede	74
12.	Dogtown	75
13.	The Old Way	76
14.	Dick Wootton at Home	77
15.	Raton Tunnel	78
16.	Raton Mountains	80
17.	Montezuma Hotel, Las Vegas Hot Springs, N. M.	82
18.	Starvation Peak	91
19.	Seal of New Mexico	92
20.	Santa Fé, from rear of Palace Hotel	94
21.	San Miguel Church and College	96
22.	The Plaza, Santa Fé	98

		PAGE
23.	The Palace, Santa Fé	100
24.	The Priest of Santa Fé	102
25.	Ship of the Desert at Anchor	105
26.	Primitive Agriculture	107
27.	Tucson, Arizona	110
28.	Indigenous to the Soil	112
29.	Indian Oven	113
30.	Adobe Fireplace	113
31.	Los Angeles, Cal.	117
32.	An Avenue at Los Angeles	120
33.	Bird's-eye View of the Loop	125
34.	Crossing the Loop	126
35.	Old Jesuit Church, California	128
36.	Palace Hotel, San Francisco, Cal.	134
37.	Cable Road and Cars	153
38.	Arch of Welcome, San Francisco	168
39.	Portrait of Past Grand Master Dean	221
40.	Cliff House and Seal Rocks	229
41.	Seal Rocks, from the Hotel	230
42.	Map of the Central Pacific and Union Pacific Railroads	276
43.	Looking up at Cape Horn	278
44.	American River Cañon	279
45.	Mountain Summits	280
46.	Snow-Sheds	281
47.	Interior of Snow-Shed	282
48.	Truckee River	285
49.	Palisades of the Humboldt River	286
50.	Ogden, Utah	288
51.	Salt Lake City	292
52.	Tabernacle and River Jordan	294
53.	Young's late Residence, Salt Lake City	296
54.	Devil's Slide, Weber Cañon, Utah	304

ILLUSTRATIONS.

		PAGE
55.	Green River City and Castle Rocks	306
56.	Pulpit Rock, Echo Cañon, Utah	308
57.	Finger Rock, Weber Cañon, Utah	309
58.	Hanging Rock, Echo Cañon, Utah	310
59.	A Dug-Out	311
60.	Approaching Council Bluffs, Iowa	312
61.	Missouri River Bridge, Omaha	313
62.	View near Stanton, Iowa	314
63.	View near Chillicothe, Iowa	315
64.	View near Ottumwa, Iowa	316
65.	Pulpit Rock	318
66.	Devil's Slide, from Union Pacific Railroad	320
67.	The Charging Bison	338
68.	Victoria Bridge, Montreal	340

BOSTON COMMANDERY KNIGHTS TEMPLARS.

CALIFORNIA PILGRIMAGE, 1883.

CHAPTER I.

PILGRIMAGES are of ancient origin and of almost universal adoption. The first Christian pilgrims of note were Constantine the Great and his mother, Helena. When the latter was seventy-nine years old, A. D. 326, they journeyed from Rome to Jerusalem, and on the authenticated sites of the nativity and crucifixion caused splendid churches to be erected, parts of which still remain. It was an easy and natural transition, when these world-thrilling events became localized, for Christian converts who had been Jews, and had made Jewish pilgrimages to the Temple yearly, or who had been pagans and had made pagan pilgrimages to Olympus, Delos, Delphi, etc., having given up their sacred spots, to revere and visit those places made sacred by the life and death of Jesus the Christ. Thus Christian pilgrimages began, and among the first was that occasioned by the dedication of the Church of the Holy Sepulchre, when an immense concourse of people, including ecclesiastics of every grade, assembled in Jerusalem from all parts of the Christian world. To Christians all Palestine became sacred soil; pilgrimages and pilgrims multiplied. For centuries they increased in frequency and numbers, until the swelling tide became a flood, and vehement devotion gave way to general superstition.

A temporary halt of the swarming multitudes was made when Jerusalem was captured by the Persians in A. D. 611. Peace having been effected by the pilgrims with the Persians, and subsequently on severe terms with Caliph Omar, the pilgrim tide began again to flow. Three centuries of cruelty and kindness, alternately exercised by the Mohammedan caliphs, followed, when (A. D. 1076) the Seljukian Turks conquered Palestine and maintained a violent persecution against the Christian pilgrims. Peter the Hermit was one of the unfortunate pilgrims. The sufferings which he saw and experienced so burned within him that, returning to Europe, he fired it with the spirit of the First Crusade. The Seljukian invaders assigned Christian churches to profanation, Christian youths and maidens to shameful slavery, and ninety thousand Christians to slaughter. Lawful toll on pilgrims became highway robbery, and insults were heaped alike on priests and people. The pilgrims still went forth by thousands and returned by tens, the multitudes having been reduced by the wanton cruelties of barbaric "infidels."

Nine Crusades were organized from A. D. 1096 to A. D. 1291. The Crusaders wended their toilsome way to the disputed field, alternately met victory and despair until A. D. 1291, when the period closed with the loss of Acre, the death of the Master of the Templars, and the reddening of the sea with the blood of the Crusaders.

Christian pilgrimages, unwarlike in character, have again risen, and annually thousands of pilgrims from all parts of the world gather on Easter day in the holy places of Palestine — notably the Church of the Holy Sepulchre — and descend to the swift

Jordan for baptism. Christian pilgrims penetrate Egypt seeking a Christian shrine. Multitudes visit Rome, with its St. Peter's and Tombs of the Apostles; others Loreto, the site of Mary's house. The churches at Treves, Cologne, Prague, Compostela, and scores of others have been considered sacred places whither repeated pilgrimages have been made. England, Scotland, and Ireland have their pilgrim shrines; so has America, — one south near Mexico, one north near Quebec. Mohammedans yearly make pilgrimages to Mecca and Medina, and in Hindostan, pilgrims resort to Juggernaut and Benares. The almond-eyed pilgrims visit Isje, and the Japanese Buddhists have as their Sinai the volcano of Fusiyama, near Yeddo. That these pilgrimages are founded on superstition and maintained through ignorance is probably true. The "Black-Stone" of Mecca, or the Rock of the Noble Sanctuary in Jerusalem, is not more sacred than the cliffs of the Golden Gate; "Santa Casa," the sacred house, than the Palace Hotel; Benares or Rome than San Francisco. "Righteousness is not in the East nor mercy in the West." The end sought by Mohammedan, Buddhist, Japanese, or Christian pilgrims may as readily be reached and enjoyed at their own hearth-stones as in circling the Caaba, climbing Sinai, visiting Isje, or grasping heaven's fire in the Church of the Holy Sepulchre from the hand of the Greek patriarch.

The early Christian pilgrims set out on their perilous pilgrimage after religious solemnities had been observed. Each pilgrim was presented with a scrip and staff and with a coarse woollen gown which bore the sign of the cross. He took with him neither money nor arms. His passport from his sovereign and letter from his bishop were his vouchers as a Christian pilgrim, and they obtained for him hospitality and protection. There were dangers on the way, however, especially when traversing Turkish dominions. Hospitals and monasteries were erected, where the wayfarers found comfort and safety, and a guard of poor Fellow-soldiers of Jesus Christ patrolled between Joppa and Jerusalem, also between Jerusalem and the Jordan.

When the arm of power was lifted by the Turks against these defenceless pilgrims, military organizations sprang into existence which were for centuries the right arm of the Church. Chiefest of these was the brotherhood of Knights Templars. Originally it was composed of nine distinguished knights, "who bound themselves by a solemn compact to protect pious pilgrims exposed to plunder and death, to aid one another in clearing the highways of infidels and robbers, and to guard the pilgrims through the passes and defiles of the mountains to the Holy City." Subsequently they added to their profession that of defending Jerusalem and the Eastern Church against the infidels. The order was speedily established in Europe. A dress was prescribed for it by St. Bernard. Pope Eugenius, some years after, added a red cross as a symbol of martyrdom. Knights journeyed from Europe and took the places of those fallen in the strife, or were added to the valiant brotherhood. The fearlessness, persistence, and valor of the Order, as displayed in the field, are beyond question.

For nearly two centuries the conflict was waged. The Crusades, begun for the protection of poor and weary pilgrims travelling from afar, who desired to offer up their devotions at the shrine of their departed Lord, developed into a Holy War, whose aim was the rescue of the Holy Sepulchre from the hands of infidels. The war was sanctified by the Church, and the knights were initiated by rites which the Church made sacred. With a zeal, sacrifice, and valor which have been the admiration of the world, the unequal contest was carried on. The Knights Templars, driven from city to city, and, finally, from Palestine, settled on the island of Cyprus, which the Order purchased for thirty-five thousand marks.

For one hundred and eighty years afterwards they continued to increase in power, fame, and wealth. In the early part of the fourteenth century Philip the Fair, an avaricious, vindictive prince, through his hatred, avarice, and jealousy, concerted with Pope Clement V. to destroy the Order and appropriate their wealth. Therefore Jacques de Molay, Grand Master, was summoned from Cyprus to Paris to consult on important matters. On arrival, he was immediately imprisoned, and soon after every Knight Templar in France was by the king's orders arrested on the charge of idolatry. "False witness, tortures, hunger, thirst, darkness, filth, and disease in sunless dungeons, were all used . . . to subdue the warriors who on the field never quailed." In 1310 fifty-four of the knights were, after a mock trial, publicly burnt, and in 1314 De Molay and the three principal officers of the Order suffered the same fate.

The Order was suppressed, but its pilgrimage was not ended. It was not annihilated. In anticipation of his fate, De Molay appointed his successor, and from that time (A. D. 1313-14) to the present there has been a regular and uninterrupted succession of Grand Masters. The Encampment of Baldwin was established at Bristol, England, by the Templars who returned with Richard I. from Palestine, and it still continues to hold its regular meetings. One Encampment at Bath, and another at York, with Baldwin Encampment, constitute the three original Encampments of England. From these have emanated the existing Commanderies in the United States, which thus directly stand related to the Knights Templars of the Crusades.

The Order of Knights Templars in the United States, as throughout the world, retains much of its ancient character. It has also changed in its character as our form of government and this peaceful era have demanded. It still professes "to protect the defenceless, feed the hungry, clothe the naked, bind up the wounds of the afflicted," to be loyal to their country, and to defend the Christian faith. It cultivates charity, social brotherhood, and hospitality. Its mission is peace and good-will among all men. The pilgrimages of modern Knights Templars result from this social and brotherly sentiment. More or fewer Commanderies in the country celebrate every return of St. John's Day (June 24) by pilgrimages to neighboring *fratres*, and some have extended their trips into different States or made a pilgrimage across the ocean to greet the Knights of Baldwin and York.

Boston Commandery has in recent years made pilgrimages to Philadelphia, New York City, thence home by Hudson River and Hoosac Tunnel, Isles of Shoals, White Mountains, N. H.; but its most extended pilgrimage, and the most successful of the times, was that of which this book pretends to give but little more than the outline. It was undertaken to escort Sir Benjamin Dean, Grand Master, to San Francisco, to attend the Twenty-second Triennial Conclave of the Grand Encampment, Knights Templars of the United States, and to bear the banner of the oldest Commandery in this country from the Atlantic to the Pacific, and to bring it back untarnished and honored. It was undertaken for pleasure, profit, and fellowship, — the pleasure of seeing our vast domain, its plains, rivers, and mountains, of realizing its diversity of climate and productions, and of beholding what the hand of man hath wrought in a century. It was undertaken for profit in new vigor of the body, new food for the mind, and new and enlarged fellowship. It was undertaken to evince the loyalty of Boston Commandery to the Order, and its cordial brotherhood towards all the *fratres* wherever scattered throughout the Union. It was begun, carried forward, and completed with a spirit of permissible pride that Boston Commandery might accomplish this unprecedented pilgrimage, bringing no reproach upon her banner, upon the Order, nor upon the city whose name it bears, but winning the respect of the brotherhood, and the good opinion of the people. It is not too much to say that all this was done; the true ends of the pilgrimage were successfully attained, and the fondest expectations more than realized.

CHAPTER II.

For some years prior to 1880, there was a desire on the part of many members of Boston Commandery that the body should make an extended pilgrimage. Both place and time were not generally considered of such moment as the pilgrimage itself. In the fall of 1877, a number of Sir Knights belonging to Boston Commandery were conversing in regard thereto, when Sir Abijah Thompson, observing the unanimity of the party "to go somewhere," asked, "Well, where shall we go?" Sir Knight John L. Stevenson, with his usual decision and directness, replied, "To San Francisco, California. Let us make a pilgrimage that will be a credit to the Commandery and worthy of being called a pilgrimage." On his return from the Conclave held at Chicago, 1880, his mind was made up that Boston Commandery ought to be present in San Francisco, at the Conclave of 1883. The above, so far as is now known, was the first suggestion of the grand pilgrimage of Boston Commandery in August, 1883.

The suggestion was developed by proper action at the beginning of 1881.

At the regular Conclave of Boston Commandery, held Wednesday, Jan. 19, 1881, Sir John L. Stevenson, Generalissimo, offered the following motion: —

That a committee of five be appointed to report, at the next regular Conclave, a plan to create a sinking fund for the purpose of defraying the expenses in part or entirely of such Sir Knights as may subscribe thereto, and are desirous of visiting San Francisco, Cal., in August, 1883, on the occasion of the Twenty-second Triennial Conclave of the Grand Encampment of the United States.

The motion was unanimously passed, and the Sovereign Master appointed as the committee, Sir John L. Stevenson, Eminent Sir Samuel C. Lawrence, Sir Albert T. Whiting, Sir Albert A. Folsom, and Sir Charles J. Hayden. Feb. 24, 1881, the committee met at Masonic Temple and organized. Sir John L. Stevenson was elected chairman, Sir Samuel C. Lawrence treasurer, and Sir Z. H. Thomas secretary.

The subject of a pilgrimage to San Francisco having been thoroughly considered by the committee, in order to give direction to its efforts, the following paper was prepared, unanimously adopted, and issued for general information: —

KNIGHTS TEMPLARS.

The committee charged with the duty of organizing an excursion of Sir Knights of this Commandery, with such other Sir Knights as may desire to join them, to visit San Francisco, Cal., on the occasion of the Twenty-second Triennial Conclave of the Grand Encampment of Knights Templars of the

United States, which occurs on the third Tuesday in August, 1883, have adopted the following rules, and now solicit your subscription thereto: —

RULES.

SUBSCRIPTIONS.

Subscriptions will be received from Sir Knights in sums of five dollars, or more, payable monthly (or any multiple of the sum subscribed may be paid in advance, if preferred), and the total amount of each individual subscription shall be applied toward defraying the expenses of the subscriber on the pilgrimage.

DEPOSITS.

Deposits may be withdrawn prior to June 1, 1883, less ten per cent for general expenses, by giving thirty days' notice thereof. After that date no moneys can be withdrawn without the unanimous consent of the committee.

In case of the death of a subscriber, however, the sum paid in shall be refunded to the legal representative of the subscribing Sir Knight on demand and without any abatement.

SIR KNIGHTS NOT MEMBERS.

Sir Knights not members of Boston Commandery, desirous of participating in the pilgrimage, can do so by presenting their names to the committee, and if accepted, by subscribing to the fund, and conforming to the rules and regulations governing the excursion.

SIR KNIGHTS:

An excursion of the magnitude projected requires time to perfect the details, money to pay the expenses, and numbers commensurate with the dignity of the occasion. Many Sir Knights will require nearly all the time now intervening to arrange for an absence of thirty or forty days from their business and professional engagements at the time specified; hence it is not premature to take the preliminary steps in this matter, and it is very desirable that the Knights should at once decide whether they will subscribe to the roll of pilgrims and thus give an impetus to the excursion which will insure its undoubted success.

The method adopted of paying money monthly toward defraying the expenses of an excursion is one that has been tried many times by Commanderies in other jurisdictions with success, and several Commanderies have already resorted to the same plan in furtherance of their contemplated trip to San Francisco. While it is an undoubted fact that the greater number of our members could at any time pay the sum necessary for the trip without inconvenience, yet upon the whole it is believed that an advantage will be gained by monthly payments, for thereby a greater interest will be created and maintained in the proposed trip, and under this method some Knights will find it more easily practicable to provide means for themselves and their wives to participate in a grand excursion which it is expected will prove one of the most interesting and enjoyable ever made by a Commandery of Knights Templars.

The rapidly increasing facilities for travelling great distances with speed, comfort, and safety fully warrant us in assuming that any number which may participate in this trip can be well accommodated on the road, and the palatial hotels of San Francisco will provide every comfort and convenience enjoyed at home. Then let the banner of old Boston Commandery be borne from the Atlantic to the Pacific, supported by such a retinue of Knights in black regalia as shall win applause from our sister Commanderies, reflect honor upon the Order, and command respect wherever it appears. If you intend to participate, let us urge you to SIGN THE ROLL WITHOUT DELAY, as by so doing you will encourage others to do likewise, and materially lessen the labors of the committee. The cost of the excursion can only be estimated at present, for many changes in fares and hotel rates are liable to occur within two years; but an approximate estimate based upon information obtained by the committee is from two hundred and fifty to three hundred dollars, including all necessary expenses. It is desirable that the Commandery should not be limited to the shortest possible time in which the visit to San Francisco can be accomplished, but that arrangements should be made whereby courtesies *en route* may be received, and points of interest away from the direct line of travel be visited.

Sir Knights, we have here given you an outline of the plans. As time passes we shall have other information to communicate, and suggestions to make in regard to matters in which we may require your support and assistance, — all looking toward the successful accomplishment of the pilgrimage at the minimum of expense and with the maximum of enjoyment. Subscriptions can be paid to either of the committee or the recorder, who as secretary of the committee will give a receipt for all moneys paid in, and promptly turn the same over to the treasurer for investment and safe keeping.

Courteously yours,

JOHN L. STEVENSON, CHAIRMAN,
    2 and 4 Faneuil Hall Square.
SAMUEL C. LAWRENCE, TREASURER,
    127 Broad Street.
ALBERT A. FOLSOM,
    Providence R. R. Depot.
ALBERT T. WHITING,
    35 Devonshire Street.
CHARLES J. HAYDEN,
    39 Court Street.

} *Committee.*

S. A. Thomas,
    Recorder, and Secretary of the Committee.

At the regular Conclave of Boston Commandery, held at its asylum, Wednesday evening, Nov. 15, 1882, the Sovereign Master, chairman of the committee on California pilgrimage, reported the progress that had been made by the committee since its organization in February, 1881.

The rules adopted by the committee, Feb. 24, 1881, were read by him, and he continued his report, saying, "More than thirty Sir Knights have subscribed to these rules or articles, and if the pilgrimage is positively decided upon, there are others who are ready to subscribe. The estimated cost of the trip, including railroad fare, hotel bills, transfers, etc., is three hundred dollars, and when the distance, accommodations, and the plan of the pilgrimage are considered, it must be thought a very low price. The committee has reviewed this subject of a pilgrimage to California in every phase possible, and unanimously concludes it is not only feasible, but desirable. It is their opinion that as the time for departure draws nigh, the requisite number will be obtained, and that the pilgrimage will not only be beneficial to those Sir Knights who participate, but also beneficial to the Commandery as a body of Knights Templars." The report was accepted, and,

On motion of Sir John H. North, it was

Voted, That the report be accepted, and that Boston Commandery visit San Francisco, Cal., at the time fixed for holding the Twenty-second Triennial Conclave of the Grand Encampment of Knights Templars of the United States, which is Aug 21, 1883, and that the committee appointed at the February Conclave in 1881, to organize an excursion to San Francisco, be constituted a committee of arrangements for the pilgrimage, with the same powers as then delegated them by the Commandery, no part of the expense of said pilgrimage to be drawn from the treasury, excepting by special vote of the Commandery to that effect.

At the same Conclave, on motion of Sir Thomas F. Temple, it was

Voted, That the Council and seven other Sir Knights, to be appointed by the Eminent Commander, be a committee to devise "ways and means" to provide a fund to be applied towards defraying the expenses of the California pilgrimage in August, 1883, and that said committee be authorized to take such action as they may deem advisable in the name of the Commandery, excepting that no money shall be drawn from the treasury on their account.

The committee, consisting of the Council and seven other Sir Knights, "to devise ways and means," authorized by the motion offered by Sir Thomas F. Temple, was announced by the Sovereign Master to be as follows: —

EM∴ SIR JOHN L. STEVENSON,
SIR EDWIN WRIGHT,   } Council.
SIR EUGENE H. RICHARDS,

SIR THOMAS F. TEMPLE.   SIR WILLIAM P. TYLER.
SIR DANIEL W. LAWRENCE.   SIR JAMES P. PHINNEY.
SIR EDWARD T. NICHOLS.   SIR JONAS G. SHILLABER.
SIR ALBERT A. FOLSOM.

The first meeting of the committee was held at Masonic Temple, Thursday evening, Nov. 23, 1882. Eminent Sir John L. Stevenson was chairman, and Sir Albert A. Folsom was elected treasurer, and Sir Z. H. Thomas secretary of the committee. After a general consultation as to the best way to devise means for the purposes of the pilgrimage, the committee adjourned to Nov. 27, when the chairman recommended giving a Knight Templar ball on a scale of magnificence hitherto unattempted in New England, and the following motion was passed: —

Voted, That the Eminent Commander be authorized to engage the Charitable Mechanic Building for the purpose of a grand Templar ball, to be given by Boston Commandery, Feb. 22, 1883, to establish a fund towards defraying the expenses of the California pilgrimage in August, 1883.

This motion was subsequently changed on account of the firemen's ball, Feb. 21, in the Mechanic Building, and the 31st of January was substituted for the 22d of February. Frequent meetings of this committee were held during the months of December and January.

The following prospectus and announcement of Sir Knight managers was issued by the committee: —

BOSTON COMMANDERY KNIGHTS TEMPLARS

⁂GRAND✠RECEPTION✠AND✠BALL⁂

— IN —

Massachusetts Charitable Mechanic Building,

HUNTINGTON AVENUE,

Wednesday Evening, Jan. 31, 1883.

All Knights Templars will be cordially welcomed to a full participation in this grand social event, to which the entire Masonic Fraternity are invited.

The entire building, having been engaged, on this occasion will be brilliantly lighted with electric lights, and appropriately decorated. The immense space at our disposal will enable us to provide properly for the comfort and convenience of all who may honor us with their presence.

The Most Eminent Grand Master of the United States, and all the Right Eminent Grand Commanders of New England have permitted the use of their names in aid of this grand gathering of Knights Templars, and the Masonic Fraternity, on a scale of magnificence hitherto unequalled.

Gen. Samuel C. Lawrence, Past Eminent Commander of Boston Commandery, and the present Grand Master of Masons in Massachusetts, will be Earl Marshal at the reception. Sir Knight the Hon. James A. Fox, Mayor of Cambridge, is chairman of the reception committee. Several Commanderies will attend in a body, with banners and jewels.

Nothing will be left undone by the management to make this reception and ball the event of the season, not only in Masonic circles, but, as a society affair, the equal of any ever given in this city. Invitations to attend the reception and ball have been extended to His Excellency the Governor of Massachusetts and his staff, the President of the Massachusetts Senate, the Speaker of the House of Representatives, His Honor the Mayor of Boston, and other distinguished civilians.

The music will be furnished by Carter's Orchestra of fifty pieces, T. M. Carter, conductor, and Baldwin's Boston Cadet Band of forty pieces, J. Thomas Baldwin, conductor. At eight o'clock concert music will be given by the consolidated bands, ninety pieces. At half past eight Boston Commandery will enter the hall in full regalia, and there receive visiting Commanderies and distinguished guests. At ten o'clock the grand march of Knights Templars with their ladies will begin. No one not in full regalia will participate in this march. At the conclusion of the march dancing will commence, in which all may join. Jewels of the several Masonic degrees will be worn.

First-class catering. Price, one dollar per plate. Tickets, admitting a gentleman and ladies, five dollars. This ticket provides the usual ball-room accommodations free. Reserved seats in the balcony can be obtained by those holding ball tickets, at White, Smith & Co.'s, 516 Washington Street, as follows: First and second rows, $2 each; the remainder, $1 each. Ball tickets may be obtained of either of the board of managers, who will cheerfully furnish any information desired.

Sir Knight Managers.

EXECUTIVE.

EMINENT SIR JOHN L. STEVENSON, *Chairman.*

SIR EDWIN WRIGHT.	SIR JONAS G. SHILLABER.
" EUGENE H. RICHARDS.	" JAMES P. PHINNEY.
" THOMAS F. TEMPLE.	" WILLIAM P. TYLER.
" DANIEL W. LAWRENCE.	" ALBERT A. FOLSOM, *Treasurer.*
" EDWARD T. NICHOLS.	" Z. H. THOMAS, *Recorder,*
	Secretary of the Board of Managers.

GENERAL.

BOSTON.

Sir JAMES M. GLEASON.
" JOHN H. NORTH.
" FRED. T. COMEE.
" EUGENE A. HOLTON.
" EDWARD COGGINS.
" CHARLES J. HAYDEN.
" ALEX. K. BRYER.
" CHARLES O. BURRILL.
" OTIS EDDY.
" CHARLES D. WHITE.
" BENJAMIN M. WEDGER.
" JOSIAH T. DYER.
" JOHN B. RHODES.
" ALBERT L. RICHARDSON.
" HENRY N. SAWYER.
" JOHN G. STEWART, JR.
" WILLIAM C. ULMAN.
" FRED S. RISTEEN.
" CHARLES E. PHIPPS.
" OSCAR A. JONES.

Sir EDWARD C. NEAL.
" CHARLES W. PARKER.
" THOMAS J. OLYS.
" ISAAC HARRIS.
" THOMAS MERRILL.
" GEORGE A. GILLETTE.
" BENJAMIN S. EASTWOOD.
" LYMAN R. MACE.
" J. GEORGE COOPER.
" JOHN BLACKIE.
" CHARLES H. BARNES.
" RICHARD A. ATWOOD.
" CHAUNCEY COON.
" JOHN H. LAKIN.
" LYMAN S. HAPGOOD.
" WILLIAM H. STACY.
" CHARLES A. FAIRBANKS.
" IRA HERBERT ODELL.
" WM. H. LAPOINTE.
" SAMUEL I. COY.

Sir HENRY W. MANSUR.
" AUGUST P. LIGHTHILL.
" LUTHER ADAMS.
" JOHN F. HAM.
" J. HARRISON ASHTON.
" JOHN C. CHAPMAN.
" SIDNEY M. HEDGES.
" J. ALBA DAVIS.
" MARTIN A. MUNROE.
" FRED. ALFORD.
" HENRY ARNETT.
" GEORGE W. BLISH.
" JOHN D. GALE.
" OTIS S. NEALE.
" GEORGE E. HALL.
" DANIEL GREGORY.
" HARRY W. CUMNER.
" WALTER W. BOYDEN.
" HENRY G. FAY.
" J. ARTHUR JACOBS.

Sir JAMES A. FOX,	Cambridge.	Sir GEORGE P. BROWN,	Winchester.
" WILLIAM A. BUNTON,	"	" ABIJAH THOMPSON,	"
" E. BURT PHILLIPS,	"	" GEORGE G. STRATTON,	"
" EDGAR F. HUNT,	"	" GEORGE F. HEWETT,	Worcester.
" GEORGE W. BUNTON.	"	" CHARLES F. ATWOOD,	Everett.
" HORACE P. BLACKMAN,	"	" SAMUEL F. TRULL,	Woburn.
" BENJAMIN HOWE,	"	" CHARLIE A. JONES,	"
" LEONARD M. AVERELL,	"	" CHARLES E. BROWN,	Concord.
" JOSEPH WILLIAMS,	"	" EDGAR O. DEWEY,	Reading.
" WILLIAM H. DOW,	"	" AUGUSTUS TOWNE,	Hamilton.
" J. CHARLES SMITH,	"	" ALFRED M. SMITH,	Dedham.
" PETER LANE,	"	" FRANCIS DOANE,	Norwood.
" FRANCIS H. JOHNSON,	"	" WILLIAM B. LAWRENCE,	Medford.
" JOHN J. CILLEY,	East Boston.	" ROSEWELL B. LAWRENCE,	"
" EMERY D. LEIGHTON,	"	" GEORGE H. MANSFIELD,	Canton.
" CHARLES H. DAY,	"	" WILLIAM H. BURROWS,	Malden.
" CHARLES B. FESSENDEN,	Arlington.	" WILLIAM DAN LAMB,	Southbridge.
" GEORGE W. STORER,	"	" WILLIAM A. HODGES,	Quincy.
" A. BARTLETT HILL,	"	" CHARLES H. PORTER,	"
" GEORGE K. HOOPER,	Somerville.	" AUGUSTUS F. BUSSELL,	"

The concise yet full reports made by the secretary, Sir Thomas, not only indicate the general plans adopted, but reveal an immense amount of details, due attention to which augmented the success of this grand Templar ball.

Elaborate arrangements for the ball were made, and the event proved a most brilliant success. The day and evening were cool, but the ardor of the Sir Knights was not abated. The following Sir Knights constituted the committees of reception, etc.: —

Earl Marshal:

EMINENT SIR SAMUEL C. LAWRENCE,

Past Eminent Commander of Boston Commandery, K. T., and Grand Master of Masons in Massachusetts.

Aids to Earl Marshal:

EM∴ SIR WYZEMAN MARSHALL,   EM∴ SIR CHARLES CHASE DAME,
EM∴ SIR CHARLES EDWARD POWERS,   EM∴ SIR SAMUEL MASON, JR.
EM∴ SIR JAMES H. UPHAM,   EM∴ SIR J. FRANCIS LOTTS,

Past Eminent Commanders of Boston Commandery, K. T.

RECEPTION COMMITTEES.

(THE GUESTS.)

SIR JAMES A. FOX.

SIR ALBERT L. RICHARDSON.   SIR FREDK. S. RISTEEN.
SIR HENRY G. FAY.   SIR CHAUNCEY COON.
SIR MARTIN A. MUNROE.   SIR J. ALBA DAVIS.
SIR AUGUSTUS TOWNE.   SIR HENRY N. SAWYER.
SIR CHARLES H. BARNES.   SIR EDGAR O. DEWEY.
SIR W. A. HODGES.   SIR PETER LANE.
SIR E. BURT PHILLIPS.   SIR L. M. AVERELL.

(THE LADIES.)

SIR ABIJAH THOMPSON.   SIR SIDNEY M. HEDGES.
SIR LYMAN S. HAPGOOD.   SIR A. P. LIGHTHILL.
SIR GEO. W. BLISH.   SIR FRED. ALFORD.
SIR FRANCIS DOANE.   SIR GEO. G. STRATTON.
SIR RICHARD A. ATWOOD.   SIR CHARLES E. BROWN.

Music for the Ball was furnished by

CARTER'S ORCHESTRA,

(Fifty Pieces,)

T. M. CARTER - - - - - - CONDUCTOR

And for the Promenade and Concert by

BALDWIN'S BOSTON CADET BAND,

(Forty Pieces,)

J. THOMAS BALDWIN - - - - MUSICAL DIRECTOR.

Committee on Music

CONSISTED OF

SIR JOHN B. RHODES.	SIR W. H. DOW.
SIR I. HERBERT ODELL.	SIR A. K. BRYER.
SIR JOSEPH WILLIAMS.	SIR LUTHER ADAMS.

The following-named Sir Knights were directors, aids, and marshals of the ball:—

DIRECTOR GENERAL.
EMINENT SIR JOHN L. STEVENSON.

ASSISTANT DIRECTORS GENERAL.

SIR EDWIN WRIGHT.   SIR EUGENE H. RICHARDS.

HONORARY STAFF.

EM.·. SIR JOHN O. SHAW, MAINE.   EM.·. SIR ANDREW BUNTON, N. H.
EM.·. SIR ALFRED A. HALL, VT.   EM.·. SIR S. O. DANIELS, MASS.
EM.·. SIR ALBERT C. EDDY, R. I.   EM.·. SIR E. C. BIRDSEY, CONN.

AIDS TO DIRECTOR GENERAL.

Sir Daniel W. Lawrence,
  Sir James M. Gleason,
    Sir William C. Ulman,
      Sir Thomas F. Temple,
        Sir George A. Gillette.
Sir Albert A. Folsom,
  Sir Edward Coggins,
    Sir Edward T. Nichols,
      Sir Fred. T. Comee,
        Sir Z. H. Thomas,
Sir Emery D. Leighton,
  Sir George F. Hewitt,
    Sir James P. Phinney,
      Sir Eugene A. Holton,
        Sir John H. North.

Sir William P. Tyler,
  Sir Jonas G. Shillaber.
    Sir Otis Eddy,
      Sir Benjamin M. Wedger,
        Sir John G. Stewart, Jr.
Sir George W. Storer,
  Sir William Dan Lamb,
    Sir William H. LaPointe,
      Sir Charles A. Fairbanks,
        Sir John Blackie.
Sir William A. Bunton,
  Sir John H. Lakin,
    Sir Horace P. Blackman,
      Sir Charles O. Burrill,
        Sir Charles F. Atwood.

SIR KNIGHT MARSHALS.

Sir Charles J. Hayden,
  Sir Charles D. White,
    Sir Josiah T. Dyer,
      Sir Charles E. Phipps,
        Sir Oscar A. Jones.
Sir Edward C. Neal,
  Sir Charles W. Parker,
    Sir Thomas J. Olys,
      Sir Isaac Harris,
        Sir Thomas Merrill.
Sir Benjamin S. Eastwood,
  Sir Lyman R. Mace,
    Sir J. George Cooper,
      Sir William H. Stacy,
        Sir Samuel I. Coy.
Sir Henry W. Mansur,
  Sir John F. Ham,
    Sir J. Harrison Ashton,
      Sir John C. Chapman,
        Sir William B. Lawrence.
Sir Henry Arnett,
  Sir John D. Gale,
    Sir Otis S. Neale,
      Sir George E. Hall,
        Sir Daniel Gregory.

Sir Harry W. Cumner.
  Sir Walter W. Boyden, .
    Sir J. Arthur Jacobs,
      Sir Edgar F. Hunt,
        Sir George W. Bunton,
Sir Benjamin Howe,
  Sir J. Charles Smith,
    Sir Francis H. Johnson,
      Sir John J. Cilley,
        Sir Charles H. Day.
Sir Charles B. Fessenden,
  Sir A. Bartlett Hill,
    Sir George R. Hooper,
      Sir Fred. Alford,
        Sir Sidney M. Hedges,
Sir George P. Brown,
  Sir Samuel F. Trull,
    Sir Charlie A. Jones,
      Sir Alfred M. Smith,
        Sir Rosewell B. Lawrence
Sir George H. Mansfield,
  Sir William H. Burrows,
    Sir Charles H. Porter,
      Sir Augustus H. Bussell,
        Sir Luther Adams.

The following account of the grand ball is from the Boston *Journal* of Feb. 1, 1883: —

THE GRAND BALL GIVEN LAST NIGHT BY BOSTON COMMANDERY KNIGHTS TEMPLARS.

A Brilliant Scene at the Mechanic Exhibition Building.

COURTLY MEN, BEAUTIFUL WOMEN, AND ELEGANT TOILETS.

In the front rank of Knights Templars Commanderies of America, in standing and enterprise no less than age, is the Boston Commandery, whose ball at the Mechanic Building last night was fully in keeping with its well-known reputation, and bespoke in a worthy style something of the taste and resources of the Fraternity. A more brilliant event, not merely in variety and radiance of color and costume, but in social aspects, has rarely been witnessed in Boston. The spectator saw on every side convincing proofs of the united effort, the tact and spirit of organization which run through the brotherhood, and nothing was spared to render the affair one for admiration and pleasure, and altogether consonant with the dignity and repute of the body under whose auspices it was carried out.

THE ARRIVALS.

Although the first ceremonies were announced for half past eight o'clock, it was long before that hour when the first carriages began to arrive, and soon they came in legions. Under the skilful guidance of Supt. Marsh all confusion was avoided, although some delay was necessarily incident, while the long line of carriages in waiting was constantly increased until it reached a considerable distance away on either side of the main entrance. The same system of checks was used which Capt. Marsh so successfully introduced early this season, and thereby was avoided much trouble and vexation at the departure of the participants in the festivities within. A long awning completely sheltered the approach to the doors, which would have sufficed had a torrent descended, but fortunately clear skies prevailed and there was not even wind enough to make the shelter welcome. Within doors were all conveniences for the disposal of outer wraps, and these incumbrances laid aside, the eye of the spectator was first attracted to the brilliant appearance of the hall.

THE DECORATIONS.

The grand hall never presented a more imposing appearance than last night, all the devices of taste and the decorative art seeming to be lavished on every part. The stage and its surrounding embellishments naturally furnished the most striking group of decorations. Just in front of the great organ, forming a sort of central figure, was a large painting in heroic style of the warrior who, in the days of early knighthood, clove through the Saracens — Richard the Lion-hearted. He was mounted on a charger, and in the background was an army of on-coming Crusaders on the field of Palestine. Above this was a trophy of arms and banners, consisting of a shield with a red cross emblazoned upon it, surmounted by a helmet, while on each side were groups of black banners, and below these were the gauntlets and crossed swords of Templars. Around the painting was a background of drapery bordered with old-gold velvet. Above this was an array of red, green, and white, in imitation of a pavilion, typical of the regal tents of the Crusaders. The banners were of the shape of the ancient French oriflamme, and on each was the ever-conspicuous red cross. A striking object on each side of the stage was a Roman altar of bronze and designed as a tripod. From each of these were emitted flames to represent the rising of incense. The banner of the Grand Commandery of the United States was erected above the altar on the right of the stage, and on the other side the banner of the Boston Commandery. The boxes and balconies were adorned in keeping with the wealth of ornament and suggestions on the stage. The central box was occupied by Earl Marshal, Eminent Sir Samuel C. Lawrence, and guests. The canopy was of red and white, with a border of red at the front figured with gold. The outer portion of the box was draped with a rich, gold-figured border. The front of the lower balcony was also beautifully decorated. Opposite the stage was a painting representing the seal of the Commandery, consisting of a cross and crown, with the words "Boston Commandery of Knights Templars," and above this there was a floral crown, around which were garlands of flowers festooned upon a white background. The entire front of the balcony was heavily hung with green, white, and red stripes upon a white background, the whole being caught up at intervals with rosettes of divers colors. Altogether the decorations, both in design and detail, were of rare beauty, for their massing of strong effects without overshadowing the many and minor beauties, and served not only to set off every outline of the interior, but to supplement and enrich it.

THE LADIES' RECEPTION-ROOM.

One of the most charming features of the occasion was the room which had been equipped for the accommodation of the lady guests, serving as it did as a commodious and tasteful boudoir. Draperies of Spanish silks, Turkish stripes, Swiss laces, and tapestries of peculiar richness were to be seen on every hand, as also furniture of amaranth, ebony, and black-walnut, upholstered in lavish style. Turkish rugs, mirrors, and ornamental woods enhanced the effect, so that in spite of its great size the room was in every sense a cosey and tempting one.

THE PROMENADE CONCERT.

At eight o'clock, the promenades being even then well filled, the first notes of the opening concert were heard.

The programme was as follows:—

No. 1. Overture, "Leichte Cavallerie" . . . . . . Suppe.
      Orchestra, under the direction of Sir T. M. Carter.
No. 2. Concert medley, "Popular" . . . . Braham.
      Baldwin's Boston Cadet Band, J. Thomas Baldwin, musical director.
No. 3. Selection, "Martha" . . . . Flotow.
      Orchestra.
No. 4. Overture, "Oberon" . . . . Weber.
      Baldwin's Boston Cadet Band.

The programme announced the following : —

AT 8.30 O'CLOCK.

Entrance of Boston Commandery.

and Reception by them of other Commanderies and Distinguished Guests.

MUSIC, BY BALDWIN'S BOSTON CADET BAND.

Reception of the Most Eminent Grand Master of the United States.

⇢ BENJAMIN DEAN, ⇠

By all the Commanderies.

MUSIC—"Hail to the Chief," • • by the CONSOLIDATED BANDS.
Under the Direction of J. Thomas Baldwin.

Grand Templar Review.

By the M∴ E∴ Grand Master.

MUSIC — "Commander Stevenson's March," • • by CONSOLIDATED BANDS
Under the Direction of J. Thomas Baldwin.

AT 10 O'CLOCK.

A Grand Templar March, with Ladies.

MUSIC — CONSOLIDATED BANDS, under the direction of Sir T. M. Carter, playing the "San Francisco March," dedicated to Boston Commandery.
Written for this occasion by Sir Carter.

THE KNIGHTLY PAGEANT.

At nearly 9 P. M. Boston Commandery appeared, with one hundred and seventy-five Sir Knights in line, seventy-five others being engaged in various capacities about the building. The officers were Em. Sir John L. Stevenson, Commander, Sir Edwin Wright, Generalissimo, and Sir Eugene H. Richards, Captain General. The Commandery presented a fine picture as it marched in to the music of the band, halting at the head of the hall, and forming two sides of a hollow square, the lines being two deep. A few minutes later

Worcester County Commandery, of Worcester, marched in, with thirty Sir Knights in the ranks, under Sir George E. Boyden, acting Commander. They were received with presented swords, and marching around the hall, halted opposite Boston Commandery. Joseph Warren Commandery, of Boston, was the next to enter, numbering forty Sir Knights, and having as officers Em. Sir D. W. Jones, Commander, Sir John Carr, Generalissimo, and Sir F. H. Spring, Captain General; then followed St. Omer Commandery, of South Boston, forty Sir Knights, with Em. Sir Jerome Smith, Commander, Sir Frederick Felton, acting Generalissimo, and Sir Charles E. Pierce, Captain General; William Parkman Commandery, of East Boston, twenty-five Sir Knights, with Em. Sir Albert C. Smith, Commander, and Sir Thomas Kellough, Generalissimo; Natick Commandery, of Natick, twenty-five Sir Knights, with Em. Sir E. F. Perry, Commander, Sir G. F. Babcock, Generalissimo, and Sir C. H. Childs, Captain General; South Shore Commandery, of Weymouth, twenty Sir Knights, with Em. Sir E. W. H. Bass, Commander, and Sir William Fearing, Captain General. Each of these Commanderies carried an elegant banner, and the Sir Knights were all clothed in the striking regalia of the Order, many of them wearing also the brilliant insignia of the various degrees and offices peculiar to the Masonic Fraternity. Hugh de Payens Commandery, of Melrose, and Cœur de Lion Commandery, of Charlestown, were represented by about twenty Sir Knights, who entered the hall as an organization, headed by Em. Sir N. J. Simonds, Commander of Hugh de Payens, and Em. Sir Joseph W. Hill, Commander of Cœur de Lion. Each of the Commanderies, after being received, halted on the left of the preceding command, and when all had entered, a hollow square was formed, Em Commander Stevenson taking command of the consolidated bodies.

RECEPTION OF GUESTS.

The formation being complete, the band and orchestra combined struck up "Hail to the Chief," and Past Em. Commander Samuel C. Lawrence, Earl Marshal, entered the hall, escorting Hon. Benjamin Dean, Most Eminent Grand Master of the Grand Encampment of the United States, who was accompanied by Right Em. Sir Caleb Saunders, Grand Commander of

Massachusetts and Rhode Island, and several other officers of the Grand Commandery. Most Em. Grand Master Dean and his companions, having been duly received, were escorted to seats on the platform, and then Gov. Butler entered, accompanied by the members of his staff, with Mayor Palmer, of Boston, and Lieuts. Learee and Lissak, of the Fourth Artillery, U. S. A. The Governor, who was in full evening dress, received a round of applause on entering, and was accorded the usual honors by the Sir Knights. The distinguished party were given seats on the platform, and then the several Commanderies passed in review before Most Em. Grand Master Dean, the band and orchestra playing "Commander Stevenson's March," and the military portion of the affair was over. The scene throughout was a brilliant one, the Sir Knights marching with a good degree of steadiness over the smooth floor, their regalia, jewels, and swords glistening in the flood of light that filled the great hall, while in the balconies bright faces watched the picture ; these, with the many colors of the ladies' costumes, making, in turn, a picture that was very beautiful, as seen from the floor.

SOME OF THE GUESTS.

In addition to the distinguished guests mentioned in the foregoing, there were present during these ceremonies, Hon. Geo. G. Crocker, President of the State Senate; R. E. Grand Commander M. A. Taylor, of New Hampshire, and the officers of the Grand Commandery of that State; V. E. D. Grand Commander E. C. Birdsey, of Connecticut; R. E. Grand Commander Edward P. Burnham, of Maine, and many others, including representatives of nearly all if not all the Commanderies in Boston and vicinity.

THE GRAND MARCH.

Ten o'clock was the time fixed for the grand march. Considering the size of the gathering, it is something to be commented on with favor that this event occurred but twenty minutes after the time fixed. At that hour the consolidated bands, under the direction of Sir T M. Carter, struck up a spirited composition entitled the "San Francisco March," composed by Sir Knight Carter, and dedicated to Boston Commandery. Commander Stevenson and daughter led the column, followed by Grand Master Dean and Mrs. Dean and a very long procession of Sir Knights and ladies. The march was an imposing one, not less than four hundred couples taking part in it.

THE SCENE FROM THE BALCONY.

The scene when the dancing was fairly opened, and the immense ball-room floor became, as if at the beck of an enchanter, alive with moving beauty and intermingling color, was such as it would be difficult to picture to the fancy. The diversity and richness of the uniforms worn by the Templars found their adequate complement in the interminable variety and manifold attractions displayed by the ladies and their toilets. The scene from the gallery afforded opportunity to note the entirety of effect, and as the mellow and varied tones of the music pervaded all, sound and motion and color seemed to be blended in a unity of result that the spectator can hardly explain. A gay waltz followed the opening quadrille, and there was a peculiar fascination which is not to be appreciated in ordinary halls in watching the rhythmic and graceful motions of the dancers. Everything on the floor seemed to become vibratile in response to the vibratory numbers of the dance, and even the on-lookers that lined the gallery felt the impulse. Next came the lancers, a galop, and Portland Fancy, each of which evoked new phases of beauty. A noticeable feature of this ball was the readiness with which the full resources of the floor for dancing were availed of, and the heartiness with which the participants entered into enjoyment. Hour after hour the moving picture maintained its charm and novelty, the hues of uniforms and oriflammes gleamed beneath the electric lights, and the scandent sights and sounds that rose over all combined to leave their impress alike on fancy and memory.

WHAT THE LADIES WORE.

Delicate and beautiful as the raiment conjured up for Cinderella were many of the toilets worn. Laces, flowers, and iridescent beads were so mingled with dainty textiles as to cause one to wonder if their fascinating wearers had not a fairy godmother to lend her magical aid on the festive occasion. Nearly all colors, with their graduating shades, were represented, from the glowing hues of Cleopatra's wardrobe to the cool tints in which

Hypatia looked so grandly beautiful. There was the usual preponderance of white costumes, many of which would have enhanced the beauty of Venus herself. One of the most beautiful of this class was of cream-white Ottoman silk, with skirt front of embossed velvet, outlined by a thick silk ruche, which also outlined the long train. Another had the skirt elaborately trimmed with pearl passementerie, while a network of fine pearl beads overlaid the white satin bodice. One of the handsomest pink toilets seen was worn by the lady who, with Em. Sir John L. Stevenson, led the grand march. It was of silk in a light shade and was made *en train*. The front and sides were trimmed with deep flounces of the silk, edged with white lace. Another of pink had the crenellations of the basque and the edge of the front drapery studded with pink pompons. A very elaborate dress of gaslight green was garnished with velvet of a deeper hue and white Spanish lace. In keeping with this age of æsthetic culture was a pink cashmere robe worn by a young lady. It was made in regular Greenaway style, the body of the dress being attached to a yoke and hanging loosely, without shirring or other device to define the waist line. The yoke and sleeves of this costume were composed of alternate stripes of pink satin ribbon and Valenciennes insertions. Another striking dress was of old-gold satin, which made its wearer look, as several spectators averred, like a picture of one hundred years ago. A superb toilet of pearl-colored satin de Lyon and ruby plush was productive in its method of arrangement of a very graceful and novel effect. A robe conspicuous for its richness was of dark blue velvet made in princesse style, with long train. The front of the skirt was of blue satin and the sleeves were slashed to show puffings of white lace. Exceedingly elegant were other toilets in blue, pink, heliotrope, crushed strawberry, écru, and various other shades, white and black. Flowers seemed an indispensable adjunct of every toilet, being displayed as rivers, corsage bouquets, or clusters to keep draperies in place. The rose, that queen of flowers, was the favorite. The gloves were long, and when not matching the costumes worn, were in the fashionable tan shades. The jewelry was noticeable for quality rather than quantity, and seemed confined to lace pins and ear-rings. Fans matched the costumes in color, many of them being dainty confections of flowers and lace.

THE MANAGEMENT.

The grand success of last evening was entirely due to the indefatigable efforts of the various committees, who are to be heartily congratulated on the result of their labors.

FRIENDLY GREETINGS.

During the evening these two telegrams were received from localities far apart, showing the fraternity of feeling all over the world: —

SAN FRANCISCO, CAL., Jan. 31, 1883.
To JOHN L. STEVENSON:
From the Pacific to the Atlantic, greeting. A continent lies between us, but we are with you in spirit to-night.

(Signed) R∴ E∴ SIR CHARLES F. LOTT,
Grand Commander of California.
R∴ E∴ SIR CHARLES H. CASWELL,
Grand Recorder.
R∴ E∴ SIR WILLIAM O. GOULD,
Past Grand Commander.
EM∴ SIR TRISTAM BURGES,
Commander of Golden Gate Commandery.
SIR SAMUEL HAND,
Boston Commandery.

ACADEMY OF MUSIC, NEW YORK, Jan. 31, 10 P. M.
To BOSTON COMMANDERY:
Warm and knightly greetings to Boston Commandery and her guests this evening. May Boston always prosper, and Christian knighthood flourish through the world. Our reception is a grand success.

(Signed) THOMAS B. RAND,
Eminent Commander, Palestine Commandery, New York.

CARD PROGRAMMES.

The order of dances, or, as they might more properly be called, the programmes of the evening's entertainment, since they contained all the information desired, were really works of art. The title-page was a fine steel engraving, representing a Sir Knight mounted upon a charger, both clothed in armor, and the Sir Knight carrying a lance and shield. Above are a trumpet, banner, shield, and sword, emblems of the Order. The back of the cover contained the following in print: "Grand Reception and Ball by Boston Commandery, Knights Templars Charitable Mechanic Building (Huntington Avenue), Wednesday evening, Jan. 31, 1883." The details of the programme were printed upon twelve pages. Mr. George M. Ardoene, of Providence, R. I., was the caterer, and the following is the *menu* of the repast he provided for the crowds of hungry dancers who flocked to his board: —

BILL OF FARE.

Salmon, with Mayonese.   Boned Turkey, jellied.

Pickled Oysters.

Chicken Patties.   Oyster Patties.

Champagne Ham.

Leg of Mutton, Caper Sauce.

Chicken Salad.   Lobster Salad

French Rolls.

English Pickles.   Olives.

Plain and Fancy Cake.

Charlotte Russe.

Vanilla.   Coffee.   Lemon.   Chocolate.

Strawberry Ice Cream.

Biscuit Glace.   Roman Punch.

Orange, Lemon Ice.

Coffee.   Tea.   Lemonade.

Bouillon.

Seats were provided for eighteen hundred persons in the galleries over the large exhibition hall. Toward midnight Gov. Butler and party were entertained, and afterward the room was liberally patronized by the dancers. It is sufficient to say that everything was of the best, and that every one was completely satisfied. The table service included over eleven thousand pieces. The waiters, all of whom were colored, wore numbered badges, and were one hundred and ten in number.

Great credit is due to Em. Sir John L. Stevenson, director general, and the Sir Knights associated with him in this grand Templar demonstration, for their untiring efforts and unqualified success. At 2 A. M. there were evidences of the "breaking up," but some continued the dance long after. As the weary and pleased revellers retired, the expression was oft repeated, and congratulations were mutually extended, that the affair was a great undertaking, yet a thorough success.

The committee to devise ways and means held six meetings subsequent to the ball, at which all matters pertaining to the ball were settled, votes of thanks were passed to the Em. Commander, Sir John L. Stevenson, chairman, to Sir A. A. Folsom, treasurer, to Sir Charles H. Barnes, who furnished the ladies' reception-room in elegant style at his own expense; and on motion, the treasurer paid over for the benefit of the California pilgrimage the balance in his hands, amounting, as per auditors' reports, to $3,104.34. July 24, 1883, at its eighteenth and final meeting, after a report upon the doings of the committee, in accordance with the above, had been prepared for submission to Boston Commandery, the committee was dissolved.

Feb. 1, 1883, the following self-explanatory letter was received by the Eminent Commander: —

GRAND ENCAMPMENT OF K. T. OF THE UNITED STATES OF AMERICA.

OFFICE OF THE GRAND MASTER,
BOSTON, Feb. 1, 1883.

JOHN L. STEVENSON, ESQ.:

Eminent and dear Sir Knight, — Allow me hereby to congratulate you upon the wonderfully complete arrangements for, and successful management of your Templar ball and reception last evening. I also thank you for your many kind attentions to me personally. You will oblige me by making known to

Boston Commandery my commendation of their gallant and knightly bearing, and my appreciation of the review, so kindly tendered and well executed.

I have the honor to be, yours in the

Bonds of Knighthood,

Benj. Dean)

Grand Master.

The committee on California pilgrimage, which suspended its meetings from Nov. 22, 1882, to Feb. 7, 1883, while the project of the grand Templar ball was being carried out by the committee on ways and means, reassembled at the latter date, when general remarks were made in regard to the pilgrimage. Previous to Aug. 4, 1883 — the time of the departure of the Commandery on the pilgrimage — this committee held twenty-seven meetings. Subsequently six meetings additional were held, the last being Sept. 27, 1883. The original committee, appointed Jan. 19, 1881, consisted of

    Sir John L. Stevenson, *Chairman*.
        Em. Sir Samuel C. Lawrence, *Treasurer*.
            Sir Albert T. Whiting.
                Sir Albert A. Folsom.
                    Sir Charles J. Hayden.
        Sir Z. H. Thomas was elected secretary of the committee.

Subsequently the following Sir Knights were added to the committee: —

    Sir Edwin Wright.
        Sir Eugene H. Richards.
            Sir James M. Gleason.
                Sir William A. Bunton.
                      Sir Abijah Thompson.
                          Sir Edward T. Nichols.
                              Sir George F. Hewitt.

The above-named Sir Knights, twelve in number, constituted the committee on California pilgrimage on and after April 24, 1883.

The above committee or members thereof conceived, planned, accompanied, and completed the pilgrimage. The Eminent Commander alone of the original committee of five, and of the subsequent committee of twelve, was present at every one of the thirty-three meetings.

No synopsis of the business which came before this committee could so clearly show what the committee did as a perusal of these pages, which contain the results of their faithful labors. Every arrangement and detail of the pilgrimage, covering the thirty-one days; also the inception and development of the plans through months of earnest thought, together with the completion of the whole by a reception at the Vendôme, Oct. 24, were all successful through the fidelity and zeal of the committee on the California pilgrimage and of the faithful secretary of the committee.

In June, 1883, the committee issued the following outline of the pilgrimage for the information of those interested, which was subjected in the grand itinerary to such changes only as the official time-tables of the several railroads required or the convenience and comfort of the Commandery rendered necessary: —

Boston Commandery Knights Templars.

CALIFORNIA PILGRIMAGE, 1883.

FROM THE ATLANTIC TO THE PACIFIC.

SATURDAY, AUGUST 4, 1883.

The Commandery will assemble in their asylum, Masonic Temple, at an hour to be hereafter designated, and, in full Templar regalia, march to the Fitchburg Depot, where the ladies going on the pilgrimage will have preceded them. Embarking on the most elegant train of

Pullman cars ever run out of this city (and the only one ever engaged to run SPECIAL from Boston to San Francisco, and return without change of cars), the party will leave the depot at 6.30 P. M. The route will be over the Fitchburg Railroad to Fitchburg; the Cheshire Railroad to Bellows Falls; the Central Vermont Railroad to St. John's, P. Q.; thence by the Grand Trunk Railroad to Montreal, passing through the celebrated Victoria Bridge, one mile and one fourth long.

SUNDAY, AUGUST 5

6 A. M.: Arrive in Montreal. — Breakfast at the Windsor Hotel. 8 A. M.: Leave Montreal *via* Grand Trunk Railroad. — Lunch on dining cars. 6 P. M.: Arrive at Toronto, Ont. — One hour and thirty minutes for dinner at the Queen's Hotel.

MONDAY, AUGUST 6.

6 to 7 A. M.: Breakfast at Battle Creek, Mich. 1 P. M.: Arrive in Chicago. — Dinner at Grand Pacific Hotel. 5 P. M.: Leave Chicago *via* Chicago, Burlington and Quincy Railroad. — Supper on dining cars.

TUESDAY, AUGUST 7.

7 A. M.: Breakfast at Cameron, Ill. 12 M.: Arrive at Kansas City, Mo., by the Hannibal and St. Joseph Railroad. — Two hours for dinner, and leave by the Atchison, Topeka and Santa Fé Railroad. 5.30 P. M.: Arrive at Topeka, Kan. — Supper at Depot Hotel.

WEDNESDAY, AUGUST 8.

8 A. M.: Arrive at Coolidge, Kan. — Breakfast at Depot Hotel. 12 M.: Arrive at La Junta, Col. — Dinner at Depot Hotel. 8 P. M.: Arrive at Raton, N. M., for supper. — The Raton Pass, where the railroad crosses, is 7,688 feet above the level of the sea.

THURSDAY, AUGUST 9

Arrive at Las Vegas Hot Springs, N. M., at an early hour. — Breakfast and dinner at the Montezuma Hotel. 3 P. M.: Leave Las Vegas Hot Springs. — Supper at Station Dining Rooms, Las Vegas. — The Glorietta Pass having been crossed after leaving Las Vegas, at an elevation of 7,537 feet, a descent of thousands of feet carries us through Apache Cañon by daylight. — 11 P. M.: Arrive at Sante Fé, N. M., the oldest city in the United States.

FRIDAY, AUGUST 10.

Breakfast and dinner at the Palace Hotel, Sante Fé. 3.30 P. M.: Leave Sante Fé. 6 P. M.: Arrive at Wallace, N. M. — Supper at the Wallace House. 8 P. M.: Leave Wallace.

SATURDAY, AUGUST 11.

7.30 A. M.: Arrive at Deming, N. M. — Breakfast at Deming House. 8.30 A. M.: Leave Deming *via* Southern Pacific Railroad. 2.30 P. M.: First Section dine at Willcox, A. T. 2.30 P. M.: Second Section dine at Bowie, A. T. 7 P. M.: Arrive at Tucson. — Supper at Porter Hotel.

SUNDAY, AUGUST 12.

6.30 A. M.: Arrive at Yuma, A. T. — Breakfast at Southern Pacific Hotel. 7.30 A. M. Leave Yuma. 2.30 P. M.: Arrive at Colton, Cal. — Dinner at Transcontinental and other hotels. 4 P. M.: Leave Colton. 6 P. M.: Arrive at Los Angeles, Cal. — Supper at Southern Pacific Hotel.

MONDAY, AUGUST 13.

Spend the day in and around Los Angeles. — Meals at hotel. 5 P. M.: Leave Los Angeles.

TUESDAY, AUGUST 14.

6 A. M.: Arrive at Merced, Cal. — Breakfast at El Capitan House. 9 A. M.: Arrive at Lathrop, Cal. — Lunch at Lathrop House. 10.30 A. M.: Leave Lathrop. 2 P. M: Arrive in San Francisco, Cal., where quarters have been secured at the Palace Hotel (the largest hotel in the world), during our stay in that city.

Aug. 15th to 25th, inclusive, will be spent in enjoying the sights in and around San Francisco, participating in excursions, and the numerous festivities arranged by our *fratres* of California for our entertainment.

Monday, the 20th, is the day assigned for the Grand Parade and Review, and is the day on which every Sir Knight parading under our banner must be in line, our position as escort to the Most Eminent Grand Master, as well as our seniority, giving us the post of honor on that occasion.

Tuesday, the 21st, the Twenty-second Triennial Conclave of the Grand Encampment of the United States will convene, and continue in session from day to day until its business has been completed.

FROM THE PACIFIC TO THE ATLANTIC.

SATURDAY, AUGUST 25.

4 P. M.: Leave San Francisco *via* Central Pacific Railroad. 8 P. M.: Arrive in Sacramento. Supper at the Silver Palace Dining Rooms. 12 P. M.: Leave Sacramento.

SUNDAY, AUGUST 26.

First Section breakfast at Colfax, Cal. — Second Section breakfast at Auburn, Cal — Dinner at Blue Cañon Hotel, Blue Cañon, Cal. — Three hours' time given for dinner. — The Sierra Nevada are crossed by day, at an altitude of 7,017 feet above the level of the sea; also the famous "Cape Horn," where the railroad runs along the mountain-side 2,000 feet above the American River. — Supper at Truckee Hotel, Truckee, Cal.

MONDAY, AUGUST 27.

5 A. M.: Breakfast at Humboldt House, Humboldt, Nev. 2 P. M.: Dinner at Depot Hotel, Elko, Nev. 7.30 P. M.: Supper at Depot Hotel, Tecoma, Nev.

TUESDAY, AUGUST 28.

5 A. M.: Arrive at Salt Lake City, U. T. — Breakfast, dinner, and supper at the Walker and Continental Hotels, spending the day in the Mormon city. — From Ogden to Salt Lake City and return, the run is over the Utah Central Railroad. — Leaving Ogden, the Union Pacific Railroad conveys us to Omaha, Neb.

WEDNESDAY, AUGUST 29.

6 A. M.: Breakfast at the Desert House, Green River, Wy. T. 2 P. M.: Dinner at Depot Hotel, Rawlins, Wy. T. The Continental Divide is at Creston, twenty-five miles west of Rawlins, at an elevation of 7,300 feet. At Aspen, on the Uintah Mountains, the elevation is 7,835 feet. 8 P. M.: Supper, Rock Creek House, Rock Creek, Wy. T.

THURSDAY, AUGUST 30.

7 A. M.: Breakfast, Union Pacific Hotel, Cheyenne, Wy. T. 12.30 P. M.: Dinner at Station Dining Rooms, Sydney, Neb. 7.30 P. M.: Supper at Station Dining Rooms, North Platte, Neb. — The highest elevation *en route* will be reached at Sherman, Neb., 8,235 feet above the level of the sea.

FRIDAY, AUGUST 31.

7 A. M.: Breakfast at Station Dining Rooms, Council Bluffs, Iowa. 8 A. M.: Leave Council Bluffs *via* Chicago, Burlington and Quincy Railroad. — Dinner and supper in dining cars.

SATURDAY, SEPTEMBER 1.

5 A. M.: Arrive at Chicago, Ill. — Breakfast, and at 12 M.: Dinner, at the Grand Pacific Hotel. 2 P. M.: Leave Chicago *via* Grand Trunk Railroad. 7 P. M.: Supper at Battle Creek, Mich.

SUNDAY, SEPTEMBER 2.

7 A. M.: Breakfast at the Queen's Hotel, Toronto, Ont. 12 M.: Dinner at Kingston, Ont. — (Those who desire it can leave the cars at this point, and, taking the steamer at four o'clock Monday morning, pass down the St. Lawrence River, through the Thousand Islands, to Montreal, arriving in time to join the Commandery as it leaves for Boston.) 7 P. M.: Arrive in Montreal. — Stop one day at the elegant Windsor Hotel. — A complimentary trip down the Lachine Rapids, and other courtesies, have been tendered the Commandery during its stay.

MONDAY, SEPTEMBER 3.

11 P. M.: Leave Montreal, returning over same line as going out.

TUESDAY, SEPTEMBER 4.

9 A. M.: Breakfast at Keene, N. H.   1 P. M.: Arrive at the Fitchburg Depot, Boston.

COST OF THE PILGRIMAGE.

The cost of the pilgrimage will be $300 for each person. Coupon tickets will be issued covering railroad fares, Pullman car service, hotel bills, and meals *en route*, from Boston to Boston.

COMFORT IN TRAVELLING.

The intention of the committee has been to secure the maximum of comfort at a minimum of cost. To provide this, they have contracted for a train of new Pullman cars (now being built), containing all the modern improvements, to be sent to this city from Chicago (headquarters of the Pullman Car Company), and to be under their pay and control during the entire pilgrimage. But two persons will be assigned to a section, thus giving to each one a double berth and a double seat. Special care has been taken in securing hotel accommodations and meals *en route*, the personal attention of the several railroad officials having been given to the same. The Windsor, at Montreal, the Grand Pacific, at Chicago, and the magnificent Palace Hotel, at San Francisco, where quarters are engaged during our stay in the several cities, are among the finest hotels in the world.

The journey out will be broken by "a day off" at Las Vegas Hot Springs; another at Santa Fé, in New Mexico; and a third at Los Angeles, Cal. The homeward trip will include "a day off" at Salt Lake City, Chicago, and Montreal. The committee understand that numerous excursions have been arranged to take place during our stay in San Francisco. The time allowed for the pilgrimage is one month, — from Aug. 4 to Sept. 4, — but the railroad tickets can be extended to and including Oct. 31 next, if desired.

SIR KNIGHTS OF OTHER COMMANDERIES.

A limited number of Sir Knights will be welcomed to our ranks on this occasion, on the same terms and conditions enjoyed by the members of Boston Commandery. Every Sir Knight going on this pilgrimage, whether a member of Boston Commandery or otherwise, will carry, and wear when required, the full Templar regalia of Boston Commandery (the black regalia), and the latest style of fatigue cap adopted by this Commandery; no other regalia will be admitted to the ranks, and no one will be allowed to go without regalia. *Black clothes must be worn on all occasions when in regalia.* A single-breasted frock coat, buttoning to the chin, is recommended to those who do not already have them, as they present a uniform appearance, and are comfortable to the wearer. A large number of ladies will accompany the Commandery, at the same expense each as a Sir Knight. The descriptive itinerary to be issued will contain details of the entertainments in San Francisco, and other valuable information. A thoroughly competent medical staff will accompany the Commandery.

Sir Knights desirous of participating in this pilgrimage, who have not already signed an order for tickets, are courteously requested to do so at once, as the number to be accommodated is *positively limited*. Blanks for orders may be obtained of either of the committee, who will cheerfully furnish any information desired.

Courteously yours,

EM.'. SIR JOHN L. STEVENSON, CHAIRMAN,
 2 and 4 Faneuil Hall Square.
EM.'. SIR SAMUEL C. LAWRENCE, TREASURER,
 127 Broad St.
SIR ALBERT A. FOLSOM,
 Providence R. R. Depot.
SIR ALBERT T. WHITING,
 35 Devonshire Street.
SIR CHARLES J. HAYDEN,
 114 Tremont Street.
SIR EDWIN WRIGHT,
 Rogers Building.
SIR EUGENE H. RICHARDS,
 7 Green Street.
SIR JAMES M. GLEASON,
 16 Sears Building.
SIR WILLIAM A. BUNTON,
 5 and 7 Commercial Street.
SIR ABIJAH THOMPSON,
 187 Summer Street.
SIR EDWARD T. NICHOLS,
 Cambridgeport.
SIR GEORGE F. HEWETT,
 Worcester, Mass.

Committee.

SIR Z. H. THOMAS, SECRETARY,
 P. O. Box 46, Cambridgeport, Mass.

CHAPTER III.

In July, 1883, Sir John L. Stevenson, Eminent Commander of Boston Commandery, issued the following order: —

KNIGHTS TEMPLARS.

A special Conclave of Boston Commandery Knights Templars will be held in Masonic Temple, Saturday, Aug. 4, 1883, at three o'clock P. M., to open a Commandery of Knights Templars, for the purpose of escorting Most Eminent Grand Master Benjamin Dean to the Twenty-second Triennial Conclave of the Grand Encampment of the United States, to be held in San Francisco, Cal. Sir Knights will report in the Knight Templar regalia of Boston Commandery, with fatigue cap (regulation style), suspended from the belt at the rear. No *back* chain will be worn in the ranks. The dress will consist of a black cloth frock coat buttoning to the throat, black vest, and necktie, and black pants. A strict compliance with this order will be observed whenever the regalia is worn. While *en route*, or when off duty, Sir Knights will dress as their comfort and taste may dictate, always wearing the fatigue cap as a means of identification. Every Sir Knight enrolled for the pilgrimage will report in strict conformity to this notice. After the Commandery has been duly organized, a collation will be served, at the conclusion of which the lines will be formed, and at five o'clock P. M. the Most Eminent Grand Master will be received with due honors and escorted to the Fitchburg Depot. The departure for San Francisco will be made at half past six o'clock P. M. Sir T. M. Carter's military band will furnish music for this parade.

By order of

John L. Stevenson,
Eminent Commander.

S. A. Thomas,
Recorder.

Accompanying this order, the committee on the California pilgrimage issued the following notice: —

The committee desire to say that in arranging for this pilgrimage they have availed themselves of the experience of those who have frequently conducted large parties across the continent, which with the ready assistance rendered by the courteous railroad officials over whose roads we pass, assure a safe and pleasant trip to our participants. No partiality has, or will be shown in the make-up of the party, our aim and desire is to have all share alike the pleasures and honors of the pilgrimage, and by mutual concessions add to each other's happiness and comfort during the time we are absent from the more substantial comforts of home.

LADIES.

Ladies going on the pilgrimage will assemble at the waiting-rooms of the Fitchburg Depot at five o'clock, where a committee of Sir Knights will be in attendance to escort them to a collation provided in the dining-room of the depot by Sir Lyman R. Mace.

PULLMAN CARS.

Sections in the Pullman cars will be assigned by the committee, who will use their best judgment in so doing. Checks for same will be ready for delivery at the armory at two o'clock on the day of the departure. The position of cars in the train is liable to change at different points. Each car will be in charge of a member of the committee, who will hold himself responsible for the conduct and comfort of its occupants as far as lies in his power.

BAGGAGE.

Baggage will be received at Masonic Temple, Aug. 4, from nine o'clock A. M. until the departure of the Commandery. Boston Commandery checks will be given for all trunks, and printed tags furnished for marking hand baggage. The trunks will be placed in the baggage car and will not be available while passing through the Canadas. The hand baggage will be called for at the depot by each Sir Knight and taken in his section of the Pullman car. The committee will be responsible only for baggage thus delivered to their care. Only one hundred pounds baggage is allowed on each ticket, hand baggage not counted thereon. A baggage master and baggage car accompany the Commandery during the entire trip without change.

BOOK OF COUPONS.

The book of coupons for the pilgrimage will be delivered on board the cars.

BADGES.

The badges for the ladies will be delivered to them at the depot, those for the Sir Knights at the asylum. A supply of badges to be used in exchange, and for souvenirs will be for sale on the train.

JEWELS.

Sir Knights will wear such Masonic jewels as they are in possession of and are entitled to wear.

MAIL.

Letters mailed to the Palace Hotel, San Francisco, on or before Aug. 17, will be due there before the Commandery leaves on the homeward trip.

By order of the committee,

F. H. Thomas,

Secretary of Committee.

In accordance therewith, during the whole of that beautiful Saturday " there were hurryings to and fro" and unusual commotion in and around Masonic Temple. At 9 A. M. baggage began to arrive at the Temple, which was systematically checked by the committee on transportation. Hand baggage was also labelled with printed tags, and taken in charge by the committee. Wagon-load after wagon-load was promptly transferred to the Fitchburg Depot, and snugly packed for its transcontinental journey. The ladies who accompanied the Commandery on the pilgrimage assembled at the waiting-rooms of the Fitchburg Depot at 5 P. M., where a committee of Sir Knights were in attendance, who escorted them to a collation provided in the dining-room of the depot by Sir Lyman R. Mace.

At 3 P. M. the "pilgrims" in full Templar regalia assembled in Gothic Hall, and a Commandery of Knights Templars was duly opened for the purpose of escorting the Grand Master of Knights Templars of the United States, M. E. Sir Benjamin Dean, to the Twenty-second Triennial Conclave of the Grand Encampment of the United States, to be held in San Francisco. The Commandery of Knights Templars then opened remained so until the return of the Commandery, Sept. 4, when it was closed in due form. This conclave or session was therefore the longest known, as it covered thirty-one days. Appreciating the great distance to be travelled, and the dangers to which they would be exposed, aware of the magnitude of the undertaking,— unparalleled in modern times,— yet thoroughly hopeful of a successful pilgrimage, the opening services were very impressive. The Eminent Commander made a timely and hopeful address, and the Prelate invoked the divine blessing upon the pilgrims, committing them, their safety, their interests, their welfare, into the hands of Him "who doeth all things well." Thus the pilgrimage was auspiciously begun, with devout trust for its happy conclusion. The Commandery then repaired to Boylston Hall, where the organization was perfected for parade, and the badges were distributed to the Sir Knights. Returning to Masonic Temple, the lines being formed, M. E. Grand Master Benjamin Dean was received with appropriate ceremony and honor; after which the Commandery repaired to the banquet hall, where a collation was served. A pleasant hour was spent at the tables in partaking of the collation, forming new acquaintances, and talking over anticipated pleasures. At 5.20 P. M. the Commandery took up its line of march, with the M. E. Grand Master under escort, for the Fitchburg Depot, being led by Carter's band, Sir T. M. Carter, leader, through Tremont, School, Washington, and Court Streets to Bowdoin Square, through Green, Leverett, and Causeway Streets, to the depot. The sidewalks along the route were lined with spectators, who frequently manifested their interest by applause, and at the depot hundreds of friends assembled to "see us off," wishing the party a pleasant pilgrimage and a safe return.

The train consisted of one baggage car, six new Pullman cars, forwarded from Chicago expressly for the conveyance of this party to the Golden Gate and return, and a special car, No. 99, belonging to the Chicago, Burlington and Quincy Railroad, the use of which was kindly tendered to Sir John L. Stevenson, Eminent Commander of Boston Commandery, for the transportation of himself and his distinguished guest, M. E. Sir Benjamin Dean, Grand Master of the Grand Commandery of Knights Templars of the United States of America. Car No. 99, thus provided and occupied, was the rear car of the train. It was furnished, supplied, and equipped at the private expense of the Eminent Commander, by whom hospitalities were freely dispensed to Sir Knights who called upon the Grand Master and Eminent Commander at various places *en route*. The special car was likewise used as the headquarters of Boston Commandery while in transit.

At 6.20 P. M. the Commandery, joined by the sixty-three ladies who were to accompany it, boarded the train and were quickly located in the respective sections assigned them. The train was in charge of the veteran conductor Kingsbury, and was drawn by the powerful engine No. 99, run by Engineer William Phelan. Mr. M. D. Birmingham, an *attaché* of the Chicago, Burlington and Quincy Railroad, had charge of the baggage car and its contents, and accompanied the party to San Francisco and return. He performed his duties with precision and despatch, and received the cordial thanks of all.

ROSTER.

JOHN L. STEVENSON,
Eminent Commander.

EUGENE H. RICHARDS,
Generalissimo.

EZRA J. TRULL,
Captain General.

REV. OLIVER A. ROBERTS,
Prelate.

JAMES M. GLEASON,
Senior Warden.

WILLIAM A. BUNTON,
Junior Warden.

JONAS G. SHILLABER,
Treasurer.

ZEPH. H. THOMAS,
Recorder.

PILGRIMAGE OF BOSTON COMMANDERY K. T. TO San Francisco, Cal., Aug. 4 to Sept. 4, 1883.

GEORGE A. GILLETTE,
Standard Bearer.

EDGAR F. HUNT,
Sword Bearer.

CHARLES F. ATWOOD,
Warder.

GEORGE G. STRATTON,
ABIJAH THOMPSON,
JOHN BLACKIE,
SIDNEY M. HEDGES,
CHARLES L. RUSSELL,
LEONARD M. AVERELL,
Guards.

DAVID S. SIMPSON,
Armorer.

CALEB BOWKER,
Sentinel.

Past Em. Sir SILAS ALDEN, Past Grand Captain General and proxy for the Grand Captain General of Maine; Past Em. Sir MARVIN S. FELLOWS, of Connecticut Valley Commandery; Past Em. Sir WM. J. ELLIS, of William Parkman Commandery; together with the

MEDICAL STAFF.

Sir Wm. Dan. Lamb, M. D., *Director.*
Sir Harrison A. Tucker, M. D. Em. Sir William S. Severance, M. D.
Em. Sir Charles E. Severance, M. D.,
supplemented the Staff of the Eminent Commander.

SIR KNIGHTS.

Atwood, Charles F., Boston.
Averell, Leonard M., Boston.
Alden, Silas, Bangor, Me.
Adams, Charles E., Lowell.
Abbott, Frank A., Fisherville, N. H.
Bowker, Caleb, Boston.
Batchelder, Henry L., Boston.
Brown, Samuel F., Fisherville, N. H.
Bailey, Jacob L., East Cambridge.
Barnard, Edwin, North Adams.
Bliss, A. L., Taunton.
Bunton, William A., Cambridge.
Bailey, Amasa W., Boston.
Blackie, John, Boston.
Bliss, James F., Boston.
Brigham, A. W., Boston.
Brainerd, Le Roy, Portland, Conn.
Brooks, E. F., Brattleboro', Vt.
Cain, Stephen, East Weymouth.
Call, Thomas E., Portsmouth, N. H.
Cook, Randall W., South Abington.
Cook, R. O., Woonsocket, R. I.

DEAN, BENJAMIN, BOSTON.

Devereaux, Charles J., Boston.
Dewell, James D., New Haven, Ct.
Ellis, William J., East Boston.
Fairbanks, Charles A., Boston.
Gleason, James M., Boston.
Gale, John D., Boston.
Gillette, George A., Boston.
Greely, Leander, Cambridgeport.
Hapgood, Lyman S., Boston.
Hedges, Sidney M., Boston.
Hewett, George F., Worcester.
Houston, James, Boston.
Ingersoll, Howard F., Gloucester.
Johnson, Francis H., Cambridgeport.
Jenks, Albert A., Pawtucket, R. I.
Kakas, Edward, Boston.
Morrill, Alfred, Cambridgeport.
Munroe, Martin A., Boston.
Montgomery, Alex., Boston.
Mathews, George W., Worcester.
Richards, Eugene H., Boston.
Russell, Charles L., Cambridgeport.
Russell, Walter, Arlington.
Roberts, Rev. Oliver Ayer, Salisbury.
Furber, Samuel N., Wolfboro', N. H.
Field, Charles W., Jr., Clinton.
Fellows, Marvin S., Greenfield.
Freeman, G. R., Bridgewater.
Garfield, Silas, Worcester.
Gibbs, William H., Clinton.
Gosling, George, Central Falls, R. I.
Goss, G. Walton, Clinton.
Hooper, George R., Somerville.
Hurd, Webster, Boston.
Hunt, Edgar F., Cambridgeport.
Haskins, C. R., Myrick's.
Lamb, Wm. Dan., Southbridge.
Lauriat, Charles P., Medford.
Lawton, Charles, East Stoughton.
Mace, Lyman R., Boston.
Miller, Wilbur F., Ludlow.
Nichols, Edward T., Cambridgeport.
Parker, George F., Winchester.
Phillips, I. B., Woonsocket, R. I.
Reed, Harry D., North Abington.
Rust, Samuel, South Hadley Falls.
Staples, Herbert M., Taunton.

STEVENSON, JOHN L., BOSTON.

SHILLABER, JONAS G., Boston.
SIMPSON, D. S., Newtonville.
SMITH, ALFRED M., Dedham.
SMITH, BENJAMIN F., Boston.
SMITH, W. H. L., Boston.
SHAFFER, STILLMAN L., Worcester.
SHERMAN, ZACHEUS, Taunton.
SMITH, GEORGE M., Springfield.
TARBELL, EVERETT E., East Pepperell.
TUCK, W. L., Boston.
WESTON, C. D., Boston.
WALKER, JOHN P., Providence, R. I.
WHEELER, LYMAN W., Boston.
WHITTAKER, JOHN, Fisherville, N. H.
WHITCOMB, FRANK H., Keene, N. H.
WHITING, WILLIAM S., Boston.
SHATTUCK, RALPH W., Arlington.
STRATTON, GEORGE G., Winchester.
SEVERANCE, CHAS. E., Shelburne Falls.
SEVERANCE, WILLIAM S., Greenfield.
THOMPSON ABIJAH, Winchester.
THOMAS, ZEPH. H., Cambridgeport.
TRULL, EZRA J., Boston.
TUCKER, H. A., Brooklyn, N. Y.
WALKER, SAMUEL H., Taunton.
WALKER, WILLIAM E., Taunton.
WALKER, WILLIAM L., Taunton.
WASHBURN, P. T., Taunton.
WILBER, WILLIAM B., South Boston.
WILLIAMS, GEO. W., Providence, R I.
WINSOR, EDWIN, Providence, R. I.
WOOD, FRANK C., East Boston.
WOOD, BAYLIES, South Abington.

WALKER, Mr. W. A., Reporter of the Boston *Herald*.

LADIES.

ABBOTT, Mrs. FRANK A., Fisherville, N. H.
ADAMS, Mrs. CHARLES E., Lowell.
ATWOOD, Mrs. CHARLES F., Boston.
AVERELL, Mrs. LEONARD M., Boston.
BATCHELDER, Mrs. HENRY L., Boston.
BLACKIE, Mrs. JOHN, Boston.
BLISS, Mrs. A. L., Taunton.
BROWN, Mrs. SAMUEL F., Fisherville, N. H.
BUNTON, Mrs. WILLIAM A., Cambridgeport.
CALL, Miss MARY E., Portsmouth, N. H.
DEAN, Mrs. BENJAMIN, Boston.
DEAN, Miss MARY, Boston.
DEVEREAUX, Mrs. CHARLES J., Boston.
DEWELL, Mrs. JAMES D., New Haven, Conn.
DEWELL, Miss JESSIE K., New Haven, Conn.
EARLE, Mrs. BELLE S., Providence, R. I.
ELLIS, Mrs. WILLIAM J., East Boston.
FAIRBANKS, Mrs. CHARLES A., Boston.
GALE, Mrs. JOHN D., Boston.
GATES, Miss A. GERTRUDE, West Roxbury.
GILLETTE, Mrs. GEORGE A., Boston.
HEWETT, Mrs. GEORGE F., Worcester.
HEWETT, Miss MABEL E., Worcester.
HUGHES, Miss MARY L., Somerville.
HURD, Mrs. WEBSTER, Boston.
HUSE, Mrs. ELEANOR, Winchester.
JOHNSON, Mrs. FRANCIS H., Cambridgeport.
KAKAS, Mrs. EDWARD, Boston.
LAURIAT, Miss ANNIE G., Medford.
MACE, Mrs. LYMAN R., Boston.
MILLER, Miss E. M., Ludlow.
MUNROE, Mrs. MARTIN A., Boston.
NICHOLS, Mrs. EDWARD T., Cambridgeport.
PARKER, Mrs. GEORGE F., Winchester.
PARKER, Miss M. L., Winchester.
PARKER, Miss SUSIE E., Winchester.
PECK, Mrs. R. C., New Haven, Conn.
PHIPPS, Miss ELIZA A., Bangor, Me.
RUSSELL, Mrs. CHARLES L., Cambridgeport.
RICHARDS, Mrs. EUGENE H., Boston.
SANBORN, Mrs. MARY S., Winchester.
SEVERANCE, Mrs. WM. S., Greenfield.

SHERMAN, Mrs. ZACHEUS, Taunton.
SHILLABER, Miss KATHARINE B., Boston.
SIMPSON, Mrs. D. S., Newtonville.
SMITH, Mrs. W. H. L., Boston.
STAPLES, Mrs. HERBERT M., Taunton.
STEVENSON, Miss GRACE A., Boston.
STEVENSON, Mrs. JOHN L., Boston.
STONE, Mrs. E. M., Springfield.
THOMPSON, Mrs. ABIJAH, Winchester.
TRULL, Mrs. EZRA J., Boston.
TUCKER, Mrs. H. A., Brooklyn, N. Y.
TUCKER, Miss N. D., Brooklyn, N. Y.
WALKER, Miss BERTHA F., Taunton.
WALKER, Mrs. JOHN P., Providence, R. I.
WALKER, Miss MARY E., Taunton.
WALKER Mrs. SAM'L H., Taunton.
WALKER, Mrs. WM. E., Taunton.
WALKER, Mrs. WM. L., Taunton.
WILLIAMS, Mrs. GEO. W., Providence, R. I.
WINSOR, Mrs. EDWIN, Providence, R. I.
WOOD, Mrs. FRANK C., East Boston.

The following committees were appointed for the pilgrimage:—

EXECUTIVE.

JOHN L. STEVENSON, EUGENE H. RICHARDS, JAMES M. GLEASON,
WILLIAM A. BUNTON, GEORGE F. HEWETT.

MEDICAL STAFF.

WM. DAN. LAMB, *Director.*
HARRISON A. TUCKER, M. D., WILLIAM S. SEVERANCE, M. D.,
CHARLES E. SEVERANCE, M. D.

LADIES.

ABIJAH THOMPSON, W. H. L. SMITH, JOHN D. GALE.

TRANSPORTATION.

EDWARD T. NICHOLS, ALFRED M. SMITH, AMASA W. BAILEY.

The Pullman cars were in charge of the following named Sir Knights, who were responsible for the safety and comfort of their occupants as far as possible:—

Car "Almeria"	SIR JAMES M. GLEASON.
Car "Modena"	SIR GEORGE F. HEWETT.
Car "Odessa"	SIR EDWARD T. NICHOLS.
Car "Albania"	SIR WILLIAM A. BUNTON.
Car "Echo"	SIR ABIJAH THOMPSON.
Car "Como"	SIR EUGENE H. RICHARDS.

BOSTON COMMANDERY OF KNIGHTS TEMPLARS,
BOSTON, May 2, 1883.

HON. CALEB SAUNDERS,

    Grand Commander of the Grand Commandery K∴ T∴ of Massachusetts and Rhode Island:

Right Eminent Sir, — Boston Commandery having made arrangements to attend the Twenty-second Triennial Conclave, to be held in San Francisco, Cal., in August next, as the escort of M. E. Sir Benjamin Dean, Grand Master of the Grand Encampment K. T. of the United States of America, I have the honor, in accordance with Templar regulations, to apply in behalf of the Commandery for a dispensation to parade on Saturday, Aug. 4, for the above-mentioned purpose, proceeding to San Francisco, and returning on or about Sept. 4, 1883. I also ask permission, through you, of the Grand Commanders of those jurisdictions through which we pass, that Boston Commandery may be permitted to parade in full Templar costume within their respective dominions.

    Courteously yours,

        John L. Stevenson,

        Eminent Commander Boston Commandery K∴ T∴

OFFICE OF THE GRAND COMMANDER,
LAWRENCE, July 17, 1883.

EM∴ SIR JOHN L. STEVENSON:

Dear Sir Knight, — I herewith send dispensation asked for in yours of May 2. Immediately on receiving your letter, I wrote to the Grand Commanders of California, and of the several States through which you must pass, asking permission for you to appear in full regalia at such points as you might desire.

Several of the Grand Commanders have expressed the wish to extend official courtesies to your command *en route*, and wish to know the time of your arrival within their jurisdiction. I enclose the address of each of them. Hoping that your pilgrimage may be entirely successful, and of great pleasure and profit to you and all the Sir Knights and ladies who accompany you,

I am, yours in Knightly bonds,

CALEB SAUNDERS.
Grand Commander.

GRAND COMMANDERY OF KNIGHTS TEMPLARS AND APPENDANT ORDERS OF MASSACHUSETTS AND RHODE ISLAND.

OFFICE OF THE GRAND COMMANDER,
LAWRENCE, MASS., July 17, 1883

JOHN L. STEVENSON,
Eminent Commander Boston Commandery:

Eminent Sir, — A dispensation is hereby granted to Boston Commandery to parade in full Templar costume, and with banners and music, on Saturday, Aug. 4, for the purpose of proceeding from Boston to San Francisco, Cal., to be present at the Triennial Conclave of the Grand Encampment, U. S. A., as escort to the Most Eminent Grand Master. Said Commandery has permission to be absent during such period as may best suit their convenience, not exceeding two months, and may parade at such places *en route* and at San Francisco as they may desire, special permission having been received by me from the several Grand Commanders of the jurisdictions through which said Commandery must pass going, remaining, and returning.

CALEB SAUNDERS,
Grand Commander.

The following is a list of the Grand Commanders whose permission was obtained, and also of their jurisdictions: —

M. A. TAYLOR, Nashua, N. H.
ALFRED A. HALL, St. Albans, Vt.
W. J. B. McLEOD MOORE,
　St. John's, Prov. Q., Canada.
J. E. SAXTON, Detroit, Mich.
HENRY TURNER, Chicago, Ill.
F. J. TYGARD, Butler, Mo.
HENRY M. WATERS, Independence, Kan.
M. H. FITCH, Pueblo, Col.
GEO. C. PERKINS, San Francisco, Cal.
WM. R. BOWEN, *Grand Recorder*, Omaha, Neb.
HENRY W. ROTHERT, Keokuk, Iowa.

The following correspondence is self-explanatory: —

BOSTON COMMANDERY OF KNIGHTS TEMPLARS,
BOSTON, MASS., Feb. 26, 1883.

M∴ E∴ BENJ. DEAN,
　Grand Master.

At the regular Conclave of Boston Commandery, held on the 21st instant, it was unanimously

Voted, "That the services of Boston Commandery K. T. be tendered to the M. E Grand Master of Knights Templars of the United States of America, as his escort *to, from, and during the session of the Twenty-second Triennial Conclave* of the Grand Encampment of the United States of America, to be held in San Francisco, Cal., commencing Aug. 21, 1883."

It gives us great pleasure to forward this *vote,* and, presenting our compliments, beg the favor of an early and favorable reply.

　　　　　Courteously yours,

Attest:
　S. A. Thomas,
　　Recorder.

　　　　　John L. Stevenson,
　　　　　　Eminent Commander.

*Grand Encampment of Knights Templars
of the United States of America
Office of the Grand Master.*

Benjamin Dean,
Grand Master

Boston, March 2, 1883.

JOHN L. STEVENSON, ESQ.,
 Eminent Commander, Boston Commandery K∴ T∴

Dear Sir Knight, — I am in receipt of your letter of Feb. 26, in which you tell me that Boston Commandery has kindly tendered to the Grand Master its services as an escort to the Triennial Conclave of the Grand Encampment of the United States, to be held in San Francisco, in August next. I accept the tender of escort of Boston Commandery with pleasure and with pride. Its services in the preservation of the Ritual and Work of the Order, and of the unity in Massachusetts and Rhode Island of the Templars during the dark days of anti-Masonry, its long-continued career of prosperity, more manifest than ever under your wise and energetic administration, should endear the name of Boston Commandery to every lover of our institution.

I have informed the triennial committee at San Francisco of your courtesy to the Grand Master and loyalty to the Grand Encampment, and have no doubt you will meet with a cordial and honorable reception.

Yours in the bonds of Knighthood,

Benj. Dean,
 Grand Master.

CHAPTER IV.

At half past six o'clock precisely, on the evening of Aug. 4, the starting bell rang, the engine began to move, and amid cheers, applause, waving of handkerchiefs, and the music of Carter's band, the special train carrying its knightly freight drew slowly out of the depot, and the pilgrimage from Boston to the Golden Gate began. Soon the familiar "landmarks" of the city faded from sight, and hills and fields welcomed us.

An evening paper of Aug. 4 recorded that "as the train disappeared in the distance, the last person that could be discerned was Eminent Commander John L. Stevenson, waving a farewell to the friends left behind."

First, each passenger was made the possessor of a ticket book, five and one half inches long, two and one half inches wide, and three quarters of an inch thick, elegantly bound in turkey morocco, and bearing the inscription in gold, on the front cover, "Boston Commandery, Knights Templars, California Pilgrimage, 1883." It contained ninety-five tickets for railroad fares, hotel accommodations, transfers, etc., sufficient for a month's tour from ocean to ocean and return. An itinerary of the pilgrimage, covering each day during the trip, was given each member of the party. This itinerary of twenty-six pages, each bearing a large Maltese cross in red, compiled and presented to the Commandery, with the compliments of the railroad companies over whose roads the pilgrimage was made, was a model of the engraver's art, and contained much valuable information. Under each day, with the hours of arrival and departure at the various stopping places, it noted the various points of special interest, and gave descriptive and historical notices of value. In addition, a very handsome souvenir, bearing Templar emblems, and containing a complete list of the pilgrims, was distributed among them.

The early evening hours were spent by the pilgrims in getting settled on the train, and in exchanging congratulations on the happy beginning of the pilgrimage.

We find the party composed of ministers, doctors, lawyers, merchants, railroad conductors, hotel proprietors, bankers, brokers, jewellers, "bondholders," manufacturers, and others; and in this party of respectable people, with his usual tact for crowding himself into good company, we find the ever-present "Sewing Machine Man." Yes, it's a fact, but *mum* is the word, and if he conducts himself like a gentleman it will be well, but should he attempt to ply any one of the tricks of the profession on this train we will "cut his thread off below the eye," and leave the "head" on some Western prairie for repairs. — *Sir S. L. S., in Sewing Machine News, December,* 1883.

Multitudes greeted us at Fitchburg, Keene, and other towns. The run during the night over the Fitchburg, Cheshire, Connecticut and Central Vermont Railroads was accomplished as per programme. Sir S. W. Cummings, general passenger agent of the latter road, having the direction of affairs, accompanied us to Montreal. Notwithstanding the grand scenery by which we were speeding, "the deep fertile valleys, gently sloping uplands, verdant hillsides, and cloud-capped summits" of Vermont, the sleep of the pilgrims, tired by the excitement and duty of the day, was undisturbed. Bright and early, we wakened and caught a glimpse of the beauty of Vermont in gazing into and across the deep, wide valley on whose farther side Lake Champlain glistened under the morning sun, when Canada with its broad fields and custom-house officers appeared.

Twenty-seven miles over the Grand Trunk were quickly run, Victoria Bridge was reached and safely passed, and we stopped in Montreal. Carriages were in waiting, by which the party was transferred to the Windsor Hotel, where breakfast was provided.

Windsor Hotel, whose external appearance immediately prejudices one in its favor, occupies a commanding site on Dominion Square, near Mount Royal Park. Our short tarry convinced us of its generous management and the homelike comfort of its guests. It was a delightful season we spent at the Windsor, and our lengthened stay on the homeward trip was looked forward to with pleasure. The souvenir *menu* cards prepared for the occasion were quite unique and remarkably appropriate. When unfolded they were in the shape of a Maltese cross, and when gathered together formed prettily draped tents, folding neatly together for carriage. The reverse of the card was printed in light tints, two of the arms of the cross representing fine engravings of the Windsor and the city of Montreal from the river, while the other two contained respectively the cross and crown monogram of the Order and the inscription.

WINDSOR HOTEL, MONTREAL.

The quiet of Montreal's Sunday hours was not disturbed by the "168," who appreciated their sunshine and peace. The reception of the party at this fine hotel was cordial and princely, and the two hours passed pleasantly.

At 10.45 A. M. the trip over the Grand Trunk Railroad, from Montreal to Port Huron, began, and ended Monday at 6.45 A. M. The special schedule time of the Templar train was made very fast,— too fast for the power applied. This, with broken-down freight trains and hot boxes, occasioned a loss of several hours. The delay was patiently endured and a general desire was manifest to make the best of it. Sunday afternoon we rode along the north bank of the St. Lawrence River, getting glimpses now and then of the great stream, with its rapids and islands.

The prairie-like fields, reaching for miles, were not what we expected to see in Canada. Quietness reigned in town and country, on the line of the road. A carriage was seldom seen, and loungers about the stations were the exception. The day was appropriately observed. Several praise meetings were held on the train. At Fredericksburg, 5.30 P. M., being delayed by a hot box, an open-air concert was given on the platform of the depot, Gospel hymn-books having been provided by a friend of the Commandery. Sir Knight W. F. Miller, of Springfield, acted as precentor very acceptably. It was not a weary Sunday, but one full of song and gratitude. The dinner and supper of Sunday were provided on two dining-cars, which added much to the weight of our train and increased our lost time. The meals were abundant and well served. At 9 P. M. we were one hundred and nine miles east of Toronto, where two engines were attached, and we were hurried along. It was, however, 1.40 A. M. when we left Toronto, the hot box of the "Odessa" refusing to "keep cool."

Crossing the St. Clair at Port Huron, at 6.45 A. M., Monday, on a colossal, three-tracked ferry-boat, we proceeded over the Chicago and Grand Trunk Railroad. This transfer across the St. Clair brought us again on Yankee soil, where Yankees cared for the road-bed and a Yankee's arm pulled the engine's lever. It was all observable by the lively manner in which our train hurried up, flying through forest, over plain, and by the neat houses and loaded grain-fields of Michigan.

Failing to reach Battle Creek for breakfast at 7 A. M., the hour appointed, coffee, tea, crackers, and other refreshments were freely served in the morning, on the special car, No. 99, by Commander Stevenson.

Our rate of speed being increased, and confidence in the railroad management having been restored, "all went merry as a marriage bell." At 10.40 A. M. Lansing, the capital of Michigan, was passed, and at 12 M. the Commandery lunched at Battle Creek. The forty-six miles between Lansing and Battle Creek were covered by the train in sixty-eight minutes. At Battle Creek engine No. 66, called Jumbo, was attached to draw the train to Chicago. By the kind thoughtfulness of friends, the locomotive was decorated with red, white, and blue streamers and festoons, with knightly spears as standards for United States flags, and on either side, over the cylinder, was placed a Maltese cross of black, bearing the letters "I. H. S. V." in white. The engine was driven by Sir Knight George Jones, of Battle Creek Commandery, and the conductor was Sir Knight Jacob A. Henry of the same Commandery, both of whom were decorated by the Eminent Commander with badges of Boston Commandery. The *Journal* of Aug. 6, Battle Creek, Mich., thus referred to the arrival, etc., of Boston Commandery at that place: —

THE SIR KNIGHTS. — A SPECIAL TRAIN ESCORTING THE MOST EMINENT GRAND MASTER TO THE SAN FRANCISCO CONCLAVE. — HONORS EXTENDED BY THE CHICAGO AND GRAND TRUNK RAILWAY COMPANY.

A special train of Pullman palace dining, sleeping, and reclining-chair coaches, consisting of eight cars and a baggage van, passed through this city at 11.30 A. M. to-day, having on board one hundred and seventy-five Sir Knights of the Boston Commandery, under Eminent Commander John L. Stevenson, accompanied by many lady friends of the Sir Knights. The Commandery was escorting the Most Eminent Grand Master of the United States, Benjamin Dean, of South Boston, *en route* to San Francisco. The pilgrimage commenced Saturday evening at 6.30 in the same coaches, which will go through to the Pacific slope with them without change, the Sir Knights being furnished transportation and all expenses during their absence for $300 each by contract.

From Grand Trunk Junction to this city the run was made in four hours and twenty minutes, making up nearly an hour of the time lost last night, caused by hot journals on one of the sleepers. The train to this city was under control of Conductor N. D. Austin, while the engine, No. 61, was run by Harry Ryan, and judging from the hand-shaking these gentlemen received as they left the train at this end of the division, they had made themselves popular with the Knights during their short acquaintance.

At this station engine No. 66, with Sir Knight George Jones, engineer, was despatched to carry the train into Chicago, where they expect to arrive at 5.30 this evening. The train was placed in charge of Sir Knight Jacob A. Henry as conductor, Supt. W. H. Pettibone having taken especial pains to select employés belonging to the Order.

Engine 66 was gayly decorated with banners, emblems, ribbons, and flags, prominent among which were the large Maltese crosses on either side, bearing the letters I. H. S. V. — "*In hoc signo vinces.*" A green flag, showing that the train was a special and was running regardless of all other trains, was also displayed.

At this station the train stopped twenty minutes for dinner, the meal being furnished by Mr. John Wilson, who has charge of the eating-house and dining-cars of the company. He was assisted by Geo. N. Potter, who manipulated the waiters and assisted the proprietor in various ways.

The tables were spread especially for the Sir Knights, and were loaded with all the delicacies of the season. Each plate had an elaborately designed bill of fare, and the napkins enfolded a button-hole bouquet, which the happy feasters displayed conspicuously on the lappels of their coats after eating.

The pilgrims expressed themselves as satisfied with their usage since coming on to the Chicago and Grand Trunk road, but said some very uncomplimentary things of the railways to the east of us. They compose one of the largest as well as oldest Commanderies in the United States, and are generally men of wealth and refinement, so that it was not a very surprising thing that they took exception to some things which might perhaps have been unavoidable.

A bugle call assembled the Sir Knights on board the cars after the dinner, and the train pulled out for Chicago with the well-satisfied party. Supt. W. H. Pettibone and Eminent Commander Wm. Andrus, of this city, accompanied the excursion to Chicago.

At Thornton, Ind., twenty-six miles east of Chicago, the train was boarded by a detachment of Sir Knights from Chicago, forty in number, who came to pay their respects to the M. E. Grand Master, Benjamin Dean, and to Boston Commandery, and welcome them to their city.

The delegation was courteously received and hospitably entertained by Eminent Commander John L. Stevenson, in the headquarters of Boston Commandery. Subsequently, the Chicago Sir Knights scattered themselves through the train, were cordially received by the pilgrims, and were safely landed in Chicago at 6 P. M. The pilgrims were immediately transferred by carriages to the Grand Pacific Hotel, where an excellent dinner was thoroughly enjoyed.

On our return to the station, the drill corps of St. Bernard Commandery drew up in line near the train and extended knightly courtesies. Grand Master Dean responded by addressing the battalion, and Eminent Commander Stevenson, in behalf of his command, acknowledged the honor. At 9 P. M. the train started on its western way, the St. Bernards, the people, and the Bostons cheering one another. The *Evening News* of Aug. 7, Chicago, Ill., notices the arrival and appearance of the Boston Sir Knights in the following flattering terms: —

TRAVELLING KNIGHTS. — THE BOSTON COMMANDERY EN ROUTE TO THE TRIENNIAL CONCLAVE AT SAN FRANCISCO.

The Boston Commandery Knights Templars arrived in the city last evening, by special train over the Grand Trunk Railroad. The party was received by representatives of St. Bernard Commandery. The pilgrims number one hundred and sixty-eight, including sixty ladies, wives and daughters of the Knights. Attired in their single-breasted frock coats, buttoned to the chin, and lappels and bosoms covered with the glittering insignia of rank, the Knights made a fine appearance.

At the Grand Pacific they scattered through the building, supping by twos and fours, everybody taking care of himself and, mayhap, his wife. There were a few dude Knights among them who had thrown aside the regulation uniform and were attired in white flannel blouses and tight pants, with monumental collars and crushed raspberry toothpick shoes.

The special train carrying the party left last night over the Chicago, Burlington and Quincy Railroad for Kansas City.

Our route westward was across Illinois, over the Chicago, Burlington and Quincy, and across Missouri over the Hannibal and St. Joseph Railroads. Monday night we crossed Illinois, 263 miles, passing Aurora, Mendota, Galesburg, Bushnell, and other thriving towns, and at 7 A. M. arrived at Quincy, where we went through with the usual breakfast motions. Proceeding, we crossed the Mississippi on one of the finest iron bridges in the world and entered Missouri, by whose empty slave cabins and through whose fields and woods we hastened towards Kansas City.

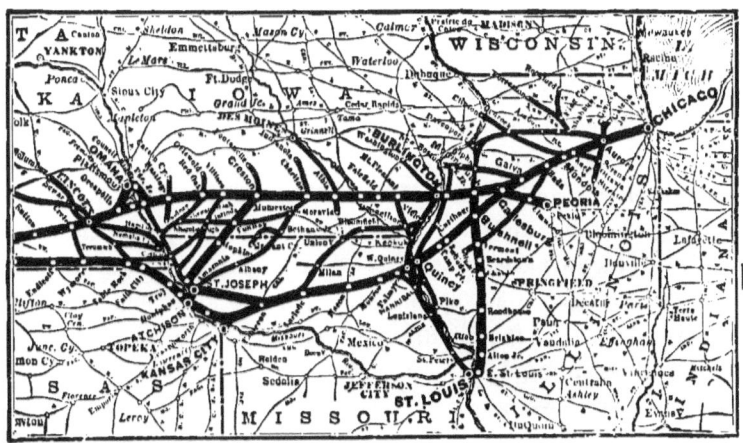

The ride of this day was greatly enjoyed by the command. A rain during the night before prevented dust, the breeze was cool and fragrant, and lost time was being regained. The fields of Missouri were very beautiful, the soil appeared fertile, and the gathered harvest seemed abundant. Sir Knight Smith and his drum corps deserve special mention for their unexpected contribution to the pleasures of the day. His purchase of toy drums and tin whistles at Quincy was thoughtful, and the natural efficiency of his performers in executing familiar airs was remarkable. There was no dearth of song and laughter on the train, for all joined in inventing proper episodes to relieve the monotony of railroad riding.

We dined at Cameron in the station dining-room, said to be the room where Jesse James, the notorious highwayman, was laid out after his tragic death.

At 4.30 P. M. we crossed the muddy Missouri and entered Kansas City, where a multitude of people awaited Boston Commandery. Sir John H. Brown, Past Grand Master of Kansas and Recorder of Grand Commandery Knights Templars of Kansas, and Sir Henry M. Waters, Eminent Grand Commander Knights Templars of Kansas, paid their respects to Most Em. Grand Master Dean and Eminent Commander Stevenson. Sir Knight Daggett, formerly of Boston, boarded the train and was warmly received, having travelled a hundred miles to meet Boston Commandery. At Kansas City we were detained some time by the recurrence of a familiar complaint — "hot box" — and the additional weakness of a broken journal.

The Russian "Odessa" is cold. For two months each year navigation sleeps — the harbor is completely frozen over. The Pullman "Odessa" could not be kept cold or cool, but its hot box was a constant annoyance. The train was stopped at the "yards," just outside the city; "Odessa" was switched out and "Mohave" was switched in. Mo-have or Mo-ha-ve? What does it mean? Mohave — a county in Arizona, named from the Mohave Indians. The county is in the vicinity of "Dry Lakes," "Death Valley," and Yuma, — hot Yuma, — where overcoats are not needed. Mohave is very suggestive of heat. Will we be further annoyed by a hot box of the Mohave, name of ill-omen? We felt somewhat relieved when we left "Odessa" at Kansas City, and, drawn by a powerful locomotive, proceeded over a superb road-bed with a clear track.

The *Journal* of Kansas City, Mo., Aug. 8, 1883, mentions the arrival of pilgrim Knights bound westward: —

PILGRIM KNIGHTS. — Three large excursions of Knights Templars passed through the city yesterday on their pilgrimage to the Triennial Conclave at San Francisco. The first to arrive was a Philadelphia Commandery, consisting of about seventy-five Sir Knights and forty ladies. De Molay Commandery, of Reading, Pa., came in *via* a special sleeper on the Wabash during the forenoon, consisting of twenty Sir Knights.

The largest excursion was that of Boston Commandery, of Boston, Mass. It came in *via* a special train, composed of six Pullman sleepers, on the Chicago, Burlington and Quincy from Chicago, in charge of General Agent J. A. S. Reed and Conductor J. S. Stephens, arriving at 4.30 P. M., and departing almost immediately *via* the Santa Fé. The party consisted of one hundred and five Sir Knights and sixty-three ladies, and it may be truthfully said that no finer body of gallant Knights and lovely ladies will be in attendance at the Conclave. The excursion left Boston last Saturday evening and came directly through without change of cars, making brief stops at Montreal and Toronto, Canada, and Chicago From here they go by the Southern route, touching at La Junta, Col., Las Vegas, Santa Fé, Tucson, and Los Angeles, arriving in San Francisco on the evening of the 14th inst.

Among the prominent members of the party was Hon. Benjamin Dean of Boston, Most Eminent Grand Master of the United States, who in a brief conversation with a *Journal* reporter expressed himself as perfectly delighted with the trip thus far, and, further, that the coming Conclave would be the most successful of any yet held. Mr. Dean was under the escort of this Commandery, which, together with the fact of its seniority, entitles the Bostons to the post of honor in the grand Templar procession. The party would not have been complete without a reporter, who was present in the person of W. A. Walker, Esq., the brilliant and versatile correspondent of the Boston *Herald*.

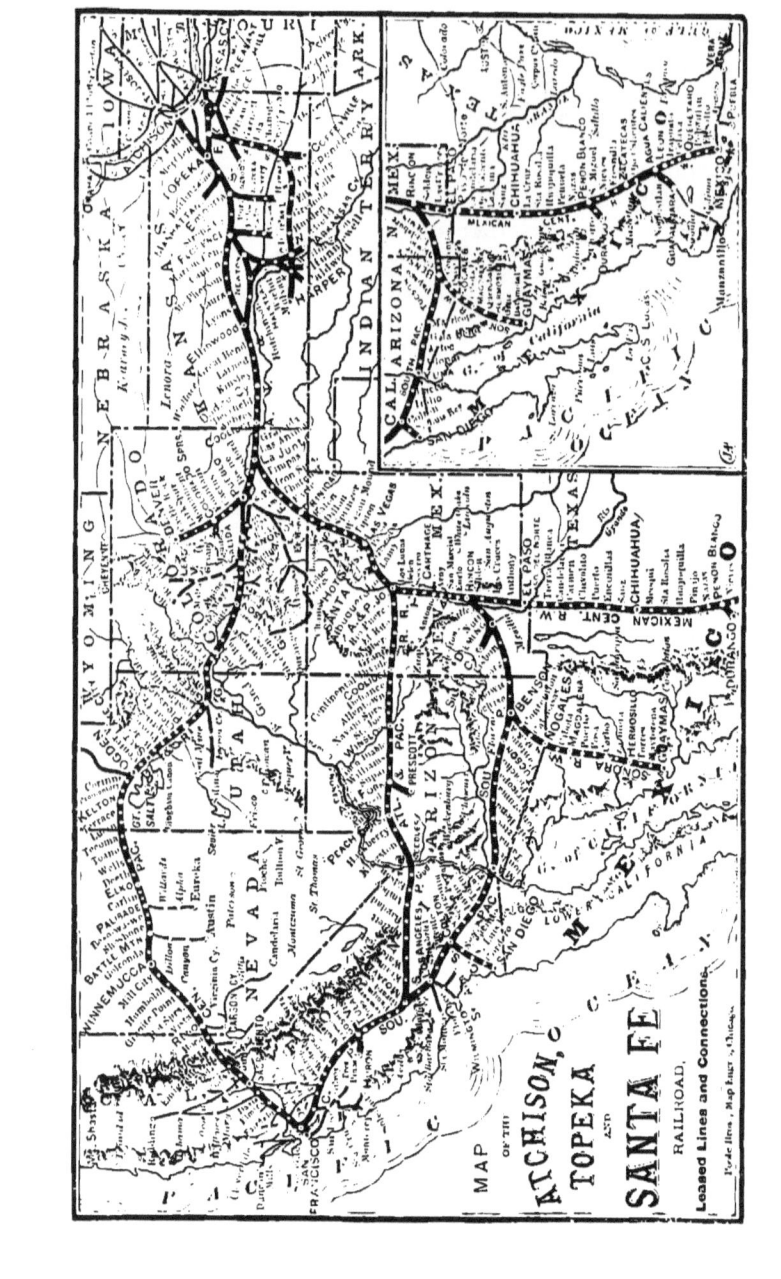

CHAPTER V.

OUR departure from Kansas City was by the Atchison, Topeka and Santa Fé Railroad, which extends its iron arm 1,149 miles westward. It was dusk when we sought a view of Lawrence, with its

DOGS ON GUARD

"Massachusetts" Street and New England people. We desired to see Lawrence, not alone because it is situated in the richest and

TOPEKA, KANSAS.

most fertile section of Kansas, nor because it is the most beautiful city in the State, but also because it bears the name and perpetuates the memory of one who truly "devoted the remaining years of life (1831-1852) to acts of exalted usefulness and pure beneficence," and because it was the headquarters of freemen in the Kansas struggle, — city of freedom, martyrdom, and victory.

Topeka, the capital of Kansas, was reached at 8.45 P. M. Topeka Commandery Knights Templars, No. 5, Bryce McMurtrie, Eminent Commander, in full regalia and accompanied by the Capital City Cornet Band, was in waiting, and tendered knightly courtesies to the Grand Master and Boston Commandery. After an extended interview, Topeka Commandery returned to its asylum for work, where the Grand Master and Eminent Commander would have returned the call had time permitted.

The courteous intentions of the Sir Knights of Topeka appeared in the *Commonwealth* of Tuesday morning, Aug. 7, which said: —

KNIGHTS TEMPLARS RECEPTION. — A special communication of Topeka Commandery, No. 5, was held last evening to perfect arrangements for the reception of Grand Master Benjamin Dean and his escort, the Boston Commandery, who will arrive *via* Santa Fé road at noon to-day, *en route* for San Francisco. The Sir Knights of Topeka Commandery will assemble at 12 M., and at 1 P. M. will march in full uniform to the depot, accompanied by the Capital City Cornet Band, and extend the courtesies and knightly honors due the distinguished visitors.

Arrangements were also made for the reception to be tendered the Galesburg Commandery, which is to arrive from Atchison on the 10th inst. The party will arrive at noon, and remain until the departure of the midnight train for the West. The reception committee consists of Sir Knights T. J. Anderson, J. B. Hibben, W. W. Manspeaker, J. V. Moffitt, G. B. Palmer, Furman Baker, H. C. Miner, J. P. Rodgers, John Elliott, O T. Welch, W. C Chaffee, Louie Dutcher, and M. R. Oswald. These gentlemen will take the visitors in charge, and show them over the city. Returning to their train, they will make preparations to attend the banquet which will be given at 9 P. M., to which they will be escorted by the Topeka Commandery, accompanied by the Capital City Cornet Band. The committee on arrangements consists of J. B. Hibben, J. V. Moffitt, Furman Baker, C. M. Atwood, and T. V. Codington.

Supper was taken at Topeka in the mammoth station dining-hall, owned and managed by the Atchison, Topeka and Santa Fé Railroad, and would have been a creditable meal in any first-class hotel. It was here that we first met Mr. Schemerhorn, who has supreme charge of the dining-rooms on this route. He accom-

A FRONTIER TOWN.

panied us one thousand one hundred and forty-nine miles, and placed the command under obligations for his efficiency and reliability. Nothing was wanting in quantity, quality, service, or price at these depot hotels. Though at some stations on the plains provisions are necessarily brought from a great distance, yet they were fresh and good, and all the meals were first class. The *Commonwealth* of Wednesday morning, Aug. 8, thus alluded to the arrival of the Bostons: —

THE JOURNEYING SIR KNIGHTS. — M∴ E∴ GRAND MASTER DEAN AND THE BOSTON COMMANDERY KNIGHTS TEMPLARS ON THEIR PILGRIMAGE.

The programme regarding the informal reception in honor of Grand Master Benjamin Dean, *en route* for San Francisco, escorted by the Boston Commandery, was varied little from that announced yesterday, except as to time. Owing to slight delays at different points the special train did not arrive at this place until last evening at 7.30. The short delay on the Santa Fé was caused by the bursting of a journal of one of the sleepers between Kansas City and Argentine, and a new car was quickly switched in. Most of the time was lost east of Chicago. At the depot they were met by Topeka Commandery, about fifty strong, in full uniform, the Capital City Cornet Band, and a very large number of our citizens, but no formal reception was held. The travellers took supper, remaining only about an hour in all, and left for the West.

There were in the party one hundred and nine Sir Knights, and sixty-two ladies, and all report a very pleasant journey thus far, and express hopes for the balance, which will doubtless be realized.

The officers of the escorting Commandery are: John L. Stevenson, Eminent Commander, in charge; Eugene H. Richards, Generalissimo; Ezra J. Trull, Captain General; Oliver A. Roberts, Prelate; James M. Gleason, Senior Warden; William A. Bunton, Junior Warden; Jonas G. Shillaber, Treasurer; Zeph. H. Thomas, Recorder; George A. Gillette, Standard Bearer; Edgar F. Hunt, Sword Bearer; Chas. F. Atwood, Warder; George G. Stratton, Abijah Thompson, John Blackie, Sidney M. Hedges, Charles L. Russell, Leonard M. Averell, Guards; David S. Simpson, Armorer; Caleb Bowker, Sentinel.

Commander Dean is a jolly, smooth-shaven, red-faced, heavy-set man, some fifty years old, who evidently enjoys life and lives well. He wore no

ARKANSAS VALLEY.—HUTCHINSON IN THE DISTANCE.

uniform or emblem of any description, was dressed in a $2.50 linen suit, and looked much more happy and comfortable than many a bearded knight, bedecked in his showy uniform.

The train, consisting of eight sleepers, a coach and baggage car, will run as a special the entire trip. They left Boston Saturday evening, came *via* Montreal, Detroit, Chicago, and thence by the Burlington route, and are to arrive in San Francisco on the 14th, stopping on the way a day at Las Vegas, one at Santa Fé, and one day at Los Angeles. Charles F. Parsons, Colorado passenger agent of the Santa Fé, will have charge of the party as far as Deming, and there they will be turned over to Mr. S. M. Miller, of the Southern Pacific.

During the thirteen hours from Tuesday, 6 P. M., to Wednesday, 7 A. M., we ran three hundred and sixteen miles, from Kansas City, Mo., to Kinsley, Kan. At the latter place we had an excellent breakfast. Afterward a few began to sing, and soon a large party gathered upon the station platform and sang familiar hymns, which constituted a suitable prelude to the pleasures of the day. The three hundred and sixteen miles were all in Kansas, first in the valley of the " Kaw " or Kansas River, and then in the valley of the Arkansas. This broad, shallow, yellow river,—the Arkansas, —rising amid the snows of the Rocky Mountains, and pursuing its windings between the treeless banks, is of untold value to Kansas. The "garden" of our country stretches on both sides of the river, fifty miles from north to south, and two hundred miles east to west, at an elevation of two thousand five hundred feet. In climate it is superior, in fertility unexcelled. Our picture of the Arkansas Valley near Hutchinson gives a good view of

. . . "the gardens of the desert, these
The unshorn fields, boundless and beautiful,
And fresh as the young earth ere man had sinned,

> "Lo! they stretch
> In airy undulations far away,
> As if the ocean in his gentlest swell
> Stood still, with all his rounded billows fixed
> And motionless forever."

At Hutchinson we first came in sight of the Arkansas River, and followed the stream for two hundred and fifty miles, through the "Garden of the West." Hutchinson is in Reno County, has a population of two thousand five hundred, and is an important shipping point. We left the Arkansas when we turned south at La Junta. Though the broad valleys and rolling, unfenced prairies of Southwestern Kansas were covered with night's darkness, we could trace our way upon the map, and imagine the vast plains which surrounded us. Our attention was called to the names of the counties and towns along our route, evincing the loyalty of the first settlers. Among the former are, Lyon, Chase, Reno, McPherson, Gray, Kearney, Stanton, Grant, and to the north or south appear the names of Presidents, generals, statesmen, the latter including Sumner, Wilson, and Lane. Just prior to our arrival at Kinsley, we passed Garfield, a new town, named in honor of the late President — himself a Knight Templar — by its first settlers, who came from his congressional district in Ohio. Kinsley, where we tarried for two hours, was named in honor of a well-known citizen of Boston.

THE NEW SETTLEMENT.

Around Kinsley the country is a gentle, undulating prairie, watered by Coon Creek and the Arkansas River. The fertility is largely due to irrigation. The ditches extend fifty miles, and irrigate seventy-five thousand acres. Garden City, as luxuriant as prosperous, owes its importance to successful irrigation. We tarried there only a few minutes.

Ditches are being constructed so as to flood the whole valley of the Arkansas, at a cost to the owner of the land of one dollar an acre per annum. The mountain streams, laden with vegetable matter, deposit it on the fields irrigated by their waters, and thus fertility constantly increases. The average crops grown on these lands — like Kansas itself — are wonderful. Coolidge was reached, our fiery horse fed and watered, and we took our last view of Kansas. Two miles west of this town we crossed the line which separates the "Sunflower" from the "Centennial" State.

WEALTH ON FOOT.

"Colorado, rare Colorado! yonder she rests; her head of gold pillowed on the Rocky Mountains, her breast a shield of silver, her feet in the brown grass, the boundless plains for a play-ground," says Joaquin Miller. The country from Coolidge to La Junta is the same as Western Kansas, a plain, well adapted for grazing, as the cow-boys and shepherds with their herds and flocks abundantly prove. Every prominent station has its cattle-pen and arrangements for loading cattle into cars. Here, also, successful agriculture depends upon artificial irrigation, except along the river bottoms. It was 6 P. M. when we arrived at La Junta, having ascended from 2,207 feet elevation at Kinsley to 4,117 feet elevation at La Junta, a distance of two hundred and thirty-eight miles. La Junta is the junction of the Colorado and New Mexico lines of the Atchison, Topeka and Santa Fé Railroad. Here we had a late dinner, and received a tiny *menu*, ornamented with a pink bow, intended as "a souvenir

STAMPEDE.

to the Boston Commandery Knights Templars on the occasion of their passage through La Junta, Colorado, *en route* to San Francisco, Wednesday, Aug. 8, 1883," from S. Leipziger, manager La Junta Depot Hotel.

We can never forget the green grass plot, made from Kansas soil, on which we sat and frolicked while we of section No. 2, hungry and thirsty, waited for the hungry and thirsty section No. 1 to appease their hunger. "We very much prefer to be in the first section every time," so all of us would say, if it were not for the cruelty to those who would have to be in the second section "every time."

Had Boston Commandery proceeded north from La Junta instead of south, it would have reached Denver, "the Queen City

DOG TOWN.

of the Plains." Its appointed route, however, lay southward, and the pleasure of visiting that "municipal miracle" and the grand scenery adjacent was unexperienced. We think it was, but the Rocky Mountain *News*, Denver, Col., Aug. 10, 1883, thought otherwise. That paper contained the following: —

BOSTON SIR KNIGHTS. — A LARGE PARTY OF MASSACHUSETTS KNIGHTS TEMPLARS EN ROUTE FOR SAN FRANCISCO.

The Boston Commandery of Knights Templars arrived in Denver yesterday morning and partook of an excellent breakfast at Major Parsons's dining-rooms in the Union Depot. They came West by the Burlington, and will remain in the State some time, visiting various points of interest.

Then followed the names of all composing the Boston party. This was a clear case of mistaken identity.

Proceeding southward we ran nearly parallel with the great chain of the Rocky Mountains. The twin Spanish peaks (one 13,718 feet high) and Pike's Peak were plainly visible. We hastened across the southeast corner of Colorado, a rolling prairie, "carpeted with

THE OLD WAY.

nutritious buffalo-grass and many-colored cacti." Around us the once-famous buffalo grounds were spread, over which prairie-dogs now hold undisputed sway. Scores were seen sitting on their cone-shaped dwellings, unscared by the hissing steam and rattling cars.

Eighty-two miles from La Junta we reached Trinidad, the last town of importance in Colorado. It is an old town, and was memorable in the days of the "old Santa Fé trail." Here we observed for the first time the adobe houses, and realized we were approaching the country of the Aztec and burro.

The wagon road— the "old Santa Fé trail," which attracted our attention in Kansas—continues to run close to the railroad track. Occasionally we saw the "ships of the desert" making slow headway over the plains, or resting at anchor for "refreshment and sleep." But things have changed, and the tedious overland journey of a few years since has become a most pleasurable excursion.

DICK WOOTTON AT HOME.

Trinidad, Col., lies at the foot of the Raton Spur. Two engines hauled us up the sharp grade of one hundred and eighty-five feet to the mile. The fires of the coke ovens we passed appeared in the distance like the torchlights of a halted procession. An intelligent brakeman consumed the evening relating many tragic traditions of the Santa Fé trail,—the great overland road to Santa Fé from the East. Unwritten are the stories of this pass over the mountains,

We noticed Dick Wootton's great square house and ponderous gate where the traveller must halt. Years ago, this mountaineer received from the American and Mexican governments a charter to maintain a highway through these mountains. He was surrounded by his "serfs," like a feudal lord, and held the pass, exacting toll from all who passed that way. Before the railroad was built, his business was very prosperous, producing, it is said, some days five hundred dollars, from tolls received at his "money-or-your-life" toll-gate. It is also said that he was in league with the Indians, and that many a dark and bloody chapter of mountain history, credited to the Indians, had Dick Wootton as its author. He is still living, and exacts tribute, but has a more moderate tariff than formerly.

The Devil's Cañon, where many an overland coach was halted, their occupants robbed, perhaps murdered, may be easily seen from the train. A trough in the trail is bordered by clefts which are level with the top of a coach passing across the trough. These clefts, smooth faced, level on top with the ground, stand about twelve feet apart, one on each side. In this strategic place, a few could dictate to the many. The brakeman concluded by saying that not a great distance from this trap is the graveyard of the Devil's Cañon, where rest the bones of scores who met their death in this treacherous trough.

RATON TUNNEL.

Five miles farther the puffing, groaning engines climbed and reached an elevation of 7,688 feet, when the train plunged into a tunnel nearly a half-mile long, running under the crest of the Raton Spur. At the north end of the tunnel, we were in Colorado; at the south end, in New Mexico. They appeared alike, both being robed in darkness. Just before emerging from the tunnel, at the highest point of the pass, the *beauseant* of Boston Commandery was unfurled by Eminent Commander John L. Stevenson and bathed in the midnight breeze 7,688 feet above the level of the sea.

We entered New Mexico,— the newest and the oldest portion of our land,— prize of Cabeza de Vaca; home of the Zunis, and territory of ruins and mystery. In an hour, flying as if on the wings of the wind, we descended a thousand feet and stopped at Raton, a railroad town having large repair shops. The descent from Raton was made

"with one engine, and for such a long and heavy train as ours, was made with danger. I sat up to view the wonders of creation in this famous pass, and when one is an eye-witness to the effect of the brakes in lighting up the whole train as with a continuous fire, and this for many miles, and knows that the railroad-men on the same train are frightened, it would seem that the railroad company should make no more experiments, but take down less cars at a time."— SIR J. D. D., *Cor. Journal and Courier, New Haven, Conn.*

Raton is also a coal-mining town, capable of producing a thousand car-loads per day.

"The hour of arrival at Raton was 2 A. M., yet the Sir Knights of Raton were at the station in their 'Knight clothes,' accompanied by a band of music. They could converse with us through open windows, and a young

RATON MOUNTAINS.

Sir Knight (?) just under mine said that 'when his father died he left his regalia to him, and he had been waiting for three months with anticipations of the greatest pleasure for the coming of this special train'" — SIR F. H. W., *in address delivered at Keene, N. H.*

At 7.15 A. M. we arrived at Las Vegas, one of the principal cities of New Mexico. Las Vegas has all the improvements, industries, churches, schools, and newspapers incident to a thriving and wide-awake city. Leaving the main line at this place by a branch road six miles in length, we rode to Las Vegas Hot Springs, where we had an excellent breakfast, and tarried until after dinner. The train stopped at the pretty depot, and by an elevated plank walk which crosses the Rio Gallinas we proceeded to the hotel.

The Commandery was delighted with its reception at this beautiful resort. The Montezuma, designed by a Boston architect, is a fine building, and owned, like the Hot Springs, by the railroad company.

Among the foot-hills of the Spanish range of mountains lies a plateau, comprising about thirty acres. Around it, the rocky cliffs tower several hundred feet, except where the river Rio Gallinas makes its entrance to and exit from the plateau. Upon the bank of the river, where it enters this amphitheatre, the Hot Springs, about forty in number, bubble forth. The temperature of the different springs varies from seventy-five to one hundred and thirty-six degrees.

It is said that the native population resorted thither with their lame and sick for centuries, venerating the springs for remarkable cures. So precious did the Indians consider these waters that they guarded them day and night, that hostiles might not destroy

THE MONTEZUMA HOTEL, LAS VEGAS HOT SPRINGS, N. M.

or injure them. The Hot Springs were visited, and the baths well patronized.

The bath-house, two hundred feet long by forty-two feet wide, is at the right of the hotel, on the opposite side of the river. These buildings are connected by a substantial bridge. Bathing experience can be best told by a bather. Sir F. H. Whitcomb said in his address at Keene, N. H.: —

The waters at Las Vegas Hot Springs are said to contain fourteen per cent of sodium sulphate, twenty-seven per cent sodium chloride, and a small per cent of soda, calcium, and magnesia, with strong traces of iodine and bromide. Benefit for cutaneous diseases is claimed for these waters, and the list of diseases cured by them is too long to enumerate. Bathers are cautioned against taking a bath without first paying a doctor one dollar for telling them it won't hurt them any. The doctors tell us we are only about seven pounds of animal matter, wet thoroughly with six or seven pails of water, and request us to exhibit faith in the water cure. In the medicated bath the patient is first brought to a profuse perspiration, in a vapor box, to extract the moisture from the body and open the pores. He is rubbed dry and cooled off in a cooling-room. Then he is put into a box, his head protruding, of course, and chloride of mercury, sulphuret of potassium, or whatever drug his case may require, is burned in the box. In case of catarrh, his head is also put in. Our party took the bath simply for cleanliness, at ninety-eight degrees. The hot bath, followed by the blanket sweat and shampoo, is given at from one hundred to one hundred and ten degrees. The temperature of the vapor bath is one hundred and fifteen degrees. Many sick people improve here, and the climate is very favorable. The winter season is short, although ice can be cut twenty-seven inches thick, and is very cheap.

A novel and peculiar feature of this place is the mud bath. The bath mud is confined in holes in the ground, which are surrounded above ground by wooden fences. The fine mud paste makes the interior look like a first-class pig pen, without the odor. It is said that this fine mud paste, through which the spring water has trickled for ages, contains powerful medicinal properties. Into some of this primeval mud, dished up into a bath-tub, the patient is put up to his neck, the head alone being visible above the black mass. This mud is heated to any temperature by means of steam conducted through pipes from a boiler. It is a ridiculous bath and a funny sight, but patients extol its virtues.

Our party were busily engaged, taking baths, visiting the bear grounds, museums of Indian relics, and collections of geological specimens, procuring photographs and souvenirs, while a few, who had plenty of time at their disposal, not being in any haste to get around, indulged in horseback exercise.

The plaza in front of the hotel is prettily laid out and adorned with flowers and shrubs. The buildings, hotels, bath-house, dwellings, and stores are all tasty and neat in architecture, which give the place an inviting appearance. The dinner bill of fare was unique. It consisted of six pages. On the first page were Templar emblems, on the last was a picture of the hotel and grounds. The second page contained the *menu;* the third, the names of "the guests of the Montezuma,[*] Aug. 9, Boston Commandery of Knights Templars and ladies"; the fourth gave the names and residences of the guests not of our party, one hundred and two in number.

The portion of the *menu* which was of personal interest was as follows: —

---

[*] A $300,000 HOTEL BURNED. — Denver, Col., Jan. 17, 1884. The Grand Montezuma Hotel at Las Vegas was burned this afternoon. The fire originated in the basement, it is supposed from a gasoline machine. In thirty minutes the hotel was in ruins. The guests, numbering one hundred, lost everything, barely escaping with their lives. Frozen fire-plugs rendered the fire department powerless. The hotel was owned by the Atchison, Topeka and Santa Fé Railroad Company, and was one of the finest structures in the West.

❧ MENU. ☙

Cream of Celery, à la Stevenson. Consommé Vermicelli, à la Richards.

Salmon Braisé, à la Trull.
Pommes, à la Gleason.

Cucumbers. Olives. Tomatoes.

Boiled Leg of Mountain Sheep, à la Bunton.
Choux Gratin, à la Shillaber.

Roman Punch, à la W. A. Walker.

Tenderloin of Beef, à la Thomas.
Currie of Chicken, à la Gillette.

Queen Fritters, à la Hunt.

Chicken Salad, à la Atwood. Shrimp Salad, à la Thompson.
etc. etc.

Vegetables.

Steamed Pound Pudding, Sauce à la Blackie.

Pound Cake, à la Hedges. White Fruit Cake, à la Russell.
Lady Cake, à la Stratton. Almond Cake, à la Simpson.
Chocolate Cream Cake, à la Averell.
Angel Food, à la Rev. Roberts. Macaroons, à la Bowker.

Melons. Oranges. Apples. Pears.
Peaches. Apricots.
Plums. Grapes. Raisins. Nuts.
Cheese. Boston Crackers.
Café noir.

Though we had travelled far away from those sacred spots where ancestral dust lies buried, yet we were still in the presence of him who wounds and destroys. At Las Vegas Hot Springs the Prelate of Boston Commandery was requested to conduct the services at the funeral of Mrs. N. J. Pettijohn, a woman highly esteemed and of rare intelligence. The Prelate officiated, and appropriate hymns were sung by a choir of Sir Knights. The memory of that funeral procession, slowly moving across the plaza, accompanying the remains, which were to be carried to Wisconsin, to the train, will not soon fade. The body was borne upon a bier, then came the afflicted husband, with friends and neighbors, walking; last, as if unconscious of all else but sorrow, her favorite horse, saddled, and wearing emblems of mourning, followed.

The Las Vegas *Daily Optic*, Aug. 9, refers to the arrival of Boston Commandery as follows:—

This morning at 6.30 a special train consisting of seven Pullman coaches, under the management of Conductor Wisner, having on board the Boston Commandery of Knights Templars, arrived, and were taken out to the Hot Springs, where they remained until 1.30 this afternoon, when they left for the Tertio at Santa Fé, where they will stay one day, and then proceed to San Francisco. The excursionists are being well cared for by Charles T. Pearson, the Colorado passenger agent of the Santa Fé road. The Boston Commandery and the ladies accompanying them are a splendid looking lot of people, and are loud in their praises of the good treatment they are receiving from the Santa Fé folks. Rev. Oliver Ayer Roberts, Prelate of Boston Commandery for the California pilgrimage, officiated at the funeral of Mrs. Dr. Pettijohn. Col. Schemerhorn is with the Boston excursionists. The *Optic* office printed a very handsome job of work for the Boston Commandery Knights Templars during their sojourn here.

We here reproduce the "handsome" work done at the *Optic* office, Las Vegas. It consisted of printing the names of the party on folding cards. These cards contained first the names of the officers of Boston Commandery for the California pilgrimage, then the names of the cars, beginning at the front. Under each car name were the names of the Sir Knight in charge, and of the occupants of the car, the number of their respective sections being opposite the names. The committees conclude the list.

BOSTON COMMANDERY KNIGHTS TEMPLARS.

California Pilgrimage, August, 1883.

BOSTON TO SAN FRANCISCO AND RETURN.

OFFICERS OF BOSTON COMMANDERY FOR THE CALIFORNIA PILGRIMAGE.

JOHN L. STEVENSON, Eminent Commander.

EUGENE H. RICHARDS, Generalissimo.   EZRA J. TRULL, Captain General.

OLIVER A. ROBERTS, Prelate.

JAMES M. GLEASON, Senior Warden.   WILLIAM A. BUNTON, Junior Warden.

JONAS G. SHILLABER, Treasurer.   ZEPH. H. THOMAS, Recorder.

GEORGE A. GILLETTE, Standard Bearer.

EDGAR F. HUNT, Sword Bearer.   CHARLES F. ATWOOD, Warder.

GEORGE G. STRATTON,   } GUARDS. {   SIDNEY M. HEDGES,
ABIJAH THOMPSON,   CHARLES L. RUSSELL,
JOHN BLACKIE,   LEONARD M. AVERELL.

DAVID S. SIMPSON, Armorer.   CALEB BOWKER, Sentinel.

CAR "ALMERIA."

Sir JAMES M. GLEASON, *Committee.*

Section.

1. { Sir JACOB L. BAILEY.
     Sir LYMAN S. HAPGOOD.

3. { Sir BAYLIES WOOD.
     Sir RANDALL W. COOK.

5. { Sir AMASA W. BAILEY.
     Sir BENJAMIN F. SMITH.

7. { Sir P. T. WASHBURN.
     Sir CHARLES LAWTON.

9. { Sir WILLIAM B. WILBER.
     Sir THOMAS E. CALL.

11. { Sir ALBERT A. JENKS.
      Sir GEORGE GOSLING.

Section.

2. { Sir ALFRED MORRILL.
     Sir LEANDER GREELY.

4. { Sir HARRY D. REED.
     Sir STEPHEN CAIN.

6. { Sir CHARLES D. WESTON.
     Sir W. L. TUCK.

8. { Sir R. O. COOK.
     Sir I. B. PHILLIPS.

10. { Sir GEORGE M. SMITH.
      Sir SAMUEL RUST.

12. { Sir JAMES F. BLISS.
      Sir H. F. INGERSOLL.

State Room.

Sir JAMES M. GLEASON.   Sir SIDNEY M. HEDGES.

Sir EDGAR F. HUNT.

CAR "MODENA."

Sir GEORGE F. HEWETT, *Committee.*

Section.
1. Sir WM. H. GIBBS. / Sir GEO. R. HOOPER.
3. Sir C. R. HASKINS. / Sir G. R. FREEMAN.
5. Sir ALFRED M. SMITH. / Sir CALEB BOWKER.
7. Sir WM. S. WHITING. / Sir LE ROY BRAINERD.
9. Sir RALPH W. SHATTUCK. / Sir WALTER RUSSELL.
11. Sir E. E. TARBELL. / Sir EDWIN BARNARD.

Section.
2. Sir G. WALTON GOSS. / Sir CHAS. W. FIELD, JR.
4. Sir STILLMAN L. SHAFFER. / Sir GEO. W. MATHEWS.
6. Sir FRANK H. WHITCOMB. / Sir JOHN WHITAKER.
8. Sir ALEX. MONTGOMERY. / Sir A. W. BRIGHAM.
10. Sir M. S. FELLOWS. / Sir E. F. BROOKS.
12. Sir SILAS GARFIELD. / Sir LYMAN W. WHEELER.

State Room.

Sir SAMUEL N. FURBER.   Sir WILLIAM DAN LAMB.

Mr. W. A. WALKER, *Reporter.*

CAR "MOHAVE."

Sir EDWARD T. NICHOLS, *Committee.*

Section.
1. Sir CHARLES L. RUSSELL. / Mrs. CHARLES L. RUSSELL.
3. Sir WEBSTER HURD. / Mrs. WEBSTER HURD.
5. Sir D. S. SIMPSON. / Mrs. D. S. SIMPSON.
7. Sir FRANCIS H. JOHNSON. / Mrs. FRANCIS H. JOHNSON.
9. Sir LEONARD M. AVERELL. / Mrs. LEONARD M. AVERELL.

Section.
2. Sir FRANK A. ABBOTT. / Mrs. FRANK A. ABBOTT.
4. Sir SAMUEL F. BROWN. / Mrs. SAMUEL F. BROWN.
6. Sir CHARLES E. ADAMS. / Mrs. CHARLES E. ADAMS.
8. Sir EDWARD T. NICHOLS. / Mrs. EDWARD T. NICHOLS.
10. Sir JOHN D. GALE. / Mrs. JOHN D. GALE.

11. Sir SILAS ALDEN. / Sir CHARLES P. LAURIAT.

State Room.

Miss MARY E. CALL.   Miss ANNIE G. LAURIAT.
Miss ELIZA A. PHIPPS.   Miss MARY L. HUGHES.

CAR "ALBANIA."

Sir WILLIAM A. BUNTON, *Committee.*

Section.		Section.	
1	Sir JONAS G. SHILLABER. Sir WILBUR F. MILLER.	2	Sir GEORGE G. STRATTON. Sir JAMES HOUSTON.
3	Miss KATHARINE B. SHILLABER. Miss A. GERTRUDE GATES.	4	Mrs. E. M. STONE. Miss E. M. MILLER.
5	Sir MARTIN A. MUNROE. Mrs. MARTIN A. MUNROE.	6	Sir LYMAN R. MACE. Mrs. LYMAN R. MACE.
7	Sir GEORGE F. PARKER. Mrs. GEORGE F. PARKER.	8	Miss SUSIE E. PARKER. Miss MABELLE L. PARKER.
9	Sir FRANK C. WOOD. Mrs. FRANK C. WOOD.	10	Sir HENRY L. BATCHELDER. Mrs. HENRY L. BATCHELDER.
11	Mrs. R. C. PECK. Miss JESSIE K. DEWELL.	12	Sir JAMES D. DEWELL. Mrs. JAMES D. DEWELL.

State Room.

Sir WILLIAM A. BUNTON. Sir CHARLES F. ATWOOD.
Mrs. WILLIAM A. BUNTON. Mrs. CHARLES F. ATWOOD.

CAR "ECHO."

Sir ABIJAH THOMPSON, *Committee.*

Section.		Section.	
1	Sir WILLIAM E. WALKER. Mrs. WILLIAM E. WALKER.	2	Sir EDWARD KAKAS. Mrs. EDWARD KAKAS.
3	Sir SAMUEL H. WALKER. Mrs. SAMUEL H. WALKER. Miss BERTHA F. WALKER.	4	Sir HERBERT M. STAPLES. Mrs. HERBERT M. STAPLES.
5	Sir ZACHEUS SHERMAN. Mrs. ZACHEUS SHERMAN.	6	Sir JOHN P. WALKER. Mrs. JOHN P. WALKER.
7	Sir WILLIAM L. WALKER. Mrs. WILLIAM L. WALKER.	8	Sir A. L. BLISS. Mrs. A. L. BLISS.
9	Sir EDWIN WINSOR. Mrs. EDWIN WINSOR.	10	Sir GEORGE W. WILLIAMS. Mrs. GEORGE W. WILLIAMS.
11	Sir ABIJAH THOMPSON. Mrs. ABIJAH THOMPSON.	12	Mrs. ELEANOR HUSE. Mrs. MARY S. SANBORN.

State Room.

Sir GEORGE F. HEWETT. Miss MABEL E. HEWETT.
Mrs. GEORGE F. HEWETT. Miss MARY E. WALKER.

CAR "COMO."

Sir EUGENE H. RICHARDS, *Committee*.

Section.
1. { Sir Ezra J. Trull.
    Mrs. Ezra J. Trull.
3. { Sir John Blackie.
    Mrs. John Blackie.
5. { Sir Eugene H. Richards.
    Mrs. Eugene H. Richards.
7. { Sir Charles E. Severance.
    Sir Wm. S. Severance.
9. { Sir Wm. J. Ellis.
    Mrs. Wm. J. Ellis.
11. { Miss Grace A. Stevenson.
    Miss Mary Dean.

Section.
2. { Sir Charles A. Fairbanks.
    Mrs. Charles A. Fairbanks.
4. { Sir Charles J. Devereaux.
    Mrs. Charles J. Devereaux.
6. { Sir George A. Gillette.
    Mrs. George A. Gillette.
8. { Mrs. W. S. Severance.
    Mrs. Belle S. Earle.
10. { Sir W. H. L. Smith.
    Mrs. W. H. L. Smith.
12. { Sir Oliver A. Roberts.
    Sir Z. H. Thomas.

State Room.
Sir HARRISON A. TUCKER.   Mrs. HARRISON A. TUCKER.
Miss NELLIE D. TUCKER.

PRIVATE CAR.

Eminent Sir JOHN L. STEVENSON, *Eminent Commander*.
Mrs. JOHN L. STEVENSON.
M∴ E∴ BENJAMIN DEAN, *Grand Master of Templars of the United States*.
Mrs. BENJAMIN DEAN.

COMMITTEES.

EXECUTIVE.

JOHN L. STEVENSON.   EUGENE H. RICHARDS.   JAMES M. GLEASON.
WILLIAM A. BUNTON.   GEORGE F. HEWETT.

LADIES.

ABIJAH THOMPSON.   W. H. L. SMITH.   JOHN D. GALE.

TRANSPORTATION.

EDWARD T. NICHOLS.   ALFRED M. SMITH.   AMASA W. BAILEY.

MEDICAL STAFF.

WM. DAN LAMB, M. D., DIRECTOR.
HARRISON A. TUCKER, M. D.   WM. S. SEVERANCE, M. D.
CHARLES E. SEVERANCE, M. D.

CHAPTER VI.

RETURNING to Las Vegas at 1.30 P. M., we continued our journey towards Santa Fé, our next stopping place. Twenty miles beyond Las Vegas we sighted Starvation Peak, and for some hours it was prominently in view, during which time we made the famous Horseshoe Bend. In order to surmount difficulties of grade, the novel sight is seen of the engine apparently going in a direction almost opposite to that pursued by the rear of the train. Often the engine could be seen from the windows of the rear cars without effort to look forward.

The Peak stands isolated upon the plain, with apparently steep, sloping

STARVATION PEAK.

sides, surmounted by a crown of ledge which seems insurmountable.
The light-colored summit of rock is in sharp contrast with the dark-
colored cone on which the former rests. The story is, that a company of Spaniards were driven to the summit of this peak by the
Indians and held there until they starved to death, with their own
fair fields in view. Some of the crosses erected there could be
clearly seen from the cars. Twenty-five miles farther, as the train
began to climb Glorietta Mountain, we looked out upon the Rio
Pecos Valley, which contains the ruins of the old Pecos pueblo or
town and church. The
ruins of the church
could be distinctly seen,
and also there were
evidences in its vicinity
of fallen walls. Once
a populous and busy
city stood there, but
now ruined and desolate
like Bethel or Jericho.

SEAL OF NEW MEXICO.

It is claimed that the church was erected by the Spaniards in
1529, and the adjacent ruins are of that pre-historic city, Cicuya,
one of the mysterious "seven cities of Cibola." Tradition says
that where the church stands there was once an Aztec temple,
built on the place where Montezuma, the culture god, was born.
Thence, upon an eagle's back, he proceeded southward; wherever
the eagle stopped at night, Montezuma located a pueblo or town.
The sign of the arrival at the site for a great city, which Montezuma was to found, was to be "the alighting of the eagle on a
cactus-bush and devouring a serpent." This event is said to have
taken place on arrival at the site of the present city of Mexico.

This tradition furnishes the subject for the territorial seal of New Mexico.

The ruins have been carefully examined. The original church was in the form of a Roman cross, one hundred and fifty feet long and forty feet wide, the transept being sixty feet. Its walls were six feet thick, built of adobe bricks. The walls now standing give no clew to their original height. There are ruins of stone and earth enclosures. For twelve hundred feet along the ridge there are evidences of fallen houses or walls.

"This spot is the traditional birthplace of Montezuma, the culture god. It was here the sacred fire was kept burning at his command until the present century. When Montezuma disappeared centuries ago, on an eagle's back, he enjoined the people of Cicuye to keep in life the sacred spark, telling them that when he returned he would descend through the flame and smoke. Warriors watched the fire in turn. Montezuma came not. Still the faithful watchers remained true to their trust. Warfare, old age, and disease decimated their ranks, but still the watch was kept, day and night. The city crumbled into ruins, and the band was reduced to so small a number that it was foreseen that the sacred fire must soon die with the faithful watchers. Then it was that the three warriors, the last of their race, took the fire into the mountains, where Montezuma is said to have appeared and received it from their hands." To these arid plains and rich mountain-sides, the culture god has indeed come, perhaps returned, in the new civilization, whose voice is heard, whose power is felt, whose strides are seen on every hand.

At 4.30 P. M. the summit of Glorietta Pass, 7,537 feet elevation, was reached, and a rapid descent was made through the Apache Cañon. Lamy, the junction of the Santa Fé branch and main

SANTA FE, FROM REAR OF PALACE HOTEL.

line, was soon passed, and a run of eighteen miles on the branch road brought us to Santa Fé, reputed to be the oldest city in the United States. On our arrival, 8 P. M., it rained very hard. Some, willing to brave the storm, sought rooms at the hotels, but the greater number remained on board the train. Next morning, Friday, Aug. 10, the remainder were transferred to the Palace Hotel, a modern and stately house, whose proprietor received his guests as well as possible.

One would naturally suppose that our party, having been exposed in the rain and swollen creek of Santa Fé, would have been wet, and the proprietor in his Palace Hotel would have been dry, but the truth is, our party was dry and he was wet.

After breakfast, the entire command, each as he pleased, proceeded "to do" Santa Fé. Carriages were in great demand.

Santa Fé claims an existence in 1325 A. D. How old the place then was even tradition cannot tell. The Spaniards occupied it in 1583, and the tertio-millennial celebration was in progress during our visit. If one can judge of the age of Santa Fé by its streets and adobes, as one judges a horse's age by his teeth, probably the earlier date is correct. Its lay-out is mediæval; its style of houses, one-story and flat-roofed, is Syrian; its covered sidewalks Bernese; its mode of brick-making Egyptian; and its general appearance Oriental. From a distance the city looks like the plain on which it stands. The houses, built of sun-dried bricks, are mud-covered and flat-roofed. The streets are narrow,—a carriage and two horses, standing crosswise, would block up a whole thoroughfare. The carriage driver in Santa Fé clears the wood-laden burros and their Mexican drivers out of the way by yelling, as the driver in Cairo clears his way of the donkeys and Arab boys. There are, however, points of real interest in the city. San Miguel Church, built in 1640,

SAN MIGUEL CHURCH AND COLLEGE, SANTA FE.

destroyed in 1680, and rebuilt in 1710, having mouldering walls without and faded pictures within, had many visitors that day. The palace, which some one has likened to a rope-walk, is, historically, the most notable building in the city. It occupies one side of a square, is one-story high, flat-roofed, and has a porch in front its entire length. It was first occupied by Indians, then by the Spaniards, next by the Mexicans, but now is the palace of the territorial governor, Lionel A. Sheldon, upon whom many Sir Knights and ladies called and paid their respects. This building has been used as fort, prison, palace, court-room, and capitol.

The Exposition Buildings were visited, and the specimens of metals, minerals, and colossal petrefactions, together with the products of New Mexico, were examined. Spinning and weaving after the native style were shown. The venerable weaver was made rich that day. There were on sale varieties of Mexican jewelry, precious stones, and native laces. There were pianos, organs, farming tools and implements, together constituting a very creditable exposition. In an adjacent building relics of various kinds were gathered: Kit Carson's original rifle; a small arsenal of ancient weapons, — knives, pistols, guns, swords; a wooden plough; paintings on skins of animals; oil paintings, dimmed by passing centuries. There must have been in this country, in some past century, something better than Indian barbarism and Mexican indolence.

A public procession, a feature of the celebration, composed of Americans, Mexicans, and Indians, civilians, scouts, and soldiers, with battery and wagon train, was very interesting. The long-haired cavaliers recalled pictures of Spain's mounted nobility; the scouts appeared to have experienced hard service; the company of United States cavalry, just returned from Crook's campaign, revived the memories of Custer and Sheridan. As the procession passed the hotel, Boston

Commandery gathered informally in front, and applauded the various companies; but the heartiest "hurrah" was reserved for the cavalry and the colors they carried.

The cathedral of stone, in process of erection, around and over

THE PLAZA, SANTA FÉ.

the old San Francisco chapel, — "the oldest house in America," said to have been built in 1542, — the college, and the most ancient part of the town, together with the jewelry and curiosity stores, were visited. All classes of citizens seemed to exert themselves to give our party a pleasant reception. It was a day of great opportunities, and they were well used.

Charlie Morris thought he was doing a nice thing when trying to deceive the Yankees from the Hub. He was known not to be a scout. He would not dare to lose sight of the adobes of Santa Fé; but in our desire to see the fun go on, we called him "Scout," — we played he was "scout." What Charlie thought is thus set forth in the *New Mexican*: —

Charlie Morris "did up" the visiting Bostonians in great shape to-day. He robed himself in a full suit of beaded buckskin, and, calling at the Palace, became an object of much curiosity and attention. The men plied him with all sorts of questions concerning border scouts, their modes of life and their trials and hardships, and the ladies shook hands with him again and again. The half-dozen citizens who stood by and witnessed the scene haven't got through laughing yet. Charlie talked to them for a good hour, explaining all the mysteries of scout-land, and informed them that little was doing in his line at present, as the border was quiet, but expressed the belief that he and all his subordinate scouts would have plenty to do before the snows came again. They called him "Calamity Charlie."

The *New Mexican*, Santa Fé, N. M., Aug. 9, has the following concerning our day in that ancient city: —

TAKING IN THE TERTIO. — THREE HUNDRED YEARS OF HISTORY CROWDED INTO A SINGLE FORENOON. — THE TABLEAUX. — CITY FULL OF VISITORS. — TO-DAY AT THE GROUNDS. — THE BALL.

To-day may justly be counted one of the most successful the Tertio-Millennial Exposition has experienced since its opening, just one month and ten days ago. Notwithstanding the unsettled condition of travel, the heavy rains, and the irregularity and unreliability of trains, visitors from far and near have left their homes, braved the difficulties, and poured into

THE PALACE, SANTA FÉ.

the ancient city by the hundreds to get a peep at our exposition, a good report from which has long since reached every quarter of the globe. The influx of travel has been greater in the past three days than during any similar period in the modern history of the city. The remarkable success of the street pageants and historic tableaux presented last month, and a desire to see them reproduced, are responsible for the gathering of visitors we have here to-day. Every available nook and corner in the city was occupied last night. Many were unable to secure accommodations at all until nearly midnight, and then not till some kindly new-made acquaintance had stirred about and found them. The stores and shops were crowded with purchasers all the afternoon and evening, and to-day the trains have all brought full loads of sight-seers, and with the Boston Knights Templars and half a dozen minor excursion parties, the streets and public places have presented a scene of life and activity that was hardly expected a week ago, when it was first announced that the exposition would continue open till the 15th inst.

The Boston excursion party arrived at eight o'clock last evening on a special train of seven palace cars. They took vehicles at the depot immediately upon arrival, and had supper at the Palace, returning to their sleepers about ten oclock, after making a brief survey of the city by gas-light. Only a limited number visited the exposition grounds and witnessed the magnificent historic tableaux. In this they missed a great treat, — such a one as is seen in a lifetime, — but they were all no doubt very much fatigued, and then, too, they desired to get a refreshing rest in order that to-day's scenes might prove all the more enjoyable. All appear to have spent an agreeable day. They had some difficulty in securing breakfast; the Palace being unable to accommodate them, many had to be content with the Grand Central and Exchange for breakfast and dinner, but they took in the situation good-naturedly and made the best of it. The party is *en route* to San Francisco to attend the Triennial Conclave. They left Boston on Saturday night last and report having had an agreeable journey throughout. They departed for the West late this afternoon, and expect to reach home about Sept. 1.

THE EXPOSITION.

The sun came out bright and beautiful and continued so till eleven o'clock. A large crowd of visitors examined the exhibits up to nearly that hour, when they repaired to the plaza, and, with numbers largely increased, watched and waited for the historic pageant. The various sections were somewhat behind time in forming, but shortly after eleven, martial music sounded from the lower end of San Francisco Street, and the procession soon made its appearance at the plaza, led by Hon. W. T. Thornton, gorgeously robed as a Spanish knight, and a very proper leader by reason of his office as president of the Knights of Coronado. The pageant proved very creditable. The various characters represented the history of New Mexico from 1550 to the present, beginning with the aborigines and running up the line of advancement and progress with the Spanish occupation, and the coming of Coronado and his plumed knights; the reconquest by Diego de Vargas; the American occupation; Santa Fé trail and its prairie schooners; the coming of the telegraph and steam engine, the Goddess of Liberty and Uncle Sam mounted on the latter; indeed, to the student of progressive history the pageant was full

THE PRIEST OF SANTA FÉ.

of novelty and unique interest. It was not characterized by as many strikingly novel features as was the first one, because of the absence of the Indians who played such a prominent part on that occasion, but this could not be helped, as all the Indians are now too busy with their crops to leave their homes under any circumstances.

The attendance at the grounds was not large during the afternoon, owing to the regular daily storm, which came up about noon and which stampeded the spectators just after the pageant had passed. This evening, however, fair weather or foul, the crowd in attendance at the ball will be all the hall can accommodate. A great many tickets have been sold, and the evening promises much enjoyment, notwithstanding the inclement weather at this writing.

In the early afternoon of Friday, Aug. 10, we forded Santa Fé Creek for the last time, and, embarking on our train, proceeded westward *via* Lamy, and arrived at Wallace, N. M., at 6 P. M. Here we tarried "for supper only," as we supposed. The manager of the depot hotel is Signor Victor Vezetta. This gentleman conceived the idea of treating the Sir Knights to the sight of an Indian dance. He sent messengers the day before to the Indian city and invited the principal Indians to come to Wallace and dance, promising them a collection and a supper if they would. The Indians accepted and were present to the number of two hundred, of all ages, sexes, dress, and decorations. They belong to the San Domingo Pueblo tribe, and live in San Domingo City, four miles from Wallace. The tribe numbers one thousand persons, and are agriculturists, but manufacture some pottery. Many specimens were procured by our party. These Indians are nominally Roman Catholics. They are not quarrelsome or immoral. The penalty with them for immorality is flaying. San Domingo is regularly laid out. The streets are narrow but very hard. The houses are adobe, with mud floors, hard as cement and scrupulously neat within. They consist of twelve large buildings, communal dwellings. There are also two council chambers, which are also used for dances. The depot at Wallace has, on the west side, a yard fifty feet square, surrounded on two sides (south and west) with a very high board fence, on one side (north) with a picket fence, and the hotel bounds the fourth side. After our supper the Indian procession was formed, east of the station, and proceeded to this yard, being led by Indians clad in all their finery, on horseback. Next came their flag of animals' skins, Indian tanned, the ancient banner of the tribe. The dancing Indians, fifty in number, came next by twos, the sexes alternating, that is, first came two men, then two women, and so on. These were followed by a crowd of seventy-five Indians, who proved to be the singers on "this interesting occasion."

On their arrival at the gate every available place for seeing was occupied by our party and the people from the surrounding country, even the top of the board fence and the roofs of the adjacent buildings. The principal Indian characters were the governor and the chief. The governor is the head of the tribe, and specially directs agricultural matters, ordering the details of men weekly for agricultural and pastoral work. The chief is the secretary of war, under whose direction the military organization is kept up, but without weapons, etc. The male dancers were bare above the waist. Their breasts, backs, and faces were gaudily painted. Their long, black hair hung down in a knot. They wore strings of beads around their necks, to which were attached crosses of tin, wood, sea-shell, etc. Below the clout their limbs were bare and painted, except they wore moccasins. In their right hands they carried a shaker, a dried gourd containing seeds, to which was attached a wooden handle. This they shook to the time of the drum-beating. In their left they carried sprigs of green. The female dancers wore a long woollen garment belted about their waist, exposing the left shoulder only. Their hair was long and flowing, and both men and women had their hair banged. Hence the modern custom is said to have been derived.

They likewise wore beads and decorations, and were barefooted. In their hands they carried sprigs of green. Their faces were painted a bright red. In stature they were all small; the faces

A SHIP OF THE DESERT AT ANCHOR.

of the men were angular and hard, but the women had pleasant expressions on their round faces. The singers were dressed in costumes civilized and barbarous. They were led by the drummer, who vigorously pounded with one stick on a drum, two and one half feet long, cylindrical in form, the heads being covered with sheepskins. On entering the yard the drum was beaten and the dancers began to dance very slowly around the yard, retaining their marching order. It was a dance in general figures. The second formation was like that in the Virginia reel. Immediately they came into sets, and proceeded with the same shuffling step as before, keeping time to the beating of the drum and to the mournful chanting of the choir. Their movements were frequently greeted with applause by the Sir Knights. The governor expressed to Signor Vezetta a desire to meet the "Capitan." Eminent Commander Stevenson was introduced to him, and the former bestowed upon the chief a new silver dollar, whereupon numerous aboriginal hands were instantly extended for a similar recognition. Subsequently the Eminent Commander decorated the Indian governor with a badge of Boston Commandery. The crowd applauded and the recipient appeared very much pleased. He was also presented with a pocket compass, which at first he hardly dared touch and seemed puzzled, but after an explanation he was profusely thankful. It was an interesting hour, some expressing the feeling that the sight was worth a ride from Boston. As we were leaving Wallace, Signor Vezetta presented Boston Commandery with a live American eagle which was captured near Wallace. This memorandum was attached to his cage: —

"UPWARD!"

This bird of emblem to our pilgrim brethren of Boston Commandery, Aug. 10, 1883, at Wallace, N. M.

VICTOR VEZETTA, *Manager Depot Hotel.*

The eagle was accepted by Eminent Commander Stevenson in behalf of the Commandery, with thanks, expressing the hope that the prestige of the bird might attend "the Bostons" in their pilgrimage, and that this "pilgrim" eagle might become famous with the Templar host as "Old Abe" was with the soldiers.

Henceforth the eagle became a "pilgrim" and shared our pilgrimage with us. A large cage was substituted for his narrow box, and in the former, upon a pole attachment, the eagle took in the whole of the Templar parade in San Francisco, and was carried in the procession of Sept. 4, 1883, in Boston, to Masonic Temple, where the pilgrimage of Boston Commandery ended.*

"The Rio Grande River," says Sir S. L. S., "which from childhood we had erroneously regarded as a river of great importance and magnitude, proved, then at least, to be a river without water, save here and there a little brook for a short distance, and then again disappeared into the earth, though the torn banks and deep gulleys plainly indicated it to be a furious torrent when fed by the fierce mountain streams during the rainy season."

PRIMITIVE AGRICULTURE.

We reached the Rio Grande at Wallace, and our night's ride of two hundred and sixty-eight miles followed that river. Agriculture is carried on by the Indians and Mexicans in the most primitive methods. Wooden ploughs are still in use, and their carts have solid wheels of wood.

---

* The pilgrims will regret to learn of the demise of the pilgrim eagle. It was thus announced in the Boston *Herald*: "A PILGRIM AT REST.—During the pilgrimage of Boston Commandery Knights Templars to California, and while stopping at Wallace, N. M., the Commandery was presented with a fine specimen of the American eagle, which was duly christened 'Pilgrim.' The bird was taken to 'Frisco,' and played a prominent part in the grand parade. It was brought thence to Boston, and has since been kept in Mr. Stevenson's store, at No. 4 Faneuil Hall Square. The bird was fast assuming large proportions, but high living and close confinement finally overcame his eagleship, and on Friday he passed to the realms reserved for Masonic eagles."

At 5 A. M. we halted at Rincon, a town of one thousand population, the junction of the El Paso branch railroad. We should have passed the junction without noticing it, had it not been for an unwelcome separation. Bro. Edward E. Stevenson, son of the Eminent Commander, who had made the journey from Boston with us, and proved himself a kind-spirited, genial travelling companion, left us at Rincon. We called him sometimes the "cow-boy." He had had experience on the plains, and was now to go south by El Paso to Abilene on the prairie, there mount, ride, herd, and watch, leading the lonely life incident to cattle raising on the plains. We wished him the best fortune, said farewell, and, proceeding, the breakfast hour found us at Deming, the terminus of the Atchison, Topeka and Santa Fé Railroad.

In leaving the Atchison, Topeka and Santa Fé Railroad, called "a child of Boston," we have none but good words for it. Good time was made over the entire road, the scenery was grand, the entertainment at all the depot dining-rooms was equal to the best we received anywhere on the pilgrimage, and the officers of the road who accompanied us were painstaking and courteous.

CHAPTER VII.

WE arrived at Deming at 7.30 A. M., had one hour for breakfast, and departed at 6.45 A. M. (one road runs by Eastern time, the other by San Francisco time).

At Deming we were obliged to part with our friends Sir Knight Schemerhorn and Mr. Charles T. Parsons. Both as officers and gentlemen they filled the measures to the brim. The entire party felt under obligations to them for favors shown. On no road were the meals better served or more abundant; nowhere were the officers of the railroad more painstaking, or the Commandery more kindly treated. Soon we entered Arizona and dined at Bowie. Proceeding, we observed the marked change in scenery and awaited the coming deserts with resignation. During the afternoon Benson was reached, where passengers for the celebrated Tombstone district change cars. The history of this remarkable name is, that the discoverer of mineral, when he first arrived, said he thought he could find mineral in the hills south of Benson. "You will find your tombstone," remarked a cattle drover, sneeringly. The prospecter persevered, and when he did "strike it rich" and was requested to name the district, he said, "Oh, it has been named before. I was told I should find my tombstone." And so to this day the place is called Tombstone. The scenery along the

Southern Pacific continued less and less attractive. The grand, tall mountains gave way to barren hills and the grazing plains became sage-fields, then sand wastes. The alkali plains are indeed desolate, but neither from dust nor heat did we suffer. At 4.30 P. M., drawn by two engines, we arrived at Tucson, the second oldest town in the United States and the largest in Arizona.

TUCSON, ARIZONA.

Supper was served at the Porter Hotel. The *menu* consisted of a four-page card, the first page containing in the centre a Masonic emblem; above it, the words "To the Conclave," while below was the appropriate couplet: —

"Across the desert on their way,
Come valiant Knights in grand array."

The Commandery was greeted with knightly courtesies. Carriages were provided and many Sir Knights viewed with pleasure the lively city of Tucson. As a party was riding near the centre of the town a dense cloud of smoke arose in front of them and an alarm of fire was quickly given. Soon a large wooden building was wrapt in flames. As the rafters began to fall a hose company with its carriage arrived. First it ran by the hydrant, then returned, attached the hose and began to reel it off. Quite unfortunately the pipe had been left at the engine house, whither a horseman was sent post haste. The building — occupied for the manufacture of ice — was entirely consumed, with its contents. It was the largest manufacturing interest in Tucson, and its product absolutely essential to the comfort of its people. Tucson is a pretty place, clean and busy. The people were social and painstaking. The streets are regularly laid out; the buildings are constructed of adobe, one story, but have an appearance of neatness and comfort within. The value of the metals shipped from this station during the year ending July 1, 1883, was fourteen million dollars. We had an Indian dance at Wallace, a great fire at Tucson, and are promised an earthquake in California. It was with regret that we were obliged so soon to leave Tucson. Bro. L. C. Hughes supplied the party with the *Arizona Star*, an illustrated annual, setting forth the glories of Arizona in general, but Tucson in particular. The *Arizona Daily Star*, of Saturday, Aug. 11, anticipated the arrival of Boston Commandery, saying: —

ALL HAIL TO THE "PILGRIM WARRIORS." — The Boston Knights will be welcomed to our ancient and honorable pueblo in their pilgrimage across the continent, and if they will stop off a few days we will show them both silver and gold in the mountains of this weird-like land, but if they must pass on we will give them such as we have, — a warm welcome and something better than cold water and hard-tack.

Starting at 7 P. M., we dared the Great American Desert. The ride across was somewhat dusty. The desert is a waste of sand, level for a few miles on both sides of the railroad, beyond which are high-rifted sand-hills. The next morning, Sunday, we halted

INDIGENOUS TO THE SOIL. — YUMA.

in the desert at Yuma for breakfast, anxious to reach the flower-land of the angels. "You ma'" be assured we saw nothing like Yuma except Yuma. Thermometer 95°. Yuma is the place where a man died, and it is said for crimes which he had done, was consigned to the "hot place," but that fiery region was so much cooler than Yuma that the very next day, it is said, he sent a message back for his overcoat.

The principal object of attraction and distraction at Yuma is the Indians. They are numerous and easily distinguished by the scantiness of their wardrobe, generally consisting of hair on the head, shirt about the waist, and moccasins on the feet. One of them had his quiver (?) of arrows slung over his shoulder and his bow in hand. He was tempted at the sight of coin to try his skill at a knightly card on a stick stuck

OVEN.

ADOBE FIREPLACE.

in the ground. The distance was sixty or seventy feet. He placed the arrow, drew his bow, and won the coin by his skill, for the card fell nearly every time. Such nude noodles were pitiable and repulsive.

We crossed the Colorado River immediately after leaving Yuma, passing from Arizona into California. Thence the road crosses the great Colorado Desert, that vast ocean-bed of past ages, at its lowest point two hundred and sixty-six feet below sea level. Occasionally there were patches of mesquite, sage, and greasewood shrubs, but principally there was a dreary, ashen desert.

As we glided by station after station, we rose above the sea level at Seven Palms, and signs of fertility appeared. Suddenly we emerged from the desert, and the foot-hills, with their scant herbage, were succeeded by green fields. We tarried a few moments at Colton, where a citizen, formerly of New England, extolled the neighboring site and thrift of Riverside — "the poor man's paradise." Here our train was boarded by Sir Knights R. R. Brown, E. F. Spence, T. J. Caystile, and F. A. Gibson, from Los Angeles, who came thus far to meet us. They brought generous donations of native productions from citizens of Los Angeles to refresh the weary pilgrims travelling from afar.

Forty-eight miles farther, past pretty villages with foreign names, is San Gabriel, the place of the old San Gabriel Mission, founded in 1771. Its orange orchard was the first planted in California. On arrival here Messrs. Weeks and Titus supplied the travellers with delicious oranges. From Colton to Los Angeles, though somewhat fatigued from the heat and dust of the desert, the party enjoyed the products of the country and conversed with their new companions. Eleven miles more, through orchards, vineyards, and beauty, and we entered the Land of Flowers, — Pueblo de la Reina de los Angeles. It was the middle of a beautiful Sunday afternoon when the train reached Los Angeles. There was an immense and orderly crowd gathered at the station to welcome us. Cœur de Lion Commandery, No. 9, of Los Angeles, accompanied by the Union Band, was drawn up in line upon the platform and received the Grand Master and his escort. The usual knightly courtesies were interchanged, and "the freedom of the city" offered was accepted by the visitors. Some of our party repaired to the hotels to rest and refresh themselves, though to many the Pullmans seemed most homelike, so attached had we become in eight days. In the same building with the passenger waiting-rooms there is a finely kept hotel, of which Sir H. A. Clawson is proprietor. This building, within and without, was profusely decorated with Templar symbols and banners. Nearly the entire command had their meals at this hotel, and nowhere on the route were the Sir Knights more hospitably entertained or better pleased.

Our arrival on Sunday evening gave us a sight not homelike, but rather European. Theatres, saloons, and stores were open, and upon the hill where Gen. Fremont planted his guns and bombarded the town, the lights of a lager-beer garden glistened like stars, while the music therefrom rolled over the town.

Sunday evening, a religious service, conducted by the Prelate of Boston Commandery, was held in the dining-room of the hotel. Mr. Nadeau had nearly completed a fine block on the principal street, in which Nadeau Hotel was to be located. A suite of rooms on the second floor was finished by his order, and the use of it generously given to Cœur de Lion Commandery, No. 9, as a headquarters during the visits of Eastern Sir Knights to and from the Conclave. The rooms were elegantly furnished, and were tastily decorated with fruits and flowers.

Sir Knights and ladies of Los Angeles were in constant attendance to welcome the pilgrims and dispense hospitality. Monday morning came bright and beautiful, bringing great anticipations, which were more than realized. Carriages were freely provided for drives around Los Angeles and into the country. The orchards, vineyards, wine vaults, and villas were visited, some parties going as far as Sierra Madre Villa and San Gabriel Mission.

"Did you ever visit an orange grove when the rich, yellow fruit surrounded you on every side? Oranges behind and in front of you; oranges on the right and on the left above you; and the ground yellow with oranges at your feet, perfuming the air with their delicious fragrance? We did, at Los Angeles, and while we were busy testing the capacity of our stomachs, our host was testing the holding capacity of our carriages after having stuffed our pockets with choice specimens until we resembled walking fruit stores." — SIR S. L. S., *Sewing Machine News*, Dec., 1883.

The different species of cacti (of which it is said there are a hundred different kinds in Arizona) increased in quantity, size, and variety as we proceeded westward. Vast quantities were seen on the route; sometimes a few scattered ones on dark soil, and again solid acres where the soil was poorest. They varied in size from a running stem to a trunk thirty feet high. The specimens cultivated at some of the stations where we tarried were wondrous in shape, but without comeliness. The principal streets of Los Angeles are level, wide, and shady, the shade trees being the pepper-tree and eucalyptus. The lawns and gardens seemed semi-tropical indeed with century plants, pomegranates, palms, and brilliant flowers. Climbing vines festooned the fronts of houses; geraniums were twelve feet high, and heliotrope grown from the ground looked down upon us from the eaves of a porch. It was fragrant, luxuriant, and seemed as if we were in a dream. Mrs. Charles A. Fairbanks, in her published correspondence, described Los Angeles as a lovely town, with orange and banana trees weighed down with luscious fruit, ready to be plucked. Flowers bloomed on every side, and white, tempting grapes hung in rich clusters within reach. She expressed delight and amazement at the profusion of double scarlet geraniums which are in bloom the year round, growing to the height of twelve feet, and at the mag-

nificent heliotrope, which covers one whole side of houses. She
confessed her inability to adequately describe the grandeur of the
scenery, or the magnificent cordiality universally manifested, and
gratefully mentioned the attentions everywhere shown to the ladies
of the party. The experience of Sir A. H. Hurlburt, as published
in the *Masonic Journal*, was similar to that of Boston Sir Knights
who made the tour of San Gabriel, Sierra Madre, and the vineyards.
He thus relates his experience in the vicinity of Los Angeles: —

LOS ANGELES, CALIFORNIA.

The city of Los Angeles is located in the most fertile part of Southern
California, and contains sixteen thousand inhabitants. Its banks, business
houses, wholesale and retail, railroad shops, factories, and hotels bespeak
the enterprise and wealth of its citizens. Its streets are fine, its public

buildings imposing, its blocks and factories extensive. It is situated on the river of the same name, about thirty miles from the sea, and is the railroad centre for all that part of the State. It sustains a public library and an organized fire department. It is supplied with water and gas, and has a well-developed system of street railroads. The climate is charming all the year round, and its soil produces all the semi-tropical fruits and flowers, with abundant garden fruits and vegetables.

Our sojourn in this delightful spot was enjoyable in the extreme, and the courtesy extended to us will never be forgotten. In our tour about the city, we visited the St. Gabriel Church at Pasadena, and endeavored, as far as in us lies, to obey the injunction which we saw conspicuously posted on the door, "*Take off your hats and behave yourselves.*" Not far from this church we were shown a dwelling whose history can be traced back to 1647.

We paid a visit to the Stem and Rose vineyard of San Gabriel. This is said to be the largest winery in the world. Its location on a hill is a most pleasant one. The buildings are of brick, and the principal wine cellar is two stories in height (or depth), with an area 226 x 146 feet and a capacity of a million and a half gallons. There is machinery for crushing two hundred and fifty tons of grapes in a day. The arrangement of the various buildings on the hillside is such that the grapes are passed through the different processes of manufacture without being handled from the time they are emptied from the boxes which received them at the vines until the wine is prepared for shipment. There are nineteen hundred acres in Sunny slope, the greater part of which is under pretty high state of cultivation, six hundred and forty acres of which are devoted to grapes and one hundred and thirty to oranges, one hundred and fifty to other fruits, such as English walnuts, figs, pomegranates, olives, pears, peaches, apricots, etc. Last year there were manufactured five hundred and sixty thousand gallons of wine and one hundred and thirteen thousand of brandy.

At Pasadena, near Los Angeles, we made a tour of the farm of Mr. Ezra Carr, where we learned the following facts : There were forty-two acres under cultivation, upon which were growing eighty-seven varieties of grapes, three hundred prune-trees, seven hundred peach-trees, six hundred orange-trees, three hundred apricot-trees, one hundred Mexican limes, and seventy-five fig-trees. There were thirteen thousand grape-vines, from which the owner sold thirty tons of grapes in the season of 1881–82, and also seven hundred boxes of raisins. Strawberries, raspberries, blackberries, and mulberries also grow in abundance. An enormous rose-bush three years old covers one side of the barn. We saw a pine-tree forty feet tall that had grown from the seed planted seven years ago. Here were a mayberry-tree, hawthorn, acacia, cedar of Lebanon, and camphor trees. The cost of the land seven years ago was seventy-five dollars per acre. Last April one acre was sold for three thousand five hundred dollars, — a larger price than was originally paid for the entire farm.

A pleasant visit to the Sierra Madre Villa, kept by Mr. William H. Rhoades, where we were served to an excellent dinner, was an occasion of pleasing remembrance. This is one of the most beautifully located hotels for the resort of invalids which it has ever been our fortune to visit. Too much cannot be said in praise of the soil and climate of this part of California. They seemed to be all that can be desired for the health, pleasure, and prosperity of man.

In the afternoon the headquarters at Nadeau Hotel were filled with the visitors, the Grand Master and Eminent Commander being present. The principal attraction was the carving and disposing of two watermelons, one weighing eighty-seven and the other eighty-eight pounds. The former was carved by our Medical Director and sundry volunteer assistants, and the latter by Grand Master Dean. To the sweetness of this pair of giants all present could testify.

Los Angeles was generous in its welcome, and the Bostons were begged to extend their visit another day. It was a royal reception, and expressions of the gratitude of the visitors were heard on every side. Sir H. A. Clawson continued his kindly offices to the last moment of our stay, then bestowing upon the Sir

Knights many banners and Templar designs with which the hotel had been decorated. These decorations were transferred to the train, and as car decorations were constant reminders of our happy hours in Los Angeles. As the time for our departure drew near

AN AVENUE AT LOS ANGELES.

thousands of people assembled at the station. The Sir Knights and ladies of Cœur de Lion and Boston Commanderies formed a circle upon the depot platform, and, joining hands, sang familiar songs. Repeated cheers were given, and the Bostons, boarding the train, proceeded towards "Frisco," 482 miles distant.

> "O Queen! I bow down before thee,
>   Allegiance unfailing to prove;
> 'Midst the mortals and saints who adore thee,
>   I offer my tribute of love."

The Los Angeles (Cal.) *Daily Herald*, Tuesday morning, Aug. 14, noticed the reception as follows:—

KNIGHTS TEMPLARS. — THE RECEPTION OF THE BOSTON COMMANDERY AND GRAND MASTER BENJAMIN DEAN.

About three o'clock on Sunday afternoon a special train of eight cars, including one special and six handsome Pullman sleepers, arrived in the city and were met at the new depot by Cœur de Lion Commandery, No. 9, of Los Angeles, who received them with all the honors of the Order in such cases. After an introduction and hand-shaking all round, the visitors were escorted to the dining-room of the Los Angeles Hotel, where a sumptuous repast was provided by Mr. Clawson in his elegant dining-room, which was elaborately decorated with the banners of the Sir Knights. The Cœur de Lion Commandery then marched back to their headquarters and were dismissed. In their march and parade they were led by the Los Angeles Union Band, in their new and elegant uniforms.

The meeting and greeting was most cordial, enthusiastic, and gratifying to all concerned. The large crowd of citizens who met the visitors at the depot showed the respect which they entertained for this fine delegation of representative men, who had crossed the continent at unlimited expense, to meet and greet their brethren of the same mystic tie on the Pacific Coast, and to renew their friendly relations and inquire into their prosperity and welfare. The Boston Commandery are a fine body of gentlemen, of ample fortune and genteel accomplishments, and largely accompanied by the wives and other lady members of their families. The ladies and gentlemen appeared much pleased with the sunny skies and the orange groves and vineyards of Los Angeles, and one lady remarked to a *Herald* reporter that it was "a very pleasant day," but on being informed that the day was three months long, she looked incredulous and amused.

After doing justice to the well-spread dinner, the Sir Knights distributed themselves about the city. Some rode around town, some went to headquarters in the Nadeau block, others went to church in the evening. The party divided up for the night, part of them going to the Pico House and the Cosmopolitan, while some remained on board of their elegant cars at the depot. Yesterday all the available carriages in the city were put into service to carry the distinguished guests about the city and over to the San Gabriel valley, taking in Pasadena, Sierra Madre Villa, and the venerable Mission San Gabriel and the great wineries They are individuals who appreciate attention and admire the beautiful, and were free to express their admiration of what they saw, ate, and drank. Many expressed their surprise and delight at the bountiful hospitality which they met from the people of Los Angeles, and declared that there was in this world but "one California and one Los Angeles."

The names of the Grand Master, officers of Boston Commandery for the California pilgrimage, Sir Knights, and ladies were appended to the above.

The following is from the Los Angeles (Cal.) *Evening Express*, of Aug. 13 : —

KNIGHTS TEMPLARS. — A SUPERB BODY OF NEARLY TWO HUNDRED MEN WITH SIXTY LADIES — THEIR DELIGHT WITH LOS ANGELES.

Sir Knights R. R. Brown, E. F. Spence, T. J. Caystile, and F. A. Gibson went out yesterday to Colton to meet a special train conveying Right Eminent Grand Commander of the Order of Knights Templars in United States, Sir Benjamin F. Dean, of Boston, and his escort of one hundred and seventy-five swords, accompanied by sixty ladies, travelling in a special train of seven palace Pullman cars *en route* to the Triennial Conclave, to convene on the 17th instant, Friday next, at San Francisco, to welcome the pilgrims to the Southern California metropolis, and escort them to this city. They took out with them generous donations of wines and fruits from citizens of Los Angeles to refresh the weary travellers. At San Gabriel Mr. Weeks boarded the train with a liberal supply of fine oranges, and on the way in at San Gabriel Mr. L. H. Titus met them with an immense supply of the same delicious fruit. Two engines brought the pilgrim train into Colton, and from there to the city the travellers, fatigued from the heat and dust of the desert, enjoyed the products of the country, and conversed with their new companions. Arrived at the depot some fifty swords of the Cœur de Lion Commandery of this city met the train, and, drawn up in line, received the Grand Commander and his escort. There was a large crowd of our citizens, of all ages and sexes, around the train. By the good sense of the people and the efforts of the police the most admirable order was maintained. It is seldom that so many people assemble anywhere and observe as good, perfect decorum as ruled round the depot The space near the cars was not encroached upon, and plenty of room was left for the evolutions of the Knights. The new chief of police, Mr. T. J. Cuddy, manifested the rarest good judgment in the admirable manner in which all was ordered. The Los Angeles Knights were in full uniform and presented a fine appearance. The Boston men wore fatigue caps, as to dress in full uniform would have been rather troublesome. They are a fine body of men, of truly knightly bearing, and made the most pleasing impression on all who saw or conversed with them. From the depot the pilgrims visited the headquarters. Many of them dispersed through the city. Some met old friends here. Parties drove through the city in all directions until late in the evening. Frequent and sincere were the expressions of admiration from many lips, as one beautiful — and to them novel — sight after another came in view. The electric lights and the general diffusion of the illumination were particularly admired. Something over fifty of the strangers registered at the Pico House. Most of them remain with the train and take their meals at the new depot hotel, which is profusely decorated with the beautiful flags and emblems of the Order. At the headquarters most of the pilgrims are registered. It is regretted that the crowded condition of these columns precludes giving all the names. The day is spent in enjoying the lovely weather on the verandas of the hotels, in visiting friends and companions in arms (it does not take long to become acquainted by the aid of the mystic ties), or in driving round the country. At seven o'clock this evening the train pulls out after the regular passenger train and proceeds to San Francisco. The Knights have been eight days *en route* here from Boston. The first few days they were behind time, owing to hot boxes and ditched freight trains, but on getting farther west they were able to make better progress They are here on schedule time, and will doubtless arrive so in San Francisco. Los Angeles people tender the gallant Knights and their fair companions a *bon voyage*.

The jewels of the Order worn by the Boston Knights are remarkably handsome. The ladies also make a brilliant display of jewels and diamonds.

From the *Evening Express*, of Aug. 14: —

The Boston Knights got off in good form last evening at seven o'clock in their splendid special train. They carry with them warm memories of Los Angeles' sunny skies, and the as bright hospitality of their companions in this city.

From the *Times*, of Aug. 14: —

BON VOYAGE. — At seven o'clock last evening the Boston Commandery bade adieu to Los Angeles and started on their way to San Francisco. They expressed themselves as being delighted with all they had seen during their short stay here. The many improvements now being made in this city filled them with admiration of the enterprise of the people, and encouraged them to believe that the time is not far distant when Los Angeles will be a formidable commercial rival to cities which make greater pretensions. The products of the county as exhibited in our markets were inspected by them, and which inspired their wonder at the variety and extent of our horticultural and agricultural resources. The Knights were entertained in a royal manner by the citizens of this city, and they expressed their gratification in many kind thanks and wishes. The Grand Commander of the Order in the United States impressed the people here very favorably by his gentlemanly conduct and refined manner. In the great Conclave at San Francisco there will assuredly not be a Commandery which can boast of a more knightly bearing than that which hails from Boston.

> " Know'st thou the land where the lemon-trees bloom,
> Where the gold orange grows in the deep thicket's gloom,
> Where a wind ever soft from the blue heaven blows,
> And the groves are of laurel and myrtle and rose?"

Such is Los Angeles, from which we so reluctantly parted. Having passed through the valleys of the Los Angeles and San Fernando, we crossed the San Fernando range of mountains by means of a tunnel 6,967 feet in length. We proceeded sixty miles

BIRD'S-EYE VIEW OF THE LOOP, TEHACHAPI PASS.

farther and reached the Mojave Desert, whose dust we left on approaching Tehachapi summit, 3,964 feet elevation. Descending rapidly, we approached one of the most remarkable feats of railroad engineering skill ever achieved in any part of the world. A group of mountain peaks and spurs belonging to the southwestern spur of the Sierra Nevada range disputed the advance of the iron horse, but by a series of complex curves, and, finally, by what is called "the loop," *i. e.*, by actually crossing its own line, a pathway was effected to the plains of Tulare and Fresno. The length of the loop is 3,795 feet, and the difference of elevation of the two tracks where they cross is seventy-eight feet.

CROSSING THE LOOP, TEHACHAPI PASS.

Through tunnels and gorges, winding around rocky points, twisting and turning in our descent, we hastened, and, having passed Fresno, entered the San Joaquin Valley. This valley of six million acres in fertility and fruitfulness is in itself an empire.

We stopped for breakfast at Merced. Here the Grand Master and his escort were welcomed to the Pacific slope by the officers of the Grand Commandery of California and the Committee on Reception. The delegation was composed of Sir William Center, chairman, and Sir William W. Morrow, vice-chairman of the Reception Committee, and Sir Knights Simpson, Dean, Dougherty, and Searles of the committee. Ex-Governor George C. Perkins, Grand Commander of California, was escorted by the following members of the Grand Commandery: Sir William M. Petrie, Deputy Grand Commander; Sir Reuben H. Lloyd, Grand Captain-General; Sir Tristam Burges, Grand Senior Warden; Sir James McDonald, Grand Treasurer; Sir T. H. Caswell, Grand Recorder; Sir O. C. Wheeler, Grand Prelate; Sir S. H. Wagener, Grand Sword-Bearer; Sir George A. Johnson, Grand Warder; Sir J. H. Burns, Grand Standard-Bearer; Sir Samuel D. Mayer, Grand Organist; Sir E. R. Hedges, Past Grand Commander; Sir W. A. Davies, Past Grand Commander; and Bro. M. D. Boruck, Journalist of the Triennial Committee.

As the train drew slowly up to the station, Grand Commander Perkins and the other officers of the Commandery, with the committee, dressed in full uniform, were drawn up in line upon the platform, supported and flanked by an immense concourse of people. When the train had stopped, these officers marched to the rear car, the headquarters of Grand Master Dean and Eminent Commander Stevenson, where the formal presentation was made, Grand Commander Perkins performing that ceremony in a short address, to which the Grand Master happily responded. Knightly sociability immediately held supreme sway,—the beginning of a fellowship we were reluctant to sever. After breakfast, the special car of the San-Franciscans was attached to the rear of the Boston train and the hours passed pleasantly. Lunch was had at Lathrop about noon. Along the line crowds of spectators were gathered, anxious, perhaps, to see the train or its occupants; but to the pilgrims their presence indicated the popular interest in this unprecedented pilgrimage.

OLD JESUIT CHURCH, CALIFORNIA.

At 4 P. M. the train reached Oakland, the terminus of the road. On disembarking, the Grand Master and Boston Commandery formed, and, preceded by the Grand Commandery of California, marched past the Oakland Commandery, the latter saluting, and embarked on the ferry-boat. The ladies of the Boston party had been meanwhile escorted to the same boat by the Reception Committee. The great *El Capitan* bore us all safely across the bay and brought us that much nearer to the realization of our hope. Upon the dock the Golden Gate and California Commanderies, each two hundred strong, were formed in double ranks. The Oaklands, Bostons, Grand Master, and Grand Commandery disembarked, and marched between the saluting lines, preceded by the First Artillery Band, playing "Hail to the Chief." Subsequently, the San Francisco Commanderies having passed to the front, the order of march was as follows: —

Platoon of Police; First Artillery Band; California Commandery; Golden Gate Commandery; Grand Commandery of California; Boston Commandery; Carriage, drawn by four horses, containing Most Eminent Sir Benjamin Dean, Grand Master; Right Eminent Sir George C. Perkins, Grand Commander of California; Eminent Sir Reuben H. Lloyd, Grand Captain General, and Eminent and Reverend Sir Osgood C. Wheeler, Grand Prelate.

Extensive decorations had been made on the high buildings and across the street. Nearly every window was filled with spectators, and the wide street was crowded with people. "The procession presented a magnificent appearance; the handsome uniforms of the Sir Knights, their gorgeous banners, and their fine marching were all alike attractive," the *Chronicle* said.

When the ferry-boat reached her dock at the foot of Market Street, the flag of the Grand Encampment of the United States was displayed from the staff surmounting the Palace Hotel. On the arrival of the column at the hotel, the escorting Commanderies formed an avenue and the visitors marched between the lines and entered the court-yard of the hotel, where an open square was formed. As the Grand Master stepped from the carriage, his escort saluted, which he gracefully acknowledged. The Eminent

Commander of Boston Commandery, in accordance with the following general order No. 4, received by him at Los Angeles when *en route* for San Francisco, reported to Most Eminent Sir Benjamin Dean, Grand Master of Knights Templars of the United States: —

General Order No. 4.

GRAND COMMANDERY OF KNIGHTS TEMPLARS OF THE STATE OF CALIFORNIA.

HEADQUARTERS OF THE GRAND COMMANDERY,
SAN FRANCISCO, Aug. 10, 1883.

To the Eminent Commander of Boston Commandery Knights Templars:

Your Commandery is hereby detailed as the special escort of the Grand Master of Templars, at the Twenty-second Triennial Conclave of the Grand Encampment of the United States.

You will therefore report to Most Eminent Sir Benjamin Dean, Grand Master of Knights Templars of the United States, at his headquarters, Palace Hotel, for orders, immediately upon his arrival in San Francisco.

GEO. C. PERKINS,
Grand Commander.

Attest: THOS. H. CASWELL,
Grand Recorder.

The Grand Master then excused the Commandery until further orders, and, accompanied by the Grand Commandery of California, retired to the rooms assigned for headquarters.

Before the Grand Commandery of California departed, Grand Master Dean feelingly requested Ex-Governor Perkins to extend to each Sir Knight of the Grand Commandery, who had done him so much distinguished honor, his heartfelt appreciation of their fraternal and personal regard. In the mean time carriages were arriving with the ladies of the Boston party, who entered the ground-floor parlor from the entrance leading from the *porte-cochère*, where they were politely received by a delegation of ladies of the Executive Committee of the Triennial Union.

Boston Commandery was immediately dismissed after the Grand Master retired, and the rooms assigned the Sir Knights and ladies were speedily occupied. The system adopted by the management, which was the assignment of rooms at the Palace by an *attaché* of the hotel on the train, simplified matters and avoided all confusion at the hotel.

The following interviews were reported in the San Francisco *Bulletin* of the 15th inst.: —

A *Bulletin* reporter boarded the train at the latter point (Port Costa). Grand Master Dean's headquarters were in the last of the six Pullman cars, and here he was found with M. D. Boruck, the journalist of the Triennial Committee. On the walls, on tables and seats were samples of California's products, — oranges, grapes, peaches, corn-stalks, etc., — presented by the Knights at Colton. The cars were as conveniently arranged and comfortable as movable palaces could be. All the visitors expressed delight at their reception. The fact of the Welcoming Committee travelling one hundred and fifty miles to meet them was a great surprise. All said the ten days' trip had been a most pleasant one. Grand Master Dean complained of the deserts, but said it was a good illustration of the magnitude of the country when you could get up in a desert, travel all day in a desert, and see desert still when you went to bed.

Subsequently the Grand Master and Eminent Commander were interviewed at the Palace, with the following results: —

Having been rested and refreshed, the Grand Master talked freely with a *Bulletin* reporter. He said that everything which he had observed so far met with his approval. He had every reason to expect that the sessions of the Grand Commandery will be well attended. He is a very business-like appearing gentleman, but withal of pleasant address. He desires to have the business of the Grand Commandery pushed ahead as rapidly as possible, and says that it depends a great deal on the various committees. So far as he has been able he has taken measures to prepare all the business he could in advance for early action. The Commandery will consider his triennial address; other business will be the acceptance of triennial reports, the triennial election and customary legislation for the benefit of the Order.

The trip of the Boston Commandery was, throughout, pleasant. The story as told by Eminent Commander John L. Stevenson to a *Bulletin* reporter is as follows: "We were ten days out, leaving Boston Aug. 4, in six twelve-section Pullman cars. We came through Montreal to Chicago, and over the Southern route. We had a perfect ovation all the way, of an informal nature. At Wallace, about two hundred Pueblo Indians treated us to a war-dance and other dances, and the Commander there presented us with a young live American eagle, which we carry with us during our journey. At Colton we were met by Cœur de Lion Commandery, who loaded us with flowers and wines and fruit. We stayed at Los Angeles twenty-four hours. The run across the Yuma desert was better than we expected; better than the run through the San Joaquin country. We lost eight hours on the Grand Trunk Railroad, but made it up by running over the Raton Mountains by night, and at Las Vegas we caught up with our itinerary. We shall leave here Aug. 25, going back by the Central and Union Pacific roads. We cannot stay longer, for the dates are fixed for our special train. We came earlier so as not to lose any of the session of the Conclave, and arrived ahead of time. We have one hundred and five swords and sixty-three ladies."

CHAPTER VIII.

CALIFORNIA'S GREETING.

We bid you welcome, Brothers, to our homes beside the sea,
Where rivers run o'er golden sands, and hills are fair to see;
Where the mountains lift their snow-caps far up the ether blue,
And the giant redwoods murmur their solemn *Sal-re* too.

Where valleys smile with vineyards and the orange groves with bloom,
And summer's sun through all the year dispels cold winter's gloom;
Where Pacific waves are roaring with never silent calls,
And Nevada's snows send answer, with thund'ring waterfalls.

To all these glories of our State, and to our hearts as well,
We bid you welcome with such cheer, no words have power to tell.
A little space abide with us, and when you homeward go,
With kindly thoughts of us and ours, may mem'ry ever glow.

No more we move, a warrior band, the Templars of to-day,
No Paynim spear nor Syrian war incites our bravery;
Our battles are with *self* alone; the Higher Law we plead—
Our pilgrim's pass, Golgotha, unto purer life doth lead.

Let us then make glad together, and strengthen heart and hand;
Pacific to Atlantic calls, across the wide-spread land;
So let mountain answer mountain, and sea reply to sea,
And thus shall live forever our knightly chivalry!

— *Pacific Coast Guide.*   J. B. H.

PALACE HOTEL is a remarkable building, colossal and majestic, and one of the wonders of San Francisco. It comprises an entire block, two hundred and fifty by two hundred and seventy-five feet, and covers 96,250 feet. Its style of architecture is modern, showing solidity, strength, and symmetry. The main entrance or double

BOSTON COMMANDERY KNIGHTS TEMPLARS.

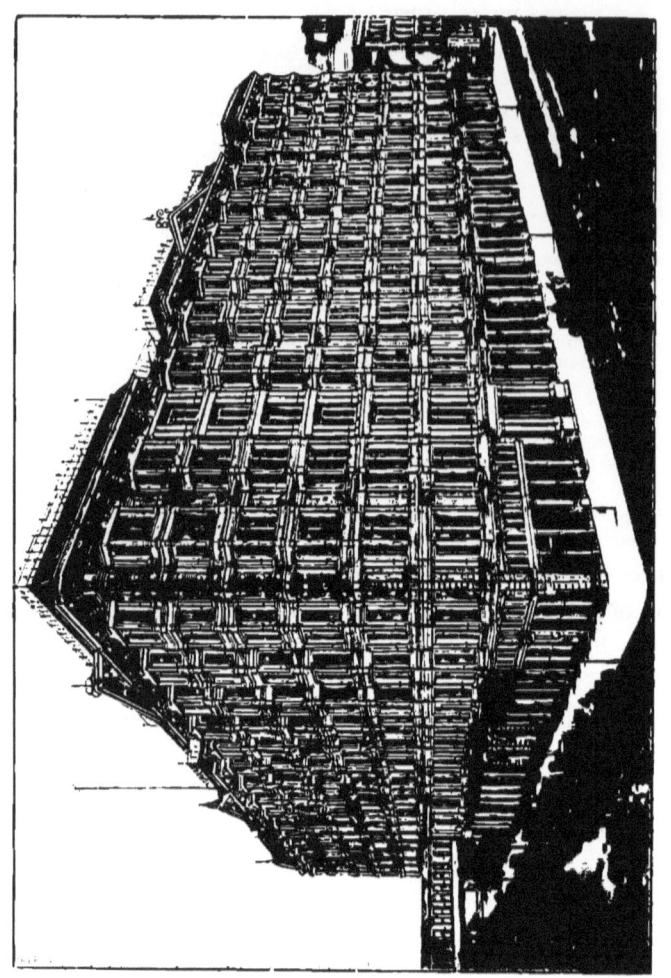

PALACE HOTEL, SAN FRANCISCO.

roadway into the court, with its walk on either side, is fifty feet wide. The distance around its outer wall is one quarter of a mile, and there is a promenade on the roof of one third of a mile. The grand central court is a noble enclosure one hundred and fifty-two by eighty-four feet, seven stories high, roofed with glass at the top of the building, and is surrounded on all sides and stories with arcaded galleries or balconies. The pavement is of black and white marble tiling, and the windows of plate glass. The lower story has a height of over twenty-seven feet, and the topmost of sixteen. Around the ground promenade are grouped the office, reception-rooms, breakfast and dining rooms, telegraph office, etc., with spacious hallways. The cost of the structure is said to have been more than six million dollars. It contains one thousand and eighteen rooms; ten thousand burners light the building; ventilation and precautions against fire are perfect. The basement contains the bakery and confectionery departments, the storeroom, butcher shop, laundry, manufactories of gas and ice, and various offices. The provisions supplied at the tables, in quality and quantity, are in keeping with the beautiful structure. It is not only the largest hotel in the world, but one of the very best. The rooms of the Grand Master and of his escort were assigned on the second floor, corner of New Montgomery and Jessie Streets. There were not more pleasant and convenient rooms in the hotel, and when the party became settled, satisfaction reigned.

The headquarters of the Grand Master, which were also the headquarters of Boston Commandery, were on the second floor, Nos. 160 and 161, corner of New Montgomery and Jessie Streets. This suite of rooms is beautifully frescoed, has heavy lambrequins over the windows, Brussels carpets on the floors, and the furniture is oak, chairs and sofas having red plush backs and seats. They were elegantly decorated for the reception of the Grand Master, by the Ladies' Executive Committee of the Triennial Union. The committee consisted of Sir Geo. C. Bromley, Mrs. J. W. Burnham, Mrs. W. O. Gould, Mrs. O. C. Wheeler, Mrs. P. T. Barclay, Mrs. H. T. Graves, Mrs. W. B. May, and Mrs. J. F. Merrill, representing Golden Gate, California, and Oakland Commanderies.

In the front parlor, over the alcove formed by a bay-window, was the word "WELCOME," made of red, white, and purple flowers, with smilax festooned across the curtains, and also hanging to the floor. Underneath, upon a table, there was a large bank of flowers, three feet square, bearing the words and figures:—

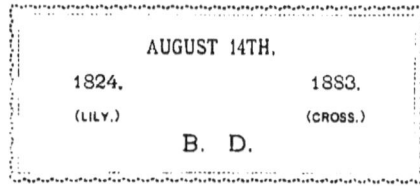

Under "1824" a little boy was represented as reposing in a large Japanese lily, and under "1883" there was a triple cross, the emblem of the office of the Grand Master. At the bottom of the bank were the letters "B. D." The groundwork of the bank was composed principally of white flowers of various kinds, the letters and figures being made of double scarlet geraniums. Around the bank was a border of lilies, roses, heliotrope, ferns, and begonias. The table on which it rests was covered with smilax. This piece, interpreted, signified that Most Eminent Sir Knight Benjamin Dean was born Aug. 14, 1824, and is Grand Master of Knights Templars of the United States, Aug. 14, 1883. This unique floral piece was devised by Sir W. O. Gould. Upon a chiffonnier there was a Maltese cross of pinks, geraniums, pansies, and other flowers, surmounted by elegant bouquets. From the arch of a second alcove a cross of flowers was suspended, and upon a table under it rested a basket of flowers. The marble mantel-pieces in both parlors supported banks of flowers of various colors, tastefully arranged. The foundations were composed of sprays of the pepper-tree, which hung gracefully from the mantels. On a centre-table in the back parlor there was an arch or gateway three feet high and two feet wide.

Upon one side of the arch was the word "Welcome" in double scarlet geraniums, and underneath it the words "To Our," while a gate made of flowers of a golden hue was easily opened and closed. The whole signified "Welcome to our Golden Gate," and was presented by Mrs. J. M. Peck, of San Francisco. There were fans made of flowers, of elegant design and great beauty; large horseshoes of rare combinations of flowers; also bouquets, wreaths, baskets, and smilax in profusion. When the Grand Master was first conducted to these apartments he found them in possession of the ladies, who had just finished the decorations. On entering, he was greeted by Sir George T. Bromley, chairman of the Ladies' Executive Committee, who, having been selected to introduce the Grand Master to the ladies, prefaced the ceremony with the following explanatory address:—

Most Eminent Grand Master: — Three years ago, upon the return of the Sir Knights from the Chicago pilgrimage, the ladies of the Sir Knights, deeming it the proper thing to do, organized an association to be known as the Triennial Union, having for its object making such perfect acquaintance with each other that the ladies from the East attending the Conclave of 1883 would be received into one united, harmonious, warm-hearted family; and we fondly hope the object will have been accomplished at the close of this Conclave. The Executive Committee of that body, having learned that your arrival here would be on the anniversary of your birthday, desired to commemorate the event by decorating these, your private parlors, with floral emblems, suggestive of the occasion. Prominent, as you will observe, are two floral designs, significant of the two great events of your lifetime. This represents your arrival on the shores of time, and this commemorates your arrival on the shores of the Pacific as our Most Eminent Grand Master. The only similarity between the first event and the present is the very large proportion of ladies who take part, and the very small number of gentlemen. My being chairman of the committee will account for my being present. And now, Most Eminent, however much we may wish to impress you with the great things of our State, we do not wish to impress you with our great speeches; consequently I will close this one of mine by tendering to you, Most Eminent, and to your wife, in the name and behalf of the ladies of the Executive Committee of the Triennial Union and of the whole Pacific coast, a warm, hearty, and right royal welcome.

Subsequently the banner of Boston Commandery and several bannerets of the Order were displayed in the back parlor.

A very pretty incident occurred at headquarters on Wednesday evening. The inscription on the "Golden Gate" device was simply "Welcome to Our," and below this was a gate of golden-colored flowers which opens on hinges. The gate was fastened invisibly. Several Boston ladies, the gate being closed, were trying to study out of the arrangement of the golden-colored flowers some cabalistic meaning to complete the inscription given above. Some jar started the "gate," which swung suddenly wide open of itself as if to extend welcome. This called forth clapping of hands, and warm expressions of delight from the ladies, who saw at once the answer. They found it difficult to find words to express their admiration fully for California flowers, and especially for the designs in Grand Master Dean's parlors. — *San Francisco Bulletin.*

The Commandery was at first somewhat crowded in the Palace,

but its obliging host allotted additional rooms, and then the accommodations were pronounced "ample and faultless." The *Chronicle* of Wednesday contained the following in regard to the accommodations of the Bostons: —

The Boston Commandery of Knights on Wednesday extended their quarters in the Palace Hotel, and their accommodations were then pronounced by them ample and faultless. On their arrival, tired and dusty, and with much baggage, some of the Knights thought that the room allowed them was not so great as they had been led to expect. Eminent Commander Stevenson said that there was no fault to be attached to any one. It had been agreed that in some rooms there should be eight and in some ten beds, but he had thought that these rooms were larger. There being room in the hotel, there was a readjustment this forenoon of rooms without any difficulty. The Boston Knights, and indeed all others, expressed themselves in admiration of the city, and say that they are enjoying themselves finely.

The flowers used in decorating Grand Master Dean's parlors in the Palace Hotel were arranged and photographed in two groups to retain their memory.

Fresh and beautiful bouquets of flowers and set pieces were at various times sent to the headquarters, complimentary to the Grand Master and Boston Commandery. Among them a set piece from Sir William Harney, of San Francisco, and another from Sir Henry A. Clawson, of Los Angeles. The flowers formed very attractive and fragrant ornaments to the marble-topped centre-table in the Grand Master's reception-room at the Palace.

Tuesday evening, the baggage having arrived promptly and in good order, the tired and dusty Knights being rejoiced at their safe arrival, with an excellent prospect of a royal visit, Boston Commandery entered at once upon the pleasures of the occasion, holding themselves ready to answer the bugle-call to duty. Early in the evening, the court and corridors of the Palace were filled with an orderly multitude,—an event which occurred every evening during the Conclave. The Gatling Cornet Band occupied the court and gave a concert complimentary to the Grand Master, whose arrival had been anxiously looked for, whose coming was an enthusiastic welcome. The human tide moved decorous and irresistible along the corridors until the approach of midnight. From the hour of their arrival until the Sunday following — when the regular plan of Conclave week began, designating the duties and pleasures — the Boston Sir Knights made good use of their time, visiting places of interest, doing San Francisco, and enjoying the hospitality of all California. The first thing to be done was to register at the headquarters of the California Committee of the Triennial Conclave, on Montgomery Street. Having registered, each Sir Knight received a certificate which entitled him to half fare by railroads and steamboats, and also free admission to all complimentary entertainments given under the auspices of the Grand Commandery of California.

On Wednesday evening fully three thousand people were congregated in the court of the Palace Hotel, or overlooked the court from the tiers of corridors surrounding it. They assembled to listen to the Royal Hawaiian Band, who gave a serenade complimentary to the Grand Master. The edges or railings of the corridors from the bottom to the seventh floor were lined with spectators, and in the court there was barely room to move. Every one of the six hundred gas jets was lighted, presenting a scene of extraordinary brilliancy. The Knights Templars in their undress suits formed a conspicuous feature, and the evening dresses of the ladies added a tinge of color to the marked contrasts of black and white. Grand Master Dean occupied a prominent place on the second story and heartily joined in the applause which greeted the various numbers. The first piece was "Kalakaua's Quickstep," the second "Grand Entrée March Knights Templars." The band numbered thirty musicians. Prof. Berger, the leader, is the only member of the band not a native Hawaiian. The continuous applause of their audience kept them busy in responding to demanded encores until 10.30 o'clock. As a variation, a quartet in the band sang several choruses, which were still more vociferously applauded.

The second number on the programme, "Grand Entrée March Knights Templars," was a new piece, composed by Sir Knight Henry Marsh, of San Francisco, and dedicated to Most Eminent Sir Benjamin Dean, Grand Master. Previous to the Grand Master's arrival, this march was published under the sanction of the music committee of the Triennial Conclave. The cover is handsomely lithographed, bearing a portrait of Grand Master Dean, a scene from the Crusades, a picture of Fort Point, and various Templar emblems. The back of the cover has handsome lithographs of Yosemite, Mt. Shasta, San Francisco, the Geysers, Cliff House, and other places of interest. A lithographed copy of this piece, enclosed in a roll of scarlet plush, with a solid silver handle, was presented Grand Master Dean by the composer.

The crowd, music, and enlivening scenes of Wednesday evening at the Palace were the same as were there experienced every evening during the Conclave. It was the centre towards which the thousands drifted. It had 2,500 guests, a crowd in itself, and, for the first time since it was opened to the public, every room was occupied. Though there were many attractions in the pavilion and at various halls in the city, yet every evening the card exchangers and badge "fiends" captured and held possession of the large office room and adjoining halls, and formed intimate and lasting friendships. The corridors of the court were occupied by promenaders, both Californians and visitors, who enjoyed the best opportunities of watching the moving multitude below, of appreciating the beautiful picture of the mammoth court illuminated by hundreds of gas jets and electric globes, and of listening to the music of various bands. The headquarters of several State and subordinate Commanderies, also of the Ancient and Accepted Rite, were at the Palace, and the hospitalities there dispensed caused not only the five elevators to be full of people, but also the broad stairways. From the evening of the arrival of Boston Commandery until that of its departure, the Palace each evening was honored with an immense crowd, music filled the air, good-fellowship reigned, and the same shifting, dazzling scenes recurred.

A book was kept at headquarters of Boston Commandery, wherein were registered the names of all visitors. They represented every State and Territory in the Union and the Sandwich Islands, every official grade in Masonry, and every profession of active life. Among the many prominent Masons who called at the headquarters of Boston Commandery was Past Grand Master J. D. Stevenson, the oldest living Freemason in California. He was present at the organization of California Lodge, No. 1, Free and Accepted Masons, in 1849, in a loft in San Francisco, so low that a man five feet six inches in height could not stand erect ten feet from the centre of the room. There were ten members. The rent of the loft was five hundred dollars per year. The chief work of the Order in those early days was the care of the sick and suffering. Hospitals were not then established. The Lodge contributed frequently and largely to relieve distress. The hat was placed upon the altar in those days, and voluntary contributions were poured into it. Sometimes one thousand dollars were collected in an evening. Masonry in California was nursed by charity, and gave a notable example for the imitation of its children. Were not the overflowing generosity, the cheerful hospitality, the royal reception manifested by the Masons of California towards their visiting brothers the direct outgrowth of that charity and self-sacrifice which stood as sponsors at the birth and baptism of "California, No. 1," the mother Lodge of the Masonic bodies in the Golden State? May the lustre of Masonic hospitality and charity, as evinced in 1849 and 1883, be never dimmed.

A full description of San Francisco does not come within the scope of this book. It should, however, be said that this cosmopolitan city is situated on a hundred hills, and is the heir of two villages dating from 1776 and 1837. The city is only thirty-four years old, but contains over a quarter of a million of people. It is well laid out, the public buildings are fine, and private residences compare favorably with those of Eastern cities. The city contains one hundred and thirteen church organizations, nineteen places of art, one hundred and ten halls, twenty-four parks and public gardens, forty-nine hotels, thirty-three literary and reading rooms, forty military organizations, sixty-nine clubs and secret societies, one hundred and sixty-eight newspapers, twelve lines of street cars, including five cable roads. Among the public buildings visited by the Bostons were the new City Hall, Mechanics' Pavilion, Post-Office, Merchants' Exchange, Stock Exchange, Masonic Temple, Free Library and the branch United States mint. This branch is twice the size of the Philadelphia mint and larger than any mint on the Continent of Europe. The process of minting is of great interest, as is also a cabinet in the reception-room. In this there is an unbroken line of American dollars from 1779 to 1877. The coin of 1804 cost fourteen hundred dollars. There were shekels and double shekels. The shekels were cast in a mould, and were the kind of which Abraham paid four hundred for a burial place, and which were the common coins 2000 B. C. A pair of gold spoons, said to have been stolen from the Temple at Jerusalem, cost six hundred dollars.

San Francisco is a grand, wondrous city. The appearance of its streets, buildings, parks, gardens, is in keeping with the generous hospitality of its people.

A city paper thus described the condition of things in San Francisco when the Conclave was at its height: —

It was imagined a few days ago that the city was full of visitors and sight-seers, but those who held that opinion then have considerably modified it. San Francisco might then have been comfortably filled; it is rammed, jammed, crowded, crushed now. Then a man could sit down comfortably; now there is standing room only. It takes five minutes to walk a block on any of the three great principal streets during the daytime, while at night they are scarcely passable even to the hardiest user of elbows and shoulders. All one can do is to get into the midst of the throng, suffer himself to be wedged into the solid mass, and then drift along with the sluggish current. The cross-bedecked caps are to be seen at every step, and the rosy cheeks of the Californian lass and the paler face of the visitor from over the mountains are now in about equal numbers. Every one wears holiday attire, the streets are gay as they never before have been since San Francisco was a city, and there is so much fluttering cambric and bunting that Market, Kearny, and Montgomery Streets appear to be actually roofed in with streamers. The city appears to be holding fair, and holding it with a spontaneity that carries everybody away with its crisp and sparkle.

One of the principal points of attraction at night is the Palace Hotel. Last evening the great court-yard was actually packed with a dense mass of humanity, listening to the music of the different bands and gazing up at the hundreds of gas jets and the electric globes which lit up the place like day. All the upper corridors were crowded with richly dressed people, and the reception-rooms of the various Commanderies which have their headquarters there were filled with a constantly flowing stream of guests and Knights. Some idea of the crowd at the Palace may be gathered from the fact that for the first time since its construction every room in the vast caravansary is occupied.

The *Bulletin*, in speaking of the elegant banners of the various Commanderies which were displayed on the corridors of the court at the Palace Hotel, said : —

The Philadelphians have four banners displayed. They stand in a row along the first gallery and nearly fill the spaces between the gallery columns as seen from below. The Philadelphians represent much capital, but probably not more than do the Boston Commandery. The latter also represents a fair share of Boston literary and musical culture. But apart from their fine personal appearance, there is little at the Palace to indicate their presence there. Extreme simplicity in decorating their quarters and making known their whereabouts is the rule. Neither will they show any particularly elegant banners in the parade. From the second gallery depends a flag bearing a monogram of the letters " B. C.," which is as plain as it can be. " We do not care much for banners," said Eminent Commander Stevenson to a *Bulletin* reporter, "and our finest one was made light and for travelling." This banner is very tasty. The upper half is black and the lower white. Above a Maltese cross are the words, " Boston Commandery K. T.," and the motto, "*In hoc signo vinces.*" On the cross are the letters, " I — N — R — I." The lower part of the banner has the inscription, " *Non nobis, Domine, non nobis sed nomine tuo da gloriam.*" The trimmings of the banner are of gilt, and handsome gilt cord and tassels depend. The cross and scroll containing the longer motto are in blue and red.

CHAPTER IX.

ON Thursday evening the festivities of the Conclave were opened by a grand ball in the Mechanics' Pavilion. This immense structure had been finely decorated for the Conclave. It was open every evening, free to all Sir Knights and ladies. The decorations were too profuse for satisfactory description. As one entered the door, the view was impressive, the native barrenness of the structure being entirely hidden by tasteful arrangements of bunting, evergreens, and flags. The first point that struck the visitor was the appearance of perspective, heightened by the arrangement at the farther end of the hall, where, through panelled archways, was obtained a view of California scenery, and above blue netting was so arranged as to give the appearance of an azure sky. The roof within was entirely concealed by decorations. A large Maltese cross supported a number of lines from which drooped flags bearing Masonic emblems from the lowest to the highest degree. They were interspersed with strips of many-colored calico, forming one huge rosette. In the centre of this was placed, on the night of the ball, Tojetti's painting of the "Babe of Bethlehem," representing the infant Jesus. The pillars supporting the gallery and roof were entwined with colored stuffs and evergreens, and the galleries were resplendent with bunting displaying the flags of all nations, among which the Stars and Stripes reigned supreme. Depending from the railing of the gallery were numerous banners of the Commanderies which participated in the Conclave, while at the back of the galleries, on the sides of the building, were displayed in evergreens the various symbols of the Order. Add to the above description numberless flags, pennants, banners, and bannerets inscribed with Masonic mottoes, or bearing Templar emblems; add also the electric light, exotic flowers, sparkling fountains, and the ever-flowing tides of melody, and a scene is produced worthy of the cause for which it was created, and one calculated to impress the minds of all visitors with the depth and warmth of the welcome and hospitality which San Francisco and California desired to tender to them.

At the extreme east end of the Pavilion was a notable piece of decorative work. Above the gallery floor on the east end, raised seats extended half-way up to the roof. Above the top seats was stretched a canvas one hundred feet long and thirty feet high, painted by Voegtlin, the subject being the entrance of the Knights into Jerusalem. The drawing was spirited and effective, the foreground figures being of heroic size, which made the distant hanging of the great canvas no disadvantage, even when viewed from the main floor, from which it was distinctly seen. Above the canvas the building was draped so as to make a frame for it. Looking west, the stage was seen to extend out on the main floor some distance past the gallery line, with raised seats running nearly up to the gallery line. Over the stage, in the centre of the west gallery rail, was the banner of the Grand Commandery of California, supported by a cross of evergreens and draped with national colors. Just above that, the eye was attracted by a very important, as well as handsomely built and decorated department, the Garden of

Welcome, on the line of the west promenade gallery and facing the main floor. From the front the garden was seen through three great arches, a glimpse of California scenery and evidences of California hospitality being had through the arches. Over the centre arch was the coat-of-arms of the Grand Commandery of California, over the one to the right those of the California Commandery, No. 1, and over the left Golden Gate Commandery, No. 16. The entrances to the inviting interior were to the right and left of these arches, the archways themselves being fenced across with a low wire fence completely woven in with ivy. Once inside the Garden of Welcome, it was found to be all that the name indicates. The back or west end of the garden was formed of two great canvases, on which were painted California scenes, one being a Yosemite view, and the other picturing the heart of the Sierras. These views were as large as the "flats" used in theatres, and formed the entire rear partition. The north wall of the garden was likewise formed of painted canvas, the centre and largest one representing the grand avenue approaching a well-known California country home, whose bountiful hospitalities have made it familiar, by name at least, to nearly every one of the Knights who entered the garden last evening. The trees of the avenue, represented as lighted at night, formed a vista, at the end of which is the home itself. This large central piece was flanked by appropriate wood and tropical views. In the centre of this handsome garden there was a cooling fountain with its base hidden in banks of flowers. The purpose of the garden, which was built, decorated, and managed by the ladies of the executive committee of the Triennial Union, was as a place to serve refreshing iced punches of California wines to the guests of the Conclave committee. The garden was a most enjoyable feature, the warm dancers gladly accepting the graciously

extended hospitalities of the ladies of the committee. To the
north of the garden, on the gallery floor, was the booth of the
ladies of the executive committee, draped with flags and furnished
in straw furniture. To the south, partitioned off by canvas hangings,
were the dressing-rooms, where every convenience for such a place
had been prepared. The main dancing floor was bounded by the
pillars supporting the galleries, and was two hundred and twenty-
five feet long by one hundred feet wide, its boundary lines, the
pillars, being twined with yellow, green, pink, purple, orange,
turkey-red, and blue bunting, and each also with evergreens, making
a bright and effective contrast with the white canvas of the floor
which they bordered. The doors opened at half past eight, and
from that time a steady stream of Sir Knights and ladies passed
into the great hall and completed a scene of magnificence.

The ladies, on arriving at the Pavilion, were hospitably received
by the reception committee of the Triennial Union, who had charge
of their dressing-rooms in the east end of the Pavilion. On repair-
ing to the main floor with their escorts, they either promenaded up
and down the canvased area or else took seats reserved for their
special benefit. During the interval before the concert the Hawaiian
band contributed some of their choicest music, which was heartily
appreciated. The Second Artillery Regiment band then rendered
as the preliminary concert some of their finest selections, including Wagner's "Tannhauser March," Verdi's "Nebuchadnezzar," Nitz's
" Americus Polka," and Conradi's "Musical Tour of Europe." While
the concert was in progress the gay throng of cavaliers and their
fair partners upon the floor was constantly being augmented by Sir
Knights in their showy uniforms, and their fair ladies, whose rich
and elegant toilets, of every conceivable hue and of fashionable
design, lent a picturesque attractiveness to the scene, outrivalling

the gaudy decorations of the Pavilion. The reserved seats about the sides of the main floor and the galleries above were well filled with Knights and their ladies in elegant toilets.

Before 10 P. M. the immense concourse was busy viewing the decorations, listening to the music, admiring the various and elegant costumes of the ladies, and receiving introductions. At that hour, Sir Reuben H. Lloyd, Captain General of the Grand Commandery of California and floor manager in chief, made his way to the committee rooms and succeeded in gathering together the reception and floor committees and formed for the grand march. The Second Regiment band was stationed at the head, and the above-mentioned committees formed two abreast in two lines in rear of the band. Then came the ladies of the reception committee, followed by Grand Commander Perkins and lady and Past Commander Tristam Burges, of Golden Gate Commandery, with Mrs. W. A. Bunton. The members of the California Commandery, who attracted much attention from their peculiarly shaped cloaks, which were heavily embroidered with silver, and bore on the left shoulder a Maltese cross of the same metal, took their station next on the right line. The Knights of Golden Gate Commandery took their station on the left line. Following these, the guests of the evening by couples formed, preceded by the Grand Officers of California. It was estimated that there were two thousand ladies and gentlemen in the lines. The Sir Knights of Boston Commandery and their ladies were well represented on the floor and seemed as happy and earnest as any. When the lines had formed, the manager in chief gave the command, the band struck up the "Grand Encampment March," and the column advanced, marching twice around the spacious floor. From the gallery the spectacle was a gorgeous scene, the beautiful toilets, attractive regalias, and rhythmic movement, intensified by the profuse decorations above and around, all glittering under the bright gas and electric lights, were dazzling. Officers of the United States Army and National Guard were in the procession, and added to its variety and beauty by their regulation uniforms. When the column returned the second time to its starting place, the Captain General and his efficient aids, by a movement unknown to military, broke up the interminable lines and formed platoons extending across the hall. The first platoons, not grasping the idea, followed the band, hesitating and ill-formed, but subsequently the platoons were readily formed and marched well, keeping a good line. The Bostons were principally in the centre and rear platoons. The platoons marched to the west end of the hall, a halt was made, and from the rear the platoons were marched to their proper places and distances, beginning at the east end. Then the first dance was called and the floor was covered by almost innumerable sets ready to commence the dizzying whirl.

The supper-room was in the western end of the building, in what is known as Machinery Hall. The walls were, with their snowy background, handsomely decorated and embellished with American flags, patriotic colors and designs, and emblems of the Order, while a tastefully looped crimson cloth extending around the large compartment lent a charming and harmonious effect. A score or more long tables, extending the width of the building, furnished a seating capacity for between six and seven hundred, whose wants were attended to by more than forty colored waiters. The tables were very neatly arranged and ornamented with California flowers and evergreens, and upon the opening of the doors of the supper-room, at twelve o'clock, the seats were rapidly filled, and the guests were profuse in their praise of Pacific Coast fruits, while not a few were heard to comment upon the reasonable charges. Overhead were the ice-cream rooms, equally beautiful in decorations.

Shortly before ten o'clock a deputation of the reception committee waited upon Most Eminent Grand Master Dean, who was escorted to the Pavilion, where his reception was rather informal. Instead of participating in the mazy dance, he took a seat as a spectator, enjoying the entertainment. During the intervals between the dances he held an informal levee, when a great many were presented to him.

The programme of music for dancing contributed by the Second Artillery band was an excellent one, which was well rendered.

The march to the supper-room took place at exactly twelve o'clock, the procession being headed by Most Eminent Grand Master Dean. The supper-room was soon filled and the excellent fare furnished was fully appreciated by the weary dancers. For supper no wines but those of this State were furnished. Supper over, the dancers sought the canvased floor once more and the band struck up. The snowy space was soon occupied by the tireless whirling figures. After each dance ladies and gentlemen commenced to leave in small parties, so that the floor looked bare towards two o'clock in the morning, and by three the last of the tired revellers had left the building in its dreary gloom.

Sir Knight Sol Smith Russell tendered an invitation to the Sir Knights of Boston Commandery and their ladies to visit Bush Street Theatre, where he was playing, upon some evening agreeable to them. The invitation was accepted by the committee on the California pilgrimage in behalf of Boston Commandery, and Friday evening, Aug. 17, was designated as the time for the visit. The Commandery was well represented at the entertainment,

—one hundred and fifty seats besides the boxes being occupied, —and all enjoyed a pleasant evening with the "original and only Sol Smith Russell." "Edgeworth Folks" was presented, which afforded a good field for the employment of Mr. Russell's droll and original acting. He was repeatedly encored, and as the play progressed the enthusiasm became intense. Gratitude to Sir

CABLE ROAD AND CARS, SAN FRANCISCO.

Knight Russell was cordially expressed for the invitation and pleasure of the evening.

Not the least of the anti-Conclave attractions was a performance given Friday evening, Aug. 17, at the Grand Chinese Theatre on Washington Street, for the benefit of the Triennial Fund. The Mongolian performers, instead of playing to a house half full of Chinese, had an audience of Caucasians occupying the whole auditorium. Knights were there from different Commanderies wearing Templar jewels and badges, and ladies from various States wearing opera hats and diamonds. When the box office was opened the Chinese were on hand, but only to be disappointed. The unobstructed entrance of "white folks" and their ladies enraged the Chinese theatre-goers, whose violence called the police. About eight o'clock the performance began. The upper gallery at the left was partly filled with Chinese women; the other galleries, boxes, and body of the house were reserved for Americans, who nearly filled it. It was all strange, unintelligible, and queer to this audience, which laughed and applauded, whether the laugh or the applause came in right or not. This must have disconcerted the actors, for they seemed surprised at something. The theatre had been fixed up for the occasion and the performers appeared in their most gorgeous robes. The newspapers of the next day called the performance an "olio," short for *olla podrida*, — selected representations from Chinese dramas. The music was sometimes soft, but usually terrific. The nearer one gets the worse the pain. The spectators persisted in going behind the scenes, to which the performers objected. To enjoy a free examination in the anteroom and survey the order and variety of their wardrobes, etc., it was necessary to come in at the rear entrance, through the kitchen and sleeping-dens. The first acts were from military dramas. Strong men are the heroes of such plays, and a Chinese audience is at once informed who the strong men are by their whirling rapidly upon the stage. He who whirls the longest advertises himself as the strongest. A Chinaman knows which hero will kill his opponent in the pending battle by the duration and speed of his whirling. Although each hero is accompanied to the battle-field by an army of four or five " supes," yet whole armies never fight. The opposing generals do the fighting, and the army of the defeated hero runs off the stage with a heroic bound. This indicates that they are dead. Each soldier in the defeated army is killed — he bounds. The first scene was that of a marriage between a king and a princess and their enthusiastic reception by the populace. Suddenly the grand joss appeared upon the scene, and, as usual, the most indiscriminate warfare began. Next the President of the United States, decked out more fantastically than ever chief of any of the various tribes of redskins in war paint, partook of a supper with the Emperor of China, this scene, too, ending up with fire and bloodshed.

One of the attractions of the evening was a stage fight between two warriors, whose method of attack was to jump up in the air, strike the adversary on the chest with the bottoms of both feet, and then fall back full length on the stage, striking on their backs with terrific force. It was a style of tumbling evidently new to most of the spectators, who applauded vigorously. Another style of gymnastics was much admired. The performer would stand on a chair, which was the apex of a pyramid of tables and chairs, turn a somersault in the air, and land on another chair similarly elevated, with his legs crossed in under him as tailors are represented as sitting. This feat was done repeatedly by two performers dressed in a bewildering multitude of baggy trousers.

skirts, jackets, and cloaks. With the ordinary dress of an athlete, the feat is calculated to break both legs of the performers, but dressed as they were it was an astonishing exhibition.

The tom-toms and tin-tins with the olio were not of sufficient simplicity to engage the attention of the audience, which wearied with noise, and, confused in mind, retired before the clatter and confusion ceased.

CHINATOWN.

The Sir Knights of Boston Commandery, with their ladies, visited Chinatown during those pleasant days, and brought from the Chinese stores very many souvenirs of the pilgrimage. Sir Knights made evening explorations, and threaded the narrow alleys where Chinamen burrow and court that sleep which opium smoking produces. The Chinese anticipated the advent of the Templars and received them kindly. At a meeting held by the Chinese merchants at the Chinese Merchants' Exchange on the Saturday evening before the Commanderies arrived, the following resolutions were passed: —

Whereas, It being the wish and desire of the resident subjects here of his Imperial Majesty the Emperor of China to do honor to the Knights Templars visting California to hold their Triennial Conclave, it is

Resolved, That all business be suspended by us on Aug. 20 and 24, and that all Chinese residents show their good-will and respect to the visiting strangers by decorating their dwellings and places of business for one week, and that this Exchange and the rooms of the Chinese Benevolent Societies, 728 Commercial Street, be kept open to Knights and their families.

The Six Companies, absolute monarchs on a free soil, caused to be placarded, in all prominent places in Chinatown, notices urging all the subjects of the Emperor to clean their houses and rooms, to burn their rubbish, and if possible apply paint and paper where needed. As a result, wall paper was in demand, paints and oil had a rise, and a general cleansing of the Mongolian quarter took place. The general appearance of the streets and alleys was much better than we expected. Chinatown covers eight squares, four by two, from Sacramento Street north to Pacific, and from Stockton Street east to Kearny, or less than a half-mile square. It is said that this district contains a Chinese population of thirty thousand. It is estimated that there are in San Francisco fifteen thousand Chinese laborers and operatives, six thousand house servants, three thousand laundrymen, and the remainder merchants, storekeepers, pedlers, etc. The female population is about two thousand.

The densely populated part is on Dupont Street, bounded by Jackson and Pacific Streets. Here one finds himself in a labyrinth of passages, where the need of a guide to thread the subterranean chambers and narrow alleys is absolute. The main artery, Sullivan's Alley, is connected with other alleys by passages only two feet wide, on either side of which and all around, above and below, the Mongolians are packed in the sty-like dens, like herrings in a box.

One evening Sir Tristam Burges, a notable guide in Chinatown, invited some Boston Sir Knights to accompany him to this "Celestial" quarter of San Francisco. It was a fête day of the Chinese, and in the evening the view was picturesque. Along the curbstones and in the gutters there were rows of punks, which threw off a pungent odor and lighted up the scenes of barbaric peculiarity. Again the dark-visaged pagan was seen bending over a fire upon which he threw sheets of cheap paper, bearing a square of gilt. These were golden prayers. At his feet were dishes of fruit, grapes, figs, rice, and a small pitcher with Chinese whiskey.

The contents of the plates and pitcher were thrown and poured upon the fire with some pagan intent, either as a sacrifice to placate deity, or to furnish provision for the departed. In those damp courts, where the walls rose black and threatening, while the swaying fire threw its flashes around, and in its flickering light Mongolian forms, like weird spectres, hastened to and fro, a gloomy scene was presented. In every apartment, large or small, good or ill, images, altars, candles, incense, prayers were seen. The altars, tiny things, were sometimes on the floor, behind the outer door, or sometimes the paraphernalia of a cathedral could be seen properly arranged in a candle-box fastened on the wall.

On entering a house a devil-fearing soul hastily passed a lighted lamp along the cracks of the doors and windows to keep the devil away. The method of packing themselves away for rest at night almost exceeds belief. Rooms filled with berths from floor to ceiling, leaving not more than enough floor space for six or eight persons to stand when crowded together, were visited. In the same proportion, Masonic Temple in Boston, in its several stories, would accommodate from five to eight thousand Celestials. The correspondent of the *Boston Journal* thus recounts a part of his experience in Chinatown : —

We visited the Chinese Theatre. Being in a narrow alley, we took advantage of the rear entrance. Entering, we were under the stage in rooms nearly subterraneous. First the kitchen, where one hundred and forty persons, all *attaches* of the theatre, have their food provided. All the actors are men ; female characters are represented by males. Ascending two flights of stairs, we reach the dressing-rooms. Extreme order prevails. The shelves and hooks contain the wardrobes and paraphernalia of the actors. Some, dressing, looked like princes in satin, silk, and gold. Several have painted faces and others are smoking. With wonderful skill a large man painted his face, with a little mirror in one hand and a camel's-hair brush in the other. A white band of paint across the head, enclosing the eyes, from which lines of black were traced down his cheeks, did not add to his personal beauty.

We entered upon the stage. There were forty actors, including a terrible band, upon it. The band was in the centre and rear, the principal actors seated in centre and front, while on either side they were flanked by gaudily dressed Celestials, who now and then in chorus had "big talk," that is, very loud. In glancing up over the audience, parquet and galleries were a sea of faces, — sixteen hundred to eighteen hundred Chinamen The theatre will hold twenty-five hundred. The play was an historical one, founded on events in the life of the last Emperor. It commenced at 5 P. M. and was continued till 12 M. Saturdays and Sundays the play begins at twelve at noon and continues until twelve at night. Plays are continued night after night until an end of the historical character is reached. The orchestra was terrible. A seat next to the fellow who pounded a large iron kettle, which was fastened bottom up on a tripod, was next to the rumbling of Vesuvius. During the progress of the play, a supernumerary made himself useful in arranging tables, seats, candles, etc., this noisy work not seeming to annoy the actors. Women occupied one gallery only, — that at the left of the stage. There are no "flies" on the stage, but a partition, with a door at each end of the stage, separates the latter from the dressing-room. One party of a dozen, royally dressed, came upon the stage and talked. They retired, and another set equally gaudy entered by the opposite door and talked awhile, then retired, when both parties returned and had a bedlam for a half-hour, the band thundering so that the plot was entirely lost to us. Having become satisfied with our experience here, we descended the two flights of stairs to the sleeping-apartments of the "one hundred and forty." It is a chamber seventy feet long, eight feet wide, and about eight feet high, having two tiers of bunks. Along the side of the chamber was an alley-way two feet wide, the only mode of entrance to their sleeping-dens. In this chamber were several places of worship, — idols, candles, punks, everywhere. The circuitous passages under the theatre, narrow and gloomy, were very similar to catacombs; the latter preferable, however, on account of the opiate fumes of the former. A general provision store — a type of all of its kind — was interesting. Everything in it came from China. Dried oysters, prepared white beans (they were boiled, dried, ground, and made into cakes in China), dried mushrooms, ducks, chickens, pork, fish, potatoes (eighteen inches long), were noticed. A dried duck was nearly transparent and thin as pasteboard. Ducks' eggs, cooked in China and preserved by being covered with clay and sand to protect them from the air, are a staple article of commerce and diet.

We visited *the* restaurant of Chinatown. It had carved ceilings and beautiful furniture The internal decorations are said to have cost twenty thousand dollars. The image and altar near the door, with burning punk and lighted candles, first attracted our notice. The proprietor, Bun Sun Low, is an affable, English-speaking Chinaman, who was very courteous to gentlemen from Boston. Near by, a cheap restaurant — Quong Loy Gony, proprietor — showed how the poorer lived. In this place were potatoes in the original earthen jars. These jars, containing about a bushel, are sealed up in China. In this restaurant everything is imported. Eels are brought over alive; so are catfish, ducks, etc. Live quails are brought over in small coops. One den, twelve by nine feet, contained bunks, except near the door, where eight could stand by crowding. The bunks — in two tiers — will accommodate twenty-one Chinamen. These bunks are not as long as the human form divine, because Chinamen never lie at full length.

In an "overall" factory we saw fifty-five sewing machines which Chinamen use. They commence work at 8 A. M. and quit at 10 P. M. They sleep on boards supported by their machines, and eat in the kitchen of the factory. Another clothing factory employs one hundred and fifty men. Six thousand sewing machines are in use in Chinatown.

Nine thousand Chinese make cigars, seven thousand work on boots and shoes. They make all the brooms, tinware, etc., control the pork market of the city, and as they are pushing into other squares adjoining Chinatown, so they are entering upon every trade and business possible. The aristocratic joss-house contains two rooms, the front one for men, the rear for women.

In the rear room (fifteen by thirty) great altars with idols occupy the ends. One idol represents a woman who lived four thousand years ago, idolized for returning good for ill. At the opposite altar there is an image of a man, worshipped for his bravery. He slew a tiger, thereby saving the lives of endangered children. There are two priests and two physicians connected with this joss-house. The priest is attired similar to an ordinary Greek monk. There are no canonical hours of service. Masses are special, costing from five to forty dollars. The cross, however, never appears. When a great Chinaman dies there are hired female mourners, as in Mohammedan countries. The Chinese mourners dress in white, Mohammedans in black. By the side of the brave man there is an altar and image of the devil, the good devil, before whom punk and candles are kept constantly burning. In the men's apartment there are images of their worship, a representation of a benevolent man, also of a great healer, who is chiefly worshipped. Their prayer service is short. The worshipper burns paper before the idol, also punk and candles, bows low, utters a few words, then goes to the luck table and shakes sticks or throws the luck blocks. In this apartment there is a fine specimen of wood carving. It represents a theatrical play in very heavy relief. The piece is ten feet long, three feet high, having two rows of figures, and is the result of the work of ten carvers during two years. During service a man beats a drum and strikes a bell near the door. The clatter of the Tan game was peculiar and the game childish, very much like "How many fingers do I hold up?" except both hold up their hands simultaneously, answer with rapidity, the fingers being quickly changed. A wrong answer enjoins a sip of Canton whiskey.

The Chinese gambling places cannot be visited during the play, because the police raid them. These dens are protected now by a series of thick doors, plated with boiler iron. Lotteries are more generally harmful. The Chinese gamble only among themselves, but their lottery tickets are on sale by all Chinamen. By this means six thousand to eight thousand dollars some days are gathered, which are used to advance the power of the Chinese. A pawn-shop kept by Pin Sho was a marvel of neatness and order. In this business he has made money enough to buy what was once the property of the First Baptist Church, at a cost of thirty thousand dollars. The building is one hundred and thirty-seven by seventy feet. He has altered it into a tenement house, wherein a thousand Chinese live, and Pin Sho receives five hundred dollars per month rent.

The society of Chee Kung Tong has eight thousand or nine thousand members. This society is for self-protection. They are blackmailers, "highbinders," and exercise an authority as fatal and secret as the Council of Ten in ancient Venice.

There are five hundred opium places in Chinatown. The proprietors furnish lamp, pipe, and opium for ten cents a smoke. The smoker crawls into a bunk, and with contracted limbs, his head resting upon a stone or wood pillow, he seeks the repose of unconsciousness. After the smoker retires the proprietor cleans the pipes, and the opium gathered is sold to second-class places or to consumers too poor to afford the best. These leavings will make a Chinaman rich. Just before the new tariff law (July 1) there was over three million dollars' worth of opium in "Frisco," most of which is now held by the banks as collateral. These people seem harmless, many of them intelligent, and all are patriotic, having great love of their country. But they are treacherous. One can here very easily understand why the people of San Francisco felt and said "that the Chinamen must go."

The *Call* of the 17th of August thus spoke of Boston Commandery, its history, and trip westward:—

The Boston Commandery claims to be the oldest of any Commandery of Knights Templars in the country, on the ground that they can show the oldest continuous record, which dates back to March 12, 1802. The history of the first meeting has quite a "Revolutionary" period sound, the meeting having been held at the "Green Dragon Tavern," and meetings were held there until 1805, when the headquarters were transferred to Sir Henry Fowle's residence. The Knights of the Red Cross, who preceded Boston Commandery, numbered among its members Gen. Joseph Warren, of

Bunker Hill Revolutionary fame. The Commandery has the exceptionally large membership of six hundred and one. The Bostonians on their way out displayed much jollity. Four Knights, dressed in women's clothes, gave a minstrel show on the cars as the "colored quartet." All of these were prominent business men, but they cracked original jokes and made the excursionists roar. The Bostonians also had sheet and pillow-case parties while running along at the rate of a mile in three minutes. Every Sunday morning the Boston musical talent was exercised at praise services, the services being held with Puritan adaptability on the cars or at stations, according to convenience.

CHAPTER X.

A GENERAL Triennial Committee consisting of over four hundred Sir Knights of California was constituted under the authority of the Grand Commandery of California, with Right Eminent Sir George Clement Perkins, Grand Commander of California, chairman. Subcommittees on transportation, reception, accommodations, finance, decorations, parade, drill, etc., etc. (twenty-five in all), were selected from the general Triennial Committee. The success which attended the efforts of these committees is evidence of their diligence and fidelity. The entire arrangements were made on a practical system, and their successful execution was effected by the care, energy, and activity of the various committees.

When the pilgrims from the Pacific coast made their excursion to the Triennial Conclave at Chicago, the ladies of their party found no one to meet them in Chicago. The Knights had their duties and parades, while the ladies were decidedly strangers in a strange land. The San Francisco ladies determined that such should not be the case at the Triennial held in their city, and on their return they busied themselves in devising some practical scheme by which they could further the social interests of the Conclave. An organization was effected Nov. 24, 1880, whose members were Knights Templars and their ladies, and whose object was to cultivate mutual friendships and aid in making the Conclave of 1883 a success. Monthly meetings were regularly held and the membership increased rapidly. In August, 1882, there were three hundred and thirty members. The ladies' Triennial Union proved a most valuable auxiliary to the Triennial Committee, and was a useful as well as attractive feature of the Conclave. At the Pavilion there was a reception committee of ladies of the Union, numbering one hundred and sixty, organized to receive every evening in the Garden of Welcome. Twenty-five ladies were on duty at a time, and the reliefs were made with military precision. These were exclusive of other ladies, who made themselves very agreeable in distributing of the productions or possessions of the bounteous garden. A *boutonnière* committee of thirty-seven ladies distributed its members throughout the Pavilion Hall each evening and presented button-hole bouquets to the guests. No Californians entered with more good-nature and zeal into the duties of Conclave week than the ladies of the Triennial Union. It was they who decorated the headquarters of Grand Master Dean at the Palace with so much forethought, skill, and beauty. It was they who first welcomed him and the ladies accompanying Boston Commandery in the Palace Hotel. In the headquarters of the Grand Encampment, of Boston Commandery, of the several Grand Commanderies, of all the California Commanderies, as well as in the headquarters of the visiting subordinate Commanderies, there could be seen evidences of the forethought and kindness of the ladies of the Triennial Union. Boston Commandery, in behalf of its ladies and itself, acknowledges its obligations and herein expresses its gratitude.

On the arrival of Boston Commandery (Aug. 14), Market Street, leading from the Oakland ferry past the Palace Hotel, appeared like a gayly decorated arbor. For several days subsequent, hundreds of busy hands, especially on the route of the grand parade, threw out more banners on the outer walls. Nearly all the business houses, great and small, displayed symbols of the Order. An observing reporter remarked: —

"The day that the Boston Commandery arrived, a Montgomery Street restaurateur seized the spirit of the occasion and conspicuously posted in all parts of his restaurant, 'Fresh pork and beans.' Well meant, unquestionably. But strange was the banner placed in front of an undertaking establishment, 'Welcome, Sir Knights.'"

It was welcome, free and hearty everywhere.

The Triennial Committee approved ten different designs of flags and banners, of which one hundred thousand were found inadequate to supply the demand, and banners with other designs were procured East. There were probably half that number on Market Street. Whichever way from the Palace entrance on Market Street the eyes were turned, and as far as they could see, Templar flags, numberless strings of streamers, crosses red and white on black and green fields, floated on the breeze. From curb to cornice the buildings were decorated. Heroic-sized portraits, colossal pictures of knights, mounted and unmounted, were displayed on the façades of the Market Street blocks, while from every window hung one or more banners. Jew, Buddhist, and Christian displayed those ancient symbols revered by all civilized nations.

Hotels, banks, ferries, newspaper and public buildings, business blocks, halls, residences, stores, and shops, all combined, presented, when in the full dress of the occasion, a scene which San Francisco never before witnessed, and which will not soon be forgotten.

"The Masonic Temple, situated at the junction of Montgomery

and Post Streets, looked like an old castle of the Middle Ages decked out in holiday attire. The exterior walls of the lofty building facing on Post and Montgomery Streets were literally covered with evergreens, shields, wreaths, and all sorts of Masonic emblems. From the very base the wreaths of evergreen twined around the tall columns of the massive Gothic structure, and crept up past the pillars of successive stories until they reached the giddy summit of the tower that crowns the edifice. Still higher than that structure rose a tall staff, from which an immense flag floated over the building and added one bit of color to the city that spread beneath the fluttering waves of yellow, red, and black. Streamers hung down from the tower and trailed past the pinnacles that lifted themselves straight and pointed as Templar spears. Vying with the great banner of the Order, the stars and stripes waved majestically over the building. The wreaths of evergreens would alone have been notable decorations, but their effect was further heightened by an abundance of emblematic flags placed at regular intervals along the walls and between the wreaths and streamers. The festooning was in conformity to the architecture of the Temple, thus appreciably intensifying the artistic grace and beauty of the picture. The total cost of the outer decorations alone of the Temple was estimated at over one thousand dollars."

All the decorations were not of cotton, cambric, or bunting. Flowers gave their beauty and fragrance to the scene. Not only cut flowers arranged with masterly skill were displayed in halls, parlors, and windows, but the lawns and gardens were a charming decoration. In a lawn upon Van Ness Avenue, the verdant incline, facing the avenue, bore the welcome sentence in living beauty, "California greets you." At either end of this sentence there was a beautiful Maltese cross, eight feet square. At the residence of

ARCH OF WELCOME, MONTGOMERY STREET

M. H. de Young, proprietor of the *Chronicle*, No. 1919 California Street, the handsome lawns were laid out in beautiful Templar designs. Upon the grassy sward to the left of the residence was a large Maltese cross in red flowers, while to the right of the house and surrounded by rich verdure, the word "Welcome" appeared in a unique figure, the syllables being divided by a cross, above and below which were respectively the letters "K" and "T," symbolic of the Templar Order. The effect was both striking and pleasing.

Triumphal arches, Gothic, Doric, or Norman, were erected at various places in the city. Two were of special beauty and interest: one at the left of the Market Street entrance of the Palace, at the junction of Market, Kearny, and Third Streets; and the other at the right of the same entrance on Montgomery Street and in front of the Masonic Temple. The first and larger arch which spanned Market Street was an immense but beautiful specimen of Gothic architecture. It measured eighty-three feet from the ground to the top of the grand triple red cross which crowned the apex. The span of the central arch was forty-three feet and of the side arches eighteen feet each. The interior of the arches were ornamented with flags, hanging and gathered in festoons and groups. Over the main arch was the inscription in gold on a black ground, "*In hoc signo vinces.*" Above this was a Maltese cross in red, and above all, resting on the architrave, there was the symbol of the Grand Encampment, or the triple red cross, the badge of the Grand Master. The Montgomery Street arch was smaller, as the street is narrower. It was, however, similar. The pedestals were decorated with Masonic emblems in blue and gold, and above and over the arch there were shields, symbols, flags, the banner of the Templars being combined with the flags of many nations.

The arch was forty feet wide and fifty feet high. On the corners and centre of the arch were figures of armed knights, and at the bases of the pedestals colossal figures of mounted knights. On one side a triple red cross surmounted the arch, and on the other the cross and crown. Both arches were erected and finished with the same close attention to detail which marked all the arrangements made by the Triennial Committee for the reception and pleasure of the visiting Sir Knights.

A prominent feature of Conclave week was the unstinted hospitality of the California Commanderies. All of them kept "open house," which was in charge of a committee, but at stated times special receptions were given, when the Commanderies, accompanied by their ladies, were present in full force to welcome their guests who had travelled from afar. It is neither necessary nor right to particularize these receptions, since all the California Commanderies were princely in their hospitality and exerted themselves faithfully for the pleasure of their many guests.

The headquarters of the California Commanderies, where visitors were so cordially welcomed, were located in the public halls of the city, some of which were quite large. All the halls thus occupied were profusely decorated; refreshments were freely distributed and bands of music were frequently in attendance. Day after day, and night after night, Sir Knights, in squads large and small, paid their respects to the Commanderies by visiting their headquarters, registered their names, left their cards, exchanged badges, — if they had the fever, — and were amazed at the ceaseless and generous hospitality of the Sir Knights of California. Visiting Commanderies, Grand and subordinate, also kept "open house" at their various headquarters at the hotels, and reciprocated the courtesies received.

California Commandery, No. 1, prepared for the entertainment of visiting Sir Knights on an extensive scale. The stage, ceiling, and sides of Platt's Hall, the headquarters of the Californias, were handsomely decorated with flags, streamers, evergreens, Templar emblems and banners. On one side of the hall a table extended the entire length. It was loaded with roast turkey, chicken, beef, tongue, ham, truffles, and with every delicacy that makes an attractive table. On the opposite side of the hall were small tables seating four people each, which were furnished with cut glass and silver. Not only were all visiting Sir Knights cordially invited to partake of California's hospitality, but the Commandery was anxious that all should avail themselves of the opportunity. At one end of the hall was an enclosed place, where iced beverages, etc., were freely dispensed. The Presidio Band was often present and discoursed excellent music. The headquarters remained open to all Sir Knights during Conclave week, and special receptions were likewise given by this knightly and generous Commandery. The Boston Sir Knights made their last call in San Francisco, just prior to leaving the city, upon California Commandery, No. 1, at Platt's Hall, and assisted in carving two mammoth watermelons.

Golden Gate Commandery had its headquarters at Dashaway Hall. The front of the hall, on Post Street, was decorated with a Maltese cross ninety feet long and forty-five feet wide. In the centre of it there was a passion cross twelve feet high. Knights with extended swords stood at each side of the main entrance, in the arch of which there was a Maltese cross with a drapery of evergreens. Above the second or inner entrance was the coat-of-arms of Golden Gate Commandery. Strings of small flags depended, while stretching from the centre of the staff to the sidewalk below were long red, white, and blue streamers. Suspended from a line stretched across the street was a canvas sixteen feet square, in the shape of a Maltese cross, in the centre of which was painted a spirited picture of the Golden Gate, with the blue waves of the Pacific Ocean, and the limitless sky above, seen in the golden light of the setting sun. The picture had the stars and stripes on each side, whence extended the various banners of the Order. Within Dashaway Hall hospitality was generous, and the multitude of guests enjoyed but did not exhaust it.

Oakland Commandery, into whose arms the Bostons first fell, had well-arranged apartments at the Pacific Club Rooms and royally sustained the reputation of California's hospitality. The other California Commanderies, though possibly less elaborate in decoration of the headquarters, were no less hearty in their knightly welcome.

The Boston Templars were particular to visit every headquarters at least once and register their names, that the Sir Knights of California might well understand that their invitations and hospitality were truly appreciated.

CHAPTER XI.

ELEGANT programmes covering thirty-two pages were freely distributed at all the Templar headquarters. The programme covered the time from 8 P. M., Saturday evening, Aug. 18, to 8 P. M., Saturday evening, Aug. 25, when the prizes won in the competitive Templar drill were awarded, — the very hour of the departure of Boston Commandery from the Palace for home.

The following is a synopsis of the programme : —

SATURDAY, Aug. 18, 8 P. M. Assemblage of California Commanderies at the Pavilion for inspection and orders.

SUNDAY, Aug. 19, 2 P. M. Divine services at the Pavilion.

MONDAY, Aug. 20, 9.30 A. M. Grand Templar Parade and Review.

TUESDAY, Aug. 21, 10 A. M. Escorting Grand Encampment to the Asylum to open the Triennial Conclave.

WEDNESDAY, Aug. 22, 8 P. M. Grand Banquet tendered the Grand Encampment of the United States by the Grand Commandery of California. Excursions.

THURSDAY, Aug. 23, 8 P. M. Grand orchestral promenade concert at the Pavilion.

FRIDAY, Aug. 24, 10 A. M. Laying corner-stone of the Garfield monument.

SATURDAY, Aug. 25, 10 A. M. Grand competitive prize drill. 8 P. M. Awarding prizes and closing promenade concert at the Pavilion.

Saturday, Aug. 18, all the Commanderies of California were on duty the entire day for the purpose of receiving and escorting the visiting Sir Knights to their quarters on their arrival. From morning until evening it was one constant pageant as the Commanderies passed up and down Market Street, and the air was constantly filled with the strains of martial music. At 8 P. M. the Commanderies of California assembled at the Mechanics' Pavilion for inspection by the Grand Commandery of California and for final orders.

Sunday, Aug. 19, was properly the first day of the Grand Masonic Conclave, and the Templar exercises of the week were commenced with religious services in the Mechanics' Pavilion. At 2 P. M. the various Commanderies formed at their respective headquarters, and soon, marching to the tap of drums, the immense lines converged at the Pavilion. California, Golden Gate, and Oakland Commanderies assembled at the Masonic building. Boston Commandery, escorting Grand Master Dean, was conspicuous by the black plumes of the Knights and the rich elegance of their silver-trimmed baldrics and regalia. When these four Commanderies turned up Market Street from Post, the former thoroughfare seemed crowded with people. The multitude increased until the Knights marched between two great columns of spectators extending back on both sides to the buildings, and as far ahead as one could see. Windows and roofs along the route, and the giddy heights of the unfinished City Hall towers, were used by adventurous spectators, who looked like specks against the cloudless sky. Other Commanderies wheeled in at the rear as the column proceeded. The Templar line, thus extended, marching with precision, the rich uniforms glittering with gold and silver, the polished weapons gleaming in the bright sunlight, and the white and black plumes nodding in the gentle breeze, constituted a rare view, and aroused the enthusiasm of the people.

On arrival at the Pavilion, the Grand Commandery of California

entered first. California Commandery following, took seats upon
the right, and Golden Gate Commandery upon the left. Boston
Commandery was seated on the right, immediately in rear of
California Commandery. It was 3.30 P. M. before the last Commandery had passed the portals. On entering, each Sir Knight
was handed a pamphlet of sixteen pages, containing the service.

The seats on the main floor, numbering three thousand two
hundred, were occupied by the Sir Knights. Invited spectators
occupied seats that ran around the floor on three sides and rose
terrace-like under the galleries. The platform was visible from
every seat. There were four thousand seats for spectators, which
were all occupied before the Grand Commandery of California
entered. Sixty gentlemanly boys distributed the service pamphlets
and acted as ushers. The audience was dignified and decorous,
and appeared to be present not simply to see but to worship.
Thousands of people who sought admission failed to enter, because
the Pavilion was already full. It was said that a merchant of
San Francisco sought on the Saturday before high and low for
a ticket of admission to these exercises. He could not find one,
but happening to mention to a Sir Knight that his wife was very
desirous of attending the service, said Sir Knight took out his
only ticket and gave it to the gentleman. The latter pulled out
his check book and wrote a check for one hundred dollars, which
he gave the courteous Knight for the benefit of the Conclave fund.

For an hour before the commencement of service the Hawaiian
band rendered numbers suited to the occasion. The platform was
neatly arranged. The invited clergymen of the city, the singers,
band, and guests seated on elevated seats around and behind the
officiating clergymen, constituted a fair-sized audience in itself.

The spectacle of seven thousand people engaged in such a

service, nearly half of them clad in the regalia of Christian Knights, was magnificent. The impressiveness of the scene, as well as of the service, grew deeper and deeper as the services proceeded. The upper windows of the immense building were open, and the breeze fluttered the long line of flags and streamers suspended from the roof. The glorious sun poured in his beams, softening and blending the colors on pillars, pilasters, columns, walls, and roof, while the pictures and knightly banners seemed blessed with a new lustre and beauty. Without any mishap or even the slightest incident to mar the order and solemnity of the services, the scene itself and the unseen but not unfelt power of the Ritual formed a most fitting and helpful prelude to the duties and pleasures of Conclave week.

The following was the order of service:—

Processional Hymn — "Onward, Christian Soldiers," clergy and choristers acting as escort to officers of the Grand Encampment. Sir Knights stand with swords reversed and blade grasped by right hand, the cross hilt level with the eyes.

Voluntary.

Exhortation — By Very Eminent Grand Prelate.

General Confession — To be said by all present after the Grand Prelate, all kneeling.

Absolution — By Right Reverend the Bishop of California, the Knights still kneeling.

The Lord's Prayer — Chanted in ancient manner.

Versicles — Psalter, with "Gloria Patri," "Gloria in Excelsis."

All standing.

The lesson — Revelation iii.

"Te Deum."

The Sir Knights stand, and firmly grasping the sword hilts in the right hand, repeat the "Apostles' Creed." "Return swords." "To your devotions." All kneeling. Prayers. Templars' Litany.

General intercession.

Hymn — "The Rising God forsakes the Tomb."

Sermon — By the Very Eminent Sir Clinton Locke, D. D., Grand Prelate of the Grand Encampment of the United States.

Hymn — "Hark! hark, my Soul! Angelic Songs are swelling."
All standing.
"Nunc Dimittis."
The Apostolic Benediction — By the Right Rev. Bishop Kip, D. D., LL. D.
Recessional — "Hierusalem, my happy Home."
"Laus Deo."

A warning note of a cornet, and then voices of sweet melody from the direction of the main entrance, indicated that the service had begun. The procession, stepping to the slow cadence of the processional hymn, proceeded up the central aisle. The procession was constituted as follows: first came sixty choristers in black cassocks and white surplices, each with a crimson cross on the breast, with uplifted banners and crosses, the sacred song growing louder and louder as they proceeded. Following them came the Episcopal clergymen of the city, all, in surplices, headed by Bishop Kip in full canonicals, accompanied by Very Eminent Sir Clinton Locke, Grand Prelate, bearing the scarf of the Order. The choristers and clergy acted as escort to the officers of the Grand Encampment, who took seats upon the platform. The Sir Knights received them in ancient style, standing with sword reversed and blade grasped by the right hand, the cross hilt level with the eyes, while the advancing procession sang: —

Onward! Christian soldiers.
Marching as to war,
With the cross of Jesus
Going on before.
Christ the royal master
Leads against the foe:
Forward into battle,
See his banners go.
    Onward! Christian soldiers,
    Marching as to war,
    With the cross of Jesus
    Going on before.

At the sign of triumph
Satan's host doth flee;
On then, Christian soldiers.
On to victory.
Hell's foundations quiver
At the shout of praise:
Brothers, lift your voices,
Loud your anthems raise.
Onward, etc.

Like a mighty army
 Moves the church of God;
Brothers, we are treading
 Where the saints have trod;
We are not divided,
 All one body we,
One in hope and doctrine,
 One in charity.
  Onward, etc.

Onward then, ye people,
 Join our happy throng.
Blend with ours your voices
 In the triumph song;
Glory, laud, and honor,
 Unto Christ the King;
This through countless ages
 Men and angels sing.
  Onward, etc.

After the hymn a voluntary was played, and at its close the Sir Knights carried swords, returned swords, and uncovered. Then the Very Eminent Grand Prelate made the following exhortation: —

Dearly Beloved Sir Knights — BRETHREN : Again we rest from the active duties of our earthly pilgrimage to sing our songs of gratitude and adoration, and renew our souls at the fountain of life. We are not strangers or servants, but children of the household of God. The Scripture, as well as the precepts of our ancient Orders, moveth us to acknowledge and confess our manifold sins and wickedness; and that we should not dissemble nor cloak them before the face of Almighty God, our heavenly Father, but confess them with an humble, lowly, penitent, and obedient heart, to the end that we may obtain forgiveness of the same by His infinite goodness and mercy. And although we ought, at all times, humbly to acknowledge our sins before God, yet ought we chiefly so to do when we assemble and meet together to render thanks for the great benefits that we have received at His hands, to set forth His most worthy praise, to hear His most Holy Word, to take counsel for the interests of our Orders, to promote the welfare of our Knight brethren, and to ask those things which are requisite and necessary, as well for the body as the soul. Wherefore I pray and beseech you, as many as are here present, to accompany me with a pure heart and humble voice unto the throne of the heavenly grace, saying:

The General Confession was said by all present after the Grand Prelate, all kneeling: —

Almighty and most merciful Father, we have erred, and strayed from Thy ways like lost sheep. We have followed too much the devices and desires of our own hearts. We have offended against Thy holy laws. We have left undone those things which we ought to have done; and we have done those things which we ought not to have done; and there is no health in us. But Thou, O Lord, have mercy upon us, miserable offenders. Spare thou those, O God, who confess their faults. Restore Thou those who are penitent, according to Thy promises declared unto mankind, in Christ Jesus our Lord. And grant, O most merciful Father, for his sake, that we may hereafter live a godly, righteous, and sober life, to the glory of Thy holy name. Amen.

The Declaration of Absolution was next said by the Bishop alone, standing, the Sir Knights still kneeling: —

Almighty God, our heavenly Father, who of His great mercy hath promised forgiveness of sins to all those who, with hearty repentance and true faith, turn unto Him, have mercy upon you; pardon and deliver you from all your sins; confirm and strengthen you in all goodness; and bring you to everlasting life, through Jesus Christ our Lord. Amen.

The Sir Knights answered here, and at the end of every prayer, Amen.

Then all chanted in ancient manner, the Lord's Prayer: —

Our Father, who art in heaven, hallowed be Thy name. Thy kingdom come. Thy will be done on earth, as it is in heaven. Give us this day our daily bread. And forgive us our trespasses, as we forgive those who trespass against us. And lead us not into temptation; but deliver us from evil: for thine is the kingdom, and the power, and the glory, for ever and ever. Amen.

Grand Prelate — O Lord, open Thou our lips.
Sir Knights — And our mouth shall show forth Thy praise.

Then all standing, the Grand Prelate said: —

Glory be to the Father, and to the Son, and to the Holy Ghost.
Sir Knights — As it was in the beginning, is now, and ever shall be, world without end. Amen.
Grand Prelate — Praise ye the Lord.
Sir Knights — The Lord's name be praised.

Psalms xxiv, xlvii, and cxlviii were then read.

GLORIA IN EXCELSIS.

Glory be to God on high, and on earth peace, good-will towards men. We praise Thee, we bless Thee, we worship Thee, we glorify Thee, we give thanks to Thee for Thy great glory, O Lord God, heavenly King, God the Father Almighty.

O Lord, the only-begotten Son Jesus Christ; O Lord God, Lamb of God, Son of the Father, that takest away the sins of the world, have mercy upon us. Thou that takest away the sins of the world, have mercy upon us. Thou that takest away the sins of the world, receive our prayer. Thou that sittest at the right hand of God the Father, have mercy upon us.

For Thou only art holy; Thou only art the Lord; Thou only, O Christ, with the Holy Ghost, art most high in the glory of God the Father. Amen.

All then were seated, when the Grand Prelate read the lesson, Revelations iii.

The lesson being over, all stood during the singing of the "Te Deum":—

> We praise Thee, O God; we acknowledge Thee to be the Lord.
> All the earth doth worship Thee, the Father everlasting.
> To Thee all angels cry aloud; the heavens and all the powers therein.
> To Thee, cherubim, and seraphim continually do cry.
> Holy, holy, holy, Lord God of Sabaoth;
> Heaven and earth are full of the majesty of Thy glory.
> The glorious company of the apostles praise Thee.
> The goodly fellowship of the prophets praise Thee.
> The noble army of martyrs praise Thee.
> The holy Church throughout all the world, doth acknowledge Thee:
> The Father, of an infinite majesty;
> Thine adorable, true, and only Son;
> Also the Holy Ghost, the Comforter.
> Thou art the King of Glory, O Christ.
> Thou art the everlasting Son of the Father.
> When Thou tookest upon Thee to deliver man, Thou didst humble Thyself to be born of a Virgin.
> When Thou hadst overcome the sharpness of death, Thou didst open the kingdom of heaven to all believers.
> Thou sittest at the right hand of God, in the glory of the Father.
> We believe that Thou shalt come to be our Judge.
> We therefore pray Thee, help Thy servants, whom Thou hast redeemed with Thy precious blood.
> Make them to be numbered with Thy saints, in glory everlasting.
> O Lord, save Thy people, and bless Thine heritage.
> Govern them, and lift them up forever.
> Day by day we magnify Thee,

And we worship Thy name ever, world without end.
Vouchsafe, O Lord, to keep us this day without sin.
O Lord, have mercy upon us, have mercy upon us.
O Lord, let Thy mercy be upon us, as our trust is in Thee.
O Lord, in Thee have I trusted; let me never be confounded.

When 'the singing had ceased, the following commands were given: Attention, Sir Knights. Handle swords.

The sword blade was sprung about six inches from the scabbard, the right hand firmly grasping the hilt, and so remaining while all repeated the ancient symbol of faith, the Apostles' Creed, as follows:

I believe in God the Father Almighty, maker of heaven and earth; and in Jesus Christ His only Son our Lord; who was conceived by the Holy Ghost, born of the Virgin Mary; suffered under Pontius Pilate, was crucified, dead, and buried; He descended into hell; the third day He rose from the dead; He ascended into heaven, and sitteth on the right hand of God the Father Almighty; from thence He shall come to judge the quick and the dead. I believe in the Holy Ghost; the holy Catholic Church, the communion of saints, the forgiveness of sins, the resurrection of the body, and the life everlasting. Amen.

The command was then given: Return swords; to your devotions. And all kneeling, the Grand Prelate said the following prayers:—

O Lord, show Thy mercy upon us.
Sir Knights — And grant us Thy salvation.
Grand Prelate — O Lord, make clean our hearts within us.
Sir Knights — And take not Thy Holy Spirit from us.

O Lord, who hast taught us that all our doings without charity are nothing worth; send Thy Holy Spirit and pour into our hearts that most excellent gift of charity, the very bond of peace and of all virtues, without which whosoever liveth is counted dead before Thee. Grant this for Thine only Son Jesus Christ's sake. Amen.

Almighty and everlasting God, give unto us the increase of faith, hope, and charity; and, that we may obtain that which Thou dost promise, make us to love that which Thou dost command; through Jesus Christ our Lord. Amen.

Almighty and everlasting God, who hast given unto us Thy servants grace, by the confession of a true faith, to acknowledge the glory of the eternal Trinity, and in the power of the Divine Majesty to worship the Unity; We beseech Thee that Thou wouldst keep us steadfast in this faith, and evermore defend us from all adversities, who livest and reignest, one God, world without end. Amen.

An impressive portion of the service next came in the following Litany of the departed: —

> Almighty and most merciful Father, through thy beloved Son we remember and beseech thee to remember and to bless the multitudes who are joined with us in one household of faith and charity — Sir Knights throughout the world.
>
> Response (*chanted*) — We beseech thee to hear us, good Lord.
>
> We remember those who have fallen asleep in Christ, and especially those who have finished their Templar course.
>
> We give Thee thanks for all thy faithful servants throughout the world, who, having fought their good fight, and having witnessed in their lives a good confession, have left the light of their example to shine before our Fraternity on earth, mercifully grant that, by Thy Fatherly blessing, we may be enabled to follow them in all virtuous and godly living, and that hereafter we may be with them and Thy glorified Son in Thy heavenly presence.
>
> Response (*chanted*) — We beseech Thee to hear us, good Lord.
>
> We remember the fathers from the beginning of the world; the patriarchs, prophets, apostles, martyrs, and the valiant and magnanimous defenders of the faith to the present day. Refresh Thou their spirits, and may we have part and lot with all thy saints.
>
> Response (*chanted*) — We beseech Thee to hear us, good Lord.
>
> We remember all such as journey, or about to journey, and them that sojourn in strange lands; may they have Thee for Their fellow-voyager and traveller; may it please Thee to abide with them wherever they abide, whether they travel by land or by water, to bring them in safety to their destined goal. Abide with those whom they leave behind, and grant that in health remaining, they may welcome their own in health returning, and rejoice with them in safety and in peace.
>
> Response (*chanted*) — We beseech Thee to hear us, good Lord.
>
> We remember all who are sick and in distress, all who suffer in body or in mind, all who are in prison and in bonds. As bound with them, and as sufferers with them, we bear them in our hearts, and pray for their relief.
>
> Response (*chanted*) — We beseech Thee to hear us, good Lord.
>
> We remember the whole family of man, beseeching Thee that the spirits of all flesh may taste of Thy grace; and that the ends of the earth may see the salvation of God.
>
> Response (*chanted*) — We beseech Thee to hear us, good Lord.

This concluded, there was next put up the following general intercession: —

> Almighty and ever-living God, who by the holy apostle has taught us to make prayers and supplications, and to give thanks for all men, we humbly beseech Thee

most mercifully to receive these our prayers, which we offer unto Thy Divine Majesty; beseeching Thee to inspire continually the universal Church with the spirit of truth, unity, and concord. And grant that all those who do confess Thy holy name may agree in the truth of Thy holy word, and live in unity and godly love. We beseech Thee also so to direct and dispose the hearts of all Christian rulers, that they may truly and impartially administer justice, to the punishment of wickedness and vice, and to the maintenance of Thy true religion and virtue. Bless, O Heavenly Father, the Orders of Knights of Malta and of St. John, the Knights of the Red Cross and of the Temple throughout the world, the various Commanderies, Grand Commanderies, and Grand Encampment of the United States here present; that with meek heart and due reverence they may hear and receive Thy holy word, truly serving Thee in holiness and righteousness all the days of their life. We beseech Thee to give Thy heavenly grace to the Most Eminent Grand Master, and to all the other Grand and subordinate officers; preserve them from all error, ignorance, pride, and prejudice; bestow upon them the spirit of truth, charity, unity, and peace, that they may never forget their solemn vows and promises, nor abandon the faith they have sworn to defend; replenish them with the grace of Thy Holy Spirit, that they may always incline to Thy will and walk in Thy way. Endue them plenteously with heavenly gifts; grant them in health and prosperity long to live; and finally after this life to attain everlasting joy and felicity. And we most humbly beseech Thee, of Thy goodness, O Lord, to comfort and succor all destitute widows, helpless orphans, and others who, in this transitory life, are in trouble, sorrow, need, sickness, or any other adversity. Grant this, O Father, for Jesus Christ's sake, our only Mediator and Advocate. Amen.

The grace of our Lord Jesus Christ, and the love of God, and the fellowship of the Holy Ghost be with us all evermore. Amen.

Then the following hymn was sung, all standing: —

> The rising God forsakes the tomb;
> Up to his Father's court he flies;
> Cherubic legions guard him home,
> And shout him welcome to the skies.
>
> Break off your tears, ye saints, and tell
> How high our great Deliverer reigns;
> Sing how he spoil'd the hosts of hell,
> And led the tyrant Death in chains.
>
> Say, "Live forever, glorious King,
> Born to redeem, and strong to save!"
> Then ask, "O death, where is thy sting?
> And where thy victory, O grave?"
>   Amen.

"The rising God forsakes the Tomb" was sung to the tune of "Old Hundred." Band, organ, choristers, and choir took up the strain, the vast audience joined with tuneful voice, and the noble choral was thundered out in a storm of sound that seemed to make the whole place vibrate. When the last heavy echoes had died away, the Very Eminent Sir Clinton Locke, D. D., of Chicago, Grand Prelate of the Grand Encampment of the Knights Templars of the United States, advanced to the lectern and preached his sermon. His theme was "The Ideal Knight." The text was from 2 Timothy, ii. 3. The discourse was as follows:—

When we say the word "knight," there troops forthwith across the stage of memory a splendid and romantic procession, a mingled gleam of banners and lances and plumes and glittering armor, pages out of Froissart, chapters of "Ivanhoe," and all the wondrous story of the Crusades. A knight, to us, is a synonyme of everything that is noble, and generous, and chivalric, and tender, and gallant. We cannot imagine a knight in his glittering steel, mounted on his charger, or kneeling at the feet of the queen of beauty, stooping to anything base, or lending his aid to anything unworthy of a Christian or a gentleman. A bright ideal, and yet only an ideal; for when we come to look into the lives of these knights, we find them very much like the lives of other men. The standard then was of course nothing like as high as it is in our time. It takes a great deal more to make a saint now than it did four hundred years ago. We certainly are not willing to think that in all that time the mercury has not risen in the thermometer of public and private life. But even according to the standard of that day, we will find many knightly names stained with cruelty, criminality, dishonor, and pride; knights betrayed each other, knights trifled with the honor of woman, tyrannized over the weak, drank deep and long, and it was the evil and vice of knighthood that made the campaigns of the Crusaders so fruitless. It was not enough to watch one's armor before the altar of the dim cathedral through all the hours of the night. It was not enough to receive on bended knees the accolade of the venerable chevalier, chosen to preside over the ceremony, nor enough to wear on the shoulders of the surcoat the emblem of the cross of Christ. There was needed then as there has been needed ever, self-restraint, self-sacrifice, the practice of the Christian virtues; and where these were wanting, there were flecks upon the polished armor and stains upon the shining sword. Centuries have passed since then. The gallant knights of the days of Cœur de Lion and the siege of Acre have long ago mouldered into dust and been blown about the streets. In venerable churches we pause before their crumbling tombs and muse over their romantic history. A vast gulf stretches between the procession of steel-clad warriors issuing from the gates of the Temple in Paris, man and horse cased in chain armor, with the crimson cross glowing on the white surcoat, every man under the most solemn vows of utter separation from every family tie, half monk, half soldier, and the procession which shall sweep through the streets of our fair city this week, gay with cross and banner, and fluttering plume and flashing sword, composed of knights who sell sugar, run railroads, stand in counting-rooms, plead in courts, practise in offices, herd sheep and oxen, many of whom never even saw a castle or touched a suit of armor.

And yet, vast as the gulf is, it is a gulf only of customs and manners and points of view. The passions of the heart have never changed. We love, we hate, we joy and sorrow, as men did in the days of Abraham. The warm tears course down our cheeks, just as they did adown the cheek of the Roman senator or English cavalier, when we stand over the dead body of one whom we have loved. The old, old story of youthful affection changes not; the sweet intimacies of happy homes change not; the relations of man to man in the varied play of human life change not; and, above all, the service of God changes not. Whether it be the twelfth century or the nineteenth, to it there is "neither circumcision nor uncircumcision, barbarian, Scythian, bond nor free, but Christ is all in all." Just as there was a terrible contrast then between the ideal knight, as described in the code of knighthood, and the real knight, living in court and camp, so is there now a like difference between the ideal knight, as portrayed in our standards, and the living, breathing representatives who crowd these streets. Just as the external, then the cross, the vow, the public profession, brought not of necessity the internal piety, righteousness, unsullied honor, and unswerving truth, so is it now. It is not enough to have uttered the most tremendous vows of upright living and holy service within the walls of the asylum, or to profess by every sign that men can use before their fellows to be soldiers of the cross. There is needed in the knight of to-day, as in the knight of old, self-restraint and self-sacrifice, faith and humility, courage and courtesy, patience and peseverance, to make his calling and election sure. Do not think I accuse you of not knowing and not feeling this, of not often lamenting your deficiencies, and wishing and praying that you were better. A man would be a poor vain fool indeed who never was lashed by the whip of conscience. But I do accuse you and myself of often forgetting our obligations, and in the wear and tear of life, in the glamour and glitter of parade, forgetting what it really is to have taken up the sword and assumed the vows of a Brother of the Temple. That we may remember them better is the object of this sacred service. Here, on this holy day, with all the reverence and devotion kindled by the noble ritual, with the authority attached to the high office which the courtesy of our Grand Master and your own approval has conferred upon me, let me ask you to follow me as I paint the picture of an ideal knight. Do you ask why I say "ideal knight"? Because, if I say a "real one," some might fold their hands and say, "I have attained unto it; I need strive no more." An ideal is something ever before us, above us, beyond us, not unattainable always, and yet as men are, never likely to be thoroughly attained; ever to be striven for, even to be imitated, and the closer the copy the more perfect the realization. We do not put before our painters some village sign-post for their imitation, but the matchless masterpieces of Raphael and Tintoret. Our sculptors do not choose for their model some ordinary figure taken haphazard from the street, but they study the faultless limbs of the Apollo of the Belvidere, or the Venus of the Pitti. So, now, it would not be wise for me to depict some ordinary character, drawn to a hair from some one who walks among us. There would be nothing then to learn. All might say, "I am as good as he, or if not, I can be without much trouble." It must be mine to draw a likeness, not so easily imitated, perhaps, in its perfection never to be reached, and yet evidently possible to be far nearer matched than we are willing to think. A real knight moving in a real atmosphere, and yet an ideal knight, as we compare him with ourselves and our fellows.

To make a statue you must have a block of stone out of which to make it, and there is the greatest difference, you know, in stone. You could not hew the pure and stainless figure of the Chevalier Bayard, which stands in the Versailles gallery, out of an ugly, discolored, cross-grained piece of marble. Not all the genius in the world could make it look well. Neither can you make Knights Templars out of every man you find. God, in his mysterious providence, has not made us all alike. Some of us are but little better than fools, and some exceeding wise; some beautiful as Antinous, some repulsive as Pan; some gracious and some ungracious; some to hew the wood and bring the water; some to build the temple; some to drive the oxen, and some to offer them in sacrifice on the altar. God did not mean every man to be equal to everything, although the average American seems to think he did. Knights of the Temple ought to be picked men, tried men, men known and read by other men to be worthy of honor and confidence, men of warm feeling and generous heart, men of a certain culture and a certain education, men of a reverent spirit and high aspirations. How ignoble it is to select them for their dollars and cents! When a Commandery sinks to that; when its doors are open simply to the rich; when its object in taking in recruits is to pay its debts, or furnish money for its display, then, as far as any real good is concerned, its "race is run, its errand done." The Hand, the awful Hand, writes on the walls of its asylum, "Thou art weighed in the balance and art found wanting." Alas that such Commanderies exist, and are not merely phantoms which I conjure up to alarm you into greater carefulness! Let us suppose that we have picked men, that our material is good, our chisels sharp, our workmen skilled, and let us proceed to build up the ideal Templar. The text I have chosen well expresses him in one single phrase, "a good soldier of Jesus Christ." "Soldier" expresses his courage, his manliness, his discipline, his *esprit du corps;* "good" expresses his honor, his virtue, his reliability, his unselfishness; and "Jesus Christ" expresses the end and aim of his service, the obedience to Jesus Christ, King of kings and Lord of lords, the

Captain of the Temple, the General of the whole army of the knights, the flower of chivalry, the rose of all beauty, the lily of all purity, the Templar's master, the Templar's ideal, the Templar's Saviour, here and hereafter. But while the text compresses in a few priceless words all that a Templar possibly can be, bear with me while I draw out in detail the features of this ideal knight. Diamonds, you know, are cut in facets, and as we turn the beautiful jewels, new sparkles flash out at every varying angle. Let us put this knight in various circumstances and consider him from each standpoint. And first let us take him in his home. One of the first words to express the knightly character is courtesy, a gentle, winning manner, self-sacrificing in all little acts, bearing calmly all the little annoyances of society, watching an opportunity to do some one a kindness, and careful ever to avoid the doing or the saying things which wound the feelings or bring up unpleasant recollections. Now this courtesy expends itself most naturally on women and children. I thank God that there is no land under the sun where that courtesy is so marked as in this free land of ours. You read of French gallantry, of Italian refinement, of English breeding; it will not for a moment compare, as far as true sacrifice of one's comfort for the sake of others is concerned, with the unvarying respect American men, even those who know but little of the thousand conventionalities of polished society, ever show a woman or a child. To be a woman, unprotected and of good character, is passport sufficient, even in the wildest West, to insure you the devotion and the loyal service of every man you meet. Now that which is common to all Americans ought to be intensified by a Knight Templar. He ought to be a mirror of courtesy, chivalrous, marked, distinguished for this protection of the weak, the defenceless, or the injured.

The ideal knight is known far and wide among all his society as a man who will never tamely stand by and see the weak under the heel of the strong; who would sooner die than insult a woman or impose upon a child; nay, who feels it his sworn place to draw his sword if need be in their defence. And his courtesy does not die upon the threshold of his own home, as is the case with some we all know. He is not suave and polite to all except those who are so unfortunate as to be linked to him by the most sacred ties. He does not think that because a woman is his wife, that therefore she needs no courtesy and is entitled to no consideration. No; it is within the precincts of his own home that he is most a knight. It is there he is the best known to be forbearing, forgiving, supporting, encouraging. It is there he is the most esteemed, because it is there the considerateness of his life is the best known. His home is such a home as only can be made by a real true man, the pillar of the house, governing it, not with any absurd assumption of an authority he knows not how to enforce, but governing it by love and justice, feeling it a headship which springs from a conscientious and broad determination to be above all things faithful to that holiest of trusts, the family which God has given him.

But let us look at the Knight Templar in business, for these soldiers of the Cross are only symbolic soldiers; the uniform, the sword, the banner, the word of command, the whole knightly discipline, are one vast emblem, setting forth before men the warfare with sin and evil which a man must continually wage if he would keep the fortress of his heart from being overrun with a foul crowd of ignoble passions. Knight Templarism is simply a splendid unending drama, played on the stage of the world, partly behind and partly before the curtain, the drama of the contest between Christ and all the powers of darkness, the battle between good and evil. Apart, then, from the soldier, the knight is taking his part in that wonderful business life, which, coursing through every vein and artery of this wide empire, keeps it fresh and saves it from corrupting. There is no division of work where you will not find the members of our Order. They fill the judge's chair. They are professors in colleges, lawyers of distinction, mechanics of undoubted skill, farmers, happy in their fertile fields; some drive the engines which brought us hither, some sail the ships which carry the wheat from these busy shores. Wherever this ideal knight finds himself in this business life, be ye sure truth and honor are to be found with him. Alas! there has been so much servility, so much corruption, so much business dishonor, but not tainting this ideal knight. To be true is his first and his last thought. He never forgets that Truth is the corner-stone on which the Order rests.

> "Whatever record leap to light,
> He never shall be shamed."

What he says is just what he says. What he sells is the thing he represents it to be. His hands are clean from picking and stealing, for dishonesty in trade is nothing less than that. His motto as a business man is the motto of old King David, in the by-gone centuries, "Lord, who shall dwell in Thy tabernacle, even he that leadeth an uncorrupt life and doeth the thing which is right, and speaketh the truth from his heart, he that hath no deceit in his tongue, nor done evil to his neighbors, and hath not slandered his neighbor. He that sweareth unto his neighbor and disappointeth him not, though it were to his own hindrance." Whoso doeth these things shall never fall; no, not even when all this world does fall.

Let us view this knight as a patriot. Of these our Order has furnished bright examples. They led on our armies in that great war which cemented our Union. They poured forth their eloquence in Senate houses and gave counsel in cabinets. The noble President who so lately fell under the shot of the assassin participated in our ceremonies and had knelt at our altar. There is no legislative assembly in our land where Knights Templars are not among the brightest ornaments. But immediately I am met by a calumny. Men say, "Yes, what you say is true, and they are where they are, not because they merited to be there, but because they are Templars. The power of their Order put them there. It is a vast combination, which uses all the powers of secrecy to advance the interests of its adherents." How often has this accusation been circulated far and wide by the fanatics who see in our society a phantom terrifying into silence all who oppose it! We who are within the sacred inclosure know how wild and empty such charges are. We are taken from all political parties. We are as fierce Democrats or Republicans, free-traders or protectionists, as any other men, and we do not lay down our cherished political opinions when we lay down our pilgrim's staff and take up our warrior's sword. I do not hesitate to say that any sensible Knight Templar would never for a moment think of voting for a man whose political creed was opposed to his own, were he ten thousand times a Templar. Such questions never weigh for a moment with a man's standing in his Commandery. He votes as he pleases, and so do all his brethren. I cannot conceive any political issue which would join in one solid mass the Templars of America, unless it should be an attempt to put down the Christian religion. Then every knight would draw his sword, and shoulder to shoulder, as one solid phalanx, we would try our strength.

Again, turn the jewel and behold the knight in his Commandery. Is he one of those who once a year lounge in to pay their dues and cast a vote for a friend who has appealed to them to come? Is he one who uses his position merely as an entering wedge to business or to acquaintance, without a thought as to the good this noble and religious Order can be to himself and through him to others? Is he a weak, disloyal, lukewarm Templar, a very millstone on the neck of those who would make the asylum one of the dearest spots to which a man can turn? Far be any such thought from him. To be sure, he does not make his Commandery a miserable substitute for the Christian church, with its ministry, its worship, its sacraments. Alas! that so many should do that, and Templarism has to take the blame of it, whereas there is not a word or a phrase in our Ritual or in our teaching which countenances such a course. Twice a year, on Easter and on Ascension, it is our pride to show by a public attendance on religious worship our devotion to the Church of Christ. It is to demonstrate that, that we are gathered here to-day, and hundreds on hundreds of the most distinguished clergymen of our land are among us. Think you they would be there if we taught that Templarism was enough for a man to profess, and that a knight could safely ignore the church of the living God? No, our ideal knight makes no such false decision as that, but he does prize as a refreshment for his soul, as a noble and beautiful way of enforcing the lessons of the life of the immaculate Jesus, as a touching exemplification of the whole gospel teaching, the ceremonial of our Order. He takes care to be regular in attendance, earnest in his demeanor, prepared for the part to which he shall be assigned. The spot on which he stands is holy ground, and when the solemn services call for his attention, he gives it as the tribute of his heart, and not as some mere lip service. Formality without heart was the vice of our ancient brethren. Outwardly, so religious, so vowed to faith and humility; really so proud, so sensual, so faithless. They fell, and we, too, if we follow in their footsteps, shall fall as low.

But there is yet one more point of view. It happened once that there were brought together, in a museum, portions, it seemed, of wondrous statues, — a foot, a hand, a leg. Gradually it was discovered that they were parts of one beautiful whole, and with joy they were put together. Lovely and perfect rose the glorious figure, but, alas! there was no head. That had not been found, and men wept to think that the matchless likeness should be incomplete, when one day a stranger appeared, drew from beneath his cloak the head, set it upon the rounded neck, and then all burst into a cry of admiration, for the statue was perfect. So I have brought together noble portions of the statue of the ideal knight. I have built up the grand figure, but, alas! it wants the head. Is it lost? Can I not supply it? Yes, thank God, it is the mission of my life so to do. The one missing part I now produce; it is the Christian profession of the ideal knight. We have Templars who are models of courtesy, beloved at home, beloved abroad; Templars who are as pure, unsullied patriots as ever breathed; Templars whose word in business is enough, no man would dream of questioning it; Templars devoted to the welfare of the Order; but unless they have added to that the humble professsion of the service of Christ, the statue is without a head, the ideal is far from realization. Can you forget, Sir Knights, the moment when a cross was hung about your neck, and into your hand was given the sacred Scriptures, with the assurance that nothing but a firm faith in the doctrines therein revealed could afford you comfort in life or death? Was that a form or did it mean something? O, did it not mean that the Christian faith was to be the faith of every true and earnest Templar? And when I say the Christian faith, I mean no weak dilution of it. I mean the faith of the Apostles' Creed, which teaches me to believe three things: in God the Father, who made me and all the world; in God the Son, who redeemed me and all mankind; in God the Holy Ghost, who sanctifieth me and all the people of God. Whatever is said here and there, it cannot be denied that so long as our Ritual is what it is, and unless our Order is torn from top to bottom, this is what we profess to believe. This is what the ideal knight believes, and he adds to it the profession of the Christian virtues, the fruits of the Spirit, "love, joy, peace, long-suffering, gentleness, goodness, faith, meekness, temperance." Would to God all Knights Templars were as this ideal one; then what an enormous power for good we would be in this land. My brethren, I have done. Piece by piece have I framed the figure of the true Templar. I pray God that I may myself come nearer to it in the future than in the past, and I offer the same prayers for you. Let us before we leave this house pledge ourselves once more to it, as we have often pledged ourselves before the altar in the asylums where we congregate. Soon we are to take part in a splendid pageant. With broidered banner and gleaming cross and waving plume and brilliant uniform, we are to march through these streets, and the standard under which we are to march is the cross of the Lord Jesus Christ, and the motto of our march is, "By this shalt thou conquer." Is the world to smile as it sees us pass, and whisper, "A vast sham, a huge whited sepulchre"? or is it to say, "God bless the Templar Order, for it makes for truth and righteousness"? It rests with you as to which it shall be, and may God give you grace to withstand the temptations which will make it the one, and to practise the graces which will bring about the other.

The preacher having closed his sermon, there was sung the following hymn, all standing: —

> Hierusalem, my happy home,
> Name ever dear to me;
> When shall my labors have an end
> In joy, and peace, and thee?
>
> When shall these eyes thy heaven-built walls
> And pearly gates behold?
> Thy bulwarks, with salvation strong,
> And streets of shining gold?
>
> Apostles, martyrs, prophets, there
> Around my Saviour stand;
> And soon my friends in Christ below
> Will join the glorious band.
>
> Hierusalem, my happy home,
> My soul still pants for thee;
> Then shall my labors have an end,
> When I thy joys shall see.

Then (all kneeling) the "Hymn of Simeon," or "Nunc Dimittis," was sung: —

Lord, now lettest Thou Thy servant depart in peace; according to Thy word:

For mine eyes have seen Thy salvation; which Thou hast prepared before the face of all people;

To be a light to enlighten the Gentiles; and the glory of Thy people Israel.

Glory be to the Father, and to the Son, and to the Holy Ghost: as it was in the beginning, is now, and ever shall be; world without end. Amen.

All still kneeling, the Apostolic benediction was delivered by the Right Rev. Bishop Kip, D. D., LL. D.

After a moment's pause the command was given: "Attention, Sir Knights; draw swords; carry swords; present swords." The Sir Knights remained at "present," until the Grand Encampment and escort retired, and the service came to a close with the following recessional: —

> Hark! hark, my soul! Angelic songs are swelling
> O'er earth's green fields and ocean's wave-beat shore:
> How sweet the truth those blessed strains are telling
> Of that new life when sin shall be no more!
>   Angels of Jesus,
>   Angels of light,
>   Singing to welcome
>   The pilgrims of the night.
>
> Onward we go, for still we hear them singing,
> "Come, weary souls, for Jesus bids you come";
> And through the dark, its echoes sweetly ringing,
> The music of the gospel leads us home.
>   Angels of Jesus, etc.
>
> Far, far away, like bells at evening pealing,
> The voice of Jesus sounds o'er land and sea
> And laden souls by thousands meekly stealing,
> Kind Shepherd, turn their weary steps to Thee.
>   Angels of Jesus, etc.
>
> Angels, sing on! your faithful watches keeping;
> Sing us sweet fragments of the songs above:
> Till morning's joys shall end the night of weeping,
> And life's long shadows break in cloudless love.
>   Angels of Jesus, etc.

The hymn following the sermon, "Hierusalem, my happy Home," was also set to a popular tune and was sung with fervor. The "Nunc Dimittis" was chanted by the choir. While all knelt, the Bishop pronounced the Apostolic benediction, and then, after a moment's pause, each plumed hat went on, and next a gleam of lightning shone as every Knight drew his sword and carried it to the present. The choristers again took up their solemn march, the notes of the recessional rang out, the white-robed clergy followed after, the Knights formed anew their ranks, the audience slowly dispersed, and the great Templar service was over.

Boston Commandery, as escort to the Grand Master, was escorted back to the Palace Hotel by California, Golden Gate, and Oakland Commanderies.

In several Protestant churches sermons were delivered by members of the Templar Order, and in others discourses were made upon topics suggested by the occasion. Prelate Locke occupied Trinity Church, and Rev. Sir Simms, the Methodist. Dr. Stebbins delivered a sermon on "Knighthood"; Rev. R. Mackenzie, at the Howard Presbyterian Church, took for his theme, "*In hoc Signo vinces*"; and Rev. H. K. Noble, of Plymouth Church, discoursed upon "A knightly Character in an unknightly Age." He dwelt upon the character of Jonathan, as one containing the qualities of a true knight, — honor, chivalry, and self-sacrifice.

CHAPTER XII.

ON Monday morning, Aug. 20, the Sir Knights of Boston Commandery were astir bright and early, and were promptly on hand for the grand parade. They left the Palace at a few minutes after 9 A. M., and marched about a mile to their place in line. The procession started with remarkable precision. Boston Commandery was at the head of the tenth or last division, Sir William F. Knox, Past Grand Commander of California, commanding, as special escort to Most Eminent Sir Benjamin Dean, Grand Master, and the Grand Encampment Knights Templars of the United States. It was preceded by the Hawaiian band, "the lion of the day." It was puzzling to discover what it was, whether it was the complexion, stature, white caps, or ordinary music of the band, that so excited the popular enthusiasm. Other bands which played as well, probably better, did not receive such a constant ovation. Boston Commandery was repeatedly applauded as it moved strong and steady over the route. The people were generous in their applause, all the Commanderies obtaining a share. They all deserved it. The *Bulletin* said of the Boston Sir Knights: "Following the band came the Boston Commandery. The simplicity and elegance of their uniform were as striking on parade as has been the entire absence of ostentation at their headquarters at the Palace Hotel; their black chapeaux, black plumes, and in their regalia is hardly a touch of color. They looked as they have been described to be, solid business men. They marched steadily, without attempting any fancy evolutions," which the instantaneous photographs taken while the column was in motion clearly prove.

"Rev. Sir Oliver A. Roberts, their Prelate, marched in line, clad in clerical robes, and was a noticeable figure. Following the Boston Commandery were the mounted officers of the Grand Encampment, Grand Master Dean riding ahead and smiling pleasantly, but without apparent consciousness that he was receiving the lion's share of notice." This division was the first to reach the position assigned on Van Ness Avenue. As the Commandery marched to its place, the streets were crowded with people. While on Van Ness Avenue, waiting for the hour of starting to arrive, they were hospitably entertained by generous residents.

At precisely ten o'clock, the hour appointed, Grand Captain General Lloyd drew his shining sword from its scabbard, and raising it to his shoulder, while his handsome black charger reared and plunged, he gave the order, "March," to which the column promptly responded and proceeded over the appointed route.

It was nearly 11 A. M. when the commander of the tenth division gave the command, "Forward." The enthusiasm was universal when the strains of the Hawaiian band were heard and the sombre line of black-plumed Knights of Boston Commandery came marching like veterans, their dark regalia being relieved by the livelier appearance of the white plumes and silver embroideries of the DeWitt Clinton Commandery, No 1, of Nevada, mounted on black horses of faultless form and beautifully caparisoned, with trappings bearing the insignia of the Order. This Commandery, bringing up the rear of the column, was mounted as a grand guard of honor. The *Chronicle* of the 20th thus spoke of Boston Commandery, when it advanced up Polk Street, and of the Grand Master and his snow-white horse: —

At precisely twelve o'clock a squad of horsemen were seen rapidly galloping up Polk Street, sending the dust in clouds about them, and it was not until they had arrived in close proximity that their identity could be ascertained. They proved to be the Grand Master Benjamin Dean and his escort, and a great stretching of necks and loud applause followed this discovery. The Grand Master was mounted on a beautiful snow-white horse, whose every move betrayed his fine blood, and its rider but helped to show off to the best advantage its beautiful proportions and fine-shaped limbs. His escort, too, was well mounted, Grand Commander Perkins's steed being little inferior to that of the Grand Master, while its trappings lent a by far better aspect to the turnout. They had no sooner taken their places, Grand Master Dean to the right and slightly in advance of his escort, when another squadron was found to be advancing up Polk Street, headed by the Hawaiian band. These soon proved to be the Boston Commandery, who, after passing the Grand Commandery with swords at present, returned and took up their station on the opposite side of the street. The bearing of this Commandery was perfect, and rounds of applause followed the manœuvres, which were executed perfectly. The interim between their arrival and the head of the first division was consumed by the music of the Hawaiian band, stationed opposite the Grand Commandery.

The animals ridden by the Commanderies were uniformly black, well trained, and had apparently been carefully kept for some weeks in preparation for the Conclave. No such body of horses has ever before been seen in California. That ridden by the Grand Master was a most beautiful animal, snow white, and so delicately groomed that his rounded flanks shone like polished marble. He was gentle, yet full of fire, with a bright, intelligent eye that seemed to understand the movements of the pageant. He carried his head nobly, never swerved at the noise of bands or fluttering of banners, and only now and then gracefully pawed the ground as the only means he had of showing under discipline the exuberant life that was in him. His rider scarcely drew rein on him, and only now and then gently patted his neck when it seemed possible that he might become restive during the tedious hours of waiting. His trappings were of royal purple and gold, like the colors of his master. The Grand Master wore over his elegant uniform a simple baldric edged with gold. His standard was borne behind him, — a small silken flag, with the three-barred cross of gold on a purple ground. But two or three beside himself were mounted on white horses.

The line of march, by actual measurement, was found to be $5\frac{11}{100}$ miles. Of the sixty-five blocks over which the route extended, $35\frac{5}{8}$ were paved with basalt blocks, twenty-two red gravel, six boards, $3\frac{1}{2}$ flat cobbles, $2\frac{1}{4}$ wood blocks, one asphaltum, and one half not paved at all. As soon as possible, after the column began to move, the line was formed for review. The Grand Master and his staff with the Eminent Sir Knights in carriages occupied one side of the street and adjacent vacant lots, while Boston Commandery was drawn up on the opposite side of the street, facing the reviewing officer and his staff. Boston Commandery thus had an excellent opportunity to observe the column, and view, as it did with pleasure, the unique movements and knightly appearance of the various Commanderies. All banners, in passing, saluted the Grand Master, which he recognized by removing his chapeau and bowing gracefully.

After the review the parade was continued by a countermarch, the wide street giving ample room to the glittering host for various evolutions while marching. Having followed the prescribed route and passed under the Montgomery Street arch, the column, composed of five thousand Sir Knights, with their banners, flags, and bands, proceeded up Market Street to the Pavilion. The crowd of people everywhere along the route was immense. All the conveyances by land and water into the city came filled with people. In fact the ferry-boats were unable to bring the crowds from Oakland in season for the grand parade. The good order was as prevalent as the people.

The army of Sir Knights was divided into ten divisions. The first division was composed of California Commandery, No. 1, escorting the Grand Commandery of California, followed by Marysville, No. 7. The second division was composed entirely of California Knights, nine Commanderies; also the third division was composed of five California Commanderies. The fourth division was headed by Golden Gate Commandery of San Francisco, as escort, which was followed by Santa Rosa Commandery of California, and the Grand Commanderies of Maine, New Hampshire, Vermont, Massachusetts and Rhode Island, and Connecticut. The fifth division was led by Oakland Commandery of California, escorting Grand Commanderies and Sir Knights of the Middle States, New York, New Jersey, followed by Bodie Commandery of California, escorting Grand Commandery of Ohio, battalion of Sir Knights of Ohio, Grand Commandery of Michigan, and battalion of Knights of Michigan. The sixth division was led by Mary Commandery of Philadelphia, followed by the Grand Commanderies and Sir Knights of Pennsylvania, Delaware, Maryland, the District of Columbia, Virginia, North Carolina, South Carolina, Georgia, West Virginia, and Florida, escorted by Mount Olivet Commandery, Petaluma, Cal. The seventh division was led by St. Bernard Commandery of Chicago, as escort of the Grand Commandery of Illinois, followed by the Illinois battalion, Raper Commandery of

Indianapolis, escorting the Grand Commandery and Sir Knights of Indiana, and the Grand Commanderies and Sir Knights of Wisconsin and Minnesota. The eighth division was led by Ivanhoe Commandery of St. Louis, mounted, as special escort to the Southern division, which consisted of Grand Commanderies and Sir Knights of Missouri, Arkansas, Alabama, Mississippi, Kentucky, Tennessee, Louisiana, and Texas. The ninth division was composed of Oregon and Walla Walla Commanderies, escorting the Northwestern division, Grand Commandery and Sir Knights of Iowa, Nebraska, Kansas, Colorado, Arizona, New Mexico, Utah, and Montana. The above divisions were heartily greeted, and each in turn received high compliments from the press and people.

The tenth division was led by Boston Commandery as escort of the Grand Encampment of the United States, followed by DeWitt Clinton Commandery, No. 1, of Nevada, as a guard of honor.

The *Chronicle* of the 21st inst. referred to the tenth division in the following words: —

The Past Grand Commander of California, Sir William A. Knox, led the head of this column, and was ably assisted by Sirs W. W. Morrow, Frederick V. Bechtel, H. D. Ranlett, Thomas C Grant, and Abraham Powell. These Knights presented an imposing appearance as they rode in procession, with the insignia of their respective ranks, and mounted on black steeds that seemed to be aware of the importance of the occasion for which they were, for the time being, called upon to do duty. The Boston Commandery acted as special escort to the Most Eminent Grand Master. Its members wore the black uniform which distinguishes the Knights Templars from other military organizations, but they showed peculiar characteristics by their hats being ornamented with black plumes as contrasted with the white which are worn by the majority of the Knights Templars. The uniform is an exceedingly tasteful one, the Maltese cross ornamenting the breast, and the star in the centre of the cross belt forming an additional embellishment of the attire. The swords embroidered on the upper part of the Knights' aprons are indicative of the calling of the members of the Order. They are emblematic of the fact that hard-fought battles must be gone through with if we wish to conquer. The lower part of the apron is still more significant, because it represents the fate which all are called upon to encounter who engage in a feud with their enemies. The skull and cross-bones show forcibly the importance of the struggle which may have to be encountered, and are emblematic of the difficulties which mankind has to contend with. The Boston Commandery excelled in their military movements and evolutions, and did great credit to themselves and to their leaders by the able way in which they acquitted themselves of their task as a military body. Among the distinguished personages who graced that part of the procession were his Excellency George Stoneman, governor of California, and his Honor Washington Bartlett, mayor of San Francisco. There were also a number of members of the Grand Encampment and Sir Knights of note in carriages, forming a part of the tenth division. DeWitt Clinton Commandery, No. 1, of Virginia, Nevada, acted as grand guard of honor. Another of the leading features of the tenth division of the procession was the Royal Hawaiian Band, composed of a body of able and intelligent natives of the Sandwich Islands. They are under the leadership of Mr. Berger, who is the only member of the corps who was not born in that part of the globe. He is a native of Germany, and owing to his untiring efforts he has succeeded in raising his subordinates to such a degree of perfection in their vocation that the dusky sons of the distant islands bid fair to outdo their competitors on this coast in regard to skill and merit as musicians. They are a fine body of men and earned well-deserved applause all along the line of march. The selection of the pieces which they played was a very felicitous one and well adapted to the occasion.

While the tenth divison was at the foot of the column when it first formed into line, they took the lead when the members of the procession entered the Pavilion in the afternoon. It is safe to say that this division is deserving fully as much credit for the part which they took in the display as any of the other organizations composing the grand procession.

Too much praise cannot be bestowed on the members of the Boston Commandery, who have given an example well worth imitating to their brothers of this coast in regard to discipline as well as in regard to the admirable way in which they acquitted themselves of their task as a well-drilled organization.

And of the review as follows: —

It was noon before the caracoling of aids, and the easy and brilliant disorder of Sir Knights, from high official to humblest soldier in the ranks, showed signs of coming to an end Meanwhile the crowd had exhibited a more than Christian patience. The long white line that trailed down the east side of the avenue, flecked here and there with red, blazing at intervals with gold dotted with green, displaying little patches of blue enriched with purple and varied at intervals by bands in uniforms sometimes gaudy, often brilliant, and always showy, lost something of its listlessness. There was a sudden movement in the neighborhood of the Grand Master. Then came a shrill bugle call, and from battalion to battalion down the long avenue passed the word of command. There was a sudden change. The bright-hued group about the Grand Master's beautiful white horse gathered closer around the standard of the cross. The escort behind them stiffened into rigid lines, the glory of the Boston Commandery showing in long yellow lines against the dark mass of their uniforms. The silver-clad Knights of Nevada brought their horses into solid phalanx beyond them. Down the long avenue flags and banners that had drooped upon their leaning staves rose quickly to an erect position, drum majors assumed statuesque attitudes, bands straightened themselves for duty, the whole waving line of white at once became rigid and straight as an arrow from end to end, and all was ready for the review.

THE SALUTE.

At the same moment the Grand Master, attended by his suite, galloped leisurely along the ranks, banners being dipped and Sir Knights presenting swords in one continuous line of steel as the cavalcade swept past them.

His escort followed, preceded by the Hawaiian band, taking the west side of the avenue. Prominent in the escort was the Prelate, in black silk robes, which, filled by the sea breeze, swelled to majestic proportions. The carriages containing the high dignitaries of the Order came next. Then began the marching and countermarching, the California Commandery following the carriages, the other Commanderies marching north to Clay on the east side and turning down on the west. The two lines of Knights passing in opposite directions left little room for evolutions, and little was attempted except occasional changes of from three to six abreast. But the double column which filled the broad and handsome street with a maze of changing movement and rich and shifting color, in which were seen grandly dressed Knights, gayly caparisoned horses, and flags, banners, arms, instruments of music, and all that can contribute to pictorial effect, made the scene the most remarkable in the day's demonstration.

A spectator on the top of the Palace Hotel thus described the scene: —

The view was a grand one. In all directions and from every house floated the bright emblems of the Crusaders. The air was filled with fluttering banners and waving flags. In the street, no matter where the eye was turned, an endless mass of humanity was slowly moving. To the eastward lay Oakland, with its pretty cottages plainly discernible through the clear atmosphere; to the westward the hills arose like huge sentinels guarding a priceless treasure; to the southward stretched out the Potrero, with its boundary of water, and before the eye towered Telegraph and Russian Hills, between which were the rippling waters of the bay; the frowning eminences that arise abruptly from the Marin County shore touched the horizon, completing the panorama of enchanting beauty. The countless vessels in the harbor were decked in holiday attire, and seemingly from every mast was flung an array of bunting in honor of the Knights. The church spires grew and lengthened out in rivalry, as though they were endowed with reason, and knew that the descendants of the heroes who fought for the Cross were passing in review. As the Grand Captain General and his mounted aids approached the arch on Montgomery

Street, their coal-black horses prancing fretfully to the swelling music and their polished swords flashing in the sunlight, the scene transported the spectators back to centuries ago, when the flower of Christendom rallied under the banner of Peter the Hermit, and with the lion-hearted Richard as their leader assaulted the gates of Acre, and with their battle-axes hewed down the infidel. Denser grew the crowds on the line of march as the pageant moved through the second arch. At various points on the route the Commanderies executed military evolutions with the precision of trained warriors. In all, the picture was a stirring one, which will never be forgotten.

The *Bulletin* thus spoke of the streets and the procession: —

One of the most imposing spectacular demonstrations ever witnessed in this city was that which occurred yesterday. Probably fifty thousand people from the near and remote towns of California were on the streets as early as ten o'clock this morning. These for the most part waited three hours to get a view of the procession. The streets for miles have been literally blocked with people. Business for the most part has been suspended, and the whole city has been given up to a holiday demonstration. There have been many military displays in this city, but nothing in the way of armed men which has been equal to the march of the Knights Templars through the streets of San Francisco yesterday. The march was well ordered throughout. The police arrangements were all that could be desired. The vast throng on both sides of the street applauded when anything especially struck their fancy. The unity of our people was never more fully exhibited. There was no perceptible difference between the men of the different States. They were all apparently cast in the same mould, — strong, stalwart, and intelligent. The graybeards appeared to predominate. The representatives of Chicago were younger men than the others. The South was not so strong relatively as the North; but the solitary Templar who carried the banner of Georgia received an ovation. The Louisiana Commandery enlivened their march with songs. No military display in richness of color can equal the march of the Knights Templars. The uniforms of those mounted were not only gorgeous but antique.

The general opinion of San-Franciscans in regard to the Templar parade was thus expressed by the *Chronicle*: —

There are two or three observations that may be made concerning the procession. In the first place, no one could help conceding that it was a grand success. In numbers it certainly was, for at the lowest computation there could not have been less than five thousand Knights in line. It was a success in point of attendance which it drew, for the most moderate count would place the spectators at a quarter of a million. Every city on the coast sent its quota; some of the more neighboring towns fairly emptied themselves. It was a success in point of arrangements, for barring a few delays inseparable to such an occasion, the vast body was moved on schedule time, and the features of the parade were carried on without a hitch. It was a success with regard to the material of the procession, for on all hands was heard the unqualified remark that the Knights were the finest set of men it would be possible to imagine. Many of them were models of physical grace and strength, while it took no physiognomist to read intellectual prominence in the faces of all. It was a success as far as the music was concerned, for never before has this city listened to such a collection of bands or heard such good military music. It was a success as far as San Francisco was concerned, for she welcomed the Knights like a royal city, decked their path in the brightest way she knew how, and made their progress like that of a triumphal army. It was a success as far as its objects were concerned, for it preached a great proselyting sermon for the Order, and it showed that there is an organization extant in this country which can bring together men of every State in the broad Union, bring their hands together in a fraternal grasp, no matter how they once might have been lifted, and bring their hearts together in an accord of courteousness and charity.

THE GRAND MASTER'S RECEPTION IN THE PAVILION.

The following is the programme: —

1. Grand March, "Knights Templars" (Marsh) — By the orchestra, the Royal Hawaiian Band of Honolulu.

2. Prayer — By the Rev. and Eminent Sir Osgood C. Wheeler, Grand Prelate of the Grand Commandery of California.

3. Templar Ode — By a select choir of twenty-four male voices.

4. Introduction — By Eminent Sir Reuben H. Lloyd, Grand Captain General of the Grand Commandery of California.

5. Address of Welcome — Right Eminent Sir George C. Perkins, Grand Commander of the Grand Commandery of California.

6. Chorus, "Tannhauser" (Wagner) — By the orchestra.

7. Address of Welcome — By his Honor Washington Bartlett, mayor of the city of San Francisco.

8. Address of Welcome — By his Excellency Gen. George Stoneman, governor of the State of California.

9. Ballad, "Morning" (Beethoven) — By the orchestra.

10. Address in response — By the Most Eminent Sir Benjamin Dean of Massachusetts, Grand Master of the Grand Encampment Knights Templars of the United States.

On the introduction of the Most Eminent Grand Master, standard-bearers will give the Grand Master's salute.

At the conclusion of the Grand Master's response, standard-bearers will quickly assemble in front of the grand stage and display their banners in appropriate groupings.

11. "America" — By the orchestra and choir. The audience is requested to rise and join in singing the national hymn.

12. Benediction — By the Rev. and Very Eminent Sir Clinton Locke, D. D., Grand Prelate of the Grand Encampment of Knights Templars of the United States.

"A hundred thousand welcomes" were the words at the head of the programme of the reception of the Most Eminent Grand Master, officers, and members of the Grand Encampment Knights Templars of the United States, which was held at the Pavilion immediately after the procession disbanded. The Commanderies and battalions marched into the Pavilion in the order in which they paraded. It took a long time to seat the vast multitude, and it was 3.45 o'clock before matters had been so arranged that the proceedings could commence. There were then seated on the platform the Grand Encampment of the United States, Sir Benjamin

Dean occupying the seat of honor. On his right sat Governor Stoneman, and on his left Sir Osgood C. Wheeler, Grand Prelate of the Grand Commandery of California. At his left, in turn, was seated Mayor Bartlett. The other officers were grouped around these four, the whole forming a semicircle. Immediately in front stood the two altars, on which there lay two crossed swords. On a table near by stood a magnificent basket of flowers. The Grand Commandery of California occupied front seats to the right of the Grand Encampment, and behind them sat the officers and representatives of the various Grand Commanderies of the States. On the main floor were seated those of the Sir Knights whom the six-hours' tramp through San Francisco's streets had not tired too much to prevent their attendance at the reception. They sat grouped about their banners, a brilliant array. The proceedings were opened with music from the Hawaiian band, which played the "Grand March of Knights Templars," composed by Marsh. When the last strain of the music had died away in the vast building, a hush fell upon the audience.

THE INVOCATION.

Rev. Sir Osgood C. Wheeler arose, and, approaching the reading desk, he said: —

Templars, pray: Most holy, wise, omnipotent, and omnipresent Lord God of Hosts, we beseech Thee under these peculiar circumstances, all known to Thyself, to ask a blessing at Thy hands, knowing that we can receive it at the hands of no other. We ask Thee to look in mercy upon Thy servant, our chosen Grand Master, as he shall be formally introduced to us. Give him, in all fulness, the spirit of the true and noble soldier, — a knight of our Lord Jesus Christ, — a knight of the cross of our blessed Master. Let similar blessing fall upon us all, according to the needs of each and every one. Bless, we pray Thee, this Order through the length and breadth of this land wherever its members may be at present. Let, we pray Thee, the principles of true knighthood spread throughout the world. Let them broaden and deepen until the whole world and all mankind shall be blessed, that all men may be drawn into closer and better fellowship with Thee; that they may glory in Thy name; carry forward Thy work in us, through us and by us, to the great honor of Thy name on the earth and thy glory in the heavens; through Jesus Christ, our God. Amen.

"So mote it be," reverently responded the host of Knights. As soon as the Rev. Mr. Wheeler returned to his seat, the choir sang the Templar Ode : —

THOU KING OF KINGS.

Thou King of kings, Thou sov'reign Lord,
    Accept our humble prayer;
While travelling on life's dangerous road,
    Oh, still protect us there!

A risen Saviour here we own,
    Who passed the silent grave,
His love immortal kindly shown,
    Who came a world to save.

When weary pilgrims travelling far
    Shall seek thy holy light,
Be Thou, O God, that guiding star
    Ne'er dimmed by shades of night.

GREETING THE GUESTS.

An address of welcome was then delivered by Grand Commander Perkins, who spoke as follows: —

Most Eminent Grand Master and Sir Knights: The pleasing duty falls to my lot as the Grand Commander of the Knights Templars of California, to extend to you and to the Grand Encampment of the United States and to all visiting Sir Knights our hearty salutation and welcome to our State and city. We rejoice that after another three-years' pilgrimage on earth we are granted the honor and pleasure of meeting you again. While we have been called ever and anon to step aside and drop a tear and a flower upon the grave of a fellow-pilgrim, we are still permitted to enjoy the privilege of helping to advance the noble mission of our Order. We join with you in rendering our homage of praise and adoration to the bounteous Giver of all good for life and health and all the manifold blessings we enjoy. We are reminded as we look over this magnificent assemblage of Sir Knights, that the Twenty-second

Triennial Conclave of Knights Templars of the United States is about to convene. Only a fervent zeal and devotion to the great cause in which you have enlisted could have brought so many valiant and magnanimous Sir Knights, whose fame for goodly deeds and knightly courtesies is fragrant in the land, so far from their homes and peaceful avocations. With great pleasure we have anticipated your coming. We felt assured that your visit would be a season of mutual profit and joyance, marked by the most agreeable associations and recollections.

Sir, we bid you a sincere welcome to our tents, and share with you our bread and water; such as we have we cheerfully give unto you. You will find the Sir Knights of California dwelling together in peace and love, loyal to the Grand Encampment of the United States and undivided in their high appreciation of you and your eminent service. With hand to hand and heart to heart we greet you, and renew our pledge to guard our sacred Triangle and redouble our efforts to spread the beneficent principles of our Order. In the presence of this mighty host of gallant Sir Knights, with glittering swords, waving plumes and banners, thought spontaneously wings its way back to that remote period when, moved by a wave of religious enthusiasm unparalleled in the world's history, the steel-clad knights of Europe mustered under their battle-flag, "the Beausant," half white and half black, fair and favorable to the friends of Christianity but dark and terrible to its enemies, took up their line of march to the Holy Sepulchre. "*God wills it!*" "*God wills it!*" was the battle shout with which they charged the opposing hosts, clove down the crescent, hurled back the mocking Saracen, and planted the cross on the walls of the Holy City. Yet it is a gratifying reflection, and one in full accord with the spirit of this occasion, that Templarism is the child of such matchless religious fervor and devotion. It was born at the Sepulchre and cradled on the shield of faith.

The age of chivalry has passed. The weary march of the Crusader is over. The song of the Troubadour is no longer heard in the land. In the history of time the memory of those eventful centuries is but as a twinkle in the dawn of eternity. But we have drifted so far away into other latitudes of thought and belief that the valor, devotion, and enthusiasm of those ancient soldiers of the Cross would seem as dim, spectral shapes, flitting through the soft haze of myth and romance, did not modern Templarism embody the substance of their faith, hope, and aspiration. The rough, harsh exterior has perished, but the truth is eternal. Christianity is the same yesterday, to-day, and forever. Sir, we rejoice to meet you under the red cross banner and the symbolic Lamb, knowing that you fling to the breeze no apocryphal device and do not come to us arrayed in legendary memories. Templarism lights its taper at the sun and bows around the altar of Immanuel, God with us. We hail you as fellow-pilgrims, clad in penitential garb, carrying the burning taper of the truth in your hand, and will join with you in singing our ascension hymn in the full glory of that hope that throws its light beyond the gloom of the grave, and in the sweet assurance of that faith that grasps the reality of that home not made with hands, eternal in the heavens, where our Divine Grand Master dwells in the majesty of power and in the beauty of holiness.

Most Eminent Sir, we cannot restrain the proud exultation that Templarism has never arrayed itself against the popular will or put itself in opposition to the advance of civilization. The whole range of history furnishes no instance where it has ever espoused the cause of the tyrant against the people. It found religion a shaded lamp in a dark and barbarous age, and placed it as a city on a hill to give light to the world. It gave purity to enthusiasm, beautified glory with generosity, taught the heart to expand as a flower in the sunshine of liberty, and smooth the rugged brow of war. We therefore contemplate with gratification this array of glittering swords, knowing that they are endowed with justice, tempered with mercy. We look with admiration on your banners as they flutter in the breeze, knowing full well that they guide to the path of honor, integrity, and truth. Well we know these swords would rest in their scabbards until consumed by rust before they would flash in defence of any law, custom, or creed that would stop human progress and turn the shadow back on the dial of time.

It seems to us perfectly meet and proper that as fellow-soldiers of an Order engaged in an uncompromising warfare against every form of injustice and oppression, that we should come together and rejoice over our victories, mourn over our defeats and failures, and stir each other up to that generous and beneficent rivalry which can make the world most bright and beautiful. Sir, we would not forget that the Grand Encampment, that august body that is about to assemble, is in its character national; that it is composed of valiant and magnanimous Sir Knights coming from all parts of this vast sisterhood of States. Here are Sir Knights from the East and the West, from the North and the South, mingling in fraternal harmony, renewing old friendships, and forming new ones destined never to be broken. Friendships formed at our altar and annealed in our glorious cause never fail. They have stood the most crucial tests. When this people were divided into two camps, and fratricidal strife dashed fire and blood like storm-spray upon every home in the land, the hearts that had beat with a kindred feeling around one common Triangle never were alienated from each other. It is the glory of our Order that the first bow of peace and mutual forgiveness that appeared on the bosom of the dark and receding storm-cloud of war was hung out by the Grand Encampment of the United States. A corresponding disposition was found. And in the renewed friendships so early made, mutually casting into oblivion the ugly memories of the past, was seen in the first glimpse of that auroral dawn upon the hill-tops and mountain peaks that now bathes the whole land in the bounteous sunlight of peace, happiness, and prosperity. As fellow-laborers in a fraternal union that knows no party lines, no sectional feelings, no latitudes, or boundaries of States, that union of hearts and hands that is the strongest cement of our noble Republic, we hail you with knightly salutation under our national flag.

May I venture to intimate that while chivalry first taught devotion and reverence to that fair being whose beauty and gentleness were her only defence, that it also owes much of its romance and success to her grateful enthusiasm and charm. History, that often neglects to gather the many pretty flowers that grow along the burnt path of war, has not forgotten to record how the unfailing and heroic faith of womanhood often revived the courage of the warrior, when the red-cross banner had begun to waver in the storm of battle and saved the honor and glory of the day. In the golden age of chivalry, when the tournament brought together the gallant and brave of all lands, the boldest and most valiant knight drew the inspiration of his valor from the smile of beauty, and asked no prouder reward than to wear upon his crest the glove or bracelet of his lady safely through the hard-contested field. You will, therefore, hear with gratification and pleasure that the wives and daughters of the Knights Templars of California, hearing of your coming, and knowing that the chivalrous gallantry that in a rough and barbarous age idealized woman, raised her from a menial, a toy, and sport of brutal lust, and made her an object of love and companionship, still grows in every knightly breast, have voluntarily come forward to enliven and refine our Triennial festivities by the grace of their presence and assistance. They early organized an association auxiliary to our Triennial committee, for the purpose of helping to give the most generous and courteous reception to the Sir Knights and their ladies. They have made the most ample preparation that the delicate taste and tact of woman can devise to enhance the enjoyableness of your visit. Sir, the ladies of the Triennial Union extend to you their most sincere welcome, and promise that no valiant Sir Knight shall go away without some token of their admiration.

Sir, knighthood, by its silent and intrinsic excellence, has ever commended itself to the admiration of the virtuous and brave, who have knelt at our shrine and received the honor of an accolade. The light has shown through its transparent drapery of signs and symbols. The world has seen enough of its teachings and principles to appreciate their beauty and value. Hence our whole community has felt the glowing inspiration of your coming, and for months the entertainment of your august body, in a manner becoming the wealth, intelligence, and good name of California for princely hospitality, has been a subject in which this whole people have taken a most lively and abiding interest. These decorated homes, these streets garlanded with flags, arches, and a profusion of evergeens and flowers, are the silent but expressive way this whole community holds out to you the hand of welcome. All classes, creeds, orders, and conditions of society, without thought of fee or reward, are delighted to have you among us, and are deeply solicitous that your visit shall be made as agreeable as possible.

Sir, California is our home, the land of our choice. We have seen its great cities spring as by the touch of a magician's rod from canvas huts and willow cabins. The wild cattle and beasts of the forest roamed at will where now run the great railroads and telegraph, and the trail of the Indian has been obliterated by the march of civilization. These spacious bays and rivers; these productive valleys abounding with fields, orchard, vineyards, and happy homes; these hills and dales and mountains of solemn grandeur, veined with the precious ores, make it indeed a land of promise. Our valleys and hillsides, with varied and prolific soil, produce the fruit and the vine, vegetables and cereals, in such abundance that the crowned prince, the peasant, and the artisan of Europe supply their tables with luxuries from our surplus store. We point with pride to our schools, colleges, churches, and benevolent institutions, as well as our increasing commerce, our growing industries, and in this line our surely coming possibilities. And of our climate, between our southern boundary where grow the orange, the pomegranate, and the vine, and our northern border where Shasta rears its majestic summit above the clouds, and, clothed in eternal ermine, reflects his sunshine to the sea, there is not a mile of latitude but what has its varied climate. The cool and invigorating breezes experienced here, and born of the breath of the Pacific, passing from its sounding shore across our valleys, warmed and softened by perennial sunshine, and finely rarefied and rising, it sighs itself away on the tops of the Sierras, to return again in God's good time laden with the odor of fruits and flowers, the product of our land and the result of our toil.

Sir, allow me to extend to you and to the Grand Encampment of the United States and all visiting Sir Knights and their families, our warm, hearty, knightly greeting and welcome. We feel assured that this meeting of this Triennial Conclave will be one of the red-letter days in our history. We welcome you to our homes, our hearts, our asylum. We greet you as our brethren, bound together by the most solemn vows of knighthood, by every aspiration of the heart, by every precept of our holy religion; as those who will stand shoulder to shoulder in grasping the mystic blade of truth and wielding it for the innocent and oppressed. And, sir, we indulge the hope that when your sojourn among us has ended, and you return to your distant homes, you will have no cause to regret your journey to this coast, and that you will often kindly think of your fellow-pilgrims encamped where the Pacific sings on a golden lea the sunset song of the nation.

The orchestra then rendered the chorus from Wagner's "Tannhauser," after which Mayor Bartlett was introduced to the assembled Knights.

THE WELCOME BY THE MAYOR.

Mayor Bartlett then delivered the following address of welcome:—

Grand Master of the United States and Templars: As chief magistrate of the city of San Francisco I extend to you a hearty welcome. Your coming has been eagerly anticipated by our people, and now that you are here one universal voice gives you a cordial greeting. The Triennial Conclave of the Knights Templars, composed as they are of representative men from all sections of the Union, serves more than to further the interests of your Order. They assemble men capable of appreciating and taking advantage of the varied resources of our country and of studying its social and political problems, thus bringing practical and lasting benefit to the whole people. You also represent the spirit of modern chivalry, which, rejecting the material and grosser ideas of the Middle Ages, keeps alive its original love of truth, justice, and humanity. The ancient knights, taking upon themselves the vows of celibacy, were bound by many monastic rules which modern chivalry has thrown aside. Still, there exists in the Order the same spirit of obedience to just laws, the same love of purity and courage, of glory and renown, and equal, if not greater, devotion to woman.

The history of Masonry in our country is closely identified with the history of the country. In the great struggle which gave us a place among nations many of the most conspicuous actors were Masons. The just and liberal spirit of our earliest laws were, no doubt, inspired in great measure by the spirit and teachings of Masonry. As the wilderness was peopled, the sphere of Masonry enlarged, and the Masonic Temple, humble though it may have been, often preceded the church and the school-house. Now there is scarcely a city in the land that does not point with pride to the temple as one of its most beautiful specimens of architecture.

The Masons of California have not been behind their brethren in the East in kindly charities and noble courage and brave fidelity. You will meet kindred spirits, Sir Knights, on this the extreme western border of our common country, and we greet you not only as the brilliant representatives of a most ancient and honorable Order, but we greet you as fellow-citizens of our glorious country. Those of us who have never been honored by the imposing titles and significant emblems of your ancient Order glory in our common birthright. We, too, are American citizens, and we behold, floating high above all banners and devices that fitly typify the lofty principles and aspirations of the Knights Templars, the stars and stripes, the flag of our Union, the flag which unites the hearts of all Americans from Maine to Florida and from Florida to California.

Again, I repeat, San Francisco bids you welcome, — welcome as Knights, thrice welcome as fellow-citizens of the United States of America. Under some circumstances I might desire that the gentle breezes of the Pacific, our bright skies and flowers and fruits which everywhere meet your gaze, might induce you all to forget your old homes and abide with us forever. But as the vow of celibacy has long since been abrogated by your Order, and no doubt many of you have left loving hearts patiently awaiting your return, I am not permitted to indulge such desire. There are, however, young Knights in your ranks, known in love and chivalry as "bachelors." To these I may safely say, would the bright eyes and "winsome ways" of our maidens incline you to tarry, it would afford me great pleasure to greet you as fellow-citizens of California, though no better provided with worldly goods than was the old knight errant,

> "Well horsed and large of limb, Sir Gaudwin hight;
> He nor of castle nor of land was lord.
> Houseless he reaped the harvest of the sword,
> And now not more on game than profit bent,
> Rode with blithe heart into the tournament.
> For cowardice he held it deadly sin,
> And sure his mind and bearing were akin,
> The face an index to the soul within."

In the struggles of life, valor, truth, and reputation are better than gold, and nowhere are the chivalric virtues of manhood more highly appreciated or more richly rewarded than in California.

I trust that you, Grand Master and Knights, who cannot be persuaded to remain, will, each and all, take with you to your several homes none but the pleasantest recollections of your visit to this coast, as I am sure that we shall ever cherish in our hearts the memory of the "very perfect, gentle Knights" who visited our city.

THE STATE'S GREETING.

Then Gov. Stoneman was introduced by Grand Commander Perkins. "When history," said the latter, "shall be written, and when a future *Chronicle* shall recount the valiant deeds of the men of the past, those of our governor, Gen. George A. Stoneman, will occupy a particularly bright page. To introduce him to you is my pleasing task. Sir Knights, I now present to you Gov. Stoneman, the executive of our State." Gov. Stoneman advanced well toward the front of the platform and spoke as follows: —

Most Eminent Grand Master, Sir Knights and Ladies: There is no one who has led an ordinarily active life who cannot recall some scenes and incidents that have so indelibly impressed themselves upon the tablet of memory that they can never be effaced by time or circumstance, and I shall ever recur with pleasure and with pride to the fact that I was a participant in the scenes now transpiring on this great and auspicious occasion. I am fully aware that I stand in the presence of moving spirits, of master minds, representatives from every quarter of our broad land, representing not only the Masonic Order, but the ability, intelligence, and integrity of the great American people; and realizing this fact most keenly as I can but do, I come before you, in accordance with the courteous invitation of your brethren of California, to perform the pleasing duties assigned me as the executive of this great Commonwealth of extending to you, Sir Knights, the right-hand of fellowship and a cordial and heartfelt welcome to our State, our hearths, and our homes. Within the long limits of our State lines you can all find a congenial resting-place. To those of you who came from the ice-bound mountain regions of old New England, we tender in exchange the pine-clad, snow-capped grand old Sierras. Should your homes be located on the prairies of the great Northwest, they can be replaced by other homes on the broad plains of the Sacramento and the San Joaquin. For the harsh salt winds of the Eastern seaboard we offer you the soft, balmy sea-trades of the Pacific coast, and for the Atlantic's roar the thunder of the everlasting waves from the distant shores of old Cathay.

It may be fitting for me on this occasion to state a few facts in connection with the history of the State whose guests you now are. The world never saw before, nor will it ever see again, the same class of men who came to California in the early days, because the same class of circumstances which produced them can never again exist. They came from the four quarters of the globe; some by the long, stormy, and dangerous cape; some by the sickly, miasmatic isthmian route; and some by the weary, toilsome journey across the burning sands, the rock-ribbed mountains, and the almost endless, trackless, treeless prairies. All were in the prime of life, and there were seen but few gray-haired men and fewer beardless boys. A large number of them were adventurers, with the world all before them and everything to learn, only intent, in the language of the times, upon "making their pile" and returning to their homes to enjoy the proceeds of their luck. A few succeeded and left, but the great majority remained. Among them was an element of eager political ambition; men who had made politics a study at home in both parties, and who, finding here a virgin field for their energy and ability, controlled the politics of the State, and won for themselves names which have redounded throughout the Union with like credit to their chosen State and to themselves. Talk of your modern "bosses," so called; they were "bosses" worthy of the name. The war with Mexico ended in 1848, and the discharged soldiers of the army, graduates of the school of arms and the tented field, became recruits for the great army of fortune-hunters coming to our shores in search of the golden fleece, like the Argonauts of yore. These have been the elements which have builded the State which you now visit and to whom the honor of the work is due. To them have been added since the unwelcome hordes from farther India, the Flowery land, and the islands of the sea.

You have, no doubt, come to the conclusion, in your short sojourn among us, that California is a land of paradoxes. Resembling every other country in the world, she yet differs from all. She yields forth almost every known product of the soil, and if these fail her she has her measureless deposits of gold, silver, and iron from which to draw, without the fear of overdraft. Should these again fail her, she has, as you all must know by this time, an unlimited supply of climate, upon which she can always rely. During the midsummer months the denizens of the East leave the cities and betake themselves to the country in search of cooling breezes. The fur-clad San-Franciscan, on the other hand, goes into the country in search of warmth. Three decades ago, as I can testify, the trip you have just completed would have required six long, weary months. Ten years thereafter it was made in the unprecedented time of six weeks by pony express. You have just made it in the usual time of six days, and rested on the seventh. Who of us will assert, in the light of the past, that some of the Sir Knights now present will not make the trip to the next Conclave held in San Francisco in six times sixty minutes by the watch? California is on the great highway of the commerce and travel of the world, midway between the East and the West, — a toll-house, as it were, for the traffic of the globe. She has had her ups and her downs, her dark days and her bright. Fate has frowned and fortune has smiled. At one time engulfed by floods and at another consumed by fire, yet notwithstanding all this her growth has been steady and rapid, fortunes have been made of fabulous extent in the short space of one generation, and palaces have been reared by nabobs and millionnaires that vie with those of the Old World in extent, grandeur, and display. In commercial circles the reckless, venturesome spirit of early days has largely given place to legitimate business methods. Where our bulls and our bears a few short years ago met in daily combat, all is now quiet and serene.

I am glad to observe that, unlike the knights of old, you have taken with you upon your pilgrimage the ladies fair, to whom you have sworn your knightly devotion, and in the heartfelt welcome which is extended to you all let them not think themselves forgotten. If there is any one thing that California is proud of, it is its wives, its mothers, and its daughters, and that they have so cordially welcomed their sisters of the East is but an evidence of that hospitality which we trust is second in California to that of no other State in the Union. If your ladies, Sir Knights, shall smile upon what efforts we have made we shall be amply rewarded; and if the attempts we have essayed to extend to you a fitting and deserved welcome shall have met with your approval and elicited your commendation, we shall ever feel more than satisfied with the efforts we have made. You will return to your homes laden with the best and heartfelt wishes of the host of friends and brothers you have left behind. You will have seen and known California and the Californians, the men whom you honored at Chicago, and who gladly do honor to you now. Sir Knights and ladies, I can only repeat on behalf of the people of California, you are heartily welcome to our State.

Grand Commander Perkins arose at the conclusion of the governor's address, and taking Grand Master Dean by the right hand, he introduced him to the assembled Knights, whereupon the standard-bearers at once arose and saluted him by waving their banners. Sir Benjamin Dean stepped forward, and bowing to the right and left in acknowledgment of the loud and prolonged applause with which he was received, he addressed the assemblage as follows: —

Most Eminent Grand Commander, Sir Knights, Ladies and Gentlemen:

I think there is no one but will agree that in the history of all chivalry that has ever been written or in the history of the world there has never been extended to any man or body of men a welcome equal to this which has greeted the Knights Templars of the United States at the hands of the Templars of California. [*Applause.*] Your hospitality could not bide the tardy speed of the railroad train. Your Right Eminent Grand Commander, the Grand Captain General, and other Eminent Sir Knights met us a day's journey off, and escorted us with open hands and hearts to our sumptuous quarters in your truly named "Palace Hotel." Upon our arrival there we were made at home by a beautiful and delicate address, so beautiful and so delicate that none but fair woman could have uttered it. They welcomed us also with tablets of flowers, representing your "Golden Gate," and bidding us enter and enjoy.

Why, sirs, having learned that the day of our arrival within your Golden Gate was my natal day, a tablet of flowers was arranged to tell the tale of my first advent into the world, and on its anniversary, my advent into all the glories of this auspicious visit to this far-away and prosperous people. [*Applause.*] Indeed, I cannot but feel that I am born again, that I am indeed the youngest son of California, the Benjamin of your tribe.

I cannot think of those tablets of flowers and of those addresses of welcome without the mind going back to the origin of the Temple. It was the first "woman's rights" society. It was established for the express purpose of protecting woman on her devotional pilgrimage to the holy shrine, and I pray that the day may never come when the Knights Templars of America will forget the origin of their society and neglect their duty to protect woman in that right dear to every American woman's heart, the right to weep over the grave and sufferings of her Saviour.

You have here alluded to the long journeys of olden times, and that brings to mind a scene I once witnessed. Having a younger brother who came here in those early days, who has received many honors at your hands (Hon Peter Dean), I was, perhaps, more than commonly interested in the events that then took place, and I remember very well the ships that were fitted out and started from the end of Long Wharf, Boston, to take that long, rough, weary voyage around the Cape to your golden State. I visited between decks, and wandered among the labyrinth of berths fitted up with coarse boards, longing, if other ties had not kept me back, to be the owner of one of those rough berths. On one occasion, I remember very well going down on Long Wharf to see a ship about to start to California. I saw such a sight, not possessing the grandeur of the one seen here, not a sight so magnificent, yet a sight calculated to make a deep impression upon any one with the heart of a man. All along the wharf, all along the bulwarks of the vessel, up the shrouds, filling the cross-trees, and extending out on the yard-arms, all were packed with human beings. In the centre of the plain deck knelt Father Taylor. Now, Father Taylor was one of Boston's institutions. He was Boston's sailor preacher, and had been for many years, and continued to keep that peculiar position for a great many years after that. At that time our sailors were composed in a measure of a very different class from those that now occupy that position. They were the sons of our New England fathers, and the office of the sailors' preacher, filled as it was by Father Taylor, a man of uncommonly strong mind, was an office of esteemed influence. Well, on this occasion there were gathered the fathers and the mothers, the brothers and the sisters, of those who were to take that voyage. There were also those who came to part with their lovers, receiving from them promises to return with plenty to take care of them for their future lives. There knelt Father Taylor, and he prayed that when the wind blew and the storms came and the subtle temptations of the devil beset them, they should put their trust in the great Captain of their Salvation. He prayed to the Great Architect of the universe, for he was a devout Mason, that they should rely upon that great light, the holy Scriptures, and be guided by its precepts, that they should steer their lives by that great light which never goes out, which never leads astray.

No fog could dim it, no headland could hide it, no distance could send it below the horizon. Such were the scenes in those times. They remind us of Peter the Hermit preaching the First Crusade, — for crusade it was, — and, like the First Crusade, to the Holy Land. They picked out and sent to your shores the strong, the brave, and firm, and much of your prosperity, Mr. Governor and Mr. Mayor, and much of the magnificence of this great city, are due to the fact that that event, as has been said, made its selection from among all mankind, and brought here the best and the strongest. [*Applause.*] But the crusade to these shores brought economic as well as other fruit. It brought untold blessings in its train, for it stimulated that enterprise which has spread a network of railroads over our country, and has furnished happy homes not only to our own people, but to the people of every country on the face of the globe.

But whatever may have been the hardships of the early settlers of California, the few short years that have elapsed have obliterated them all.

Our way hither was without toil or trouble. This our visit may be called the second crusade. But how different from the first crusade. No long, weary journey across the plains, no six months' voyage around the Cape. We came with the speed of the gale, we came in palaces to your palace city, we came to your hearts, we came to your homes; we are welcomed as friends and we are welcomed as relatives, and that great crusade brought all this about.

There is something in the heart of every man looking for adventure. One seeks adventure nowadays by climbing mountain crags; another braves the torrents of Niagara; others seek to find an open sea at the North Pole; and others again are spending their lives and their strength in marching from one end to the other of the dark continent; but no such circumstances can ever again take place like those which have built up this great State. Why, it has not only built railroads, established telegraphs, covering the whole country with them, but it has furnished beautiful homes to millions of people of other lands as well as ours, covering this whole land, which not long ago was a barren wilderness, with a multitude of people. We meet here a happy people. There is no such people in the world. There never has been such a people in the world, and there never will be such another people. We have had a quarrel, it is true, but it was a love quarrel. It was a family quarrel, none the less severe on that account, but it taught us how dear we were to each other. It seems to me that we love each other better because of the quarrel, and no power on earth can part us hereafter. But I am talking too much. This cordial coming together of all parts of our great country we may claim as largely due to our widespread societies teaching, as they do, love of country, obedience to law, and brotherly love towards each other and towards all mankind. We have had long, weary marches that have been pleasant. They have not wearied us so much as they would have under other circumstances, because our hearts are full of rejoicing, chock full and brimming over with the milk of human kindness. Our institution is one that tends to home kindnesses. It preaches peace on earth and good-will toward men. There is something in the heart of man — I don't know how to describe it — there is something in the heart of man which awakes a responsive throb in the bosom of his fellow-man, which this institution fills as no other institution can, and that is why we are here in such numbers. That is why we are here so united, and I trust we shall go on fulfilling our mission, and causing this country to grow in honor, in chivalry, in all those arts and amenities which make up the prosperity of a great nation in the future as it has grown in the past. May the God of our fathers be with us in the future as He has been in the past, and bring about and continue that great consummation. [*Applause.*]

And now, Right Eminent Grand Commander, permit me gratefully in behalf of myself and my companions of the Grand Encampment to acknowledge our obligations to yourself and the Grand Commandery of California, and to the Knights Templars of San Francisco, for this princely welcome, the inspiration of which has added so much earnestness to your eloquent address.

I cannot but heartily approve, Mr. Mayor, of your suggestion for those closer connections between the younger of our Templars and the fair daughters of this happy shore which form the firmest of ties and will surely keep up a friendly and constant intercourse between your city and all portions of our widespread jurisdiction.

And, Governor, I assure you we shall return to our distant home laden with pleasant memories of your great and favored State, and of the valuable friendships we have formed here. If we came too late to make some of the colossal fortunes of which you speak, we have not come too late to enjoy the hospitalities those fortunes have made possible. For the labors for our comfort, for the manifestation of friendship everywhere exhibited, and for this outpouring of patriotism as well as fraternal love, I again and again thank one and all. [*Prolonged applause.*]

At the conclusion of the Grand Master's response, the standard-bearers assembled in front of the grand stage and displayed their handsome banners, the line extending across the Pavilion, the Grand Master remaining standing. The whole assembly then arose, the Sir Knights bared their heads, holding their plumed chapeaux over the left shoulder, while the band struck up "America," the audience joining in the singing of the national hymn. When the last note had passed away, Grand Prelate Locke stepped forward and pronounced the benediction. The Knights bowed reverently, and when the amen was pronounced they responded, "So mote it be."

CHAPTER XIII.

At 11.30 A. M. Tuesday, Aug. 21, Boston Commandery responded promply to the bugle call and formed in line. As usual there was a great crowd attracted hither to hear the Hawaiian band and witness the ceremonies preceding the opening of the Conclave.

The Royal Hawaiian Band accompanied Boston Commandery at all its public parades, etc., and was present at the reception given by the Commandery at the Palace Hotel, having been assigned to duty with Boston Commandery by the courtesy of the Triennial committee.

The California, Golden Gate, and Boston Commanderies, together with representatives from other Templar organizations, acted as escort to Grand Master Dean and the other officers of the Grand Encampment. The procession, headed by the Royal Hawaiian Band, proceeded from the Palace Hotel to Masonic Temple. Boston Commandery was the special escort of the Grand Master. On Post Street — the Temple is situated on the corner of Post and Montgomery Streets — double lines were drawn upon either side, and the Grand Master with the Grand Officers passed through the avenue, the Sir Knights being at the present, and entered the Temple ascending to King Solomon's Temple on the third floor, where the sessions of the Twenty-second Triennial Conclave were held.

Boston Commandery was escorted back to the Palace Hotel by the Commanderies before mentioned. After Eminent Sir John L. Stevenson, Commander of Boston Commandery, had, in behalf of the Grand Master, expressed his thanks for the escort, the lines were dismissed.

The story of the pilgrimage seems to demand some reference to the Conclave and its transactions, though but few of the Boston Templars attended its sessions. Shortly before 12 M. the Grand Organist played a voluntary, and at 12 M. precisely the Grand Master rose and said,—

"The hour has arrived for the Grand Encampment of the Twenty-second Triennial Conclave of our Order to open. The proper officials will see that only those entitled to remain are present. All others will at once retire."

Immediately after opening with appropriate services, the routine business was done, roll called (all Grand Officers, each Grand Commandery, and the several charter Commanderies being represented), and standing committees were appointed. The Grand Master then began to read his address, which was exhaustive in its treatment of those matters (as ritual and tactics) which are of practical interest and importance to the Order. As of special interest and appropriate to have a place on these pages, we quote from the address of the Grand Master his remarks concerning Boston Commandery. In discussing the relative claims to priority in Templar work in this country, he quotes from the records of St. Andrew's Royal Arch Chapter, of Boston, Mass., and comments as follows:—

"At a Royal Arch Lodge Held at Mason's Hall, Boston, New England, August 28, 1769.

"Present, The R. W. Brother James Brown, M.; Charles Chambers, S. W.; Winthrop Gray, J. W.; William McMullen, Henry Glynn, William McKean, John Waddington, Joshua Loring, D. S.

"The Petition of Brother William Davis coming before the Lodge begging to have & receive the Parts belonging to a Royal Arch Mason, which being read was received & he was unanimously Voted in & was accordingly made by receiving the four Steps, that of an Excell¹, Super Excell¹, Royal Arch & Kt. Templar."

These degrees, or "parts," or "steps," are in the subsequent records alluded to as the "four degrees of a Royal Arch Mason."

There could not be four degrees of a Royal Arch Mason without including Knight Templar.

The Lodge was a "Royal Arch Lodge," and the words "Royal Arch Mason" included the possession of the Order of the Temple.

The record of the 14th of May, 1770, has this:—

"*Voted*, That the Most Worshipful Joseph Warren, Esq., should be made a Royal Arch Mason this evening, and he was accordingly made. Gratis."

Thus it appears that Gen. Joseph Warren, who was slain at the battle at Bunker Hill, was a Knight Templar.

The record of another meeting reads:—

"June 21, 1770.—The Most Worshipful Bro. Warren, G. M., present: he gave his opinion for holding the Royal Arch Lodge, till instructions from Scotland, or otherwise as he should think fitt, & if directions from thence he will then grant a charter therefor."

He was present on the 14th of September, 1770, and once again in 1773, when he was chairman of a meeting which seems to have been called to consider the interests of the body.

Paul Revere received the degrees in December, 1769. The record reads:—

"The petition of Bro. Paul Revere coming before the Lodge begging to become an Arch Mason, it was rec'd, & he was unanimously accepted & accordingly made."

So he, too, was a Knight Templar.

> "Listen, my children, and you shall hear
> Of the midnight ride of Paul Revere,
> On the eighteenth of April, in seventy-five.
> Hardly a man is now alive
> Who remembers that famous day and year."

The only reference to Knights of the Red Cross is the following record made Feb. 8, 1797, when it was

"*Voted*, That the Knights of the Red Cross by Bro. Benjamin Hurd, Jr., be, and they are hereby permitted to make their records on the books of the Chapter."

This was not done, however, and there is no subsequent notice in the records of Knight Templar or Knight of the Red Cross.

How long the Knights of the Red Cross had been at work there are no means of ascertaining with certainty. The record speaks of the Knights of the Red Cross as already existing, and Benjamin Hurd, Jr., was made a Templar, March 20, 1789, eight years before the "Red Cross" record last quoted. There can be no question that the Royal Arch Masons and Templars of St. Andrew's Royal Arch Lodge were also Knights of the Red Cross.

These Knights, thus made in St. Andrew's Royal Arch Lodge, subsequently, when the time arrived for the separation of the Chivalric from Craft Masonry, formed Boston Encampment, first as a Council of Knights of the Red Cross, and afterwards embracing the three Orders of Knighthood.

Boston Commandery, by its present Eminent Commander, John L. Stevenson, claiming a continuous existence as a body of Knights, though under different organizations, from 1769, puts forth the right to rank from that date.

That gallant body of Templars is here as the escort of your Grand Master, from ocean to ocean, from farthest east to farthest west. Commencing with the meeting of March 12, 1802, it has held one thousand and forty meetings, has conferred the Orders of Knighthood on one thousand four hundred. Its present membership is six hundred and one. Its meetings have been continuous and uninterrupted from 1802 to the present time.

Under the head of "the Ritual" the Grand Master calls attention (*vide* pages 78, 79, and 80, Grand Master's Report, 1883) to a convention of three representatives from each Commandery within the jurisdiction of the Grand Commandery of Massachusetts and Rhode Island, held in A. D. 1871, A. O. 753, for the especial purpose of considering the work and lectures. When the present Grand Master was Grand Commander in that jurisdiction, he laid before the Grand Commandery of Massachusetts and Rhode Island a manuscript copy of the lectures carefully prepared. This manuscript was reviewed and considered by Sir Knights Dame and Moore, Past Grand Masters, by Sir Knight Nurse, Past Grand Generalissimo, and by Sir Knight Harwood. Thirty-five years before (1836), Sir Knight Harwood wrote a key to the lectures in an abbreviated cipher, unintelligible except to himself. This key was found to correspond to the manuscript of Sir Knight Dame with almost undeviating uniformity.

Sir Knight Fowle, the first Deputy Grand Master, was Grand Generalissimo during the entire administration of Sir Thomas Smith Webb, 1805 to 1817. He was also Commander of Boston Commandery from 1805 to 1823, during a portion of which time Sir Abram A. Dame was his Junior Warden, and from him (Fowle) he (Dame) learned the lectures and work. From that time to the present Sir Knight Dame has been active in his attendance upon the meetings of Boston Commandery, and has been the teacher of the work and lectures to his numerous successors. Sir Knight Nurse is second only to Sir Knight Dame in the jealous preservation of the ancient ritual in its integrity. "This manuscript," said the Grand Commander in 1871, "which I now produce, has the entire sanction of all the eminent and learned Sir Knights to whom I have alluded, as the lectures taught and used in the days of the founders of Templar Masonry in this Commonwealth. It is impossible that there should be anything more authentic."

"A copy of these lectures, obtained, approved, and adopted in the manner I have narrated, attested by Eminent Sir Knight Alfred F. Chapman, Grand Recorder of the Grand Commandery of Massachusetts and Rhode Island, I now present to this Grand Encampment. At this time, when there is so much interest and desire for uniformity in the rituals of the Order, I feel that I could do no act more acceptable to this Grand Encampment. More than that, I have no doubt whatever that in presenting this manuscript of the work and lectures, I present the only adopted and authorized work of this Grand Encampment. They are the lectures and work of those who were mainly instrumental in establishing this Grand Encampment. Boston Commandery, which has honored me by its escort upon this occasion, is the body that preserved these lectures and work, by weekly rehearsals at its members' houses, during the entire anti-Masonic period, and furnished half of the money required to pay the expenses of the delegates to the convention which formed this Grand Encampment."

It is worthy of notice that the Eminent Commander of Boston Commandery was appointed a member of the committee on rituals for the ensuing three years; also, a member of the committee on tactics.

The Conclave continued until Friday evening (four days), considering those matters demanding its attention. Thursday the election of officers took place, which resulted as follows: —

Grand Master. — Sir Robert E. Withers, of Virginia, succeeding Most Eminent Sir Benjamin Dean.
Deputy Grand Master. — Sir Charles Roome, of New York.
Grand Generalissimo. — Sir John P. S. Gobin, of Pennsylvania.
Grand Captain General. — Sir Hugh McCurdy, of Michigan.
Grand Senior Warden. — Sir J. LaRue Thomas, of Kentucky.
Grand Junior Warden. — Sir George C. Perkins, of California.
Grand Treasurer. — Sir J. W. Simons, of New York.
Grand Recorder. — Sir Theodore S. Parvin, of Iowa.

Before vacating the office of Grand Master, Most Eminent Sir Benjamin Dean issued the following order: —

GRAND ENCAMPMENT OF KNIGHTS TEMPLARS OF UNITED STATES OF AMERICA.

OFFICE OF THE GRAND MASTER,
SAN FRANCISCO, Aug. 23, 1883.

☩ *Benj Dean*
   Grand Master.

[General Order No. 8.]

It would not be fit for the Grand Master to retire from office without in his official capacity, in behalf of the Grand Encampment, expressing the obligation of the Knights Templars of the United States to the Grand Commandery and to the governor of California, to the mayor of San Francisco and to its citizens at large, for a heartiness and a universality of welcome and a generosity of hospitality almost without a parallel. The Knights Hospitallers of old, with whom hospitality was a specialty, backed by the wealth of Europe, could not have outrivalled it. The committees of ladies, in the many beautiful and delicate and interesting attentions that none but themselves know, have captivated the Templar hearts and run away with the affections of their wives and daughters. If too late to reap the colossal fortunes which have been described to us, it has not proved too late for them to share in the fruits of the accumulated wealth of these happy shores. The Grand Master cannot omit his own personal acknowledgments of the many kind attentions and courtesies to himself and family. Fruit and flowers and invitations in flowers and gold, adorned with tasteful and costly workmanship, have welcomed him, and stored his mind and heart with lasting memories. It would not be just if in this, one of the last of his official acts, the Grand Master should omit to express his obligations to his escort, which has been unremitting in its endeavors to discharge its self-imposed duties. To Boston Commandery, to its Eminent Commander, to all its members, and to those of their ladies who accompany them, he returns his heartfelt thanks.

Done at the place and on the date above written.

CHAPTER XIV.

A SERIES of excursions was arranged by the committee on excursions, which was successfully carried out. Thousands of visitors took advantage of their opportunities to visit Napa Valley, Santa Rosa, Santa Cruz, Menlo Park, the Geysers, Monterey, etc., and to enjoy a sail down the bay. Many also made excursions of a private nature to nearer points of interest, as the Cliff House and Seal Rocks, Oakland, Vallejo, etc. The following was the programme as arranged by the committee on excursions: —

GRAND EXCURSIONS TO SIR KNIGHTS AND THEIR FAMILIES.

TUESDAY, Aug. 21. — To Napa Valley, the great wine growing region of the State. Free entertainment will be tendered at Yountville and St. Helena. . . . The excursion will be under the direct charge of Sir Abraham Powell.

WEDNESDAY, Aug. 22. — Grand complimentary excursion tendered to the visiting Sir Knights and their families, to the Golden Gate and points of interest in the bay, on board of the yachts of the San Francisco and Pacific Yacht Clubs, tendered for this occasion by their owners, and the steamers "Newark," "Ancon," and "San Rafael." . . . This excursion will be under the immediate control of Sir Stewart Menzies.

THURSDAY, AUG. 23. — Grand excursion to Santa Cruz, the Giant Redwoods of Santa Cruz Mountains, passing through the finest scenery of California to the most beautiful seaside in the world. The citizens of Santa Cruz tender a grand California barbecue. . . . This excursion will be under the control of Sir R. M. Garratt.

MONDAY, Aug. 27. — Grand excursion to Monterey, the famous summer resort of the coast. The world-renowned hotel Del Monte. Complimentary to the Grand Master and officers of the Grand Encampment of the United States. . . . This excursion will be under the sole control of Sir J. A. Fillmore.

SIR H. B. SMITH, JR., *Chairman Excursion Committee*,
116 Montgomery Street.

One of the chief attractions near San Francisco is the Cliff House and Seal Rocks. It was one of the first places visited by the Sir Knights. The Cliff House is situated on the Pacific shore, at Point Lobos, near the entrance of the Golden Gate. The hotel is built on a cliff at the ocean edge and about one hundred feet above sea level. The hotel on the water side has a wide

CLIFF HOUSE AND SEAL ROCKS.

veranda from which there is a fine sea view. About eight hundred feet from the cliff there rise out of the ocean seven rocky islets, and these, at least on the sides toward the hotel, were covered with sea-lions, crawling, barking, rolling, and tumbling. They can be distinctly seen and often heard by persons on the veranda. As they come up out of the water they appear "black, sleek, and slippery," but when dry they look dirty and yellow. The sea-lions are strictly seals, very large, awkward and clumsy on the ledges, but very nimble in the water. They rolled around in the strong current, they climbed up the rocks, they clung upon the shelves in

SEAL ROCKS FROM THE HOTEL.

the almost perpendicular sides of the rock islands; some ascended to the very summit, seventy-five or one hundred feet above the water, and basked in the sunshine. Far beyond extends the restless Pacific, and at the right is the famous Golden Gate. It is a pleasant drive to the Cliff House, by way of Golden Gate

Park, which is beautifully laid out. One is well repaid for visiting "La Punta de los Lobos Marinos," the Point of the Sea-Lions.

We visited the Geysers and rush down to Monterey and Santa Cruz. A carriage ride of six miles brings us to the famous redwood-trees. In the base of one, the "Fremont," the proprietor wisely informed us that the "Pathfinder" passed all one winter when on an exploring tour. This is the story, and we tack our card on to the general, as thousands have done before, and hastily return to the station over a dusty but romantic pike, having time to ride over to the cliff and see the sea waves. To reach that section we pass through Santa Clara Valley, a garden in fact. Wheat in some sections here grows one hundred bushels to the acre. I don't believe it, but a Methodist divine stationed at Waterville says it is true.— SIR J. D. D., *Cor. Journal and Courier, New Haven, Conn.*

Some of the Boston party visited the Geysers. They are situated in Sonoma County, about one hundred miles from San Francisco. The route is from San Francisco to Oakland, thence to Calistoga by rail, passing through Napa Valley, with its stretches of vineyards, orchards, and beautiful scenery, with Napa and Sonoma Mountains on either hand. From Calistoga to the Geysers, twenty-five miles, the trip is made by stage. Leaving the hotel and passing through the gate "TO THE GEYSERS," one first comes to the Iron Spring. Crossing the little Pluton River (seventeen hundred feet above sea level), the traveller enters the Devil's Cañon, trembling, boiling, steaming, with a hundred springs of all sizes, depths, colors, and temperatures. The most important of these have received suggestive names, as Eyewater Spring, Devil's Inkstand, Devil's Pepperbox, Devil's Kitchen, Devil's Machine-shop, — the entire gorge seems to be given up to devils' names.

"The Witches' Caldron," seven feet in diameter, by its black, boiling waters, holds a temperature of 195° Fahr. There are hot alum and sulphur springs, and springs containing ammonia, epsom salts, magnesia, soda, etc. The Devil's Inkstand flows with incarnate fluid. The Lemonade Spring is bad to drink. The Temperance Spring, within a few feet of the boiling sulphur springs, flows with clear cold water. These springs are of various temperatures, hot and cold being in some places adjacent. The Steamboat Geyser sounds like a locomotive blowing off steam, so heated as to be invisible six feet from the mouth. The Geysers are a great natural wonder, and the Sir Knights expressed themselves as perfectly delighted with the trip.

The excursion to Napa Valley took place Tuesday, Aug. 21, as per programme, under the charge of Sir Abraham Powell, of Golden Gate Commandery. Napa Valley, the garden spot of Napa County, is about thirty-five miles in length and from one to five in width. The great product of the valley is wine. The natural beauties of the landscape in peaks, vales, creeks, hillsides, and fields are rich and inspiring. At 8 A. M. about a thousand Sir Knights and ladies, the Bostonians being well represented, embarked on the steamer "Amador" at Market Street Wharf, for Vallejo. Music was furnished by the Stockton band of sixteen pieces. At Vallejo (10.40 A. M.) the party was transferred to two special trains, one of nine cars and the other of twelve. At 11.15 A. M. the first train arrived at Napa station, where the excursionists were heartily welcomed. Business was suspended, schools dismissed, and the people from miles around gathered at Napa. An excursionist described the trip in the following language: —

The reception committee ushered the knights into the depot, where a fine collation of fruits was spread, which rapidly disappeared from before the hungry Knights. In the midst of the general rejoicing, Morris M. Estee was introduced, and in the name of the residents of Napa Valley extended a welcome to all the excursionists. A response to the greeting was made by Gen. C. H. Grosvenor, Past Eminent Commander of Athens Commandery, of Ohio, and Speaker of the House of Representatives of that State. He returned thanks in the name of the Knights for the hearty welcome tendered by the residents of Napa, and stated that since he reached California he had not drunk cold water nor tasted dry bread.

Among the fruits furnished were the following varieties: Apples, Hoover and Gravenstein; figs, California and Turkey black; peaches, Strawberry, Snow, Chinese Cling; plums, Washington, Early Crawford, Green Gage, Bradshaw, and French; pears, Bartlett, Madeline, Clairgeau, and Beurre; grapes, Muscat, Sweetwater, Zinfandel, and Hamburg. Watermelons, muskmelons, and almonds were also furnished in profusion.

The second train arrived, and the occupants were subjected to similar treatment, but the first train had proceeded to Yountville, where the excursionists were the recipients of the really splendid hospitality of one man, G. Groezinger. This gentleman's large wine vaults and distillery are situated directly opposite the Yountville station. The Knights and ladies were bade welcome, and after a wondering, hasty stroll through the cool vaults, where over half a million gallons of wine are stored, ascended to the second floor of the winery, where wine actually flowed like water. Pails filled with iced wines were on all hands, and hundreds of bottles of the red and white vintage of the valley were opened and served by the employés of the generous host.

Luncheon was also laid on long tables, and around this the guests ate and drank enjoyably, while the host, from a raised platform, formally welcomed them. All the wine served had been in casks for over five years, and the guests expressed themselves as greatly pleased with it.

At Yountville a committee from St. Helena met the excursionist, and one of them, Wm. H. Jordan, in a happy speech, welcomed the guests and urged them to reserve a little of their capacities for the hospitalities of the St. Helenaites.

The latter place was reached at two o'clock, and there another large crowd of citizens, with committee-men and a band, met the train, and conducted the excursionists to Hunt's Grove, a little distance from the station. An evergreen arch of welcome was passed on the way thither, and within the grove a scene of what the visitors must have considered peculiarly California hospitality greeted them. Beneath a madrone grove were long tables loaded with materials for a substantial repast. Near that was a long booth, stocked with a score of casks of red and white wine, all tapped and yielding their rich contents in streams at the bidding of the guests. A committee of ladies and gentlemen served the excursionists to the contents of the booth and table in a generous manner. This inspiration of hospitality was thus inscribed on an arch over the wine booth: "To weary pilgrims travelling from afar: Greeting from the wine growers of St. Helena district." After hunger and thirst had been satisfied, there were music and speeches, and lounging under the madrone-trees for half an hour, when the trip was continued over to Calistoga. At the latter place, and at Krúg's, *en route*, the same generous welcome to the strangers was given. The day and circumstances attending the trip were both calculated to impress the beauty and fertility of the valley, and the generosity of the valley residents, upon the excursionists.

The second train passed through the same ordeal, when the return trip began. Hospitalities were again extended to all. At Vallejo a crowd of Napa Valley citizens gathered to bid farewell to the Sir Knights and ladies. As the boat left the pier, cheer after cheer was given by the happy citizens and the happy Templars. Soon after their departure, the Knights were called together in the cabin of the "Amador," an organization was effected, and a committee appointed to draw up resolutions, thanking the residents of Napa Valley for their hospitality. Each State and Territory was represented on the committee by one Sir Knight. Sir C. E. Severance, M. D., of the medical staff of Boston Commandery, represented Massachusetts. Addresses were made, cheers were given for Napa Valley, California, etc., which were brought to an end only by the report of the committee and adoption of a series of very complimentary resolutions.

The excursion was marred by no accident or unpleasant incident, and all the members of the party were loud in their praises of the beauty of Napa Valley and the generous hospitality of its people.

On Wednesday, 22d inst., Sir Knight William Harney, of California Commandery, No. 1, earned the lasting gratitude of a hundred ladies and Sir Knights of Boston Commandery, by a most generous and graceful act. He chartered a special train of two passenger coaches, to which was attached a commissary car, laden with all the delicacies of the season in bountiful supply, and invited the party to Menlo Park for the day. Menlo Park is about thirty-five miles from San Francisco, and contains the beautiful country residences of many of the wealthiest citizens of California. Arriving at the station, lunch was served on board the train; after which, the twenty-five or thirty spanking teams in waiting at the depot conveyed the sight-seers to Palo Alto, the stock ranch of Leland Stanford. Palo Alto, Spanish for tall timber, suggested by a redwood-tree on the bank of the creek, is the name of the rural home of Mr. Stanford. Here Mr. Stanford has set apart fourteen hundred acres for the breeding and training of horses, of which he has seven hundred of the best thoroughbred and trotter blood. Two of his horses cost him twenty-five thousand dollars each. He employs seventy-five men to take care of his horses. For the pleasure of the visitors several of the horses were speeded around the track, while others were paraded for their inspection. Among these horses were the well-known Electioneer, Piedmont, and Gen. Benton.

The Templars and their ladies then proceeded to the residence of Col. Harney, and through the grounds of several magnificent estates. The residences are in the midst of spacious grounds, which are planted with a large variety of ornamental trees, and are intersected by extensive drives. The royal house of J. C. Flood was thrown open to the visitors, who entered and were shown through the stately halls and magnificent parlors of that noted residence. The party returned to the train loaded with the choicest flowers contributed by many citizens of Menlo Park, and, after a really happy day, with hearty cheers for their generous host, the train was taken for the return to San Francisco.

The greeting extended to the seventy-five guests who visited Menlo on Wednesday was a surprise to the Eastern tourists. Gentlemen owing handsome turnouts drove to the depot, exchanging cards with those who filled their carriages, and explained the peculiarities and development of the country to the tourists. Charles Felton handled the ribbons of his four-in-hand, and four teams from Gov. Stanford's place, and the carriages of James Flood and William J. Adams awaited them. The guests alighted at the residence of Mr. Spreckels, and were received by the ladies of the house, and the four young ladies visiting there. An impromptu luncheon was served from the veranda tables, consisting of champagne, cake, and fruit.

The ladies were presented, as souvenirs, with the badges of the different

Commanderies, the hostess receiving a golden medal. Those indebted for the use of private carriages thoughtfully left their cards at the different residences. The Bostonians particularly expressed their astonishment at the beauty and extent of the private grounds through which they drove. — *The Call, of Monday, Aug. 27.*

Wednesday was set apart by the Triennial excursion committee for excursions down the bay, and thousands improved the opportunity to make the trip, view the harbor and fortifications, take a look through the Golden Gate, and try the placid Pacific. The steamer "Newark" left her berth with about fifteen hundred ladies and Sir Knights and the Fifth Infantry band. The steamer "Sausalito" had five hundred guests, with the Eighth Infantry band. The steamer "Mary Garrett" had on board the Stockton Commandery and their friends, with the Stockton band. The steamer "Ancon" ploughed the bay with a party of two thousand guests and the Hawaiian band. A number of yachts, each carrying from fifteen to seventy-five excursionists, were taken in tow by steam yacht "Thetis" and the Pacific Steamship Company's tugboat, by which they were towed to the ocean. Steamers, yachts, and harbor shipping were all profusely decorated. The crowd on the docks cheered, the guns on the yachts were fired, and the bands played their loudest if not their best as the Templar fleet headed for the Golden Gate. Having reached the Heads, the rocky posts of the Golden Gate, yachts were cast off, sails were set, and the crafts bowled back into the bay, with a fair wind, to the place of starting, in less than an hour.

The yacht "Lurline" had a pleasant party of ladies and gentlemen aboard. The commander, Sir William Center, directed that the main brace should be spliced every half-hour, beginning at 10 A. M., but as some of the watches indicated Boston time, another Pittsburg time, and several San Francisco time, the splicing had to be done with a little more rapidity than the skipper expected.

Among the guests on board were ex-Congressman A. R. Cotten and wife, of Iowa, ex-Congressman Hopkins, of Pennsylvania, Past Grand Commander of the United States, and Sir Knights A. L. Richardson, Boston, and John Haigh, Somerville, Mass.

The steamers proceeded farther out, passing beyond the Gate. When near the Seal Rocks, off the Cliff House, the " Ancon's " cannon was fired to frighten the seals, which made a grand scramble for the water, much to the delight of the excursionists. A return salute of twenty-one guns was fired from the Cliff House bluff, which was answered with music and cheers. Refreshments were supplied in great abundance, and everybody returned perfectly delighted. Mass meetings were held on the steamers, speeches were made (some verbose passengers received permission to have theirs printed without delivery), thanks were expressed, and the hinges of the Golden Gate were sufficiently oiled to last until some other Triennial Conclave meets in San Francisco.

Thursday, the 23d of August, was barbecue day at Santa Cruz. Two trains, one of seventeen cars and one of ten, occupied by eighteen hundred Sir Knights and ladies, left Almeda Point for Santa Cruz. The ride of three and a half hours was through long tunnels and amid picturesque scenery. Santa Cruz was once the fashionable seaside resort of California. Grace Greenwood called it "a beautiful, smiling town, seated on the knees of pleasant terraces, with her feet in the sea." Mountains, gardens, bay, and town unite Italian and Swiss beauty, Naples and the Alps.

When Santa Cruz was reached it was evident that the event of the visit of the Knightly party was considered a jubilee occasion.

Nearly two thousand people, many from the country around, swarmed in the depot and streets, and on the High-School bluff overlooking the depot. It was nearly one o'clock, and the excursionists were hungry, therefore the notable absence of speech-making or formal reception at the depot was favorably commented upon. Without any delay, every one fell in behind the Santa Cruz brass band, and marched the half-block to the barbecue grounds. Here was a scene calculated to bring great peace and joy to the minds of the eighteen hundred tired, hungry, and thirsty invaders. A large vacant lot had been walled in with tall branches of evergreens. A canopy of evergreens, supported on decorated poles, prettily shaded and cooled the entire space. In the centre was a great standard of flowers, surmounted by an immense passion cross of crimson flowers. But best of all were the thirty-one long tables, each with seating capacity for forty, and each loaded with fruits and flowers, and many evidences that something more substantial was quickly coming. About the tables stood fifty Santa Cruz ladies, many of them with aprons made of Knight Templar flags, and all looking cheerful, willing to begin their service of waitresses without delay. The Knights and ladies filed into the grounds with many expressions of delight with the pretty and hospitable picture, took seats at the tables, as many of them as could, and fastened on the dainty *boutonnières* laid on each plate. There were 1,240 plates, and before each plate a hungry guest, and behind each hungry guest another hungry guest waiting. The arrangements for one of the biggest barbecues ever given on the coast, except that it was simply impossible in the space to seat every one at once, were simply perfect. Unlike such affairs usually, the work of barbecuing the meats was entirely separated from the tables, and the result will surely make that plan of serving barbecues popular, as there were no squeamish appetites destroyed, as is frequently the case, by the sight of the cooking carcasses.

In an adjoining lot, over the usual long earth ditch, were roasted sixteen sheep and four beeves. The barbecue had been well timed, for the dozen carvers found the meat just ready for their knives and axes as the guests sat down, and in a very short space there was delicious barbecue meat steaming hot, with goblets of wine, fruit, loaves of French bread, and coffee before every plate. Luscious fruits of all kinds, delicious pastries, meats of all kinds, coffee, tea, and wines, composed the bill of fare, and to give some idea of the execution done it is only necessary to state that the following is a partial list of the good things partaken of: Three thousand pounds of beef and mutton, done to a turn; eight hundred loaves of bread, one hundred boxes of peaches, twenty crates of watermelons, forty gallons of milk, five hundred gallons of wine, etc.

An open-air concert was given by the band, which occupied a handsomely decorated platform. After the barbecue the guests strolled about town or proceeded to the beach. Many availed themselves of the opportunity for a plunge in the surf. The weather was delightful, business was suspended, and a holiday was enjoyed by all. As the time for departure drew nigh, the excursionists held an informal meeting at the depot, and appointed a committee, which presented resolutions of thanks to the Lodge, Chapter, and Commandery, to railroad, excursion committee, citizens, and ladies of Santa Cruz. The resolutions were adopted with deafening cheers. It was 10 P. M. before the excursionists arrived at the city.

The excursion to Santa Rosa was not so largely attended as others, but the hospitality was no less. Three hundred Sir Knights and ladies, accompanied by the Royal Hawaiian Band, took passage on the steamer "Sausalito," which was gayly decorated. An hour by water brought the party to San Rafael, where the train was taken for Santa Rosa. On arrival there were gathered at the depot fully one thousand persons, including Santa Rosa Commandery, No. 14. Members of the Commandery received the visitors, when the line was formed on Fourth Street, the principal thoroughfare, in the following order: Parks's Santa Rosa Band of fifteen pieces; Santa Rosa Commandery; the Royal Hawaiian Band; visiting Sir Knights; citizens in carriages. The business streets of the city were handsomely decorated, and from the depot to the local Commandery asylum — the line of march taken by the column — the thoroughfare was lined with people from all parts of the county. There were at Santa Rosa several thousand non-residents brought together by the holding of the Sonoma County Agricultural Fair, and these, with the persons assembled to witness the Templar ceremonies, made the little city present an animated appearance. The Knights marched along Fourth Street to the Plaza, when they came to a halt in front of the rostrum. Past Eminent Commander G. A. Johnson, of Santa Rosa Commandery, No. 14, then mounted the rostrum and delivered a brief address, in the course of which he said: —

Ladies and Sir Knights: In behalf of our citizens and Santa Rosa Commandery, I bid you a cordial welcome to our city, whose residents are a cosmopolitan, contented, and happy people, and to a country of wonderful natural resources and climate. Our county is fifty miles long and twenty miles wide, larger than the State of Rhode Island. It is a country of beautiful landscapes and blooming vineyards. It is close to such natural wonders as the Geysers and Sulphur Springs and the far-famed redwoods, which are only some twenty miles east of here. It is told in a legend of our State that away back in 1833 or 1834, when the possession of this country was a topic of dispute between the Russians and the Mexicans, that Friar Amorosa, after having established a mission at San José, met, half a mile east of town, on the banks of Santa Rosa Creek, with an unsophisticated but beautiful Indian maiden, whom he baptized, and that she, then becoming frightened, fled to Rincon Hill, nine miles to the southeast, and there lay down underneath a tree, the two lower limbs of which, in connection with the trunk, form a perfect passion cross, one of the mystic emblems of knighthood. The friar, when he baptized the maiden, named her St. Rose or Santa Rosa, and it is from this source that our city derived the name which it now bears.

The visiting Knights were next escorted by the Santa Rosa Commandery, led by Eminent Commander T. P. Baxter, to the Masonic Temple, at the corner of Hinton Avenue and Fourth Street. Refreshments of fruit and wine were served in the asylum, and the freedom of the city was then courteously extended to the excursionists. The party visited the fair, and beheld with wonder the resources and products of Sonoma County. The visitors were enthusiastic in their praises of the people of Santa Rosa for their hospitality, and expressed warm thanks for the kind treatment received.

A special train brought the excursionists back to the city, leaving Santa Rosa at six o'clock, connecting with the boat at San Rafael, which arrived at San Francisco at 9.30 P. M.

At an informal assembly of Sir Knights in the steamer's cabin the usual resolutions of thanks were adopted.

The excursion to Monterey occurred on Monday, the second day after the departure of Boston Commandery for home; but as reference to it seems necessary to complete the excursions, the following account is taken from the San Francisco *Chronicle*: —

The excursion to Monterey, in compliment to the Grand Encampment of the United States, was taken yesterday by the Knights Templars who still tarry in San Francisco. Sir Knights Fillmore, Powell, Knipe, Burns, and Graves were the gentlemen composing the excursion committee, and thanks to them, none of the arrangements necessary to the comfort and entertainment of the excursionists were neglected. At 7.30 A. M. a special train, consisting of twelve commodious coaches, left the depot of the Southern Pacific Railroad, and after a pleasant run of four and one half hours arrived at noon at its destination. The aggregate number of the excursionists was seven hundred and fifty, including officers and members of the Grand Encampment, Knights belonging to various Pacific coast and Eastern Commanderies and their families and friends. The music was supplied by the First Infantry band, the members of which were fancifully attired in scarlet coats and white-striped pantaloons, and wore swords. The train on the way down passed the smaller stations, and halted only at such places of interest to strangers as Menlo Park, where are the summer residences of many capitalists, San José, the garden city of California, and the old Spanish town of Gilroy. Leaving the Del Monte depot, the visitors, after a short walk, reached the hotel, where luncheon was eaten. The Knights and their ladies then strolled around the grounds for a time, admiring the green lawns and the beautiful flower-beds. Then the excursionists divided themselves into small groups, and were conveyed in carriages to the old Carmel Mission of Monterey, Point Cypress, Moss Beach, Pebble Beach, the Point Pinos Lighthouse, and the Pacific Grove, located on the ocean beach, five miles from the town. About five hundred persons, from all sections of the State, were there seen by the excursionists encamped for the summer, and living in tents and cottages. The tall pine-trees of the grove grow down to the water's edge, and appeal strongly to the tastes of the æsthetic. Surf bathing was indulged in by many of the visitors, and the old adobe convent, the Catholic church, and like curiosities and landmarks in the ancient town of Monterey also claimed a due share of attention. Purchasing a supply of abalone shells, the excursionists took the return train at 4.30 P. M., and arrived in the city soon after nine o'clock, witnessing on the way one of the brilliant and gorgeous sunsets so characteristic of the climate of California.

Private excursions were likewise made to Sacramento, Oakland, Vallejo, Alameda, Monterey, Yosemite, and other places, also to the petrified and redwood trees. The valleys at the north and the vineyards at the south alike rejoiced the hearts of California's guests.

San Francisco was thoroughly explored, — some climbing Russian and Telegraph Hills, enjoying the superb cable roads, lounging in Woodward's celebrated garden, visiting the Safe Deposit and Diamond Palace and other places of interest. The participating in the regular excursions, with the additional rambles which the Sir Knights and ladies made, enabled them to see very much of California, and to leave with a hearty wish to again visit the golden shore. When it is remembered that the Bostons were obliged to be in the city certain days for duty, it is a matter of surprise that they were enabled to see so much of the State. The hours were filled with duty or pleasure; no day or hour was permitted to run to waste, but, without error or disappointment, the various plans were carried out, and an uninterrupted season of pleasure and profit was enjoyed. It is not possible to describe all the tours in detail, or paint in words all the glorious scenes which greeted the eyes. Sufficient has, we trust, been rehearsed to re-enliven pleasant memories of the Templar excursions in California.

Wednesday evening, 22d of August, the grand banquet tendered by the Grand Commandery of California to Most Eminent Grand Master Benjamin Dean and the officers and members of the Grand Encampment of the United States took place at the Palace Hotel. About eight o'clock the guests, Sir Knights and gentlemen prominent in all the walks of life, assembled in the grand parlor, where they spent a most agreeable hour in cordial conversation while awaiting the summons like knights of old to the festive banquet board. There were present the Grand Encampment officers, the Grand Commandery of California, Eminent Sir John L. Stevenson, Boston Commandery, Sir Knights from near and afar, and gentlemen well known in all the leading movements of the day. About nine o'clock, Captain General Lloyd and his chief of staff, Past Grand Master Gould, marshalled the guests in line, and to the stirring strains of a grand march, performed by the Second Artillery band, they marched to the grand dining-room, the Sir Knights and officers presenting a beautiful sight in their gay trappings and gaudy uniforms.

The commodious dining-hall was beautifully arranged for the banquet. There were seven tables, and arrangements made for the accommodation of four hundred and fifty guests. The festive boards fairly glittered with crystal and polished silver ware. The ornaments were tasty, though not gaudy, being beautiful exotics, and clusters of choice, luscious fruits. There were royal and sefortia palms, artillery ferns, silver-leaved pandanus, coleus, and dracæna set at intervals along the tables, while smilax was strung in tasty curves and loops. About the halls were rich banners,— rich not only in material but rich in historical associations, carrying memory back for centuries, when Sir Knights, instead of gathering about tables decked with good cheer and resplendent with cut crystal and glittering silver, performed valiant deeds on arid plains, and refreshed themselves with frugal fare. There was the beautiful banner of the Grand Commandery of California, supported on the right by that of St. Albans, and on the left by that of St. Bernard. The rich banners of the various Commanderies in attendance upon the Conclave were grouped about the spacious dining-hall.

The *menu* was in the form of a four-page pamphlet with an ornamental cover. The front outside was covered with an elegant composite lithograph representing the great Yosemite Fall, and Big Trees, and underneath, an arch, spanning a view of the Golden Gate, with a mounted knight charging with his poised lance. In the centre, a Masonic key-stone, the face showing Templar devices against a Maltese cross. In the centre of the back outside was the heraldic device of Templarism. The first inner page showed a red passion cross at the top, underneath which was the inscription: "Grand Banquet given by the Commandery of California, complimentary to the M. E. Benjamin Dean, Grand Master, the Officers and Members of the Grand Encampment of the United States, Wednesday evening, August 22, 1883, Palace Hotel." The second page contained the *menu*. On the third page was the wine list, naming California wines almost exclusively. The fourth page contained the toasts proposed, with the names of the Sir Knights who were to respond to them.

Grand Commander George C. Perkins presided. Sir O. C. Wheeler, Prelate, invoked the Divine blessing. After the viands of the Palace had been fully discussed, the Grand Commander of California Knights Templars welcomed the guests as follows: —

Most Eminent Grand Master and Fratres: The California Knights, in accordance with that long-honored custom, desiring to show their respect and appreciation for their guests, have invited them to sit around the banqueting table with them, not because we offer you viands the products of this prolific soil, not because we offer you this wine, rich and fragrant, if not with age, it is with the odor of our friendship for you; it is not for this that the Grand Commandery of California has extended this banquet to the officers and members of the Grand Encampment of Knights Templars of the United States, but it is, in addition to all this — it is because we are proud to have you amongst us. It is a time which each of us in California realizes; it is a Conclave that our State has never witnessed before, where so many representative people from every part of the great sisterhood of States have visited California and this city on the Pacific coast. You have left your professional avocations and your commercial pursuits, and have come here to work together, advancing the best interests of the Order at whose sacred shrine we have all bowed. It is an occasion upon which we may congratulate ourselves upon having so many representative men among us here, who have come thousands and thousands of miles across dreary deserts, over the far Rocky Mountains, across the snow-clad Sierras to visit us here on our western shore. We welcome you most heartily. We hope when you return to your distant homes again that you will feel with us you have an abiding interest in the people of California. I assure you that wherever you go you will have our warm personal friendship and love for each and every one of you. [*Applause.*] California extends to you a most hearty, a most cordial greeting; and while we are proud of our own State, proud of all that nature has done for it, proud of our snow-capped mountains, proud of old Mount Shasta, towering up into the clouds, proud of our orange groves, fragrant with sweet odor and laden with luscious fruit, proud of our great plains, yielding fruits and cereals, supplying to-day the demands of Europe; but prouder far are we of our people, prouder are we of our Knights Templars, whose hearts respond with that generous friendship that they hope you feel for them. Such as we have, have we given unto you. As I said before, our wine is not as old in years, but if it had lived a century it might not be older in friendship than that we feel for you. [*Applause.*] We have done all we could for you. If any of you have lacked for personal attention to your wants, I assure you it is an error not of the head nor of the heart. Our Most Eminent Grand Master comes from one of the hubs, and California is the other hub, and all the other States make up the spokes and felloes, — a grand union and sisterhood of States that shall go on round and round till time shall be no more. [*Applause.*]

I remember when a boy our ancestors used to send missionaries away out in the islands of the Pacific, and I am also reminded of the fact that when the people of California, in their enterprise, not satisfied with the boundary of this golden shore which the Pacific continually lashes, went down to the islands of the Pacific and found some, more beautiful than Venice, luxuriant with eternal verdure, we found the Sandwich Islands, and we are now sweetening all this great Union. We are sweetening all of you, not only with our sugar, but we have sent down there and brought up one of the practical results that have come in the way of missionary work, — we brought up for you a Kanaka band that is giving you music. [*Laughter.*] As I said before, it is the only practical result that has come back to us from all that missionary work. Once more, my friends, once more, Most Eminent Grand Commander, we thank you for honoring California and our city with your presence, and I now propose this sentiment: "The Grand Encampment of the United States. The head of the Masonic chivalry, — brave and true as the knights of old."

Most Eminent Grand Master Dean in responding said: —

Right Eminent Grand Commander and Sir Knights: Our Right Eminent Grand Commander of California has been pleased to speak of Boston as one of the hubs of the universe, and of San Francisco as the other. I can only say that Boston, after this exhibition, will be truly proud to be at one end of the axle, just so long as San Francisco is at the other [*applause*]; and if anything could take place in the future that would equal the wonderful performance of the last thirty years, it will be the drilling of a hole from Boston to San Francisco to run the axle through, on which this universe shall work. [*Laughter.*] As long as you invite us here by such cards of invitation as I have received, to such a banquet as you now spread before us, then I say, let the deserts spread themselves, and let the alkali plains broaden in their extent; they cannot grow so broad but that we will come to see you. You have spoken, sir, of your vine-clad hills and of your plains, and I may add to them your cities. There is nothing that so strikes one on coming from the East for the first time, remembering as he does in his lifetime your short history, nothing so strikes one as so remarkable as this fine city, so magnificent, full in every respect, with its surroundings and its suburbs, of every possible convenience that belongs to civilized life. You have spoken not only of your hills and of your mountains, of your fruits and wines, but you have spoken of your men — of your men! Why, Right Eminent Grand Commander, there were men here before the Anglo-

Saxon came here. There were other men here, and they had their mines before the Anglo-Saxon came here, but what of it? The Spaniard came and he extended up into those beautiful regions, but what came of it? Nothing whatever. But when the Anglo-Saxon came from the Eastern coast, the gold could not be hidden from him. He took it from your plains and from your streams. He bored holes into your mountains, and he took it from the heart of your mountains. Then he washed your mountains clean in order to take every particle of gold from them. That exhibits the difference between peoples, and when we came here we could not but be surprised on finding such wonderful results of a mere change of the nationality of inhabitants. It is blood that tells. Blood will tell, and the blood of the East and the blood of the West, the blood of the Pacific and the blood of the Atlantic, will not be divided so long as lives the spirit of fraternity that leads to such entertainments as this. [*Applause.*] But I am reminded by your toast that I must speak of something else. I must make some reference to the institution to which we belong,— Knight Templary. What purpose does it serve? What is it? It is an Order of Christian knighthood. I remember once a yacht came into our Eastern waters, and on going into the cabin we found over the door in the owner's state-room the words, "Stand up for Jesus." He had to whistle up his courage by putting over his door these words That phrase has become quite common for the purpose of encouraging the faithful, lest they remain not true to their faith. Then what shall we say of a society that never needs any motto of that kind, that never needs to be told that you must have a motto to keep you faithful to the Christian religion, a society whose history goes back and emblazons it with everything that is brave and noble, a society with which the Christian religion is blended, embracing everything that belongs not only to gentle women, but to brave men? That, Right Eminent Grand Commander, is the fraternity of the Temple, and of Malta. We need no encouragement. We need not be told that so far as the Christian religion is concerned we have got to brave everything. It is associated in our breasts with the knights of old who went to the field of battle to defend the Christian religion by sword and battle-axe, clad in armor, not standing at rifle-shot distance, but braving the foe, face to face, shield to shield, sword to sword, and axe to axe. He then made brief reference to the ritual of the Knights of Malta, declaring that it best describes the duties of the Templars, the Hospitallers, and the Knights of Malta. With the age that gave them birth, their adventurous and warlike spirit has passed away; but their moral and beneficent character still remains, bright in all its primitive beauty and loveliness, to excite, as in the days of their greatest glory, that spirit of refined and moral chivalry which should prompt us to press onward in the cause of truth and justice, stimulate us to exertion in behalf of the destitute and the oppressed, to wield the sword, if need be, when pure and undefiled religion calls us in her defence and in a brother's cause to do all that may become men. They also teach the triumph of immortality; that though death has its sting, its infliction is but for a moment; that this frail organization, though here subject to the many "ills that flesh is heir to," possesses an ethereal principle that shall soar to the realms of endless bliss, and beyond the power of change live forever. Right Eminent Grand Master, I can only say, if this institution goes on and performs its apparent destiny, it will not only be a helpmeet to the church, but it will be a blessing to mankind.

To the toast, "Our Visiting Fratres," Deputy Grand Master Robert E. Withers said:—

Right Eminent Grand Master: By the inexorable fiat of the committee of arrangements, the pleasing yet arduous duty of giving expression to the feelings of this splendid array of Knights Templars has devolved upon me. Futile, indeed, will be the effort adequately to depict them. The tongue of inspiration and the "fine frenzy" of poetic fancy could alone hope to rise equal to the occasion. As the trumpet calls, the Sir Knights of the magnanimous and noble Order of the Temple have assembled from every State and Territory of this nationality. From the dark and sombre forests of the North, where Boreas, blustering railer, "ceases not to charm the ear with grand and solemn monotone"; from the rock-ribbed and wave-washed shores of the Atlantic, whose sounding surges ceaseless swell the sonorous diapason ; from the coral reefs of that beauteous land of flowers, where tropic breezes with melodious breath woo to hushed repose the willing senses of the languid listener; from vine-clad hill and rugged mountain side; from smiling savanna and alluvial plain ; from silent prairie and rustling woodland ; from the pellucid waters of our inland seas, and along the turbid tide of the rushing "father of waters"; from arid wastes and perforated mountain, where the delving miner with ponderous blow wrests from nature's stern embrace the precious ore and gives to civilization its glittering treasures, — from every country and from every clime we come, knowing no North, no South, no East, no West, separated by no sectional lines, divided by no political dogmas.

With hearts glowing with fraternal love, and hands tingling from the electric touch of the knightly greetings, this band of weary pilgrims, travelling from afar, has traversed the sands of the desert, bathed their aching limbs in the placid waters of the Dead Sea, escaladed those mighty ramparts which, snow-capped, guard the entrance to your El Dorado, until now we stand in sight and hearing of the gently rippling waters of the great Pacific, and pause to receive at your hands the typical bread and water. But now there seems to be a hitch in our ritual. We listen in vain for the greeting, "Silver and gold have we none." We find no bread in our scrip, no water in our cruise. On the contrary, from the gates of your city to your cards of courtesy, all is golden. Viands the most luscious are moistened by the potations of nectar which Hebe herself might have served. The corn of nourishment, the wine of refreshment, and the oil of joy are with lavish prodigality poured out for our delight. As peace is within your walls, so is plenteousness within your palaces. Our scant vocabulary fails us; we surrender. Whatever may hereafter befall us, whether our pathway is rough and rugged, or adorned by pleasant memories which will arise in after years and cheer our recollections, the remembrance of these knightly courtesies and this fraternal welcome, of these gorgeous pageants and this princely hospitality, will march in grand procession through the fields of memory, and hang a wreath of laurel on each feature of this

Triennial as they slowly pass. If it be true that one touch of nature makes the whole world kin, then have we brothers innumerable of every color and of every clime. There is a time which comes to all when all ranks shall be abolished, all distinctions done away; a time which it well behooves all Knights Templars to remember, even at the festive board, where hilarity abounds, when joyous greetings are exchanged, and when wit and laughter hold highest carnival. Even now let us recall the words of one of the poets of our Order: —

> "There 's a land where all are equal,
> We are hurrying toward it fast;
> We shall meet upon the level there,
> When the gates of death are passed.
> We shall stand before the Orient,
> And our Master shall be there
> To try the blocks we offer
> By his own unerring square."

To the toast, "Our Past Grand Masters," Sir John Q. A. Fellows, Past Grand Master, paid an eloquent tribute to the worth of those who had presided over the Encampment, declaring that "without the first of the Grand Masters, DeWitt Clinton, we might say the Order would not have had an existence. He and his contemporaries saw something in the institution that was worthy of preservation, and they perfected the organization and started the Order on its onward career." He went over the list of Grand Masters, bestowing words of praise, and maintained that so far as lay in their power they performed their duty faithfully and well.

"Masonic Law" was responded to by Past Grand Master James H. Hopkins, who said that —

God's law is one of regularity, of seed-time and harvest and plenteousness and beauty, and when these are absent it indicates that God's smile has been withdrawn, and as a consequence desolation and barrenness ensue. And so with our organization. We may expect to be overwhelmed and buried by a similar calamity unless we remember our obligations to the fundamental principles of Masonry. This earth on which we live and the innumerable stars that stud the sky above us, all move in their prescribed orbits, chanting the sublime anthem of the music of the spheres. If the law which holds each in its course were disturbed, a wreck of matter and a crash of worlds would fill all space with darkness and despair. So Masonry, the one institution, and the only one, that looms up in the gloom of prehistoric centuries, and which towers its head above all the civil institutions of to-day, owes its perpetuity and power to the steadfast adherence of its members to its fundamental principles and laws. And the law of Masonry is not enforced by physical power, but its potency consists in the fact that its essential element is love. That, Right Eminent Sir, opens a theme which I dare not discuss to-night. [*Applause.*]

"Knight Templarism" evoked an eloquent response from Sir Knight N. Greene Curtis, in the course of which he said:—

Our mystic swords are always leaping from their scabbards in the defence of the innocent, the oppressed, and the distressed, but should the time just spoken of ever occur, the keen ring of the old Damascus steel will be heard all over the land, from the orange groves in the South to the throne of the snow-capped peaks of old Maine, the valiant Knights walking shoulder to shoulder, fighting for the grand old flag again. I told you a few minutes ago to watch our Grand Commander. I am not certain but he will have me before a court-martial of Sir Knights for divulging a secret. He intends to place a silver cup in your sacks when you start away, and he will demand of you some Benjamin to be returned.

Most Eminent Sir Benjamin Dean, the Grand Master: "I'll come back."

Sir Knight Curtis: "I know you will, and stay with us." [*Laughter.*] Continuing he said:—

Sir Knights, I believe you understand the great principles of the Order too well for me to attempt to illustrate them. Charity. Oh! that a Mason should require any other Mason to tell him the beauties of charity. You all understand that. When you leave us, remember that we have an abiding faith in the principles of our Order; that the light that flows from the Star of Bethlehem has warmed the heart and illumined the path of every Christian warrior. Then let our lives be that of the Christian soldier, and when the grim old tyrant issues his command, "Sir Knight, halt! disarm!" then you will hear, as I hope and believe, the Grand Master, saying, "Come up into the asylum and receive your reward." The toil-worn pilgrim and the battle-scarred warrior will find in that asylum eternal rest. [*Applause.*]

"The American Pioneer" was responded to by Sir Peter Dean, who spoke eloquently of the pioneer discoverers, of all ages, and paid a tribute to the worth of the men who came to this coast in '49.

To the toast, "The Key-stone State," accompanied by the sentiment, "May the key-stone of Masonry never drop out," Sir J. P. Gobin, of Pennsylvania, the Grand Captain General, responded, and Sir John W. Simons, the Grand Treasurer, reviewed "The Past, Present, and Future."

"The Grand Commanderies of our Sister Jurisdictions," was honored by Grand Recorder Theodore S. Parvin; and Past Grand Commander Enoch T. Carson, of Ohio, responded to the toast, "Masonic Lore." Sir Henry Vallentine honored "The Twenty-second Triennial Conclave in San Francisco"; and Sir Vance Knight, of Rhode Island, paid his devotions to "Woman, God bless her." Past Grand Commander Love then, in a few brief sentences, dismissed the banqueters, who parted after singing "Auld Lang Syne."

The ticket of invitation to this complimentary banquet given to the Grand Master was a plate of solid gold, five inches long and three wide, upon the upper left-hand corner of which was a raised oval, on which was enamelled the portrait of the Grand Master. On the right upper corner was the coat-of-arms of the Grand Encampment of the United States, enamelled in colors. The plate bore the following inscription: —

M∴ E∴ Sir Benjamin Dean, Grand Master Knights Templars of the United States:

The Grand Commandery of California requests the honor of your presence, together with the officers and members of the Grand Encampment of the United States, at a banquet to be given at the Palace Hotel on Wednesday evening, Aug. 22, 1883, at eight o'clock.

G. C. PERKINS, *Grand Commander.*

On the other side of the plate was engraved the following: —

GRAND BANQUET.

Committee — M. J. Keating, chairman; James Simpson, vice-chairman; F. H. Day, secretary; Samuel Foster, Thomas M. O'Brien, C. F. Bassett.

The plate was made from gold obtained from Grass Valley quartz, such as is used in the manufacture of jewelry.

Californians spoke of the banquet as surpassing in splendor everything before attempted in the city of San Francisco.

On Wednesday, the 22d, the following invitation was sent to the headquarters of the various Grand and Subordinate Commanderies represented in San Francisco, and personal invitations were extended to as many Sir Knights and their ladies as possible.

OF

KNIGHTS TEMPLARS.

PALACE HOTEL, SAN FRANCISCO, CAL.,
Aug. 22, 1883.

Boston Commandery Knights Templars will cordially welcome the Sir Knights and their ladies at a Templar reception, in the ladies' parlors, first floor, Palace Hotel, Thursday evening, Aug. 23, 1883, at eight o'clock.

Courteously yours,

John L. Stevenson,
Eminent Commander.

S. H. Thomas,
Recorder.

Thursday, at 11 A. M., Marysville Commandery, No. 7, tendered a breakfast to the Most Eminent Grand Master and the officers of the Grand Encampment, at the Palace Hotel. Several members of Boston Commandery were invited, but pressing duties detained them. The Prelate, Rev. O. A. Roberts, represented the Commandery by request of the Eminent Commander. Judge P. W. Keyser, Grand Generalissimo of the Grand Encampment, presided. The tables were arranged in the form of a passion cross, and were elaborately decorated with tropical plants, flowers, and smilax. Among other prominent guests

AT THE CONCLAVE IN SAN FRANCISCO.

were Gov. Stoneman, Mayor Bartlett, and Ex-Gov. Perkins. The music was furnished by the Hussar Band, of Sacramento, which accompanied Marysville Commandery on its pilgrimage. The presiding officer proposed the health of the Grand Master and Grand Officers of the United States, which was drunk with enthusiasm. The *menu*, which presented a very neat appearance, was complete in all its details. The breakfast was provided with the same generous hospitality which marked the receptions of the Sir Knights of California during the Conclave.

At the close of the Conclave, Marysville Commandery presented each lady who accompanied Boston Commandery with a beautiful souvenir. It consisted of a card of four pages. On the first page was the monogram of Marysville Commandery, No. 7, Knights Templars, with the words, "Souvenir, Triennial Conclave, San Francisco, 1883." The second page contained Templar emblems and the names of the officers, Past Commanders, and members of Marysville Commandery. The third contained a beautiful picture of Marysville Buttes. In the foreground there was represented a partially wooded shore, on whose open places were several Sir Knights mounted, beyond which a river flowed. On the opposite shore was Marysville, situated on a gently sloping hillside, while the jagged mountains forming the background rose far beyond.

The reception given by Boston Commandery in the grand parlors of the Palace, in accordance with the foregoing invitation, was a grand success. The three parlors, engaged for the week by the Grand Commandery of California at an expense of eighty dollars a day, were kindly given up for this reception. The rooms are furnished with drab, crimson, and blue furniture, curtains, etc., and are the finest in this finest of hotels. The middle and largest parlor is fifty feet square, and lighted by five eight-light chandeliers. There are two smaller parlors, one on each side of the large parlor. The Commandery further beautified them by elaborate decorations. In the large parlor there was a very large ball of flowers suspended from each chandelier, and the ceilings, cornices, and chandeliers were festooned with smilax. There are two large mirrors in the principal parlor. Across the larger were the words, forming an arch, "Boston Commandery." Beneath, in the centre, a cross and crown, the former of white and the latter of scarlet flowers. On the left, "1769"; on the right, "1883." Under the cross and crown were two crossed swords of white stock flowers. On the left, a large Maltese cross of scarlet geraniums on a white ground; on the right, a triple cross of violets on a white ground. On the mantel there was a great mat of beautiful flowers and smilax. In front of the second mirror, which is opposite the entrance to the parlors, was the word "Welcome," in stock flowers, and underneath it a Maltese cross of scarlet flowers with a green border. Below the cross were the words "Sir Knights," in white and scarlet. A pyramid of flowers nearly four feet high stood upon the floor immediately in front of the mirror. Bouquets of crimson tacsonia and agapanthus and Jacqueminot roses, great vases supporting pot plants in bloom, palm-trees, and stars of flowers upon the walls, completed the finest decoration seen in any one parlor during the Conclave. They were admired by all. The Royal Hawaiian Band was present, and called together a crowd filling the corridors and much of the court below. They gave selections of instrumental music, and also sang specimens of their national songs. Their strange melodies, now dolorous, then rapturous, were listened to with pleasure by hundreds of the people who gathered in the corridor before the parlor.

A vocal quartet added to the enjoyment of the evening. Mrs. Tippett, who formerly sang in the Old South Church, was present,

AT THE CONCLAVE IN SAN FRANCISCO. 259

and gave her well-rendered selections for the pleasure of the guests. Mr. Tippett and Mr. Mayer also took part in the entertainment. Refreshments, which were abundant and well served, were provided in a large dining-room upon the same floor as the reception parlors. From 8 to 11 P. M. it was a procession of guests, who first paid their respects to the Eminent Commander, who, with Mrs. Stevenson and Past Grand Master Dean and Mrs. Dean, stood in front of the larger mirror. Immediately the guests mingled in a happy way, and cordial sociability marked the fleeting hours.

Among the guests were Gov. Stoneman, of California, Gens. Dimon and Carr, of the National Guard of California, Col. Harding, the Russian consul, Charles Brooks, of San Francisco, Gov. Trippet, of Arizona, and Chas. B. Rutherford, Esq., of Oakland. The various Commanderies were well represented by Sir Knights and ladies, as were also the Grand Commanderies and Encampment.

Among the many pleasant little affairs was the presentation to Sir Knight Dr. H. A. Tucker, of Brooklyn, N. Y., of a Knight Templar's cross of California quartz, with native gold fastenings for the watch-chain, by one of the doctor's friends.

At ten o'clock a march was played by the band, and the ladies and gentlemen, in couples, threes, and groups, repaired to the banquet-hall, where liveried waiters served the guests. Here fruits, wines, and every delicacy of the season were spread, and all were partaken of freely. Even the dishes on the table were so arranged that long strings of vines were woven around, and formed squares, stars, several styles of crosses, and other Masonic emblems, with a centre here, a base there, or a crowning on the figures made of bright flowers.

As midnight came the guests retired, well pleased with the reception given by Boston Commandery.

The delicious fruit used on this occasion was a present to the Commandery, and was accompanied by the following note:—

BOHEMIAN CLUB, SAN FRANCISCO,
Aug. 24, 1883.

EMINENT SIR J. L. STEVENSON,
Eminent Commander Boston Commandery:

Sir Knight,—Please accept the accompanying boxes of fruit with the compliments of

Yours courteously,

J. E. TIPPETT.

Of the reception given by Boston Commandery at the Palace, the *Bulletin* remarked: "It was one of the most carefully arranged affairs of all that have been given, complete in every detail." And the *Chronicle:* "Though each reception and social gathering given and received by the Knights merits the praise bestowed, none are more deserving of praise than the reception of the Boston Commandery given to friends last evening at the Palace."

CHAPTER XV.

Friday, the 24th of August, was set apart to "the memory of our dead President," and was made the occasion of a military and civic pageant which proceeded to Golden Gate Park, where the corner-stone of a "monument to the nation's martyr was laid, with elaborate Masonic ceremonies." The people crowded every thoroughfare; every available place from which to view the procession was occupied. Good order prevailed; the weather was delightful for marching, and perfect success crowned the efforts of the Garfield Monument Association. The project of erecting this monument first took form Sept. 24, 1881. On the thirtieth day of that month a preliminary organization was effected, and Oct. 3, 1881, the Garfield Monument Association was organized. Subscriptions were immediately secured, which on the day of laying the corner-stone amounted to twenty-five thousand dollars. The statue will represent President Garfield standing with hands crossed before him, one holding a half-opened manuscript. The figure will be of bronze, of colossal size, standing on a pedestal of Penryn granite, the whole being twenty-four feet high. The front will be inscribed with the name "Garfield." Below, on one of the steps on which the pedestal stands, will be a bronze figure of Columbia weeping; on either side bronze eagles and the national shield, and on the latter prominent events of the President's life will be inscribed.

It was eminently fit that this solemn service should occur during Conclave week, for President Garfield was a Knight Templar. Columbia Commandery, No. 2, of the District of Columbia, the Commandery of which President Garfield was an active member, bearing the only national colors in the Templar parade, was represented by several Sir Knights, who formed an interesting feature of the fine procession.

Most Eminent Sir Benjamin Dean, Grand Master, in his report to the Grand Encampment, after speaking of the death of President Garfield, and his attendance (accompanied by many Eminent Sir Knights) upon the obsequies and the final deposit of the remains at Cleveland, Ohio, continues:—

> The President's remains had been accompanied from Elberon, the place of his death, to Washington, attended during the lying in state in Washington, and accompanied thence to Cleveland, Ohio, by his fellow-members of Columbia Commandery, whose devotion to their lost comrade challenges our admiration. Thus ended the career of a great man, cut off in the midst of his usefulness.
>
> From Nov. 19, 1861, when on his thirtieth birthday he was made an entered apprentice in Magnolia Lodge, No. 20, in Columbus, Ohio, he had been an active Mason.
>
> There is something singularly striking in the manner of his death. He had passed through the dangers of a long war without injury. Seldom has there been a life of more striking contrasts. Born in obscurity, he became famous; under every disadvantage, he became learned; a scholar, he became a soldier; from "the applause of listening senates" he passed to the magistracy of a mighty Republic.
>
> President Garfield said "the unexpected always happened to him." Dreadful and true was this in the manner of his taking off. The choice of

a nation, with all his blushing honors thick upon him, was slain by the hand of a lunatic.

> "A falcon towering in her pride of place
> Was by a mousing owl hawked at and killed."

He has been called a martyr. This is in no sense correct. A martyr is one sacrificed at the demand of a strong opposition Garfield had the good-will of all. Of him dead it is well said, "Such a spectacle has never before been presented as the mourning with which the whole civilized world is honoring the late President Garfield. Emperors and kings, senates and ministries, are in spirit his pall-bearers; but their people, from the highest to the lowest, claim to be equally visible and audible as sorrowing assistants."

The tender sympathy of the Queen of Great Britain and Empress of India was not merely a tribute to a departed ruler and his sorrowing widow; it was also in honor of departed worth. Who can estimate the value to the world of the example of such a life? Who the value to this Republic?

> "The rank is but the guinea's stamp,
> The man 's the gowd for a' that."

The pageant was formed in four divisions: military, the Grand Army of the Republic, the Templars, and Ancient Free and Accepted Masons. The military division was composed of the National Guard and United States troops, batteries, regiments of artillery, San Francisco Hussars, and Governor's Guard. The second division, of Grand Army Posts, was very large, containing nearly two thousand veterans. The Templar division was brilliant with its long array of Knights. The representatives of President Garfield's Commandery followed the Grand Commandery of California as a guard of honor. This division attracted the most attention apparently, and received the most liberal applause. It seemed as if all San Francisco had assembled to do honor to the

Knights. The last division was headed by the Grand Consistory, Ancient and Accepted Rite, led by the Union Gatling Band. There were eighty members of the Consistory in full uniform, whose rich colors, resplendent emblems, and gold jewels were very attractive. Rose Croix Knights followed, marching in the form of a square, enclosing eight carriages containing Masons who have received the thirty-third degree. The Royal Arch Masons followed, having in line a magnificent representation of the Ark of the Covenant on a decorated platform car drawn by four horses handsomely caparisoned.

The Ark of California Chapter, No. 5, of Royal Arch Masons, is probably the most elaborate, beautiful, and costly structure of the kind ever used by a Masonic body. It is probably as near a *fac-simile* of the Ark of the Covenant as human hands ever devised. It is made of brass, covered inside and out with pure gold; the cherub upon the top is also covered with gold, as well as the rods by which it is borne. It has been universally admired as a work of art. When carried in public procession it is always the centre of attraction. It was designed by the late Sir Samuel Graves, and constructed by the most skilful workmen in San Francisco. Its cost was twenty-five hundred dollars.

The Grand Lodge of California was then followed by the various Lodges of the city, who marched by twos, forming a line that extended for squares. The procession was grand, inspiring, imposing. It had not the beauty, precision, and splendor of the Templar procession of Monday preceding, but it was doubtless the longest ever seen in San Francisco. There were about twenty-five thousand persons in the procession. The highways to the park were filled with people, and during the ceremony the park was literally jammed with people. The impressive ceremonies of laying the corner-stone passed off satisfactorily, under the direction of the Grand Commandery of California, and according to the Masonic ritual. After prayer and an ode sung by the Masonic choir, the Garfield Monument Association, through its vice-president, Hon. Horace Davis, invited Most Worshipful Clay W. Taylor, the Grand Master of Masons in California, to lay the corner-stone of the monument. The Grand Master accepted the duty in a short address, and, with solemnity and sympathy, the stone was duly laid. After which, Sir Henry E. Highton, Grand Orator of the Grand Lodge of California, A. F. and A. M., delivered a eulogy upon the deceased President. At its conclusion the procession was dismissed, and the thousands wended cityward, grateful that this memorial work had been so auspiciously commenced.

Saturday, the time for the competitive drill, dawned beautifully, with the promise of a suitable day. Five magnificent prizes were offered by the San Francisco Triennial Committee. St. Bernard, of Chicago, Raper, of Indianapolis, and De Molay, of Louisville, were booked for the competition.

The conditions of the drill were as follows: —

First. That no California Commandery should compete.

Second. The trophy becomes the property of the Commandery winning it, which means that California makes an out-and-out gift of a magnificent present to the best men.

Third. The schedule of movements prepared was not known to the Commanderies until it was read off in orders by the commanding officers.

Fourth. The judges selected were not known to the competitors until they appeared on the ground.

The judges were Col. Alanson M. Randal, ranking captain of the First United States Artillery; Major Joseph P. Sanger, commander of the Light Battery of the Fourth Artillery of the United States Army, and First Lieut. John K. M. Davis, adjutant of the First Artillery Regiment, United States Army, who were present in full uniform, and discharged their duties with satisfaction to all.

The Bay District track was selected as the place for the trial. Each Commandery was obliged to drill with at least twenty-seven men. The Rapers drilled first, the St. Bernards second, and the De Molays last. At 12 M., the hour appointed, the Rapers marched on to the track, headed by the First United States Cavalry band, and saluted the judges. The order of evolutions having been given the commander by the judges, the Rapers proceeded to their work,—falling into line, marching, wheeling, breaking up, attention, dressing, sword manual, etc.,—during which the spectators several times enthusiastically cheered. Subsequently, but not as a part of the competition, the Rapers exhibited fancy movements, triangles, crosses, squares, etc., when the applause was universal and hearty. The Commandery also gave an exhibition of drill by bugle call, and seemed as proficient as in drilling by orders.

When the Rapers retired, the St. Bernards, headed by Lyons and Healy's band, filed into the enclosure. The method of procedure was as before, and the movements of the Commandery, its manual of arms, exercise, and fancy drill, called forth similar applause.

After the St. Bernards, the De Molays, headed by the Eighth Infantry band, appeared, and went through the evolutions as arranged by the judges. This Commandery elicited great applause, doing its work with wonderful precision and promptness. Each figure of its fancy manœuvres brought forth prolonged cheering. The crowd was immense. Good order prevailed, and the competition was pronounced a grand success.

The exercises of the week closed with the awarding of the prizes at Mechanics' Pavilion, on Saturday, at 8 P. M. At that hour eight thousand people were seated in the Pavilion, and "standing room only" could be obtained by thousands of others. The De Molays occupied an hour in exhibiting their manœuvres, and at 9 P. M. the ceremony of presentation began.

Grand Captain General Lloyd then advanced, and, calling the three Commanders up to the stage, he asked, "Eminent Commanders, are you all satisfied with the manner in which the drill was conducted?" They answered, "We are." The Grand Captain General then turned to the audience, speaking as follows: —

Ladies and Gentlemen: As you are all aware, the Triennial Committee selected some time ago three competent men, officers in the United States Army, to be judges of the competitive drill. Their names were kept from the public, so that the matter could be carried on entirely without any influence being brought to bear in the slightest degree to in any manner swerve their judgment in this matter. They are men of high standing and are entirely competent to fulfil the duties they have undertaken. I may say they are the peers of any in the United States. They have fulfilled their duty and are now ready to announce their judgment.

Ladies and gentlemen, I ask you to remain as quiet as possible until the entire award is read.

Ladies and gentlemen, I take pleasure in introducing to you Col. R. M. Randal, chairman of the committee of awards.

Having concluded, he retired, but returned immediately, leading Col. A. M. Randal, of the United States Army, the chief of the committee on awards, and introduced him to the Eminent Commanders. The colonel, producing the decision of the judges, read as follows: —

SAN FRANCISCO, CAL., Aug. 25, 1883.

To the Triennial Committee of California Grand Commandery, of California:

GENTLEMEN,—The judges of the competitive drill of Knights Templars, held this day, have the honor to recommend that the competing Commanderies be ranked in the following order of merit: No. 1, De Molay Commandery, of Louisville, Ky.; No 2, Raper Commandery, of Indianapolis, Ind.; No. 3, St. Bernard Commandery, of Chicago, Ill. The judges take this opportunity to congratulate the competing Commanderies and the Conclave of Knights Templars assembled in San Francisco upon their great efficiency in drill upon this occasion.

COL. A. M. RANDAL,
MAJOR J. P. SANGER, } *Judges.*
LIEUT. J. K. M. DAVIS,

When he read, "No. 1, De Molay, of Louisville, Ky.," a wild and prolonged shout went up that seemed to lift the Pavilion itself; then "No. 2, Raper Commandery, of Indianapolis, Ind.," was as warmly welcomed; and last, "No. 3, St. Bernard Commandery, of Chicago, Ill.," received a hearty and warm applause.

The De Molays, being awarded No. 1, the Commander was instructed to make his selection from the five prizes offered. He selected "The Vase and the Miner." Applause followed, which was supplemented by the peculiar cheer of the De Molays. Then the Rapers, awarded the second choice, through their Commander, made the second selection, and chose the "Mounted Knight and the Column." The audience cheered again, supplemented by the Rapers' "hurrah" and the De Molay's "refrain." St. Bernards, awarded the third choice, as their selection pointed out the "Globe and the Knight in Armor." Once more the audience cheered, and the Commanderies likewise supplemented the applause. Immediately after, the three Commanders advanced to the centre, extended their right hands, and shook heartily, burying whatever feeling of rivalry may have existed between them.

Hon. N. Greene Curtis, of Sacramento, then presented to the competing Commanderies the prizes selected by them. Each Commander in accepting the prize made an appropriate reply. In conclusion Mr. Curtis bid all the Sir Knights farewell in the following words:—

California has done all she could to make your visit pleasant, to make you feel that you were with your friends, that we met you with warm hearts, that we were glad when you came, and that we are sorry when you go; and fellow Sir Knights, who have travelled from gallant old Massachusetts away over here to the Pacific, coming from the rocky hills of New England, from the great Middle States, from the prairies of the West, from the savannas of the South, from the lakes to the gulf, it must have been pleasing to you to come over here and find that the pioneers ahead of you had established a mighty empire.

We are proud of our Commonwealth. We are proud of our agriculture, of our commerce and manufactures,— three great elements constituting a great State. We are proud of our gallant men, of our —oh! beautiful ladies. [*Laughter and applause.*] We are proud of our princely residences, our cosy cottages, and our happy homes. We are proud of the ore in our mountains, yielding up its treasures to reward the horny-handed sons of toil. We are proud of our valleys, where the grain grows in golden luxuriance, gladdening the hearts of the husbandmen. We are proud of our orchards, our vineyards, our flocks and herds. We are proud of our schools and our churches. We are proud of our Eden home out here, and would be glad if you could stay and see more of us. You have seen us in our city life. Go with us to the country, and see us there. There is one proud consolation that we are all American citizens. We all live under the same flag,— even all have our happy homes here in one common country.

Fratres, it is the earnest prayer of every Christian Knight that no conflict will ever occur in our broad, free, and beautiful country. If it should, the soldier Knights would be turned instantly into the soldiers of our country, for under this Constitution and this government we are protected in our rights; and let us remember, by all that is pure, holy, and sacred, to uphold the integrity of these things by our faith, by our liberty, by our love of law, by the memories of our dead heroes and patriots, by our Washington, Warren, and Montgomery, by the blood of all those men who fought and died for our liberties, to stand by our old flag for ever and ever.

In your capacity as Knights Templars never draw your swords in the cause of wrong or oppression, but be ever ready to draw them in defence of the innocent, the helpless, and the distressed. And should it ever happen that you have to draw your swords, the enemies of the Christian religion will find that you are ready to die as your fathers died for the faith your foes denied. Now, Sir Knights, if we should never meet again, tell our brethren over there in the East that you have knelt at our altars, and that the incense burns as pure upon them to-day as it did in the days when old Peter the Hermit preached the Crusades, and that we will ever keep its sacred flame.

If we never meet again, if the grim tyrant should pronounce his command, "Halt, Sir Knight, disarm!" and order you into the little green tent whose curtains never outward swing, then we hope, we have the right to believe — for we cling to our faith with all the tenacity of spiritual life — that we shall realize the dying Christian's hope of a home in heaven. And if we never meet here again, Sir Knights, when our Great Captain shall call us to the grand asylum not made with hands, may we all meet there and enjoy that eternal rest vouchsafed to the toil-worn pilgrim and the battle-scarred soldier of Jesus Christ. Forever may this grand old Order flourish.

When you go home, Sir Knights, tell the people how you were met, and how you were treated, and I know that when the St. Bernard Commandery gets back to Chicago, you will remember the fratres here with the same kindly feeling that we cherish towards you.

Again, Sir Knights, thanking you for your presence at this Conclave, and assuring you of the love and confidence of your fratres and the respect of the whole community, when you must go we bid you God speed and farewell. [*Applause.*]

AT THE CONCLAVE IN SAN FRANCISCO.

Immediately at the conclusion of the farewell address, California Commandery, No. 1, was presented with a handsomely engraved slab of marble, commemorative of the Triennial Conclave of 1883, by Mrs. A. E. Austin. The gift was accepted by the Commandery, and an appropriate reply was made by Sir Knight Day, of the Californias.

The order for the grand march was then given, music arose, and sociability ruled the closing hours of the Twenty-second Triennial Conclave.

Saturday the Sir Knights of Boston Commandery spent most of the day in preparing for their departure, especially in packing the souvenirs of their California pilgrimage. At 5 P. M., by special invitation, they visited the headquarters of California Commandery, No. 1, whose receptions in Platt's Hall had been continuous during the Conclave. At the appointed hour the various Commanderies in the city and the Ancient and Accepted Rite nearly filled the large hall. The assemblage was called to order by the chairman of the reception committee, who introduced Judge Bromley, of San Francisco, the Mark Twain of California. After his funny speech, Past Grand Master Dean was called upon. He made a short address pertinent to the occasion, remarking that while sitting at his dinner with the Eminent Commander of Boston Commandery, he was waited upon by his brother Peter in behalf of California Commandery, No. 1, requesting his attendance here to cut one of California's mammoth watermelons. Now, his brother Peter could always command him, and without him, if a watermelon could n't, California Commandery could. So he instantly obeyed, accompanied by Brother Stevenson. Now this was a pleasant episode. In fact, we have had many such. One was the presentation to Eminent Sir Stevenson, for Boston Commandery, of an

American eagle, captured at Wallace, N. M. Now, in the Orders of the Knights of Rhodes and of Malta there was a very distinguished office, second in rank in the English language, the first of them being that of Turcopilier, occupied by a succession of distinguished Knights. The office was Bailli de Aquila, or the Bailli of the Eagle. Now, Boston Commandery in its pilgrimage to the Golden Gate having been presented with a live American eagle, in order that it may be cared for with the dignity that ought to attend the national bird, and being freed from constitutional restraint, it is not an unfit procedure to nominate our Eminent Commander Stevenson to the newly re-established office, on this side the Atlantic, of Bailli de Aquila. He therefore took great pleasure in appointing Eminent Sir Knight Stevenson to the office of Bailli de Aquila. He would also call upon him to perform the duty of cutting this splendid specimen of California fruit. When you have seen and heard Brother Stevenson, you will recognize the fitness of this appointment.

The Bailli de Aquila was called for and received with cheers. He made a speech, not of the "eagle" order, but especially thanking the Grand Commandery of California, all the Sir Knights, ladies, and citizens of San Francisco and California, for the more than hospitable reception that Boston Commandery had received. Immediately this officer proceeded to cut an eighty-eight pound watermelon, which was soon disposed of, and the seeds were scattered among the audience, to be preserved for planting in the various States represented. After cheers, hand-shakings, and fraternal words, the Bostons withdrew to their headquarters at the Palace Hotel.

Previous to leaving San Francisco, Eminent Commander Stevenson directed Sir Z. H. Thomas, the recorder, to tender his personal thanks and the thanks of the Boston Commandery to the Triennial Conclave Committee, to California Commandery, No. 1,

Oakland Commandery, No. 11, Golden Gate Commandery, No. 16, the railroad officials, the managers of the Palace Hotel, and the citizens generally, through the Sunday *Chronicle*, of San Francisco, for the unbounded kindness, courteous and true knightly hospitality shown them on their reception and during their stay in San Francisco.

The treatment and accommodations received by the Bostons at the Palace were very satisfactory to the Commandery. The committee drew a check for over eight thousand dollars to pay the hotel bill of the Commandery for the eleven days of our stay, which, with the individual bills paid the hotel, amounted to over ten thousand dollars, constituting probably the largest amount ever paid to one establishment by any Commandery for entertainment.

The bugle call at 7 P. M. summoned the Sir Knights to their posts, preparatory to their departure. The alignement being made, the Commandery marched to the large court below, and formed in a hollow square. Past Grand Master Dean, accompanied by Most Eminent Grand Master Robert E. Withers, of Virginia, entered the square, and the former introduced the Grand Master to Boston Commandery, which received him with the proper military salute. The Grand Master thanked Boston Commandery for the compliment of the salute, and congratulated them on their successful pilgrimage across the continent, on their fine appearance on parade, and thanked them for the knightly and courteous conduct which had especially marked their stay in San Francisco. The command was then given "Threes right! march!" and Boston Commandery, taking Past Grand Master Dean, and Past Grand Master Hopkins, of Pennsylvania, under escort, commenced their homeward pilgrimage, being escorted by California Commandery, No. 1, to Oakland Ferry. The column was led by the Gatling Cornet Band, which played appropriate airs, — "One Wide River," "Home, Sweet Home," and "Auld Lang Syne."

On leaving the hotel court rounds of applause were given by the crowds. It was repeated at many points on the line of march. On the ferry-boat a congratulatory speech was made by Col. Sherman, of Oakland, which awakened much enthusiasm. He said that even the trees of California, and the great pines of Yosemite, all bend toward Bunker Hill and Plymouth Rock. The special train of Boston Commandery was in waiting on the Oakland side, which the Sir Knights and ladies boarded, and were off for Boston. Previous to our leaving Oakland, friends from San Francisco placed on board of the Eminent Commander's car, as complimentary to the Commandery, a colossal Maltese cross of scarlet and white flowers. The foundation was white, with a scarlet Christian cross in the centre, the arms bearing in scarlet the words, "Pleasant trip home, B. C. and ladies." At Oakland, Companion Chas. B. Rutherford, formerly of Salisbury, Mass., and wife, and other friends came to the station, who, having bestowed upon the travellers "corn, wine, and oil," bade them "God speed." At 9 P. M. the train started, and passing through Oakland, hastened toward Sacramento.

CHAPTER XVI.

The Sacramento *Bee*, of the 28th of August, contained the following editorial, suggested by the many train-loads of Templars hastening homeward: —

Yesterday the plumed Knights turned their backs reluctantly upon the golden coast. They came, in many cases, unwillingly. The journey was long; it more resembled a veritable pilgrimage or a real crusade than any undertaking in the history of the Grand Body. It was over mountain and desert, it was through many a stretch of wilderness, it was in somewhat of peril, too; but they came, to find a land where the rose and lily combine in a beauty that would have soothed the love-sick sorrow of Calypso; they reached a coast where the ocean counts its pulse-beats on near a thousand miles of beach and cliff, but where on sunlit bays the tides come and go as gently as the breathing of a child; they found a land where nature always smiles, and the garners are full of corn and the cups brim with wine; and they go home to carry back such tales as were told of old by pilgrims to the promised land. With the name of California the world associates generous wealth and sumptuous hospitality, and our visitors can certify to the verity of our fame.

As for us, we are lonesome. The Conclave has been a holiday. We long for some stranger on whom to wreak our hospitality. We have had the first chance to lavish upon many the social capacities heretofore displayed to the few, and as hosts, it can, without egotism, be declared we are a success. But it is hard to take down the banners, strip the decorations, and look upon the

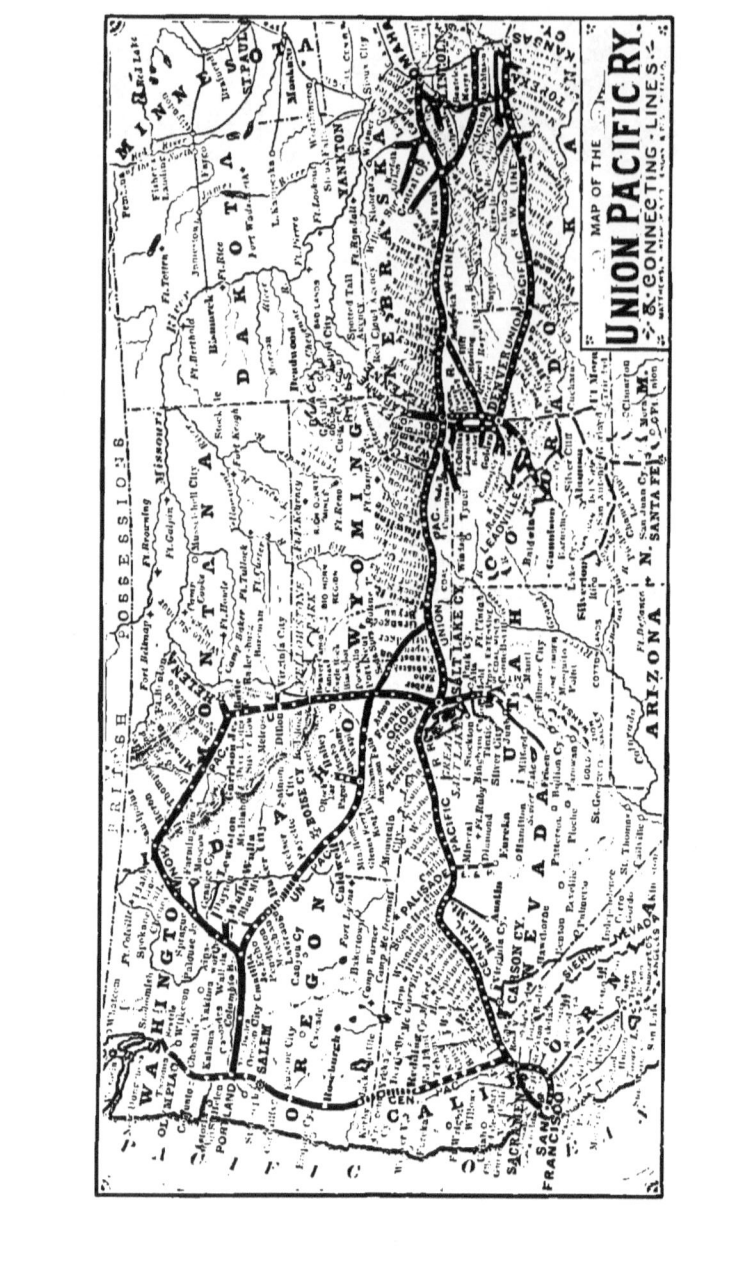

streets now given over to prosy commerce, which lately shook under the tread of belted men, and to hear only the rattle of trucks where lately brass music volleyed and thundered. After so much plume and baldric, so much embroidered cloak and vestment, the plain crowd in business suits does not stimulate the vision; but we cannot have the pilgrims always with us, and so must put the high and mighty days behind us, and begin to figure on the harvest, the vintage, and take up the great problem of daily bread where we dropped it to take this week's holiday with the Knights, who bring their diction, their ritual, and their good clothes down from the traditions of Malta and Jerusalem.

Passing San Pablo and Vallejo Junction, running thirty-two miles, we reached the Straits of Carquinez, which are about one and a half miles wide. To cross these, the train was run on to the "Solano," the largest steam ferry-boat in the world. This mammoth boat is 424 feet long, 116 feet extreme width, 18 feet 5 inches high in centre. She is propelled by two vertical steam engines capable of two thousand horse-power each, and has eight steel boilers with a heating surface of 9,816 feet. She registers $3,541\frac{31}{100}$ tons. There are four tracks over her entire length, with the capacity of forty-eight freight or twenty-four passenger cars. A million and a half feet of lumber were used in her construction, each of the four timbers in her keelson measuring 4,032 feet. Safely crossing the straits, we hastened homeward, reaching Sacramento, the junction of Sacramento and American Rivers, at about midnight. We looked out into the darkness, wishing to see once more, at least, the face of Sir Knight Petrie, of Sacramento, Deputy Grand Commander of Grand Commandery of California, who was among the first to greet us at Merced, and the last to say good by under the Palace arch as the Bostons were marching to the ferry-boat. He was unremitting in his kindnesses and industry during the occupation of San Francisco by the Templar army. Proceeding, we climbed the mountains, and morning brought us the charming view from Cape Horn,

LOOKING UP AT CAPE HORN.

seventy miles from Sacramento. The train stopped on the cape to give all an opportunity to realize and enjoy the scene. The mountain-side is precipitous, and the American River, appearing like a thread of silver, traced its circuitous way two thousand five hundred feet beneath us. Far above and behind us the black mountain crests were lifted, and beneath and before us trees waved and waters flowed. We seemed to be between heaven and earth. On the mountain-side, where from its steepness no Indian trail could

AMERICAN RIVER CAÑON.

run, a road-bed has been well constructed, whereon, swiftly and safely, living freight is carried from shore to shore.

For twelve hundred miles eastward the road is continued at an elevation of four thousand feet or greater, except once on the alkali plains of Nevada, where the elevation is slightly less.

We tarried at Blue Cañon, a freight and lumber station, for breakfast, in whose vicinity grand old pines were very conspicuous. The Sacramento *Bee*, of Aug. 27, contained the following:—

BROKEN COUPLING.— The special train going east, carrying the Boston Commandery, composed of Pullman sleepers from the Chicago, Burlington and Quebec Railroad, while just this side of Blue Cañon at an early hour

MOUNTAIN SUMMITS. (10,000 feet high.)

yesterday morning, broke a coupling which detached the four rear sleeping-coaches from three others and the baggage, which continued with the engine. The cars detached were provided with the new automatic air brake, which at once sets upon the wheels of any and all cars which, by accident or otherwise, become detached from the train. The brakes in this instance fulfilled their duty, and saved what might otherwise have proved a disastrous "wild run" down the mountains. The loss of the cars was quickly noticed by the engineer, and after about a half-hour's delay the coupling was renewed and the train proceeded. No one was injured except a woman of the party, who was struck in the face with a brass coupling upon the bell-rope, which threw back with great force when the rope broke from the strain of the cars becoming separated. A cut was made upon the cheek, which was properly cared for by the physicians upon the train. A peculiarity of the make-up of the party was that it included four doctors and three undertakers, but it is claimed that they did not come out expecting to be needed.

Passing through Emigrant Gap, by the cascade where during the summer the Yuba leaps in a shower of spray, we came to the tunnels and snow sheds. The train slowly crept over the summit of the Sierra range, 7,017 feet above the level of the sea,—not the highest part of the Sierras, of course, for they rise ten thousand feet above the track. It is the dividing ridge of the Sierra Nevadas. The summit tunnel is 1,659 feet long, and there are others from one hundred to eight hundred and seventy feet in length. The snow sheds are solid structures built of sawed and round timber, bolted together, completely roofing the road, originally costing ten thousand dollars per mile.

SNOW SHEDS.

The line of sheds is about forty-five miles long, or the entire distance of the deep-snow line on the dividing ridge. During a wet winter snow falls along the summit from sixteen to twenty feet deep. The track is kept clear of snow in winter by these sheds, and in the springtime the avalanches of snow and soil pass over the sloping roofs, protecting the track, and plunge into the chasms

INTERIOR, SNOW SHED.

below. The sheds are protected from fire by watchmen who dwell far up on a mountain, from which an extensive view of the road is obtained. The watchmen, in case of fire, give the alarm and location of the fire by signals. An engine with steam on constantly, attached to water cars, is stationed at the summit ready for every emergency.

Geo. A. Crofutts, Esq., relates in his "Overland Guide" that Oct. 17, 1872, as an excursion train, loaded with passengers, most of whom were women and children, rounded the curve close below the tunnel, and with No. 6 train thundering along close behind, the timbering in the tunnel was discovered by the fireman to be on fire. The engineer, Johnny Bartholomew, comprehended the position at a glance, made one of the most brilliant dashes, under the circumstances, on record. The train passed through the tunnel safely, when to have stopped short would have been sure death. G. H. Jennings, Esq., of Brooklyn, N. Y., has put the following words in the mouth of the brave engineer:—

"I ain't very much on the fancy,
 And all that sort of stuff,
For an engineer on a railroad
 Is apt to be more 'on the rough':
He don't 'go much' on 'his handsome,'
 I freely 'acknowledge the corn,'
But he has got to 'git up' on his 'wide-awake,'
 That's 'just as sure's you're born.'

"Now, I'll tell you a little story,
 'Bout 'a run,' we had for our necks,
When we thought 'old Gabe' had called us,
 To 'ante up our checks.'
We came 'round the curve by the tunnel,
 Just beyond the American Flat,
When my fireman sings out, 'Johnny!
 Look ahead! My God, what's that?'

"You bet, I warn't long in sightin':
 There was plenty for me to see,
With a train full of kids an' women,
 And their lives all hangin' on me.
For the tunnel was roarin' and blazin',
 All ragin' with fire an' smoke,
And 'Number Six' close behind us,—
 'Quick, sonny! shove in the coke.'

"Whistle 'down brakes,' I first thought;
  Then, thinks I, 'old boy, 't won't do';
And with hand on throttle an' lever,
  I knew I *must roll 'em through!*
Through the grim mouth of the tunnel,
  Through smoke an' flame as well,
Right into the 'gateway of death,' boys,
  Right smack through the 'jaws of hell'!

"The stanch 'old gal' felt the pressure
  Of steam through her iron joints;
She acted just like she was human,
  Just like she 'knew all the points,'
She glided along the tramway,
  With speed of a lightning flash,
With a howl assuring us safety,
  Regardless of wreck or crash.

"I s'pose I might have 'jumped the train,'
  In hope to save sinew and bone,
And left them women and children
  To take that ride alone;
But I tho't of a day of reck'nin';
  And whatever 'Old John' done here,
No Lord ain't going to say to him then,
  'You *went back* as an engineer.'"

The scenery of the Sierras — the mountains, gorges, precipices, and lakes — was grand and interesting. Passing the summit and descending the mountains, Donner Lake, a silver sheet set in the shadows of green forests and brown mountains, appeared. It is called the "Gem of the Sierras." It is three and a half miles long, about one mile wide, and two hundred feet deep. It is said that the water is so clear that pebbles may be seen on the bottom where the water is fifty feet deep. Towering mountains, covered with spruce, fir, and pine, surround it on three sides; on the fourth side the land gently slopes to the shore, and there are a few cabins scattered here and there on the lowlands. This lake was made memorable by the terrible suffering of the Donner family and party, which consisted of sixteen souls, all but one of whom perished near its banks. Mr. Donner, though urged to advance, because winter was approaching and the sky threatening, halted for the night at this fatal spot. That night the storm burst upon

TRUCKEE RIVER.

them, the snow fell heavily and fast. For several weeks the storm continued, the imprisoned could not escape, and the hand of help could not reach them. In the spring a party of brave men, after weeks of effort, reached the camp of the Donners. One alone, a German, was alive, but he was a maniac. The lake is a famous resort in summer, and in winter is a sleighing and skating park. Bierstadt has made Donner Lake the subject of one of his finest paintings.

Truckee City, the last California town of importance, was reached at 12 M., where a good dinner was provided. One could hardly see the town on account of the piles of ties, wood, and

PALISADES OF THE HUMBOLDT RIVER, C. P. R. R.

lumber which covered the ground. Truckee is the headquarters for tourists who desire to visit Donner and Tahoe Lakes, and other points of interest in the vicinity. Swiftly we descended fifteen hundred feet in running thirty-three miles, and at 3 P. M. reached Reno, Nev., a bright and active town, named in honor of

Gen. Reno, who was killed in the battle at South Mountain. A late Reno newspaper accuses the squaws in that vicinity of becoming civilized, as it is informed they have learned to powder their faces. Virginia City, twenty-one miles southeast, is the centre of the greatest mining region in the world. Leaving Reno, we rode over a sandy desert, bounded by dirt-hills from five hundred to one thousand feet high, while, looking over their summits, snow could be seen on the peaks beyond. During the evening and night the desert spread around us. One town at least, "Desert," was fitly named. In the morning of Monday, Aug. 27, still desert girt, we became well acquainted with the Great Nevada Desert, whereon are Humboldt, Carson, Walker, Pyramid, and other lakes. Sand-hills and flats alternated, but the bed of the desert is lava and clay combined. The action of the elements has covered these clay and lava deposits with a coarse dust or sand, which is blown about and deposited in curious drifts by the wind.

At 10 A. M. breakfast was had at Terrace, a small railroad town. Bare beds of alkali or wastes of gray sand continued to accompany us. We traversed the bed of a saline lake, perhaps an annex to Salt Lake. The line of water wash was generally noticed. At noon, as we hurried along, we observed a little cemetery, isolated in this valley of death. At five of the graves white head-boards had been erected, and the dreary place was surrounded by a painted picket fence. There was no village near. Who was here surprised by the murderous red men? Who here, in deep distress, left father, mother, or children, in this barren waste? What a death-robed place in which to meet death! The lesson of these lonely graves, in the midst of this lifeless solitude, not only awakened surprise, but taught important and serious truth. Tri-mountain and the Nevada Desert alike are in death's empire.

288   BOSTON COMMANDERY KNIGHTS TEMPLARS.

OGDEN, UTAH.

It was a hot day on the desert (thermometer 102° Fahr. in the cars), and very dusty, but good-nature and resignation prevailed among the pilgrims.

Promontory, fifty miles from Ogden, was reached at 2 P. M., where the train was boarded by Mr. F. R. McConnell, general passenger agent of the Union Pacific Railroad, and Mr. W. C. Borland, general ticket agent of the same road at Salt Lake City. These gentlemen extended an invitation, on behalf of the Union Pacific Railroad, complimentary to Boston Commandery, to visit Salt Lake City.

At Promontory, May 10, 1869, "the last spike was driven." The last tie, a beautiful piece of workmanship, of California laurel, with silver plates on which were suitable inscriptions, was put in place, and the last connecting rails were laid by the Union and Central Pacific Railroads. The spikes were then driven, one of gold from California, one of silver from Nevada, and one of gold, silver, and iron from Arizona. The completion of the herculean work was duly celebrated.

At 4 P. M. the train reached Ogden, the present junction of the Union and Central Pacific roads, where dinner was served. Here the Commandery again met Major Silva and his estimable lady, who were decorated with badges of Boston Commandery. The citizens of Ogden are mostly Mormons. The waters of Ogden River are conducted through the streets and thence into the gardens for purposes of irrigation. The invitation to visit Salt Lake City, was gratefully accepted by the committee on the California pilgrimage, in behalf of the Commandery, and the entire party rode in their special train from Ogden to Salt Lake City, and returned over the Utah Central Railroad, on one special ticket, "good for one hundred and sixty-six persons," presented by the Union Pacific Railroad Company. The ride through the Salt Lake Valley, so different from the alkali beds near Corrinne, white, hot, and dazzling, gave us a welcome change. The air was fresh and cool, the fields green and fertile, and the houses were neater than those upon the plains. There was an appearance of industry and thrift on all sides. The Wasatch range of mountains rose grandly over all. At 7 P. M. the train arrived at "Zion," as the Mormons call Salt Lake City.

CHAPTER XVII.

SOME of our number immediately repaired to the Continental and Walker Hotels, the remainder slept on board the cars. On Tuesday morning the headquarters of the command were established at the Continental Hotel, and the entire party were tranferred to the two hotels mentioned. Like old Zion, new "Zion" disappointed. We had the impression that clear water ran along the shaded streets, and that an air of coolness and comfort spread around. The mountain water passing through the main streets was vitiated by sewer or sink water; the shade trees in clusters were separated by hot distances; the dust was deep and everywhere, and there was neither "coolness, comfort, nor repose." The streets are wide, hence wider dust; the buildings as a whole are inferior. There are a few first-class buildings, notably Odd Fellows' Block, but the principal streets where the business is done are occupied by buildings such as in Eastern cities give way to the march of improvement.

The forenoon of Tuesday, Aug. 28, was spent in doing the city. The Tabernacle, the new Temple, the Co-operative Institution, Brigham Young's grave, and his late residence, etc., were visited. They have been described so many times that it seems unnecessary to insert a description of them here. The impressions of Salt Lake

SALT LAKE CITY.

City, its Mormon people, and its prevailing religion (if we should designate their system by that word) made upon the minds of the visitors were similar. It happened that a funeral service held over the remains of City Marshal and High Priest Burt, who was killed on the Saturday evening previous by a creole, gave those interested an opportunity to listen to presidents, apostles, and bishops of the Mormon hierarchy, and to look upon the faces of a Mormon multitude in the Tabernacle. There was nothing either brilliant or objectionable in the exhortations of Sharp, Smith, or Taylor. They are not men of culture or magnetism. They refrained from such disloyal statements as they have made at other times in the same and other places.

Their personal appearance and that of the confraternity about them evinced more of that which was gross than spiritual, more of that which was obstinate than charitable. The congregation was composed of several national types, yet one general cast of features seemed to predominate, implying intellect, refinement, and devotion of a low order. The men appeared stolid, workful, but ignorant. The women seemed burdened, sad-faced, as if carrying a secret they would disclose. Very many of them appeared unhappy, smileless, heart-broken. The whole service and congregation seemed to lack true human sympathy, — at a funeral, too, where human sympathies are generally easily touched, — and there seemed wanting a spirit of devotion. It seemed like a great caucus to declare loyalty to the Republic on the part of the speakers, and, on the part of the people, like a mass meeting of representatives of various nationalities, who did not realize for what they had gathered. The social ulcer of Mormonism seemed to chill and embitter everything. Nature, when we came up the valley, seemed beautiful and smiling, but a pall lies over this city of Brigham. The very streets and houses reveal it. The people have not that sprightly way, that polite address, that willing conversation, met with in other towns where the Commandery tarried. The Mormon women one

TABERNACLE AND RIVER JORDAN.

meets seem all on their way to the cemetery, without a single emotion, good, bad, or indifferent, except the face reveals a burdened heart.

It was with no regrets that we departed from Salt Lake City, except the leaving of intelligent Gentiles, whom business or duty compels to abide in this fetid atmosphere.

A pleasant half-hour was spent in the Masonic Public Library. It is called Masonic, not because it is composed of Masonic works, but because it was established and is controlled by the Grand Lodge of Utah. It contains six thousand volumes, and is the only public library in the Territory. Freemasons can take out books free of expense, but others are charged a small amount. Eastern people perhaps do not appreciate how speedily and far Mormonism is spreading. Utah is buried under it. Mormons control Idaho, Wyoming, and Arizona. It is said that the election of the Gentile-Democratic delegate from Wyoming was effected by a bargain with Mormonism.

The schools in Salt Lake City are of two kinds, the public schools and the mission schools. The latter are largely supported by contributions from the East; the former, like ours, are supported by a general tax. Though the Gentiles pay their proportion into the general fund, yet their children attend the mission schools, because all the teachers in the public schools are Mormons; the control is Mormon, and the Book of Mormon and Mormon Catechism are taught therein. A visit to the Mormon cemetery was suggestive. It is the burial-place for children indeed. On inquiry, we were informed that the funerals of little ones in Salt Lake City are from two to eight per day. Mormons generally do not call physicians to attend their sick children, but seek to restore them "by laying on of hands." Brigham Young lies alone beneath an enormous block of granite, enclosed in a grassy yard; the little ones of the kingdom lie in the cemetery thick as pansies in my neighbor's garden.

The ground of Gentile opposition to Mormonism is simple in

YOUNG'S LATE RESIDENCE, SALT LAKE CITY.

its statement and direct in proof. "They build up Zion with blood and Jerusalem with iniquity. The heads thereof judge for reward, and the priests thereof teach for hire, and the prophets thereof divine for money: yet will they lean upon the Lord and say, 'Is not the Lord among us? None evil can come upon us.'"

Gentile opposition arises on account of the Mormon priesthood. It is usurping. It assumes to be the priesthood of Aaron. That priesthood descended only from father to son. A Mormon claiming himself an Aaronic priest can but be a usurper and fraud. It deceives the people in telling them they must defend and embrace polygamy as given of the Lord, whereas everybody who has investigated the matter, even superficially, knows whence and how polygamy was introduced into the system.

Financially it is a fraud. During twenty years more than twenty million dollars have been paid by this industrious people into the hands of the priesthood, by whom no itemized report is ever made; and burdened toilers understand that, as the tithes "go to the Lord," it is not their business to inquire as to the expenditure. Politically it is deception, burning into the hearts of the people that the United States government would rob them of their religion. The Mormon priesthood is vindictive. All outside are Babylonians. One of the twelve apostles remarked, "I do pray for our enemies; I pray God will damn them and send them to hell." It is tyrannical. It claims to control the keys which open and close heaven and hell. It tells the people with whom they must trade, what newspapers to read, what school to patronize, and how much every man must contribute to the priesthood. It is criminal. Facts, notorious and well authenticated, prove it. Mutilations, blood atonings, assassinations, and massacres confirm it. Individual Mormons may be intelligent, honest, and good; the mass is ignorant, superstitious, and fanatical, and the priesthood cherishes this condition. The system encourages disloyalty to the United States. Mormon allegiance is first to the church.

In San Francisco, Sir Knight Major V. M. C. Silva made himself known to Boston Commandery, and was very cordial in his attentions. The major is the most extensive wool buyer in Utah, and has a warehouse corner of Hartford and Pearl Streets, Boston. He met Boston Commandery again at Ogden, and accompanied us to Salt Lake City. The Utah Western Railroad (narrow gauge) runs west from the city and across the river Jordan with its adjacent bottom lands, along the shore of Salt Lake. This is the old Utah and Nevada road, and was built by Apostle John W. Young, second son of Brigham. It is now under Mormon control, and the employés are all Mormons. The distance from the city to the lake is twenty miles. Major Silva chartered a special train, having three open cars and one closed, and invited the Sir Knights and their ladies to visit the lake and enjoy a bath. The invitation was accepted, and a very enjoyable afternoon resulted. Passing the Black Rock, we tarried at Garfield, a resort for picnic parties, where the bath-houses were immediately occupied, and about fivescore Knights and ladies swam and frolicked in the clear salt water. Among other guests were Gen. Agramonte, K. T., Christopher Diehl, K. T., and Grand Secretary of the Grand Lodge of Utah.

Returning to the city, we had dinner and repaired to the station to return to Ogden and thence homeward. Previous to our departure from the depot the Opera House band visited the train and serenaded the Commandery. While it was in progress, Eminent Commander Stevenson was called for by the people present, and responded in a very pleasant speech of thanks to the band and to the various individuals who contributed so much to make our stay in Salt Lake City so agreeable. He concluded by introducing Past Grand Master Benjamin Dean, who also addressed the multitude. After cheers for the Eminent Commander, Past Grand Master, the band, Major Silva, and others, the train slowly started, and the city was soon wrapt in darkness and lost to sight.

The following is from the *Daily Tribune*, Salt Lake City, Tuesday, Aug. 28, 1883:—

BOSTON KNIGHTS—THEY ARRIVE IN THE CITY LAST NIGHT, AND WILL TAKE IN THE LAKE TO-DAY.

Last evening the special train of nine cars of the Boston Commandery arrived in the city at seven o'clock, and they will remain until this evening. This Commandery left Boston on Aug. 4, and will return to that city on Sept. 4, after having crossed the continent from the far East to the far West and back again, occupying just one month. To make the trip as pleasant as possible, the Commandery secured a train of nine cars, consisting of Pullman palace sleeping-coaches, dining-car, commissary and baggage cars, all being fitted up in the finest style and supplied with everything desirable. Going West they went via the Atchison, Topeka and Santa Fé, taking in various points of interest in Colorado, thence to New Mexico, Arizona, and Southern California via the Southern Pacific. In California they were treated as honored guests by their brethren, and given every opportunity to see the country and learn of its wonders and resources.

The party is composed of some of the best and most prominent citizens of Massachusetts, all of the gentlemen being well-known business men. Yesterday they were met by Messrs. Borland and McConnell of the Union Pacific at Promontory, to escort them to the city and look after the comfort and pleasure of the party. They travel in a thoroughly organized style, having an executive committee of ladies and gentlemen, a transportation committee, and a medical staff, the general management being with Eminent Sir John L. Stevenson, Eminent Commander, who occupies a

Chicago, Burlington and Quincy directors' car, said to be the finest of the kind ever built.

To-day the party will visit places of interest in the forenoon, and at one o'clock will go by special train to Garfield to take a bath in the lake. Major V. M. C. Silva, of Ogden, who had many acquaintances in the party, and spent much time with them in California, organized this excursion to the lake and tenders it to the Commandery, who go as his guests. They will return to the city about four o'clock and go East in their train over the Union Pacific, leaving here at eight o'clock to-night. The Knights of this city will do what they can to-day to entertain the brethren.

The issue of the *Daily Tribune*, Salt Lake City, Wednesday, Aug. 29, 1883, contains the following:—

COMMANDERY EXCURSION—THE BOSTON KNIGHTS VISIT THE LAKE AND BASK IN ITS WATERS.

The excursion to Garfield, given to the Boston Commandery yesterday, was a very enjoyable affair and was highly appreciated by the Knights and the ladies accompanying them. The train of three well-filled cars left the Utah and Nevada Depot at one o'clock, and arrived at Garfield fifty minutes afterwards. After arrival it was not long until most of the party were bathing in the lake. These persons were all used to bathing in the Atlantic, and many good swimmers were among them, but this lake bathing was something entirely new to them. Those who delighted at home to ride the waves as they came in found a new element to contend with in our great inland sea, and made every effort to keep their heads above water and feet below. Being good swimmers, however, they soon learned to float with ease. They were the jolliest crowd we have ever seen at this resort. Every member of this Commandery is a business man, and many are of the most prominent and wealthy class, embracing the mercantile, manufacturing, and other interests. In all their trip from Boston, through Canada, the various States and Territories of the Union to California, and their return thus far on an eight thousand mile trip, nothing had pleased them better than this excursion to the lake and the bath therein. Citizens who accompanied the party were plied with questions, and gave an attentive audience about the lake, Utah, and kindred subjects. One gentleman said, "This is the most noted thing we have seen on our trip, and if this bathing-place was near Boston it would be improved and return to the owners millons of dollars."

We are of the opinion, and have often so expressed ourselves, that the property should be made the greatest resort in the West by being improved in such manner as to make it as attractive as possible.

The special train returned to the city at four o'clock, and the party went directly to the Continental and Walker Hotels, took supper, and again embarked on their train, via the Union Pacific, at eight o'clock, for their homes in the East.

Although this is called the Boston Commandery pilgrimage, the members of the excursion reside in several of the New England States.

This pleasant excursion was planned and paid for by Major V. M. C. Silva, of Ogden, and he could not have done anything which would have given more satisfaction to the party. We are pleased to have citizens of the East visit the great West. It gives them a better idea of what the West is than they could obtain in any other manner. We learned from some of the party that the Chinese question, which has been so much agitated, looks to them very different from what it did before they visited the streets and houses of the Chinese in their quarters in San Francisco. They have not that love or sympathy for the race they had when they viewed the question from afar. Indians in New Mexico and Arizona were brought to their notice, and they were given some opportunities of investigating the Indian question. They return home less firm in their views in favor of the policy of governing and managing these wards of the government by what has been termed the church rule.

While in Utah they obtained some insight into into the polygamous question, and discovered that a handful of Americans were upholding the flag against a foreign and Asiatic institution planted in the great heart of the Republic.

The following editorial is from the *Daily Tribune*, Salt Lake City, of Aug. 29, 1883, and is eminently worthy of knightly consideration: —

THE KNIGHTS.

To a great many people this gathering of the Templar Knights, with their somewhat ostentatious display, has a look of extravagance and foolishness. But we see in them and their brothers, the Masons, the possible force which at last in America is to stand between popular government and warring creeds, a safe and sure defence. History is prone to repeat itself. In every age there are Saracens and Crusaders. Somehow in nature's economy the great reforms of the world come in shocks and violence, and even as the earth, through convulsions inconceivable, was moulded at last into a habitation for men, so through the discipline of suffering man is made better. The Order of these Knights was founded upon a fanaticism, and the cry which swelled their numbers, until suddenly they blazed out a terrible host, was that the Saviour's sepulchre must be defended from the unbeliever. As though any sepulchre needed a defence, much less that of the Saviour! But in that defence thousands and tens of thousands died, — died with triumph songs upon their lips. The Knights move West now instead of East. To many of them their coming and going seem but a pleasure excursion, but with them goes the recorded oath of every one that he believes in the divinity of the Messiah, and every one is trained in the rudiments at least of war's discipline. What if it should transpire at last that unconsciously to themselves they are rounding into an army form; and that their mission is to guard a temple, and to keep secure something more sacred than a sepulchre? By the temple we mean the temple of freedom on the earth; by that sacred thing we mean the manhood and womanhood of America. The death of Jesus Christ is not the most impressive event in his history. For a principle many a man and many a shrinking woman have looked upon death with unblanched face, and calmly passed from the scaffold to glory. It was the *life* of the Master that left its impression upon this world, the most vivid impression that in all the rolling ages has been made. Through him real manhood had its birth; that manhood which was devoid of cruelty and of fear; that manhood which was at once clothed with independence and with mercy, which claimed the right to think and act, but which forever has pity for suffering. That manhood did not belong to the ancient world: that came first from Nazareth. But as we study still deeper that history, we find that the same hand was stretched out to touch the chains which had worn deep scars in the brow of woman; that at its touch not only did the chain crumble and the brow grow white and pure, but by the act, as woman advanced to man's side, by the splendor reflected from her, man was glorified. There are all the symptoms of warring sects in our land; pride and envy and jealousy, and the love of ostentatious display, have all crept into the churches; the love of wealth and of power has its influences with them all.

At last there has an organization risen up which in the name of religion seeks to kill that manhood which the Saviour first revealed, and seeks to burn again the brand of shame into the white brow of woman. By and by these things will culminate in fury. The wild beast which lies dormant in most souls will spring to active life, and to the morals of men will come something which will be to them what a geological period is to the earth. When that time shall come, we expect that the Masons and the Templars will first fully realize what subtle power has incited them to keep up their organization and discipline; that they will see that as the hope of the early Christian world hung on them, so the hope of liberty on earth is to be surrendered to their keeping. We like their coming and going. By it they gain a better idea of the land which may, sooner than they imagine, require defenders; with a deeper patriotism they will renew their vows, and, with a fuller realization of the fact, they will understand that the world's present hope centres in this Republic, and that to be on the alert to guard it is a duty as sacred as ever knight set lance in rest to defend.

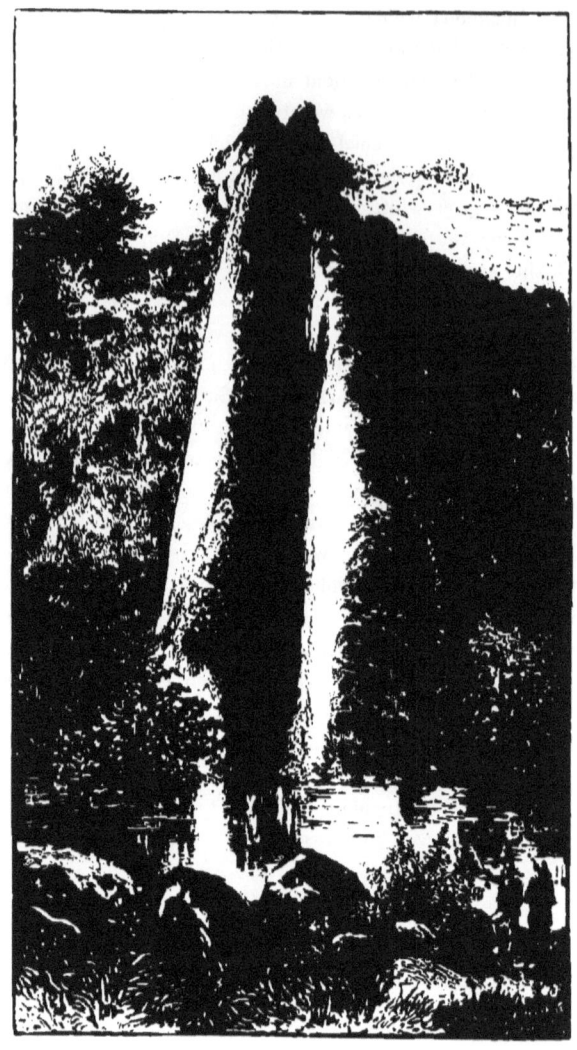

DEVIL'S SLIDE, WEBER CAÑON, UTAH.

CHAPTER XVIII.

THE train arrived at Ogden in due time, when the Commandery took formal leave of Sir Knight Silva, and at "11 P. M., Aug. 28," the precise moment laid down in the itinerary, we left Ogden for Boston. During the night we entered the portals of Devil's Gate, where massive rocks rear their crests far up toward the star-lit sky. Then came Weber Cañon, with its deep gray and grotesque rocks, often rising to great heights and seemingly about to close in upon the train. The Devil's Slide, of which we are enabled to give accurate pictures, consists of two parallel ledges of granite, fourteen feet apart, and about fifteen feet high, jutting from the mountain-side. The thousand-mile tree, "1,000 miles to Omaha," is in this cañon. Weber Cañon is left at Echo City, a pretty place clustered amid ravines and waters. Echo Cañon is entered here and left at Wasatch, nine hundred and sixty-eight miles from Omaha. The sandstone crags rising on either side assume grotesque shapes. Every jutting ledge, every fantastic form, has received a name, appropriate or otherwise. Pulpit Rock and Hanging Rock are easily discerned, and the fitness of their names is apparent. Echo Cañon itself is well named. The whistle of the engine and the rattling of the wheels wakened the echoes, until at times the cañon reverberated with deafening sounds.

GREEN RIVER CITY AND CASTLE ROCKS.

The following morning we were in the Sweetwater country of Wyoming, upon the banks of Green River, whose strange rock formations were of great interest. We stopped at Green River station for breakfast. The regulations of the depot hotel, as printed on handbills like an executor's sale of "farming tools, hay, and stock," were intended to be funny, probably, but were rather coarse.

Petrified wood, agates, etc., were seen here in abundance; there was also a small menagerie, lion and two bears, caged and lonesome, which once roamed at will on these bare hills. Caged wild beasts in this free and boundless wild country seemed anomalous. Previous to our departure the ubiquitous photographer put in an appearance, and the ladies and Sir Knights, forming a large semicircular group upon the station platform, were enabled "to see themselves as others saw them," in about a month afterward, when the artist forwarded very good photographs of the party.

Fifty-four miles from Green River to Rawlins, where the pilgrims dined, were accomplished at 3.30 P. M. We followed the celebrated Bitter Creek, an alkali stream unfit for man or beast. Sage brush and alkali beds, artesian wells, and general desolation were the rule that day. Near Creston we crossed the backbone of the continent. A sign advertises "the Continental Divide," 7,100 feet above the level of the sea. The whole region is rugged and barren. A good dinner at Rawlins atoned somewhat for the desolation between the stations. A gentle shower laid the dust, and all were made happy. During the afternoon heavy showers with lightning were seen around us. It was grand to see the rain-storms sweep down the mountain-sides and over the parched plains. Dustless and cool, we congratulated ourselves upon our repeated blessings.

Laramie was reached at 10 P. M., where we were ushered into

PULPIT ROCK, ECHO CAÑON, UTAH.

an airy, cheerful dining-room, and an excellent supper was set for us. Upon the front of the hotel a knightly welcome was displayed: "Pilgrim: I greet thee; walk thee in and refresh thyself. Silver and gold have I none, but such as I have give I unto thee."

FINGER ROCK, WEBER CAÑON, UTAH.

On entering the dining-room a copy of the *Daily Boomerang* lay at each plate, complimentary to the Sir Knights and ladies from "Bill Nye," the funny man of the *Boomerang*. The head-lines of the leading article were "Howdy." "Wyoming steps to the front and asks to be introduced to you." In this article the editor wrote of the resources of Wyoming, its climate, soil, scenery, stock, etc., and also of Wyoming's "future great" Laramie, "the Queen City of the Plains."

The *Boomerang* of Aug. 29 said: —

KNIGHTS TEMPLARS. — Another delegation of pilgrims whose banners bear the strange legend, "*In hoc signo vinces*," which interpreted means, "Have n't had a square meal since I left Laramie," passed here yesterday morning. This evening the Boston boys pass East by special train. Every regular train also bears its quota of gallant Knights back to their Eastern homes.

HANGING ROCK, ECHO CAÑON, UTAH.

The *Boomerang* of Aug. 30 was pleased to say: —

The Boston Commandery Knights Templars passed East last night. They were a fine-looking lot of people.

After ninety minutes' delay, a Taunton engine hauled our heavy train up the mountain-side. At midnight we reached

Sherman, 8,242 feet above the level of the sea. The clouds were black. Now and then the lightnings flashed and brought into weird view the pyramidal monument which suggests and will perpetuate the work and memory of Oakes Ames and Oliver Ames, the projectors of the Pacific Railroad. At this point, the highest reached by Boston Commandery in its pilgrimage across the continent, the Eminent Commander, surrounded by several Sir Knights, unfurled the beauseant of the Commandery and gave it to the midnight breeze. The gentle shower descended upon it, the lightnings played around it, and the cheers of the Sir Knights greeted the white and black ensign of Templarism. Our descent from Sherman was at a fearful rate.

At 8.30 we arrived at North Platte, Neb., the terminus of the mountain division of the railroad, where our attention was called to the fine residence of Hon. William F. Cody, "Buffalo Bill." After breakfast a Sir Knight, said to be a member of the Boston National Lancers, essayed to ride a prairie horse which

A DUGOUT.

was the pet of the boys and girls of the village. Unused to such exercise, the Lancer lost his seat, came to the ground, and the crowd were so cruel as to laugh.

Thence we proceeded along the valley of the North Platte River, parallel with the emigrant road of olden time. The rude forts that once surrounded the now deserted ranches, wherein frontiersmen defended themselves and their property from the Indians, were occasionally seen. Also those strong cabins roofed with turf, whose loopholed walls still remained, suggested those days when the savage held possession of this favorite hunting-ground.

Thursday, Aug. 30, at 1 P. M., the Commandery arrived at Grand Island, where dinner was served. Immediately after, we continued our advance on Omaha. The country was fertile, rolling, and fine. The harvesters were busy, and the plains presented a scene of activity. On our right was the river Platte, through whose valley the road runs over three hundred miles. Passing Columbus, which George Francis Train said was the geographical centre of the United States and should be the site of the national capital; North Bend, and other busy towns; having a view of spendid Nebraska at its best, we reached Omaha in the evening at ten o'clock.

VIEW APPROACHING COUNCIL BLUFFS, IOWA.

The present site of Omaha was selected as a homestead, in 1853, by Wm. D. Brown, who had previously ferried the California gold-hunters across the river at this point. Omaha was founded in 1854. In previous years the locality had been known as the "Lone Tree Ferry." The schools of Omaha are her pride. The high-school building, standing on the summit of a lofty hill back of the city, on the site of the old Capitol building, cost $250,000. Its tall spire reaches three hundred and ninety feet above the level of the river, and can be seen for miles in every direction. The city, situated on a commanding bluff, contains at this time over forty thousand inhabitants, and has doubtless a brilliant future. Halting but a moment at Omaha, the train proceeded across the Missouri River by a magnificent iron bridge that cost $1,600,000.

MISSOURI RIVER BRIDGE, OMAHA IN THE DISTANCE.

Having arrived safely at the transfer grounds, two miles west of Council Bluffs we tarried until 1 A. M. This is the terminus of the Union Pacific Railroad. The Union Depot, wherein we obtained a late supper, is a model structure, built of brick, furnished with hot and cold water, gas, and other modern conveniences. Council Bluffs, which doubtless receives it name from councils held by Indians on the bluffs, was originally (in 1846-1853) called Kanesville, in honor of a brother of the Arctic explorer. Council Bluffs was laid out in 1854, and now has a population of over twenty thousand. It is a flourishing city, and a considerable shipping point of wheat, cattle, and hogs. From Council Bluffs east, we proceeded over a principal line of the Chicago, Burlington and Quincy Railroad. This corporation is one of the wealthiest and most powerful in the world. It owns or controls over four thousand miles of track, which, with the bridges, rolling stock, etc., is first class in every respect. Its various lines, starting at Chicago, Peoria, and St. Louis, "like a massive drag-net, sweep every part of the West, from the eastern edge of the Mississippi Valley to the golden State of California." We anticipated a fine run across the State of Iowa, but, after passing Red Oak, encountered a smash-up of freight trains, which detained us four hours at Prescott, ninety miles east of Omaha.

VIEW NEAR STANTON, IOWA.

Leaving Prescott at 7 A. M., we breakfasted at Creston at 10 A. M., making seventy-four miles in three hours. The *Daily*

Advertiser, Creston, Iowa, Aug. 31, thus referred to our arrival and delay: —

This morning, between eight and ten o'clock, a special train, consisting of six sleepers, baggage, and dining car, stopped at the depot in this city, conveying the Boston Commandery Knights Templars on their return home from San Francisco, where they had been attending the Triennial Conclave.

The travelling Knights and their ladies took breakfast at the Summit during their stay, and then took a look at our beautiful city while waiting for the train to leave. They were met at the depot, the Summit, and on the streets by Knights of Bethany Commandery, No. 29, this city, who made themselves known, and enjoyed a social chat with them concerning their trip, the Conclave, their Commandery, Knight Templar work in general, and other topics, making their short stay in our city as agreeable as possible, and their recollections of it pleasant to refer to in the future.

VIEW NEAR CHILLICOTHE, IOWA

The special was accompanied by J. A. S. Reed, general agent of the Hannibal and St. Joe road, of 59 Clark Street, Chicago, who was looking after the welfare of the travellers very closely. The reporter had the pleasure of making his acquaintance at the Summit, and found him to be a very agreeable gentleman. The reporter also met Sir Knights E. F. Brooks, of Beauseant Commandery, No. 7, of Brattleboro', Vt., accompanying the Boston Commandery, and Z. H. Thomas, recorder of Boston Commandery for the California pilgrimage. They were both very pleasant gentlemen. Mr. Thomas is also secretary of seven different bodies, and has had his hands full during the pilgrimage, as well as for months previous.

All of the Knights expressed themselves as highly pleased with the hospitable treatment received from Sir Knights here, and were pleased that the wreck west delayed them so they were compelled to stop here for breakfast, which was not upon their programme. Several of them were invited to the Commandery's lodge-room here, and enjoyed a few minutes socially with the brothers of Bethany before taking their departure. They expressed themselves highly pleased with their trip, yet complained of its being a tedious one, and were very impatient to reach home.

Chariton, a sprightly town, was soon reached, where the local baggage-master with a large bundle of late Boston papers awaited our coming. Next in importance, Ottumwa, on the Des Moines River, came to view. This town has doubled in population in ten years, has one hundred and ten manufacturing establishments, an enormous wholesale trade, and all conveniences and luxuries of metropolitanism, except a debt. Forty-seven miles farther east is Mount Pleasant, "the Athens of Iowa," famous for its schools and colleges; and at 7.30 P. M. our train halted at Burlington, Iowa.

VIEW ON LINE OF C., B. & Q. R. R., NEAR OTTUMWA, IOWA.

The Burlington *Hawkeye*, Sept. 1, noticed our arrival as follows:

BOSTON COMMANDERY. — At half past seven o'clock an elegant train of Pullman cars arrived at the Union Depot, containing Boston Commandery

Knights Templars. The party included one hundred and five Sir Knights, their wives and daughters. A *Hawkeye* reporter met Sir Harrison A. Tucker, of Brooklyn, N. Y., who stated "the pilgrimage had been a grand success; that nothing had occurred to mar the pleasures of the junketing pilgrims; that the Triennial Conclave was one of the grandest events he had ever witnessed; and that much praise was due the Chicago, Burlington and Quincy Railroad for its courteous treatment and its efforts to provide for the comfort and convenience of the Commandery." After giving the roster of the command, it concludes: The Sir Knights tarried in Burlington an hour, and during this time a number of them, accompanied by their wives, were conducted through the Burlington Boating Association building, and pronounced it the finest of the kind they had ever seen. At half past eight o'clock the Sir Knights boarded their special train and departed for the Hub.

At 9 P. M., leaving Burlington, the Mississippi was safely crossed and the pilgrims were speedily carried to Chicago, arriving at five o'clock on the morning of Saturday, Sept. 1. The Commandery and ladies proceeded by carriages to the Grand Pacific Hotel. The Sir Knights were warm in their praises of this fine hotel, where every effort possible was made to please them. After breakfast the command separated, and the forenoon was spent in seeing Chicago. Stock-yards, tunnels, public buildings, etc., were visited, and the Boston Templars cordially welcomed everywhere.

The Boston *Globe* of Sept. 2 contained the following despatch:

[Special Despatch to The Sunday Globe.]

CHICAGO, Sept. 1. — Boston Commandery of Knights Templars arrived here this morning, and this afternoon all left the city for home. No demonstrations were made here in their honor, nor was there any organized march to the hotels where dinner was partaken of. The Knights expressed themselves highly pleased with their reception in San Francisco, but, like Commanderies from other cities, are extremely indignant at the manner they were ignored by Chicago brethren All of the party, one hundred and sixty-eight in number, are well and in the best of spirits.

A laughable incident transpired at the Grand Pacific this afternoon. One of the Boston Knights, having just left the dining-room, was standing in the corridor picking his teeth, when a British lord, who had never seen the uniform before, thought he was one of the porters of the hotel, and ordered him to go and look after his baggage. The Knight stared at the lord amazed, and the indignant lord, thinking the porter was putting on airs, repeated his request in no well-chosen language. The Knight consigned the lord to hades,

PULPIT ROCK, ECHO CAÑON, UTAH.

and serious trouble was imminent, when an American friend of the lord's came up and explained. The lord was profuse in apologies, but highly disgusted with his own inability to make, after several weeks spent in America, so simple a social distinction as that between a pilgrim and a baggage smasher.

At Chicago the "Mohave" had exhausted the patience of the railroad-men. True to its name, it kept in a warm condition,—a hot one,—and it was necessarily abandoned. The car "Spokane" took its place. "Spokane" is the name of a river, far north in the cool Territory of Washington. Its axles stood the friction, and we had no further trouble with hot boxes during the trip.

The Pullman cars had received a renovation, when, at 1.15 P. M., the Commandery stepped on board for its ride to Montreal.

From Chicago to Battle Creek, Sir Knight George Jones was engineer, and drove engine No. 66 with remarkable speed, considering the very heavy train. This engine empty weighs fifty-one and one half tons; filled, with tender attached, it weighs over ninety tons. The one hundred and seventy-six miles were made in five hours and forty-five minutes, including stops. One section of ten miles was covered in twelve minutes.

At Battle Creek, Mich., the platform of the depot was crowded with people who had come to welcome Boston Commandery. The German band of Battle Creek was present, by the kindness of the Sir Knights of Battle Creek, and gave good music during our stay there. We arrived at 7 P. M. and departed at 9 P. M. On entering the supper-room a pretty buttonhole bouquet was found on each plate and an elaborate *menu*, tastefully printed and ornamented with Templar designs. Prior to our departure all the members of Battle Creek Commandery Knights Templars who were present were, by the Eminent Commander of Boston Commandery, decorated with Boston badges. Our reception at Battle Creek was cordial, our departure cheery.

The Battle Creek *Journal* thus spoke of the arrival and reception of the Bostons at Battle Creek: —

The Boston Commandery, composed of one hundred and five Sir Knights, with their ladies, sixty-three in number, arrived in this city at seven o'clock Saturday evening via the Chicago and Grand Trunk Railway, on their return from their pilgrimage to San Francisco.

The train consisted of six Pullman cars, a Chicago, Burlington and

Quincy coach, and the baggage van, drawn by an engine in charge of Sir Knight George Jones. The train was the same in which they went West some weeks ago, and was in charge of Sir Knight J. A. Henry, who was held in Chicago four days to meet them and conduct them through the State to Fort Gratiot, while the Pullman cars were in the hands of George A. Chapman, conductor.

VIEW OF DEVIL'S SLIDE, FROM UNION PACIFIC RAILROAD, WEBER CAÑON, UTAH.

The train left Chicago at 1.15 P. M. and reached this city promptly at 7 P. M., making the quickest run ever made over this road,— one hundred and seventy-six miles in five hours and forty-five minutes, including the stops.

Among the passengers was the Past Grand Master of the United States, Benjamin Dean, of Boston, for whom the Boston Commandery acted as an escort, under command of John L. Stevenson.

Upon the arrival of the train at this station they were met by members of the Battle Creek Commandery, who tendered them a serenade by the German band during the hour that the train stopped for supper. The music was well spoken of by the excursionists, many of whom joined in a dance on the platform to settle their supper. The supper was especially provided for the guests, and consisted of the rarest and most seasonable dishes to be procured in the city, and prepared under the direction and supervision of the caterer, who is making the railway restaurant popular and famous with the travelling public.

Boston Commandery is one of the most ancient, if not the very oldest in the United States, and can claim a working Lodge as early as 1769; but as they did not receive their charter until 1806, it is perhaps proper to date their existence from that time. It is older than the Charleston, S. C., Commandery, or the St. John's, of Providence, R. I., in date of organization, although the latter Lodge's charter is dated 1805. Both of the Lodges here mentioned contested priority, but have finally conceded it to the Boston Commandery. The latter Commandery is composed of the wealth of the "Hub" and is its "crack" Masonic organization.

The train left this station at eight o'clock and arrived in Fort Gratiot at 1 A. M. The party were profuse in their praise of the management of the Chicago and Grand Trunk Railway, and said they had not had more attention and gentlemanly favor shown them during their whole travels than while in hands of the Chicago and Grand Trunk officials and employés.

Mr. W. A. Walker represented the Boston *Herald*, and blew the bugle to notify the passengers that the train was ready, an appropriate and happy combination of duties, the blowing and the newspaper; while Dr. W. Dan Lamb, of Lawrence, Mass., had charge of the health of the party, and dosed out the quinine to fortify the gentlemen against the fevers of Michigan, a thing that exists in the imagination only, and for which they appeared to like to take the liquid remedy. Sir Knight Wheeler conducted the vocal music, and assisted in keeping his fellow Sir Knights happy throughout the pilgrimage.

The excursion ended early this morning, when they were landed at their homes in Boston, having been absent since Aug. 4. They report a very pleasant trip throughout, and speak in high terms of the repeated courtesy which has greeted them at every point.

Our ride across Michigan was completed at 1 A. M., and we proceeded over the Grand Trunk homeward. Mr. J. A. Richardson, travelling passenger agent of the Grand Trunk Railway, joined us at Chicago, and continued with us till our arrival at St. John's, a terminus of the Grand Trunk. He was very welcome, having made the outward trip with us as far as Chicago. He was social and gentlemanly, and used all his authority and persuasion to put the train through to Montreal on time. Going West there were six or seven hours lost on the Canada road, but on our return we came into Montreal only an hour behind time. Mr. Defries, the conductor on the Grand Trunk, did all he could to make the day's ride comfortable and enjoyable.

At Toronto, at 7.45 A. M., the Commandery breakfasted at the Queen's and Rossin's Hotels. The quiet of the early Sunday hours in Toronto and other Canadian towns, when compared with the doings of our own Western towns, was very striking. Evidently it was Sunday in Canada; in the railroad towns in the far West there is no Sunday. On Sunday dinner was well served in the dining-cars of the Grand Trunk road. At 8 P. M., Boston Commandery arrived in Montreal. The train was immediately deserted, and quarters taken at the Windsor. The Sir Knights were soon provided with rooms and supper was served. While here the cars received further attention, and entered Boston as bright and clean as when they left.

CHAPTER XIX.

SUBSEQUENTLY in the spacious rotunda of the Windsor House, in the presence of Past Grand Master Dean, Eminent Commander Stevenson, Sir Knights, ladies, and guests of the hotel, a religious service was conducted by Rev. Oliver Ayer Roberts, Prelate of Boston Commandery during the California pilgrimage.

There were the usual introductory services, congregational singing, led by Sir Knights Wilbur F. Miller and Henry L. Batchelder, prayer by the Prelate, who then read, as a Scripture lesson, Revelation i. and ii. 8–12. After another hymn had been sung the Prelate delivered the following sermon: —

Leaving Rhodes with its dismantled dwelling of the Grand Master, with Templars' coat-of-arms sculptured on the fronts of the ancient houses, with its scattered fragments of the once fair church of St. John, — a memorable spot, where for one whole summer six thousand knights defended their city against two hundred thousand Moslems, — we steamed by the isle of Patmos, bare and brown, where John the Evangelist beheld unutterable things. The next morning we anchored in the magnificent harbor of Smyrna. The city, containing two hundred thousand people, is situated upon a plain and upon the first swellings of the hills, which lift their summits high above the shore. The bay, the city, the Cyclopean walls, the ruins of the old apostolic church, with the high surrounding hills, constitute a rare view.

Everything becomes more interesting when we remember Smyrna was the birthplace and home of Polycarp, "the angel of the church in Smyrna," and there is pointed out not only the site of his church, but the spot where this eminent man suffered martyrdom.

"And unto the angel of the church in Smyrna, write: These things saith the first and the last, which was dead, and is alive; I know thy works, and tribulation, and poverty, and I know the blasphemy of them which say they are Jews, and are not, but are the synagogue of Satan. Fear none of those things which thou shalt suffer. Behold, the devil shall cast some of you into prison, that ye may be tried; and ye shall have tribulation ten days. Be thou faithful unto death, and I will give thee a crown of life."

These words, quoted from the Revelation of St. John the divine (ii. 8-10), are the language of one who announces himself as follows: "I am Alpha and Omega, the beginning and the ending, saith the Lord, which is, and which was, and which is to come, the Almighty" (i. 8); also, "I am the first and the last: I am he that liveth, and was dead; and behold, I am alive forever-more" (i. 17, 18). The speaker by name and description is identified as Jesus, the Messiah, concerning whom we believe and teach: "He was born of the Virgin Mary; suffered under Pontius Pilate, was crucified, dead, and buried; the third day he rose from the dead; he ascended into heaven and sitteth on the right hand of God the Father Almighty; from thence he shall come to judge the living and the dead." It was he who condescended to commune with the beloved disciple on Patmos; it was he who as Lord and Judge reviewed the condition of the church in Smyrna and pronounced his decision; it was he who foresaw and foretold the suffering and tribulation that were to wound and scatter the youthful church; it was he who dictated these helpful, hopeful words for the encouragement of Polycarp, the angel of that church, viz., "Fear none of those things which thou shalt suffer. . . . Be thou faithful unto death, and I will give thee a crown of life."

The waves of persecution rolled over Smyrna's shore. The disciples were sorely tried. Polycarp stood forth an illustrious example of unshaken fidelity to the truth and of saintly trust in a crown of life. His work was harassed, his steps dogged. His life was sought, nevertheless he trod the path of Christian duty, believing in "the crown of life, which the Lord hath promised to them that love him." Brighter than flame or earthly crown glows the fidelity of the angel-bishop. Polycarp evaded not the enemies of the cross, but received them cheerfully and kindly. He invited them to banquet. Afterward by every persuasion he was urged to renounce his faith. He would not trample upon the cross. When entering the stadium, a voice came from heaven, saying, "Be strong, Polycarp, and contend manfully." The proconsul, again urging him, said, "Swear, and I will release thee! Reproach Christ!" Hear the reply of the aged saint: "Eighty-and-six years have I served him, and he has done me nothing but good, and how could I curse him, my Lord and my Saviour? If you would know what I am, I tell you frankly, I am a Christian." The populace then demanded that he should die at the stake. Preparations were therefore made. Fagots were brought. Polycarp refused to be nailed to the stake, but deliberately placed his hands behind him and prayed. The murderers kindled the fire: the flames leaped and sighed. In the midst thereof Polycarp was not like flesh burning, but like gold and silver purified in the furnace. A fragrant odor like the fumes of incense spread around. He was crowned with a crown of immortality. Such is the origin and immediate application of our text: "Be thou faithful unto death, and I will give thee a crown of life." (Revelations ii. 10.)

I have selected these words as a text for this hour from several considerations: *First*, They are the words of the chiefest among ten thousand. *Secondly*, They express an unvarying law, fidelity brings its reward: after the cross the crown. Again, they are calculated to check the faithless and encourage the faithful. Moreover, they constitute the motto of Boston Commandery of Knights Templars. They encircle the cross and crown upon its seal. They are borne upon its banner. The tribe of Judah marched through the wilderness at the head of the chosen people, bearing aloft its banner emblazoned with a lion as its symbol, denoting courage, strength. Boston Commandery takes its place at the head of the Templar host bearing upon its banner a motto infinitely more significant and precious. "Be thou faithful unto death, and I will give thee a crown of life," held by their strong arms, has floated in the gale upon the summit of Mt. Washington, and, higher than Templars' banner was unfurled before, has been displayed upon the mountains of the West. This motto is appropriate. Heaven's Prince uttered it. It inspires to utmost obedience, and promises a crown of life when pilgrimage and warfare on earth are completed. Fling wide its golden folds. Let the mountain breezes baptize and kiss it. Let the valleys hear it. Let villages and hamlets read it. Let the whole world drink of its blessedness.

> "Fling out the banner! Heathen lands
> Shall see from far the glorious sight;
> And nations, crowding to be born,
> Baptize their spirits in its light.
>
> "Fling out the banner! Sin-sick souls
> That sink and perish in the strife
> Shall touch in faith its radiant hem,
> And spring immortal into life.
>
> "Fling out the banner! Wide and high,
> Seaward and skyward, let it shine;
> Nor skill, nor might, nor merit, ours:
> We conquer only in that sign."
>
> *Bishop Doane.*

As the brave crusader exclaimed when, on the field of Acre, pierced to his death, he passed the banner of the cross as he reeled in his saddle, to the knight by his side, "Men fall, but the banner of Christ never goes down." The staff may break, but the banner, with its beautiful folds, and more with its golden truth, never let that droop; bear it aloft with strong arms and trusty faith, and thou shalt find on the other side, when the crowns are given to the faithful, that this banner with its cross and crown and promise is the banner of our God.

The crown of eternal life was promised Polycarp on condition of his faithfulness. Obedience on earth was to culminate in victory in heaven. His it was to prove faithful, to proclaim the truth, to counsel the church, to converse wisely and walk uprightly, to endure with patience and die with fortitude. The result, a crown of life, was the promise of the Almighty.

The temporal duty was Polycarp's, the eternal gift was God's. It is thus with all men. It is their duty to be faithful to their opportunities and light, and as effect succeeds cause, so there will come to every sincere life the promised blessing. Ours it is "to run the race," "to endure to the end," "to be faithful unto death." God is the author of the course. He placed us in the race. We are not responsible for its length, "its rough and rugged ways," its wild mountain passes, its paths in deep and chilling glens. We are responsible for the spirit in which we enter it, and for the energy and fidelity with which we push onwards towards the goal. Fidelity to life's best aim and end should be our battle-cry. The illustrious Duke of Wellington, when some one said that a Frenchman had noticed that the word "glory" never appeared in his despatches, remarked, "How foolish must that man be not to see that if I wished to get the rich harvest of glory, the way to do it was *to do my duty*." Duty, present duty, the duty of this and of each moment, truly done, is the course to the crown. The post of honor, of success, of power, of final triumph, is the post of duty.

We, Companions and Sir Knights, have made a great profession. Serious and important duties rest upon us. Though convened from various States, though taught in different "asylums," clad in unlike regalias, and differing as men, in habits, circumstances, and opinions, nevertheless, the same vows bind us all, the same duties are before us, the same scenes of mortality and life have impressed us, the same unsectarian and inspiring truth of God has received the plight of our protection and love. We are held by our profession to the highest manifestation of every virtue and to the truest portraiture of the Christian life. We are pledged to care for our bodies, to regard our neighbor, feed the hungry, clothe the naked, bind up the wounds of the afflicted, to perform our earthly pilgrimage with patience and perseverance, to carry on life's warfare with courage and constancy, and to endure the pains and afflictions of life with faith and humility. It is our duty to be faithful unto death, inspired with such moral firmness as George III. displayed when speaking on the Roman Catholic question. He said, "I can give up my crown and retire from power, I can quit my palace and live in a cottage, I can lay my head on a block and lose my life, but I can *not* break my oath."

Let me rehearse some of those principles and duties which we professedly accept, to which it is necessary for us to prove faithful if we would obtain a crown of life.

1. Vividly have we been reminded of human weakness and mortality. There was a motto on the walls of the Delphian Temple, ascribed to Chilo, one of the seven wise men of Greece, "Consider the end." The royal road that monarchs travel, attended by their courtly train, the way whereon the learned walk, the path whereon the warrior leads his multitude, the roads whereon humanity loiters without nerve or hope, or rushes onward with ambitions boundless, lead to one place. All terminate in that "house appointed for all the living." The pride of beauty, the strength of manhood, are no unconquerable defence. We hail the appointed dissolution. Weak and mortal, chained in this clayey tenement, we complain not of the bound we cannot pass, remembering that while travelling the rough and rugged paths of this life, a firm reliance on Divine Providence can alone afford us that consolatory satisfaction and peace of mind which this world can neither give nor take away. The emblems of mortality, with helpful word, encourage us to improve this span of life, that when our weak and frail bodies become cold and inanimate, our spirits may soar aloft and dwell forever in realms of light and everlasting bliss. Mortality demands the support, comfort, and blessing of divinity. We recognize this truth as fundamental; and therefore,

2. The Holy Scriptures are accepted as our authority and guide. The Book of books is ever open upon our altar. From its wisdom we draw our lessons, upon its truth we found our ritual. From it we formulate no creed; upon its interpretation we seek the decision of no council or synod; from its deep revelations we weave no scholastic system; concerning its shadowed mysteries, over which sects wrangle, we recognize the largest liberty; but the great light blazes upon our altars, sheds abroad its light and truth, and begets its unspeakable hope in the hearts of our communion. To the broadest freedom in its interpretation, to the cheerful defence of its truth, to the embodiment of its wisdom, to the attainment of its promised crown, we are severally and solemnly pledged.

> "Most wondrous Book! bright candle of the Lord!
> Star of eternity! The only star
> By which the bark of man can navigate
> The sea of life, and gain the coast of bliss.
> The only star which ever rose on Time,
> And, on its dark and troubled billows, still,
> As generation, drifting swiftly by,
> Succeedeth generation, throws a ray
> Of heaven's own light up to the hills of God."   *Pollock.*

The Bible is our Malakoff. It is our chiefest light. It is the inestimable gift of God to man, the image of himself. It has been cast into the fire, but it is not burned. It has been thrown into the water, but it is not drowned. It has been ostracized by papal edicts, but in every clime it is welcomed. Fire may consume our altars, water may extinguish all other lights, but no crafty hand can rob us of our great "Light," whose author is God, whose subject is truth, whose happy issue is a crown of life. Without it would be darkness, chaos, dissolution; with it there are light, love, and life. The knightly host here marshalled, our knightly companions throughout the world, are morally pledged to maintain the integrity and sacredness of this Book of books, and esteem it as the gift of God, teaching "the best way of living, the noblest way of suffering, and the most comfortable way of dying."

3. We believe in the Son of God, who humbled himself to be born of a woman, to endure all the pains and afflictions incident to human nature, and finally to suffer a cruel and ignominious death upon the cross. We believe that, after having suffered the pains of death, he descended into the place of departed spirits; that on the third day he burst the bars of death and triumphed over the grave, and in due time ascended with transcendent majesty to heaven, where he now sits at the right hand of our Heavenly Father, a mediator and intercessor for all those who put their faith in him. This is the lever that lifts the world. This is the great song of apostles, martyrs, and saints, which has wakened multitudes from death to life, and girdled the globe with new impulses and new hopes. This is the living flame by whose light and warmth our Order has outlived centuries without knowing the weakness of

age. This is the eternal truth, by whose inspiring power Templarism has survived the scimitars of the Saracens, the confiscations by popes and kings, the fires of martyrdom, and the torments of the Inquisition. It is on account of its present Christian character, deficient though it be, more than by its solemn service and impressive ritual, that its influence still widens and its membership multiplies. To the defence of the Christian religion on the tented field and in our daily walk, to the acceptance of Him who is the way, the truth, and the life, we are unqualifiedly committed.

In a small chapel in the Church of the Holy Sepulchre, the servitor may be induced to show you an ancient sword, with which the Knights of St. John are girt when invested with that honorable Order. Vulgar curiosity sees nothing but an old belt of leather, a black, rusty scabbard, and a sword not beautiful. Its edge is keen, its blade wide, and still bears the marks of the blacksmith's hammer. Stupid ones call it "another of those pious frauds." The unreflecting look, then pass along, to wonder at the crown of thorns, the bloody spear, or some other invention of the place. The servitor says, "This is the sword of Godfrey de Bouillon." The fact is apparent, and the sword becomes invested with intense interest. What a history it has! With this same sword did Godfrey slay the Emperor Rudolph on the field of Molsen? Girt with this did Godfrey plant Henry's banner on the walls of Rome? With this did he cut his way through phalanxes of Greeks and hordes of Turks, till the City of Peace rose in sight? With this did he cleave horsemen from head to saddle, and with one stroke cut off an ox's or camel's head? The begrimed sword is an historic treasure. It represents the strength of a giant, the heroism of a dauntless knight, the leadership, power, and self-abasement of one who declined to assume a royal crown on that spot where the Saviour had been crowned with thorns. The cross, the universal symbol of the Christian system, ever signifying the obedience and sacrifice of Jesus Christ, has been the badge of knighthood since the days of Bohemund and St. Bernard. The first cut his coat-of-arms, the latter his outer garment, into small crosses, which as badges were distributed among the knights of the First and Second Crusades. Subsequently, —

> "In glorious Christian field,
> Streaming the ensign of the Christian cross,
> Against black pagans, Turks, and Saracens."

The intrinsic value of our symbol, whether made of gold, wood, or cloth, is of minor account. We wear it for what it symbolizes. By the unanimous assent of the civilized world, the cross represents certain great truths, which we accept. The cross symbolizes the brotherhood of man ; forgiveness, even toward enemies ; life's mission fulfilled ; love, universal and perfect ; self-sacrifice, cheerful and complete ; and obedience, even unto death. It signifies faith, — courageous, conquering faith ; it signifies hope, — patient, steadfast hope ; it signifies charity, — amiable, universal, and everlasting charity. The cross signifies Christ, — all he was, all he did, all he endured. It signifies discipleship. He, therefore, who wears the cross as the symbol of his faith, should be thereby continually reminded of that nobility of manhood, that perfection of character, that fidelity unto death, so essentially necessary to gaining admission where the once crucified but now living Saviour abides forever.

4. Charity and hospitality are the distinguishing characteristics of our Order. "Though I speak with the tongues of men and of angels, . . . though I have the gift of prophecy, and understand all mysteries, and all knowledge, . . . though I bestow all my goods to feed the poor, and though I give my body to be burned, and have not charity, it profiteth me nothing." Charity is the corner-stone of our temple ; it is the cement which binds us all as friends and brothers. The nine knights, who called themselves "poor Fellow-Soldiers of Jesus Christ," formed a brotherhood on Christian charity. They protected the pious pilgrims in Palestine who, travelling from afar, were exposed to plunder and death. They bound themselves by a solemn compact to protect the innocent, relieve the distressed, feed the hungry, and to distribute alms to the poor and needy. The humane work thus begun was consecrated with blood. During the nine centuries of its struggle, it has been rebaptized in fire and blood again and again ; but the passing years dull not the knightly blade, nor stay the fountains of knightly charity.

Charity is more than generosity : it is love. It is more than the bestowal of aid, or the sentiment of commiseration ; for, as the apostle declares, "charity suffers long and is kind." True knightly charity includes not only the guarding of dangerous passes, and the making of tedious journeys to relieve distress, when necessary, but also the thoughts we coin, the words we speak. Charity in giving is abundant; charity in thinking and speaking is comparatively scarce. The spirit of resentment, the spirit of aversion, the spirit of jealousy, the spirit of indifference, are alike opposed to charity. These we are taught to shun, and to cultivate that charity which covers a multitude of sins. The ancient councils, when they deposed any bishop, never recorded the offence, but buried it in perpetual silence. Knightly charity should lock in charitable breasts the faults of brother-man and cover his foibles with charity as with a garment. A painter was commanded to sketch the Macedonian emperor. In one of the emperor's battles he had been struck with a sword upon the forehead, and a very large scar had been left on the right temple. The painter, who was a master in his art, sketched him leaning on his elbow, with his finger covering the scar on his forehead; and so the likeness of the king was taken, but without the scar. Sketch men — their faces and their deeds — in memory, without their scars. Draw the finger of a tender and forbearing charity over the healed wounds of men.

> "Teach me to feel another's woe,
> To hide the fault I see;
> That mercy I to others show,
> That mercy show to me."   *Pope.*

"And now abideth faith, hope, charity, these three; but the greatest of these is charity."

Faith may be lost in sight, hope ends in fruition,

> "But charity, serene, sublime,
> Beyond the reach of death and time,
> Like the blue sky's all-bounding space,
> Holds heaven and earth in its embrace."   *Montgomery.*

Such are the fundamental tenets of our Order, — mortality, Christ, the Bible, and charity, — which invest us with the most important duties of life. Grander principles were never avowed, more important were never revealed. We ought to accept them in sincerity and manifest them with fidelity. Let "not our profession be but a painted pageantry; not like the trappings upon the black horses which draw men to their graves; not a thing of ornament, a passport to respectability, or a cheap substitute for a warfare never truly made" and for a crown never truly striven for, but with that zeal which characterized the ancient knights, with that feeling of self-sacrifice which distinguished the lone pilgrim-guard among the defiles of Palestine; with the whole armor of Christian knighthood on, buckled and burnished, let our profession be made our practice, and the sublime tenets we are taught become the sincerely attempted standard of our living; then we will, with Polycarp and De Molay, prove obedient to the counsel of our great Teacher, namely, "Be thou faithful unto death."

II. "I will give thee a crown of life." The crown is ancient and well-nigh universal. Since the mythological days of Jupiter, "the first crowned by the gods," since Nimrod, the mighty hunter, wore this symbol of power, crowns have been in use. In the Old Testament era kings and priests wore them, though differing in form and material. In the New Testament reference is often made to the crowns of laurel, pine, or parsley, given to victors in the great games of Greece. But in the vision of St. John the most precious metal shines on every hand. The city appeared "to be of pure gold like unto clear glass." The street of the city was pure gold. John speaks of the golden censer, golden candlesticks, golden vials, golden girdle, and *golden crown*.

"I will give thee a crown of life"; also 1 Peter v. 4, "When the chief Shepherd shall appear, ye shall receive a crown of glory that fadeth not away"; and Paul, in 2 Timothy iv. 8, declares, "Henceforth there is laid up for me a crown of righteousness, which the Lord, the righteous Judge, shall give me at that day: and not to me only, but unto all them also that love his appearing." Herein crown is used figuratively, denoting a place, a power, a dignity, an authority bestowed as the gift of God. The crown thus promised to those faithful unto death is not of earthly texture, for it is fadeless and eternal. A crown of life prefigures the best, the deepest, the highest, the most glorious thing the Supreme Architect of the universe can bestow upon the creatures of his love. "A crown of life!" It does not signify the wreath of green won by the victorious runners of Greece. "They do it to obtain a corruptible crown, but we an incorruptible." It does not signify the golden circlet, the jewelled mitre, or the imperial diadem. These all tarnish, and like all human glory pass away, but the promise of the Almighty is an eternal, unfading, ever-precious crown of life.

> "A crown with peerless glories bright,
> Which shall new lustre boast,
> When victors' wreaths and monarchs' gems
> Shall blend in common dust." *Doddridge.*

The promise is crowns of glory and of life, — not literal crowns of fashioned gold, glittering on the brows of saints, but the crown of life is sainthood exalted to a perfect state, and immersed forever in the unspeakable glories of the spirit life. "I will give thee a crown of life," or "a crown of glory that fadeth not away." It symbolizes peace : crown-bearers shall never hear war's wild alarm, nor the disputes of contentious men. It symbolizes beauty : crown-bearers "will shine like so many suns in the kingdom of the Father." Heaven full of earth's faithful toilers each emitting a splendor like the glorious body of our Lord. It stands for dignity : crown-bearers constitute a congress of sovereigns, a commonwealth of kings, a royal priesthood, heirs of God and joint heirs with Christ to an inheritance that will never fade away. They are kings and priests unto God, and shall reign for ever and ever. A crown of life symbolizes love : crown-bearers dwell in God, and God in them, but God is love. It symbolizes activity : crown-bearers look forward into an eternity of untiring action. Fields of knowledge far outreaching, heights of perfection unattained, inspiring the glorious activity of immortal powers. It stands for praise : crown-bearers pray not, but praise. The whispering of adoring love, the greeting of kindred spirits, the full chorus of the redeemed, are only praise, praise to "Him that sitteth on the throne, and to the Lamb forever." A crown of life symbolizes knowledge: crown-bearers realize that "that which is in part is done away" and "the perfect is come." "Then shall I know even as I am known." "We shall be like him, for we shall see him as he is." It symbolizes triumph and victory. Battles are over. The sword forever sheathed. Conquests all complete. Death slain, sin overthrown, and universal victory will thrill and delight all hearts. A crown of life symbolizes a city, New Jerusalem, never built with hands, nor hoary with the years of time. "A city through whose streets will rush no tide of business; no nodding hearse will slowly creep with its burden to the tomb. A city across whose firmament will roll no sun; around whose people will gather no night." A city where sorrow will never come, tears never fall; a city without grief or graves, mournings or marriages, whose walls are salvation, whose gates are praise. A crown of life symbolizes infinitely more: crown-bearers shall see Jehovah, and greet their risen Lord. They shall mingle with the good and great of by-gone centuries, and revel ever in unspeakable delight.

Be patient, O cross-bearer! If faithful unto death, thou wilt become a crown-bearer, and then the glory of that crown of life, which now it cannot enter into the mind of man to conceive, thou shalt know, and its wealth of blessedness thou shalt possess.

"These are the crowns that we shall wear,
    When all the saints are crowned;
These are the palms that we shall bear,
    On yonder holy ground.

"That is the city of the saints,
    Where we so soon shall stand,
When we shall strike these desert tents,
    And quit this desert land.

"Then welcome toil and care and pain,
    And welcome sorrow, too,
All toil is rest, all grief is gain
    With such a crown in view.

"Come, crown and throne; come, robe and palm;
    Burst forth glad stream of peace;
Come, holy city of the Lamb,
    Let these thy blessing share."   *Bonar.*

The sermon was listened to with close attention, and, after singing and a benediction, the last Sunday of the pilgrimage was fittingly closed.

CHAPTER XX.

MONTREAL papers of the following day thus referred to the visit of Boston Commandery to that city: —

A special train of Pullman cars arrived in the city from the West last evening, having on board the Boston Commandery of Knights Templars, *en route* for Boston, on their return journey from San Francisco, where a gathering of the Order was held about the middle of August. The party, numbering nearly two hundred, are all stopping at the Windsor. After leaving here on Aug. 5, the party went through to San Francisco, arriving there on the 14th of August, and having spent a day at Las Vegas, Los Angeles, and Santa Fé *en route*. After stopping eleven days at San Francisco, they left for the return trip on the 25th of August, and spending a day at Salt Lake City and another at Chicago on the way, they arrived in Montreal last evening and put up at the Windsor. The members were summoned together in the hotel last evening for religious service, when an eloquent address was delivered by the acting Prelate, the Rev. Oliver A. Roberts, from the text, "Be thou faithful unto death, and I will give thee a crown of life." To-day will be spent in visiting the various points of interest in the city, and the party will leave for Boston this evening. The Commandery acted as an escort to Most Eminent Benjamin Dean, now Past Grand Master of Templars of the United States, and was the largest in the grand procession of some five thousand swords, the Commandery itself numbering one hundred and five swords. — *Montreal Gazette, Sept.* 3.

Last evening an interesting event took place on the arrival in town of the Boston Commandery of Knights Templars, numbering some one hundred and sixty-nine persons, including ladies, John L Stevenson, Eminent Commander. The Commandery are on their return trip from their pilgrimage to San Francisco, where they attended the Grand Triennial Conclave held on Aug. 21, which extended over a week. The party, it will be remembered, left Boston on Aug. 4, *via* the Central Vermont Railway, arriving in Montreal on Sunday, the 5th, and proceeding on their journey to the golden city. Since then they have travelled over some seven thousand miles of country, without accident or sickness of any kind, and have spent a most enjoyable time. On their journey West, stoppages were made at Las Vegas Hot Springs, N. M., Santa Fé, Los Angeles, and on their return trip one day at Salt Lake City. The Commandery, numbering one hundred and five swords, was the largest Commandery in line in the grand procession at San Francisco, which included some five thousand Sir Knights. This Commandery had also the honor of being the escort to the Most Eminent Benjamin Dean, Grand Master of Knights Templars of the United States, who accompanies them on their return journey. On arrival in town last evening the party at once proceeded to the Windsor Hotel, where, after supper, divine service was held, an elegant address being delivered by Rev. O. A. Roberts, Prelate, which clearly defined the tenets of the Order, under the text, "Be thou faithful unto death, and I will give thee a crown of life." This morning the Commandery ran the Lachine Rapids, and after spending the rest of the day in viewing the principal sights of Montreal and its vicinity, will leave for Boston by special train of eight elegant Pullman cars at eight o'clock this evening. — *The Montreal Herald, Sept.* 3.

The Knights Templars who arrived in this city Sunday evening from an extended trip to San Francisco and other points on the Pacific slope passed yesterday very agreeably. They were astir at an early hour yesterday, and proceeded to Lachine at eight o'clock, in order to run the Lachine Rapids. On their arrival at Lachine, the steamer "Prince of Wales" was in waiting for them. They shortly afterwards embarked, and ran the rapids in safety. In conversation with a member of the party this afternoon, our reporter was informed that all on board were delighted with the run. The party left for Boston last night at eight o'clock.

A party of the Knights Templars visited Joe Beef's yesterday to inspect the menagerie, and whilst there one of them, weighing twenty stone, was carried round the place on the horns of the buffalo, from which precarious position he was safely rescued by Joe himself. — *The Daily Star, Sept.* 4.

The latter item, clipped from the *Daily Star*, is interpreted in the racy correspondence of Sir J. D. D., published in the *Journal and Courier*, New Haven, Conn. He wrote as follows: —

Monday, the 3d, was spent in the usual sight-seeing fashion so familiar to all, yet I venture to say that one of our entertainments will be new to many. At a resort in the lower section of the city, kept by a man named Joe Beef, the male portion of the pilgrims found more fun to the square inch than at any other place this side of Sundown. This Joe sells gin, beer, etc., and has a curiosity shop as well. Among the rubbish in one corner is a huge bath-tub where Joe dips his victims if drunk, and *he does it* when occasion requires. Behind the counter or bar is a human skeleton, upright, wrapped in the British flag. There are other curiosities too numerous to mention, for his crib and its contents can- not be explained in a brief letter. What we went to see was his menagerie, com- posed of bears, wolves, wildcats, etc., the main attraction being a huge buffalo. Joe invited all of us, eight Sir Knights, to en- ter the den, with the assurance there was no danger. At the first crack of the whip the small animals set up a howl and Mr. Bison charged on the crowd. By a desperate effort I escaped by the door, Sir Knight W. close to my back.

W. declares that one horn grazed his back. Two of our party, Sir Knights M. and B., jumped up to a high window and remained there a long time before venturing down. Joe claims that all of his collection is tame, but we all expressed ourselves as better satisfied to stay outside the cage in the future. *Moral:* Don't believe all that people tell you, and shun bad company.

Monday morning came, but the halls of the hotel were quiet. The tired Knights were improving the opportunity of making up lost sleep. The porters were called into service and the command was wakened for breakfast and the shooting of the Lachine Rapids. At 7 A. M. carriages were in readiness to take the party to Bonaventura Street station, where cars were taken for Lachine. Sir Silas W. Cummings, general passenger agent of the Central Vermont Railroad, to whom Boston Commandery is under many obligations, was on the train and distributed among the Sir Knights and ladies a souvenir of this excursion.

Embarking at Lachine on the steamer "Filgate," with the veteran Jean Baptiste as pilot, one hundred and twenty-five of the Commandery and its friends made the safe descent of the rapids among projecting rocks, over angry waves, and through foaming eddies. From the flag-staff on the bow of the steamer floated the *beauseant* of Boston Commandery. Accompanying the party were Mr. T. H. Hooper, superintendent Montreal Division, Grand Trunk Railroad, and Sir Col. A. A. Stevenson, commander of the Montreal Field Battery. All were very much

VICTORIA BRIDGE, MONTREAL.

pleased with the "shooting," notwithstanding the cutting blast, which made overcoats and wraps a necessity. The continuance of the ride down the river and under Victoria Bridge gave us a better appreciation of that wonderful structure. This bridge was constructed on the plan of the Britannia, is nearly two miles long, cost over five million dollars, and contains ten thousand five hundred tons of iron. It is a huge tube, eighteen feet high by fourteen wide, of wrought iron. From the railroad track to the water at high tide, the distance is one hundred and fifty feet, thereby forming no obstruction to the tallest masts. The floor is slightly curved, for the purpose of increased strength. This curve or the raising of the centre prevents one from seeing through the bridge. There are twenty-four piers, which contain no stone weighing less than two tons. Most of them weigh five tons each. The central span is four hundred feet long, about double the length of the others. It was two years in its erection. A royal dinner was given within the bridge at the completion of the work. The Prince of Wales was present, and with a trowel gave the finishing touches, when the bridge was pronounced finished. It was at the time of his memorable visit to this country, A. D. 1860.

Returning at 10 A. M., the remainder of the day was occupied in doing Montreal. Churches, charitable institutions, monuments of her Majesty Victoria, and of Lord Nelson, and other places of interest were visited. The Church of Notre Dame, with its lofty towers, many chapels, imposing sanctuary, and main altar, was leisurely examined and much admired. Some, by a corridor back of the altar, found their way into the sacristy, where a courteous sacristan for a small fee displayed the gorgeous vestments used on great occasions. Mount Royal Park was also visited, and its fine view of the city and river enjoyed. Some entered the Gray Nunnery and witnessed the procession of the gray nuns at noon, and made a call upon the foundlings, whose little hands were uplifted for a gift. Older boys and girls sang and performed gymnastics, in order to get pennies, handfuls of which followed their entertaining efforts. The day was greatly enjoyed. It was a restful season, preparatory to the last day and march of this successful pilgrimage.

On its homeward journey the party was increased by the addition, at San Francisco, of Mrs. Caroline Davenport, sister of Sir

Knight Edward T. Nichols, who returned to Boston after an absence of more than thirty years; at Port Huron, of Mrs. Oliver A. Roberts and children, Oliver B. and Stephen H. Roberts; at Montreal, of Sir Knight A. A. Folsom, superintendent of the Boston and Providence Railroad, and wife, and Misses Nellie and Maud Stevenson, daughters of Eminent Sir John L. Stevenson, and Past Most Eminent Grand Master James H. Hopkins, of Pennsylvania, who joined the party at San Francisco, but left it at Chicago. On arrival at the Windsor, the warm greetings of Sir Knight James A. Rich, Palestine Commandery, No. 18, New York City, and of Sir Knight Charles E. Pierce, Captain General of St. Omer Commandery, Boston, were received by telegraph. After supper, "all present or accounted for," the party boarded their palace cars for the final stage of their pilgrimage.

Boston Commandery, having made excellent progress during the night, arrived at Keene, N. H., on time, 7 A. M. The command was sent to the Cheshire, City, and Eagle Hotels for breakfast. An excellent meal was provided, and the Sir Knights and ladies were presented with an elegant souvenir *menu* of the breakfast, a card of four pages. The last bore Templar emblems, the second and third the *menu*; the first, on a background of purple satin, bore a shield, on which there were symbols of the Order. The train started promply at 9 A. M., previous to which it was photographed. The Commandery at Keene intended a reception for Boston Commandery, but the early hour of our arrival prevented. Immediately upon our departure a pleasing episode occurred. Sir Knights E. T. Nichols and Charles E. Adams presented the compliments of the party riding in the car "Spokane" in the form of a card, which contained the names of the three cars they have occupied, "Odessa," "Mohave," and "Spokane," worked into a double cross, also the names of the occupants of the car, bearing at the bottom the words, "Hot boxes and broken journal." It was from these causes that the "Odessa" was left at Kansas City and the "Mohave" at Chicago. The ladies received a beautiful card of invitation bearing a gilt Maltese cross in the centre, of which the following is a fac-simile: —

SPOKANE
MOHAVE
ODESSA

The forenoon ride from Keene to Boston was delightful. The ever-changing scenery, the many towns and cities, busy and progressive, which we passed, and the expectation of soon reaching the end of the pilgrimage, gave new interest to the trip. During these last hours the porters of the cars were remembered pecuniarily. A substantial testimonial was presented Sir Z. H. Thomas, recorder, as a recognition of his services; and preparations were made for a suitable souvenir of the high consideration in which the Eminent Commander was held, and in recognition of his earnest, faithful, and unequalled labor in the interest of the pilgrimage. The pilgrims passed from car to car, shook hands, bidding each other good by, and packed their wares and goods preparatory to disembarking. The last miles quickly vanished; the train made its last stop. With grateful hearts the party disembarked, greeted by hosts of friends. Unspeakable the emotions of standing once more on our native soil after a journey of eight thousand miles, without accident or loss. The ladies were escorted to Young's Hotel by Sir A. A. Folsom, and the Commandery speedily formed its lines for its reception and march.

"De Molay Commandery had determined to receive its brethren in a fitting manner, and accordingly assembled in Masonic Hall, Tremont Street, soon after noon, about one hundred Sir Knights responding to the call. Shortly before one o'clock the company was marshalled on the Common, the Boston City Band, F. A. Hersey, leader, at their head. Eminent Sir H. P. Hemenway was in command, and was assisted by Generalissimo F. T. Dwinell and Captain General George T. Ambrose; the military movements being under the direction of Senior Warden H. G. Jordan. The companies present were commanded by Sir Knights John Mack, George H. Maynard, E. R. Frost, W. H. Chester, A. C. Betteley, and A. K. Timson. The route taken to the Fitchburg Depot was through Tremont, Sudbury, Canal, and Causeway Streets.

"Promptly at 1 P. M. the train bearing Boston Commandery Knights Templars, on their return journey from their grand pilgrimage to San Francisco, rolled into the Fitchburg Depot in this city, where was assembled a large number of persons to greet them, the gathering including many ladies, relatives of members of the party. As the train stopped and the first glimpse was caught of a plumed chapeau, a hearty round of applause was given the travellers, and the next moment there was a scene of congratulation and friendly greeting, here and there, denoting relationship. A short time was spent in arranging for transportation of baggage and the minor details to be looked after when journeying, and then line was formed under command of Eminent Commander John L. Stevenson, Sir E. J. Trull acting Captain General, as executive officer, the lines numbering one hundred and four men, headed by the Cadet Band, Sir J. Thomas Baldwin, of Boston Commandery, leader. Outside the depot the De Molay Commandery, one hundred men in line, was drawn up in Canal Street. After the customary courtesies in the reception by the escort, the line of march was taken up through Canal Street, Haymarket Square, Union Street, Faneuil Hall Square, South Market, Commercial, State, Washington, School, and Tremont Streets, to Masonic Temple. Most Eminent Sir Benjamin Dean, who accompanied the party, was also under escort, being seated in a carriage, accompanied by Eminent Sir William Parkman and Sir Joseph M. Russell, of De Molay. A feature of the parade was the appearance, borne aloft in a cage, of the eagle captured in New Mexico and presented to the Commandery at Wallace, N. M. Having arrived at the Temple, the Knights with little ceremony repaired to the banquet-hall, where the Sir Knights of De Molay and Boston Commanderies were seated side by side at the tables.

"Commander H. P. Hemenway presided, while on his right sat Past Grand Master Benjamin Dean, and upon his left Commander John L. Stevenson, of Boston Commandery. Brief prayer by Rev. Oliver A. Roberts, Prelate of Boston Commandery during the pilgrimage, was followed by a vigorous attack upon the well-loaded board. The appetite being fully satisfied, Eminent Commander Hemenway said: —

"*Eminent Commander and Sir Knights of Boston Commandery:* Our hearts have throbbed with joy as we have read of the ovation accorded you in a journey unprecedented in our history. It is appropriate that Boston Commandery, the oldest in the country, should attend the Triennial Conclave, and I wish to offer you as a proper sentiment, 'Boston Commandery, the oldest Templar organization in America. May its future career be as proud and harmonious as its past has been honorable and useful to the Fraternity.' [The toast being drunk standing, the Eminent Commander continued:] It would ill become me to take up more of your time, and, therefore, I have pleasure in introducing to you Eminent Commander John L. Stevenson, of Boston Commandery. [*Great applause.*]

"Commander Stevenson replied: —

"*Eminent Sir and Sir Knights of De Molay Commandery:* I have a deep sense of the honor which has fallen to my lot, to be the recipient at your hands of these courtesies, which I know are appreciated by all the members of Boston Commandery, who fully join in thanking you for every kind word and thought which you have had for us. It is, indeed, the ending of a remarkable pilgrimage that a Commandery of Knights Templars has traversed this continent from the far East to the far West, from Boston to San Francisco, and paraded there with a larger number of Sir Knights than any other Commandery, except those of San Francisco. We have had no accident of any kind to mar our pleasure, but instead there have come to us all the blessings that ever fell to the lot of man. With all these circumstances is it remarkable that we should survive and return in good health and at the very instant at which we promised we would thirty-one days ago? Our trip has been unprecedented in many ways. The train was the first that was ever run from Boston to San Francisco on a special time schedule, without change of cars, and with a right of way across the continent. We have been the recipients of many favors, which have been equally and impartially bestowed. We have not travelled to display our regalia or our proficiency in drill. We went, first, as an escort to the Most Eminent Grand Master [*applause*]; and second, that, when the Triennial Conclave was held at the farthest point in our country from Boston, the oldest Commandery might be represented. And of our conduct on this trip I challenge any one to point to any act of ours which would not redound to the credit of the Commandery, to the credit of the good city of Boston, to the credit of Massachusetts, and the jurisdiction of Massachusetts and Rhode Island, and to the credit of the New England States, for they were all represented in our lines with dignity and honor. This glorious reception is a fitting conclusion to a glorious pilgrimage, one which will become historical, and which has left along its line mile-posts marking an increased love and admiration for our chivalric Order, a deeper sense of loyalty to our glorious Republic, and a closer fellowship with its generous people. [*Prolonged applause.*]

"Past Most Eminent Grand Master Benjamin Dean was received with great applause and hearty cheers, and said: —

"I feel somewhat dazed at this hearty reception. I look upon this pilgrimage as an era of no small importance in the history of Knight Templary in New England. It is the first occasion when any body from Massachusetts has visited the Grand Encampment at its Triennial Conclave. It is a curious fact, that, so far as the Grand Encampment of the United States is concerned, no great attention has been paid to it by the Templars of Massachusetts, although they played an important part in its establishment. It is eminently fitting and proper that the Commandery that had so much to do with the creation of the Grand Encampment should at this time send so great a delegation to its Conclave, in spite of obstacles almost insurmountable; but it only shows that there is nothing that can keep the hearts of the Templars on the one side of the country and on the other from beating in unison. The speaker dwelt at length upon the importance to the Order of its Grand Encampment, which is necessary to take care of and maintain the honor and dignity that belong to it. He spoke also of the magnitude of the enterprise just brought to a happy close, and gave the highest praise to Commander Stevenson, to whom he said were due the thanks, not only of himself but of the entire Grand Encampment. [*Applause.*] Boston and Massachusetts have occasion to be proud of him, and of this honored Commandery that now returns to tender to you its well-earned laurels. The address closed with a reference to the protection which the organization affords Christianity, not only for its members, but for their wives and children, for this generation and for the generations to come.

"Past Eminent Commander William Parkman, who received the orders of Knighthood in Boston Commandery in 1848, and one of the charter members of De Molay Commandery, spoke pleasantly of the fresh bonds of union of which the pilgrimage has been productive, and, taking a humorous strain, kept his hearers laughing for some minutes. In closing he took up the argument of Most Eminent Grand Master Dean, on the importance of the Grand Encampment, many of the founders of which he knew personally, and in the welfare of which he had a deep interest.

"Most Eminent Grand Master Dean asked leave to make a supplementary address, called forth by the allusion of the previous speaker to Webb and others. He said they had formulated a ritual which was adopted by the original Grand Encampment, and which was preserved during the anti-Masonic excitement, by weekly meetings at the houses of members of Boston Commandery. It had been argued that no ritual had ever been adopted by the Grand Encampment, but it was a mistake, and he had offered the one thus preserved to the Conclave just closed, at which it was unanimously approved.

"Sir Knight Richards, acting Generalissimo of Boston Commandery, fired his hearers with the statement that, however much he had enjoyed his travels, he had found no place like New England, cold and rough as it may be, to live in. He spoke in the highest terms of the enjoyments and hospitalities of the trip, and invoked a hearty blessing on the Sir Knights of California.

"Sir Knight Roberts, Prelate of Boston Commandery during the pilgrimage, said that he was struck by the influence which he found Boston exerted upon the country, and instanced several cases where strangers were eager to see and clasp the hands of Boston men. Alluding to the eagle presented to the Commandery, he gave the sentiment, 'As the eagle soars above the clouds, the loftiest of all birds, so may the influence of Boston, in the years to come, be the highest of all among the sister cities of our Republic.'

"Brief addresses were made by other Sir Knights. Three hearty cheers were given for the ladies of San Francisco, the Grand Commandery of California, and the Eminent Commander of Boston Commandery; the two Commanderies cheered each other in turn; and after Sir Knight Miller, of Springfield, had led them in the 'Sweet By and By,' the familiar strains of 'Auld Lang Syne' denoted that the last formalities were over, and that the curtain had fallen on the last public act of this most eventful pilgrimage. During the festivities the members of Boston Commandery who occupied the car 'Almeria' during the pilgrimage stepped into a side-room and presented Sir Knight Gleason, executive officer of the car, with a massive gold Knight Templar charm as a token of appreciation of his services during the trip. The presentation speech was made by Sir Knight Baylies Wood.

"The ladies of the party were dined at Young's Hotel in the afternoon by the Commandery. The dinner, as the souvenir *menu* stated, was 'complimentary to the ladies with the Boston Commandery. Home again. Sept. 4, 1883.'"

After the banquet, Boston Commandery repaired to the asylum, where this, the longest Conclave ever held by a Commandery of Knights Templars, was closed in accordance with the ritual; prayer was offered by the Prelate, who expressed the sincere gratitude of the pilgrims to Him who had kept, guided, and blessed them during the pilgrimage. Expressions of congratulation and thankfulness and the parting words closed the eventful pilgrimage.

The Boston *Journal* referred editorially to the return of the pilgrims as follows: —

THE RETURN OF THE BOSTON COMMANDERY. — The Knights Templars made a fine appearance yesterday as they marched up Washington Street. Bright skies and bracing air greeted their return from what has been a very enjoyable and noteworthy trip. On their way to and from San Francisco, and during their stay in that city, the Knights have had a very delightful time, and have been treated everywhere with great courtesy and cordiality. Their bearing and conduct have reflected credit upon their organization and the city which they represented, and it is with a sense of sincere pleasure that they are welcomed home again. Bright with many pleasures and new experiences as the days of their absence have been, doubtless they are glad to be again among familiar scenes and to see familiar faces. The holiday is over, and the common but pressing cares of business and professional life follow it, but the trip to the Pacific coast will always be a cherished memory among all who have enjoyed it.

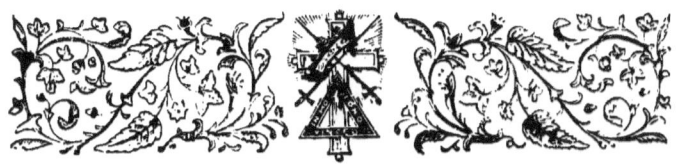

CHAPTER XXI.

A PILGRIMAGE so comprehensive in its plan, so successful in its completion, with such an endless variety of details, some of which could not be foreseen, necessitated the forethought and attention of many persons. The general features were arranged by the executive committee in connection with Sir Knight S. W. Cummings, general passenger agent of the Central Vermont Railroad, Mr. J. Stephenson, general passenger agent of the Grand Trunk Railroad, Mr. J. Q. A. Bean, general Eastern agent Chicago, Burlington and Quincy Railroad, and Mr. S. W. Manning, New England agent Atchison, Topeka and Santa Fé Railroad, as representatives of their respective roads. These gentlemen did all in their power to assist the executive committee and advance the interests of the pilgrimage. They arranged and compiled the itinerary for the pilgrimage, which constituted a very serviceable guide for the pilgrims. Their continued good services in the preparation of this story of the pilgrimage have been valuable.

MEDICAL STAFF.

The director of the medical staff, Sir William Dan Lamb, M. D., carried his valuable "kit of tools" which accident might have made needful, and the medicine chest was carefully packed with

restoratives. Sir H. A. Tucker, M. D., was well prepared for
emergencies. His preparations were very popular with the sick
and well, male and female. The remainder of the medical staff
constituted the consulting board in extreme cases. The box of
instruments was uncalled for during the pilgrimage, but the stock
of medicines was drained to its last milligramme. During the pilgrimage
the need of a surgeon's skill was not experienced. There
were several cases of illness resulting principally from colds, which
the physicians successfully managed, and brought the party into
Boston "all well." The kindness of Drs. Lamb and Tucker was
gratefully appreciated. The relief rendered was gratifying, but their
cheerful responses to every call made upon their time and stores
enhanced the gratitude of all.

TRANSPORTATION.

The committee on transportation carried forward and executed
their work with the same precision indicated in their notice issued
prior to the departure, Aug. 4. No trunk or parcel committed to
their charge was lost, but all the baggage was promptly delivered
in San Francisco at the Palace Hotel on arrival, and as promptly,
with its additional pine boxes, returned to the train on Saturday,
Aug. 25. While *en route* they were called upon for many favors
in the delivering and receiving of baggage, all of which were cheerfully
attended to. Too much praise cannot be awarded Mr. M. D.
Birmingham, an employé of the Chicago, Burlington and Quincy
Railroad, for his fidelity and kindness as train baggage-master.

LADIES.

The Sir Knights to whose care the ladies in the party were
intrusted when their liege Templars were otherwise engaged were

faithful in the discharge of their duty, and were watchful to provide for their welfare. From the first gathering in the dining-rooms of the Fitchburg Depot, Aug. 4, until the last gathering at Young's Hotel, Sept. 4, nothing was left undone by the committee which could add to the pleasure of the pilgrimage. While the ladies were thus the recipients of knightly care and attention, their presence enhanced the interest of the trip and their influence was helpful. The ladies endured temporary disappointment without murmuring, and if the train was delayed, they submitted without complaint. A party of ladies more patient during delays, less fretful when the dust arose and the sun blazed, less complaining when the first table was full, or more grateful for attentions shown, it would be difficult to gather together. Whether the efficiency of the committee tended to produce these conditions or not, it is true that they used every means possible to make the pilgrimage both a pleasure and a surprise to the ladies. The latter doubtless desire the reappointment of the same committee for the same duties when the next pilgrimage of Boston Commandery shall occur.

RECORDER.

Sir Zeph. H. Thomas, the Recorder of Boston Commandery, was the secretary of the committee on ways and means which conceived and conducted the Grand Templar ball, and also of the committee on the California pilgrimage. He was present at nearly every meeting of these committees, and discharged his duties with his usual promptness and efficiency. The expressions of appreciative regard on the part of the pilgrims were universal and cordial. Just before our arrival in Boston, the officers of the several cars assembled in the car "Como," where Sir Knight

Thomas was presented with a valuable testimonial as a recognition of his services in connection with the pilgrimage. The committee on the pilgrimage likewise presented him with a substantial token in appreciation of his faithful services as their secretary, and Eminent Sir John L. Stevenson, Oct. 24, expressed his personal gratitude to his "right-hand man" by the presentation of a jewel of Boston Commandery set with brilliants.

COMMITTEE ON CALIFORNIA PILGRIMAGE.

The committee on the California pilgrimage are entitled to great praise and gratitude for their faithfulness and efficiency. With one of their number the pilgrimage was an original suggestion. It found a response in many minds. A less enterprise would probably have failed. This would be heroic. The faith of a few became first the hope, then the pleasure of many. During more than thirty months there were strong brains cogitating the grand scheme. The organization of this committee (January, 1881) gave the project shape and direction; it also increased the anxiety and burden, and presented new questions for solution and new difficulties to be overcome. For a part of this time two committees, having the same chairman and secretary, were busy reaching the same end, but by different methods. They worked harmoniously, the one materially strengthening the efforts of the other. Prior to the departure, during the days of travel, and while in San Francisco, the committee held frequent meetings, and gave its attention to the most minute details of the pilgrimage. The committee must be conscious, not only of the hearty gratitude of the party, but that their efforts were crowned with perfect success. The way to it, however, was through toil and doubt, difficulty and sacrifice. The obstacles were more than a hot box or broken journal. In the development of the scheme, when the sky was bright and circumstances seemed favorable, all interested Sir Knights felt the pilgrimage was to be a grand success. Again, when the clouds gathered and circumstances seemed unfavorable, as was natural, doubt arose in the minds of many, and occasionally it was whispered that "the success of the pilgrimage is doubtful." Whether under the star-lit sky or the thick cloud, one, at least, the Eminent Commander, stood firm in purpose, undismayed by temporary defeat, as if thoroughly conscious of the ultimate and triumphant success of the pilgrimage. He, fruitful in resources, strong to shape circumstances, gave the full strength of his mind to the work, and, through the aid of the Sir Knights who gathered around him, realized the satisfactory achievement of the greatest and most successful pilgrimage in the history of modern Templarism.

To Eminent Sir John Lindsay Stevenson, the originator of the pilgrimage, the chairman of the committees on the Templar ball and on the California pilgrimage, also of the executive committee, and the Eminent Commander during the pilgrimage, the party is under great obligations. Previous to their arrival in Boston the pilgrims conceived a method for the suitable recognition of these obligations, as will appear in a subsequent chapter. The pilgrimage, however, in its inception, development, and success will ever remain a monument to the forethought, energy, ability, and devotion of the Eminent Commander.

In a review of the pilgrimage as outlined in the preceding pages, there is much to be remembered, little to be forgotten. The transportation of one hundred and sixty-eight persons across our country on a train with the right of way of the various roads, with a complete itinerary for thirty-one days to be observed, was a remarkable feat, hitherto unprecedented. Such a train neither before nor since has traversed the continent. The delays were slight when compared with the distance to be travelled. The mishaps, caused by the excessive weight of the train, and the high rate of speed attained, were less and fewer than the average on an eight-thousand-mile run. The meals, with a very few exceptions, were furnished at the appointed time, and all were good, most were excellent. The people in the small towns along the route welcomed the advancing Knights, as well as those in the larger towns and cities. Crowds in the busy East, the fertile West, the desert stations, and the golden shore bade them "God speed." Frequently the command was royally welcomed by courteous *fratres*. In San Francisco the reception was everything any one could ask for, and the attentions shown the command were many and cordial. Boston Commandery during the pilgrimage did no discredit to its historic prestige, but added to its renown. Its name was unsullied and its banner untarnished. It brought no breath of uncourteous demeanor against the Commandery's bright fame, nor against the illustrious city whose name it bears, nor against New England, from whose thriving towns and cities the pilgrims gathered. There is much to remember, to rejoice in; little to forget, to be sorry for. The success of the pilgrimage assures it the highest place among the celebrated pilgrimages of modern times.

CHAPTER XXII.

THE first Conclave of Boston Commandery after the return of the pilgrims was held in Masonic Temple, Wednesday evening, Sept. 12, 1883. The attendance was so large that many could not be seated. Eminent Commander John L. Stevenson was in his accustomed place, and the Order of the Red Cross was worked. The notices for the Conclave bore the following: —

THE CALIFORNIA PILGRIMAGE.

The Eminent Commander takes this opportunity to extend his congratulations to the members of Boston Commandery on the unparalleled success of the California pilgrimage, it being historically and socially one of the most brilliant ever made by any Commandery of Knights Templars. At the July Conclave the Commandery generously voted,

That the committee on the California pilgrimage be authorized to draw on the treasury of Boston Commandery for a sum not exceeding one thousand dollars, provided any exigency should arise which may require the use of the same to maintain the reputation of Boston Commandery for knightly courtesy and hospitality.

The Sir Knights in charge of and participating in the pilgrimage have proved equal to every emergency, and the reputation of Boston Commandery for knightly courtesy and hospitality has been placed infinitely higher than ever before, *and without the use of any part of the money so courteously placed at their disposal by said vote.*

The Eminent Commander devoutly hopes that the position which Boston Commandery now enjoys may in the future be maintained; and to the courteous Sir Knights who are ever ready to support and maintain the reputation of Boston Commandery, he extends his heartfelt thanks. A report in part of the doing of the committee will be made at this Conclave.

In accordance therewith Sir Z. H. Thomas, Recorder, in behalf of the committee, submitted a detailed report of the pilgrimage, which was received with approbation by the Commandery.

It was a pleasant sight to see the pilgrims, after their long and eventful pilgrimage, so warmly greeted by their knightly brothers. It was no less joyful to the pilgrims, having survived the perils by the way, and experienced the fellowship of so many Sir Knights from different parts of the Union, to gather once more in health and safety around their own "vine" and under their own "fig-tree."

CORRESPONDENCE.

Prior to the closing of the Commandery, Sept. 4, 1883, it was

Voted, That the committee on the California pilgrimage be authorized and instructed to tender the thanks of Boston Commandery to such Templar organizations and persons as have by their courteous acts laid the Commandery under obligations to them.

In accordance therewith, Sept. 27, the committee instructed the Recorder to forward letters of thanks to the following persons: —

Sir Sol Smith Russell, Boston, Mass.; Sir S. W. Cummings, St. Albans, Vt.; Sir V. M. C. Silva, Commonwealth Hotel, Boston; Sir William Harney, San Francisco, Cal.; J. Q. A. Bean, Esq., Boston; S. W. Manning, Esq., Boston; F. R. McConnell, Ogden, Utah.

The following is a copy of the letter of thanks forwarded by Sir Z. H. Thomas, Recorder, to Sir Sol Smith Russell: —

OF

KNIGHTS TEMPLARS.

BOSTON, Oct. 6, 1883.

SOL SMITH RUSSELL, ESQ.:

My dear Sir, and Sir Knight, — It is with much pleasure that I inform you that at a recent Conclave of this Commandery it was unanimously voted, That the thanks of Boston Commandery be and are hereby tendered to Sir Sol Smith Russell for the knightly courtesy extended to us by him while in San Francisco, in August last.

With kind regards I am,

Courteously yours,

Z. H. Thomas,

Recorder.

Letters of like purport were sent to the other Sir Knights and gentlemen designated.

The following replies were received: —

SHERMAN, TEXAS, Oct. 18, 1883.

Z. H. THOMAS, *Recorder:*

My dear Sir, — Your communication of Oct. 6, relative to the action of the Boston Commandery, reaches me here in the genial, sunny South. To me it was a real pleasure, that we were happily permitted to contribute a few songs and funny things, and add something pleasant to your visit to "Frisco."

Thanking you for the kind recognition of our efforts, and with good wishes to all,

Fraternally,

SOL SMITH RUSSELL.

CENTRAL VERMONT RAILROAD, PASSENGER DEPARTMENT,
ST. ALBANS, VT., Oct. 13, 1883.

Z. H. THOMAS, ESQ.,
Recorder Boston Commandery K∴ T∴, Boston:

Dear Sir, — On my return, I find your very courteous favor of the 6th inst., conveying resolutions voted by Boston Commandery, relative to the humble services it was my good fortune to be able to render them on their California pilgrimage.

I thank you, and through you the Commandery, for this very kind and flattering remembrance, although in the discharge of my duty only.

It will always be looked back upon as an honor, in addition to the pleasure enjoyed at the time, that I was in any way connected with the most remarkable feat of transportation ever undertaken up to the present time in this country. May it prove to be only one of still more brilliant and successful pilgrimages of Boston Commandery.

Remaining, dear sir,

Very courteously yours,

S. W. CUMMINGS.

BOSTON, MASS., Oct. 16, 1883.

SIR Z. H. THOMAS, *Recorder Boston Commandery:*

My dear Sir, and Sir Knight, — I beg to acknowledge the receipt of your favor of the 6th inst., conveying to me a copy of the vote of thanks of Boston Commandery.

While I am not insensible of the honor thus conferred by so distinguished a body of Sir Knights as Boston Commandery, I would say that while the beautiful valley of Salt Lake offered but poor facilities for enjoyment compared with the grandeur and beauties of California, it gave me great pleasure to have the privilege of greeting in that far-off region weary pilgrims travelling from afar.

To the officers and Sir Knights of Boston Commandery convey the acknowledgments of,
Yours fraternally,
V. M. C. SILVA.

SAN FRANCISCO, Oct. 15, 1883.

SIR Z. H. THOMAS, *Recorder of Boston Commandery K. T.:*

Sir Knight and Frater, — Yours of the 6th of this month, conveying to me the kind expressions of thanks from Boston Commandery to myself, I have this day received. I feel, indeed, highly complimented, and cherish beyond expression this kind feeling of gratitude on their part towards myself. I, with others of our Order, as well as our citizens generally here, share in the unanimous sentiment which has been frequently expressed, that no body of people has ever visited our coast that merited higher commendation for gentlemanly and ladylike bearing and deportment than the Boston Sir Knights and the fair ladies accompanying them to our shores. I heartily share those sentiments and feel proud of the Boston Commandery and the lady visitors.

Be pleased to convey sincere thanks to Boston Commandery for their kind remembrance and friendship towards me, and I only regret that I could not have done more to make the visit agreeable and pleasant to them during their sojurn here; for it is a great satisfaction to our Order, and those outside of it here, to know that their visit to us has been agreeable to them.

With kind remembrances to all Sir Knights and ladies, and a sincere hope that we may all meet again at the next Triennial of our Order,

I remain,
Yours fraternally and courteously,
WILLIAM HARNEY.

ATCHISON, TOPEKA AND SANTA FÉ RAILROAD CO.,
NEW ENGLAND AGENCY,
197 Washington Street.

BOSTON, MASS., Oct. 20, 1883.

Z. H. THOMAS, ESQ.,
Recorder Boston Commandery:

My dear Sir, — Your letter conveying a vote of thanks from Boston Commandery for courtesies received on its late pilgrimage is gratefully received. As an agent of the Atchison, Topeka and Santa Fé Railroad, I am only conscious of having done my duty towards the Commandery as patrons of our line. It is a great pleasure to know that our efforts were crowned with success, and that on your return you expressed perfect satisfaction with the treatment received and accommodations furnished by our company.

I am, yours very truly,

S. W. MANNING,
N. E. Agt.

UNION PACIFIC RAILWAY CO.,
GENERAL AGENT'S OFFICE,
SALT LAKE CITY, Nov. 6, 1883.

Z. H. THOMAS, ESQ.,
Recorder Boston Commandery K. T.:

My dear Sir, — Your very kind and most unexpected favor, 30th ult., came to hand in this morning's mail, and I beg to express my thanks for the kindly expression of your Commandery. Your people did not know it, maybe, but right down in my heart I had registered a vote of thanks for the good time and generous courtesies extended to me last August by the Boston Commandery.

Am glad you enjoyed your ride over our line; glad to indulge the hope that it is only an initial trip for all of you, and that as the weeks go by I may have the recurrent pleasure of seeing some of the good-natured faces of the most notable Commandery at the Conclave of '83.

I shall always remember most pleasantly the few days that you were here, and will always be glad to welcome you or any other member of Boston Commandery to Salt Lake.

With assurances of my high regard for yourself and all others of your party,

I am, yours very truly,

F. R. McCONNELL,
General Agent.

GENERAL EASTERN AGENCY,
CHICAGO, BURLINGTON AND QUINCY R. R. CO.,
BOSTON, Oct. 13, 1883.

Z. H. THOMAS, ESQ.,
Recorder Boston Commandery K∴ T∴, Boston, Mass.:

Dear Sir,—I thank you, and, through you, the Boston Commandery, for your very kind remembrance as given in your favor of the 6th inst. I did all I could to assist in arranging your California pilgrimage; and that all returned safe and well from your long and successful trip, and now remember me as aiding in your arrangements, is exceedingly gratifying to

Yours very truly,

J. Q. A. BEAN.

Boston Commandery

OF

KNIGHTS TEMPLARS.

OFFICE OF THE EMINENT COMMANDER.

Boston, Aug. 4, 1883.

R∴ E∴ Caleb Saunders,

Grand Commander of the Grand Commandery of Massachusetts and Rhode Island:

R∴ E∴ Sir, — I have the honor of offering the services of Boston Commandery as an escort to yourself, and other officers and members of the Grand Commandery, on your arrival in San Francisco, Cal., to attend the Twenty-second Triennial Conclave of the Grand Encampment of the United States. We shall have preceded your arrival several days, and it will give us pleasure to attest our loyalty to our Grand Commandery and its officers by receiving them on the shore of the Pacific Ocean with all the honors due their exalted position.

Courteously yours,

John L. Stevenson

E∴ C∴ Boston Commandery K∴ T∴

DENVER, COL., Aug. 11, 1883.

E∴ SIR JOHN L. STEVENSON,
 E∴ C∴ Boston Commandery:

Eminent Sir Knight, — Your favor of 4th instant, tendering to me and the officers and members of the Grand Commandery who accompany me an escort on our arrival in San Francisco, came duly to hand on Monday last. We shall arrive in San Francisco on Sunday. And as in our own jurisdiction it would be considered highly improper for members of an institution founded upon the Christian religion and the practice of the Christian virtues to publicly parade for escort duty on that day, I must decline the pleasure of an escort by Boston Commandery.

Courteously yours,
CALEB SAUNDERS,
Gr. Commander, Mass. and R. I.

TESTIMONIALS.

The committee on the California pilgrimage caused suitable testimonials to be prepared and forwarded to the following Commanderies: California Commandery, No. 1, San Francisco, Cal.; Cœur de Lion, No. 9, Los Angeles, Cal.; Oakland, No. 11, Oakland, Cal.; Golden Gate, No. 16, San Francisco, Cal.; and De Molay Commandery, Boston, Mass.

On the following page will be found a copy of the engrossment on the testimonial sent to California, No. 1, of San Francisco, Cal.: —

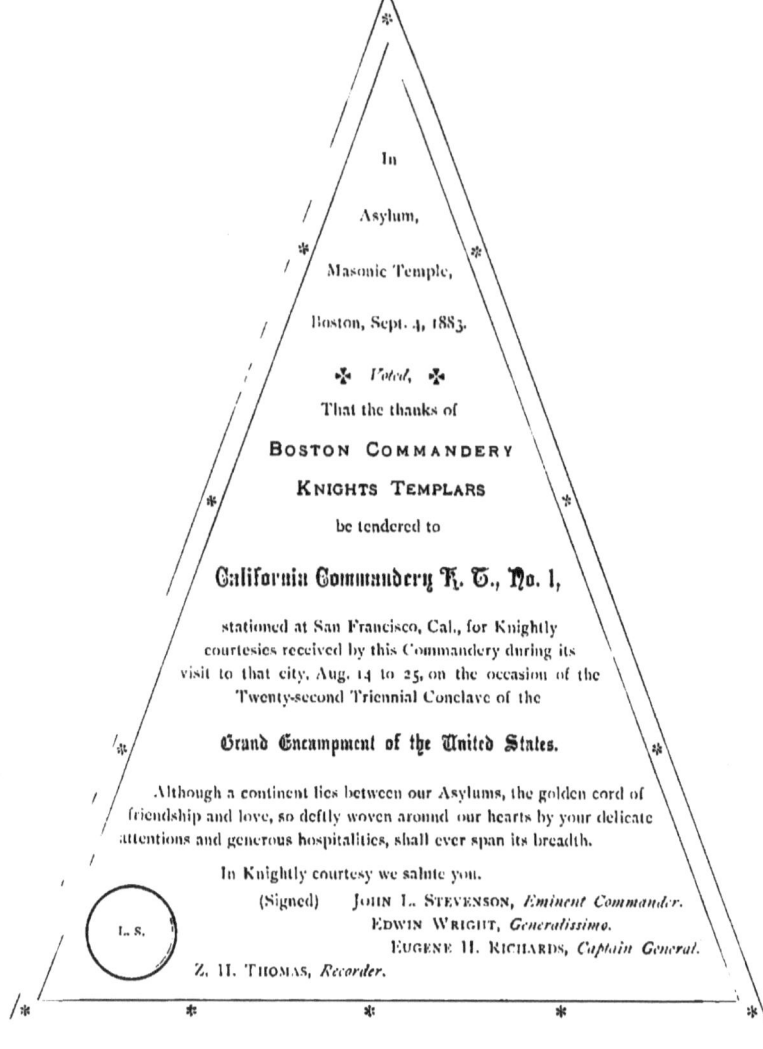

In Asylum, Masonic Temple, Boston, Sept. 4, 1883.

✠ *Voted,* ✠

That the thanks of **BOSTON COMMANDERY KNIGHTS TEMPLARS** be tendered to

𝕮alifornia 𝕮ommandery 𝕶. 𝕿., 𝕹o. 1,

stationed at San Francisco, Cal., for Knightly courtesies received by this Commandery during its visit to that city, Aug. 14 to 25, on the occasion of the Twenty-second Triennial Conclave of the

𝕲rand 𝕰ncampment of the 𝖀nited 𝕾tates.

Although a continent lies between our Asylums, the golden cord of friendship and love, so deftly woven around our hearts by your delicate attentions and generous hospitalities, shall ever span its breadth.

In Knightly courtesy we salute you.

(Signed) JOHN L. STEVENSON, *Eminent Commander.*
EDWIN WRIGHT, *Generalissimo.*
EUGENE H. RICHARDS, *Captain General.*
Z. H. THOMAS, *Recorder.*

L. S.

The testimonials, five in number, were alike in design and finish. A triangular parchment, as represented on the opposite page, elegantly engrossed, contained the vote of thanks passed by the Commandery, followed by a suitable sentiment, and bore the signatures of the first three officers and Recorder, and the seal of the Commandery. The parchment was surrounded by a black border, in which were set twelve silver stars, the whole being enclosed by a gold mat. Over the apex of the triangle was cut in the mat a Christian cross in red, and on either side thereof a Greek cross in the same color. The heavy frame of bronze and gold, thirty-six by thirty-six inches, was of elaborate workmanship, skilfully carved and moulded, and bore appropriate symbols. Both in general appearance and in their minute details they received the commendation of all who saw them.

The other testimonials differed in the sentiment only, as follows: —

OAKLAND COMMANDERY.

"From the *Silvered Sands of the Atlantic to the Golden Sands of the Pacific*, our banner has waved in love and honor, amid the applause of our *fratres*.

"To your Commandery, and to the generous Sir Knights of California, are we indebted for many acts of courtesy and boundless hospitality.

"Remembering which we salute you."

GOLDEN GATE COMMANDERY.

"The *memorable Pilgrimage across the Continent*, and the generous reception accorded us in your city, will ever be remembered by our Sir Knights. We indeed found the *Golden Gate of Friendship* on *Golden hinges turning*, while your many and varied hospitalities shall ever shine the *brightest gem* in memory's diadem.

"Generous *fratres*, we salute you in love."

CŒUR DE LION COMMANDERY.

"For the Knightly courtesies and hospitalities extended to us August 12th and 13th, while tarrying in that beautiful city *en route* to San Francisco. We were indeed weary Pilgrims, travelling from afar, when you bade us rest and refresh ourselves, and when, having partaken of your good cheer, we resumed our pilgrimage, our hearts were light and happy, and pleasant recollections of the happy hours spent in your company welled up an ever-living fountain of love in our grateful memories.

"Presenting these thanks we salute you."

DE MOLAY COMMANDERY.

"For the Knightly courtesies and cordial reception given us this day on our arrival home from San Francisco, Cal.

"Your magnificent escort and your fraternal greeting will ever be cherished in our memories as the highest of many honors, and the warmest of all welcomes received by us during our memorable *Pilgrimage across the Continent*.

"In love and honor we salute you."

On the evening of Jan. 23, 1884, at a regular Conclave of De Molay Commandery, the testimonial before described was presented to De Molay Commandery by Past Commander John L. Stevenson, of Boston Commandery. It was received by Eminent Sir H. P. Hemenway, Commander of De Molay Commandery, in behalf of his Commandery, in an address expressive of his thanks and of the knightly fellowship existing between the two Commanderies.

In response to the testimonial sent to Cœur de Lion Commandery, No. 9, Los Angeles, Cal., a set of resolutions, engrossed and beautifully framed, was received, of which the following is a copy: —

ASYLUM OF CŒUR DE LION COMMANDERY, No. 9, K∴ T∴,
STATIONED AT LOS ANGELES, CAL., March 20, 1884.

At a stated Conclave held on the above date, the following resolutions were unanimously adopted: —

Whereas, We have received from the Sir Knights of Boston Commandery K. T., an engrossed copy of resolutions adopted by that Commandery expressing thanks for the attentions they received at our hands while they were sojourning in our city on their way to attend the late Triennial Conclave held in San Francisco;

Resolved, That we return to the Boston Commandery of Knights Templars, and to each and every Sir Knight thereof, our sincere thanks for this elegant token of their remembrance of us, and that we hereby extend to said Commandery, and every member thereof, a perpetual invitation to visit us, that we may have an opportunity by acts rather than words to express our regards for the oldest Commandery in the United States, and our esteem for the Sir Knights we learned to respect and love during their short stay in our midst. And be it further

Resolved, That said engrossed resolutions be hung in a conspicuous place on the walls of our asylum, and that an engrossed copy of these resolutions be transmitted to Boston Commandery.

E. F. SPENCE,
Eminent Commander.

[SEAL]   W. W. ROSS,
Recorder.

The presentation of the testimonials to the San Francisco and Oakland Commanderies was delegated to Eminent Sir Tristam Burges, Grand Senior Warden of the Grand Commandery of California, who, having discharged that duty in his usual courteous manner, reported as follows: —

SAN FRANCISCO, CAL., Feb. 28, 1884.

EM∴ SIR JOHN L. STEVENSON,
Past Commander Boston Commandery K∴ T∴:

My dear Frater, — On the sixth instant I received the several testimonials of Boston Commandery, and in compliance with your instructions I have presented them to the Commanderies named, at their first stated Conclave; namely, on Friday evening, Feb. 8, 1884, I presented your testimonial to California Commandery, No. 1, as follows: "Eminent Commander, among the various testimonials California Commandery, No. 1, has received from the Commanderies present at the last Triennial Conclave, none, I am sure, will be more highly prized than the one which, as the representative of Boston Commandery, I have now the honor to present. Beside its artistic beauties, the fact that it comes to you as an honest and knightly expression of the esteem of the oldest Commandery in the Union, must make it doubly valuable. I am charged by the members of this venerable institution to say to you, in their behalf, that, one and all, they were delighted with their visit here, especially with the kind attentions and open-handed hospitality with which they were received, and which everywhere among the Sir Knights of the Pacific were extended to them. They regard it as most satisfactory evidence of a growth in our Order of that fraternal feeling which should naturally flow from our principles, and as a grand illustration of the progress of a universal brotherhood. In this our day, societies are constantly multiplying, whose leading objects are to promote among men an increasing regard for each other, to bring them together in fraternal union, to provide for their material welfare, and to make a family of the race. Our Order, one of the oldest, is also one of the most zealous in the good work, and as it is founded upon Christianity, the time can never come when it shall cease to be an important factor in the cause of civilization. Accept then this memorial of the great Conclave, in the spirit in which it is intended Give it a place in your asylum, and its donors a place in your hearts. May it ever serve to remind you of the grandeur of Templarism, and be handed down to your successors in the great institution."

Eminent Commander Sir Franklin H. Day appropriately responded, accepting, in behalf of his Commandery, your testimonial, and by a unanimous vote the Council and the Recorder were directed to properly acknowledge the same, as follows:—

ASYLUM OF CALIFORNIA COMMANDERY, NO. 1, KNIGHTS TEMPLARS,
SAN FRANCISCO, Feb. 15, 1884.

To the Em∴ Commander, Generalissimo, Captain General, Recorder, and Sir Knights of Boston Commandery K∴ T∴, Boston, Mass.:

California Commandery, No. 1, sends joyful greetings and acknowledges with feelings of gratitude and sincere pleasure the receipt of the beautiful testimonial commemorative of their pilgrimage to our "City by the Sea." In a few well-chosen words the presentation was made in our asylum by Grand Senior Warden Sir Tristam Burges, to whom the pleasing duty had been assigned by the generous donors.

The expressions of admiration from all present for the exquisite design and artistic execution of the splendid gift could only be equalled by the high regard and warm fraternal affection felt for the givers, who so kindly remembered those they left behind when returning to their far-off homes.

It will be prized for all time to come as a memento of the grandest Masonic gathering ever witnessed on the Pacific coast, and, as a token of the fraternal tie which we trust will ever bind Boston Commandery to us, will be cherished as the fairest gem that adorns our asylum.

In behalf of California Commandery, No. 1, Knights Templars, we are
Courteously and fraternally yours,

[SEAL] FRANKLIN H. DAY, *Em∴ Com∴*
J. M. LITCHFIELD, *Generalissimo.*
H. H. PEARSON, *Capt∴ General.*
HIRAM T. GRAVES, *Recorder.*

On Monday evening, Feb. 18, 1884, I presented to Golden Gate Commandery, No. 16, your testimonial, as follows: "Eminent Commander, one of the most pleasing duties of my life now devolves upon me, having been requested by Boston Commandery of Knights Templars to present to you, Eminent Sir, and through you to the officers and members of Golden Gate Commandery, No. 16, this testimonial. I assure you, Eminent Sir, that Boston Commandery has in this slight manner endeavored to show her appreciation of the many courtesies and knightly hospitality received at your hands during the recent Conclave."

Eminent Commander Sir Columbus Waterhouse, in accepting of your testimonial, responded as follows: "Eminent Sir Tristam Burges, Grand Senior Warden, in being called upon to receive this beautiful testimonial tendered to us by you in behalf of the Boston Commandery, I cannot easily find words to express the sentiments of fraternal regard and esteem which the members of Golden Gate Commandery entertain for our courteous visiting Knights of the 'Hub,' who honored us by their pilgrimage to the Golden Gate during the Grand Triennial Conclave of 1883. I accept of this beautiful testimonial, in behalf of my Commandery, and we will appreciate and treasure it, not alone on account of its beauty, but because it speaks to our hearts, keeping a memory fresh that will linger in our minds forever. It will ever be a token of our friendship for them that will endure until the last grand pilgrimage is over."

By a vote of the Commandery, the Recorder was directed to properly prepare an acknowledgment of its receipt, and the first three officers and the Recorder to sign the same, under seal of the Commandery, viz : —

GOLDEN GATE COMMANDERY, No. 16, KNIGHTS TEMPLARS,
No. 131 POST STREET, SAN FRANCISCO, CAL.,
February 28, 1884.

Golden Gate Commandery, No. 16, K∴ T∴, stationed at San Francisco, Cal., to Boston Commandery, of Boston, Mass., Greeting:

We send our sincere acknowledgments for the handsome testimonial received from you through Eminent Sir Tristam Burges, and in this we recognize another proof of your "unwearied spirit in doing courtesy." We realize that the generous motives of chivalry are as strong to-day as they were centuries ago; and these fraternal wishes, coming so far, and from the oldest to one of the youngest Templar bodies, shall be ever valued and forever cherished. *May this fellowship ever last.* When your pilgrims take up the staff for a pilgrimage to our shores, they shall find an asylum and true friends and *fratres.* In knightly courtesy we salute you.

On behalf of the Commandery as voted at the regular Conclave, Monday, Feb. 18, 1884.

[SEAL]

COLUMBUS WATERHOUSE, E∴ C∴
FRANK WM. SUMNER, Gen∴
WILLIAM C. STROUD, Capt∴ Gen∴
WM. T. FONDA, Recorder.

On Tuesday evening, Feb. 19, 1884, I went to Oakland, and in behalf of Boston Commandery presented to Oakland Commandery, No. 11, your testimonial, as follows: "Eminent Commander, having been requested by Boston Commandery of Knights Templars, it now becomes my pleasing duty to present, through you, to Oakland Commandery, No. 11, this beautiful testimonial of their appreciation of the hospitality and many courtesies of your officers and members to them during their recent pilgrimage to the Pacific coast.

"Accept it, Eminent Sir, and permit it to adorn the walls of your asylum, as a beautiful memento of the Twenty-second Triennial Conclave of the Grand Encampment of the United States."

Eminent Commander Sir George D. Metcalf, in accepting, responded as follows: "Eminent Sir Tristam Burges, you are always a welcome visitor to Oakland Commandery, but to-night doubly so, because you come as the bearer of knightly greetings from across the continent, as the representative of the old, the tried, and the true Boston Commandery. This beautiful token which you present in their behalf revives in our minds tender memories of delightful associations, and strengthens, if anything could, the cords of love, the bonds of esteem and respect which unite us, the younger with our elder *fratres*. Permit me, Eminent Sir, in behalf of Oakland Commandery, No. 11, Knights Templars, in accepting this eloquent memento, to extend through you, to Boston Commandery Knights Templars, our cordial greetings, and the assurance that among all the delightful recollections of the Triennial Conclave of 1883, none are more sincerely cherished by us, or live with greater freshness and vigor, than those we have and shall continue to retain of Boston Commandery, and that, like the place reserved for them in our memories, so shall there always be in our asylum a most prominent place reserved for this gem of beauty, this mute but most expressive offering."

By vote of the Commandery, resolutions were adopted, and the Recorder directed to communicate the same to Boston Commandery, as follows:—

ASYLUM OF OAKLAND COMMANDERY, No. 11, K∴ T∴.
OAKLAND, CAL., Feb. 19, 1884.

At a meeting of this Commandery held this evening, the following preamble and resolutions were adopted unanimously:—

Whereas, This Commandery has been presented, at the hands of Eminent Sir Tristam Burges, Grand Senior Warden of the Grand Commandery of California, with resolutions adopted by Boston Commandery K. T., acknowledging courtesies of this Commandery to them during the Twenty-second Triennial Conclave of the Grand Encampment of the United States;

Resolved, That the Recorder of this Commandery is hereby instructed to acknowledge the receipt of the same, and to inform our *fratres* of Boston Commandery that we shall ever cherish with satisfaction the effort on our part to extend to them a fraternal welcome to our Pacific State, and assure them that it is the ambition of the Sir Knights of Oakland to imitate the sturdy character and Christian virtues exemplified in the lives and character of the Pilgrim Fathers who raised the standard of religious and political freedom on Pilgrim Rock; and our sincere wish is that the Boston Commandery, its members and their families, may "live long and prosper."

[SEAL]   SAMUEL T. BLACK, *Recorder*.

In presenting the testimonials, I have endeavored to impress upon the minds of the members of the several Commanderies that the sentiments expressed in the resolutions are but a reflection of what every Sir Knight in your ranks feels in his heart for the Sir Knights on the Pacific coast. All of which is courteously submitted.

TRISTAM BURGES,
P∴ C∴ <i>Golden Gate Commandery, No. 16, and</i>
Grand Senior Warden Grand Commandery of California.

CALIFORNIA GRAND COMMANDERY,
SAN FRANCISCO, February 12, 1884.

EM∴ SIR JOHN L. STEVENSON,
Past Commander of Boston Commandery:

My dear Sir Knight, — In compliance with the request of our mutual friend, Em. Sir Tristam Burges, it is with great pleasure I recall the pleasant week of the Conclave. As you must be aware, this grand gathering, from the day it was appointed at Chicago, to the hour of its close, was a subject of intense interest and solicitude to the Templars of this city, and indeed of the entire Pacific coast. No effort or means were spared on their part to make it a success. After it was over and we recalled the scenes of the week, the decorations, the receptions, the pageants, the literary exercises, and the apparent good feeling and knightly bearing of our guests, I assure you we all felt that it had proven a success, and we were as well satisfied with our efforts as we had hoped to be. This feeling on our part has since been so strongly intensified by the frequent assurances and testimonials we have received from the Commanderies in attendance, that we feel more in the humor of returning thanks to them for their expression of kindness and good-will, than receiving thanks for anything we did to render the occasion a success. It was an event that will ever be memorable in the history of the Pacific coast. It called together in council many of the leading and substantial men of the nation. Every State and Territory of our great Union had here her representative. They saw our State, our city, our immense commercial and agricultural advantages, and our great mining resources; and were able from actual observation to form correct ideas of the great future in store for us. We enjoyed their society socially and fraternally, and in turn were proud and happy to be numbered among the members of a society which everywhere was composed of such grand material.

It would seem almost invidious in me, where all were so unexceptionable, to single out any one of the numerous bodies which met here for special commendation. We were delighted with all; but then I remember when we met your honored Commandery as the escort of the Most Eminent Grand Master, shortly after you had crossed into the dominion of the Golden State, that yours was one of the first organized bodies of Templars in the Union, that as long ago as the middle of the last century the first Templars had been made by you, that you have had an uninterrupted existence of more than three quarters of a century in organized form, that indeed you were the De Payens and St. Aldemars of American Templarism. These facts and the knightly bearing of your officers and members made your Commandery an object of special veneration, and added much to the interest of the great occasion. In view both of the present magnitude as well as future growth of our great Order, your Commandery has reason to be proud of its origin and age. It is a living testimony to the pure principles and exalted religious sentiments which animated the fathers of the Order in its early history in this Republic. They were good, honest, pure men. Surely I can wish nothing better for our Order for all time to come than that we, their successors, should imitate their virtues, and strive to transmit this glorious heritage to our posterity as pure and unspotted as it came from them to us.

With fraternal greeting, I remain,

    Courteously yours,

      GEO. C. PERKINS,

       Grand Com∴ G∴ C∴ of Cal.

CHAPTER XXIII.

SOON after the return of Boston Commandery from its pilgrimage to California, Sept. 4, 1883, it was decided by the committee that, to renew the memories of the pilgrimage and make the forthcoming story of the event complete, it would be well to hold in October a reception of the pilgrim Knights, and the ladies who accompanied them on the pilgrimage. Arrangements were accordingly made to that end, and Hotel Vendôme was decided on as the place and Oct. 24 as the time. Accordingly the following invitation was issued: —

CALIFORNIA PILGRIMAGE BOSTON COMMANDERY K.'. T.'.

Aug. 4, 1883.   Sept. 4, 1883.

RECEPTION AND DINNER AT HOTEL VENDOME,

Wednesday, Oct. 24, 1883.

Enclosed please find ticket (not transferable) to a complimentary reception and dinner at Hotel Vendôme, Wednesday, Oct. 24, at 5 P. M.

This dinner has been arranged by the committee as a medium of exchanging congratulations at an early day over the many happy events connected with the pilgrimage of Boston Commandery K. T. to California in August last. As one of the participants you are courteously invited to be present. The committee hope you will kindly accept the invitation and meet them while the pleasant recollections of the pilgrimage are yet fresh in our memories.

Please reply not later than Oct. 20, to the enclosed address.

Evening dress.

Courteously yours,

John L. Stevenson

For the Committee on the California Pilgrimage of Boston Commandery K∴ T∴.

BOSTON, Oct. 10, 1883.

Of one hundred and sixty-eight persons constituting the original party, over one hundred and fifty were present. Invitations were also extended to the Sir Knights of the committees on pilgrimage, and on ways and means, who did not go on the pilgrimage; to Right Eminent Sir Caleb Saunders, Grand Commander Knights Templars of Massachusetts and Rhode Island, Most Wor. Samuel C. Lawrence, Grand Master of the Grand Lodge of Massachusetts, Eminent Sir Edwin Wright, Commander of Boston Commandery, Sir Charles E. Pierce, Generalissimo of St. Omer Commandery, Boston, and Sir V. M. C. Silva, of Ogden, Utah, at whose invitation the pilgrims visited Garfield, the bathing-place on Salt Lake. The entire party gathered at the Vendôme numbered one hundred and seventy-five.

At 5 P. M. carriages began to arrive at the private entrance, where a canopy had been erected to protect the ladies from the rain, bringing the invited guests, and in a very few moments the parlors of the hotel presented a very brilliant appearance. Many toilets were very elaborate, and all appeared happy. The greetings were hearty, and all seemed to feel at home as if back once more in their "Pullmans." An hour having quickly passed in greetings and conversation, the party repaired to the main dining-room, which was filled. After places had been assigned to all, a short prayer was offered by Prelate O. A. Roberts, and the party proceeded to discuss the viands of the Vendôme. Two hours and twenty minutes were spent while the various courses were being served. The dinner was excellent and well prepared. The bill of fare bore on the face the following: "California pilgrimage, Boston Commandery Knights Templars, Aug. 4, 1883, Sept. 4, 1883. *In hoc signo vinces.* Reception and dinner at Hotel Vendôme, Boston, Oct. 24, 1883."

During the dinner, and also subsequently, instrumental music was finely rendered by a select orchestra, Sir Knight T. M. Carter, leader, stationed in an adjacent corridor. On entering the dining-room the orchestra played the "San Francisco March," composed by Sir Knight T. M. Carter, and first played at the Grand Templar ball, January, 1883.

At 8.20 P. M. Sir Knight John L. Stevenson, Past Eminent Commander of Boston Commandery, arose, and welcomed the pilgrims and guests as follows: —

Sir Knights, Ladies, Pilgrims, — We dine in one section to-night! And I tender you my sincere congratulations that your ranks are yet unbroken by disaster, and your loving hearts, free from sorrow or bereavement, are throbbing with pleasure as you greet each other on this pleasant occasion.

I also congratulate the committee on the happy fruition of their well-timed efforts in arranging thus early this reception while every incident connected with the pilgrimage is fresh in your minds, and its many pleasures continually welling up, an ever-living fountain of joy in your memories.

This is our family party; no orators have been invited, no speeches prepared; more eloquent than either are your bright faces, and the memories of our grand pilgrimage from the orient to the occident.

So far as is known, all who went with us are in the enjoyment of health, and no one has been found who regrets that he took part in the California pilgrimage of Boston Commandery. [*Applause.*]

In bidding you a warm and hearty welcome to the pleasures of the evening, and giving you renewed assurance of my appreciation of your friendship, I desire to return my sincere thanks to the Sir Knights composing the rank and file of the Commandery during the pilgrimage. Whether members of Boston or of other Commanderies, each seemed to vie with the other in knightly courtesy, and all combined to maintain the standard of the Order, to preserve unsullied the reputation of the Knights Templars of New England, and with a chivalric ardor determined to enhance the honor and glory of old Boston Commandery.

In this the several officers also earnestly and faithfully joined, the whole constituting a body of Templars the command of which was an honor worthy of any man's aspiration, and one which I shall recall with pride while life lasts. [*Applause.*] To the ladies who accompanied us, and by their welcome presence added so much more pleasure to the pilgrimage than we should otherwise have enjoyed, I beg to say, your kindness, patience, and forbearance were in the highest degree commendable. Little I apprehend did you realize at the time how much you encouraged and strengthened me in the discharge of my somewhat arduous duties, by your ever-kind words and cheerful looks, and by your ready acquiescence in any change rendered necessary by the vicissitudes of railway travelling. He must be a false Knight indeed who would not enter the lists willingly to serve so fair and agreeable a constituency, and no such Knight am I. [*Applause.*]

How many times have we all in our imagination lived the pilgrimage over again, and how the many and wonderful sights we saw and pleasures we enjoyed come rushing back in our thoughts! — the triumphant march through the streets of Boston; the crowds assembled at the depot to cheer us onward; that quiet ride on Sunday through Canada; our arrival and departure at Chicago; our crossing the Mississippi River, which many of us saw that morning for the first time; on through the State of Missouri we sped our way, the ride enlivened by song and story, and anon with music by the band; across the river into Kansas City, thence to Topeka for supper, where, alas for my military renown, I allowed the Grand Master to be nearly captured by Topeka Commandery before I was apprised of their proximity,— we were indeed surprised, he in his seersucker suit, I in my linen duster; how on the succeeding day we flew across the rolling plains of Kansas, making up lost time in good earnest; passing over the Raton Mountains at midnight, in order to make schedule time, which we overtook at Las Vegas Hot Springs, New Mexico, and did not lose again during the round trip; the breakfast and elegant dinner at the Montezuma Hotel; the burros riding by our most rotund Sir Knights, at the imminent risk of their feet rather than necks, and many other scenes, all pleasant to review; over the Glorietta Pass, through Apache Cañon, we rush along, and at early twilight reach Santa Fé. What you saw there you all know much better than I can tell, for I predict that the ancient city was never more completely "done" by any party than we did it, and some of you must have vivid recollections of certain incidents which occurred, especially those Sir Knights who had the temerity to ask for clean plates from which to eat their frugal meals. [*Laughter.*]

Leaving Santa Fé we are whirled onward speedily. Wallace presents us with the "bird of freedom"; Deming, Bowie, and Tucson are passed, after a good square meal at each place, and we reach Yuma for breakfast. The great American desolation is passed. The perfume of flowers, the luscious fruit, the wonderful cacti in endless variety, the cooling breeze, all announce our arrival in California, and soon we are at Los Angeles. Our reception here by our *fratres* of Cœur de Lion Commandery, their continued courtesies and hospitalities so delicately bestowed, will never be forgotten. [*Applause.*]

With regret we left "the town of the Queen of Angels," and our kind, generous-hearted hosts behind, and "on to Frisco" was the refrain warbled by our "Angelica" minstrels; through the tunnel of the San Fernando Range, across the Mojave Desert, on to the Tehachapi Pass, through the intricacies of the famous "loop," we safely wend our way, and early morning finds us entering the San Joaquin Valley. The reception of Grand Master Dean at Merced by the officers of the Grand Commandery of California, headed by Ex-Gov. George C. Perkins, Right Eminent Grand Commander, the day's ride to Oakland, our arrival there on schedule time, the escort to the Palace Hotel, the floral decoration of headquarters arranged by the ladies of San Francisco, are, I am sure, indelibly impressed on your memories.

Then came the time spent so delightfully in and around San Francisco, the rounds of duty so few, the tours of pleasure so many. The courtesies shown us by Right Eminent George C. Perkins, Grand Commander of California, and by all the officers, committees, and members of that body, the hospitalities of California, Oakland, and Golden Gate Commanderies, the many and varied attentions showered upon us by individual Sir Knights, and the delicate services of the ladies' committee so charmingly rendered whenever and wherever they could strew the flowers of welcome in our paths, were experiences so grand and captivating that the heart must be cold indeed that does not exult in great joy as we recall them. And to the generous list of fraternal courtesies we can truly add those received from State and city officials, and of the thousands of private citizens with whom we came in contact. It was difficult to determine from casual observation whether they were or were not members of the Order, so universal was our welcome from all the people of glorious, generous California. [*Applause.*] What a striking contrast exists between the management of the affairs of and incident to the Conclave of 1880 in Chicago, and the Conclave of 1883 in San Francisco! Truly and nobly have the Sir Knights of California redeemed the pledges given by them. Chivalric, generous, and true-hearted *fratres*, we left you feeling that our lives would be the better for having met you. And rest assured, Sir Knights, that the precious minerals within the borders of your State will sooner be exhausted than the golden memories of our visit to California shall be effaced. [*Cheers.*]

Our stately and orderly departure from the Palace Hotel, the magnificent escort again accorded us, the hearty expressions of good-will and wishes of "God speed you on your journey" from the Sir Knights of San Francisco, are never to be forgotten

At length we were homeward bound. After crossing the straits of Carquinez on the mammoth steamer "Solano," quiet reigned supreme. Tired and weary, the pilgrims sought their respective berths, and slept the sleep of the innocent until called on that bright Sunday morn to gaze from "Cape Horn," high up on the mountain-side, down the precipitous cliffs two thousand feet into the American River at their base. We breakfasted at Blue Cañon, on the top of the Sierras, then leisurely resumed our homeward course. Through snow-sheds we bowled along, now and then catching glimpses of deep ravines and distant mountain peaks. Lake Donner in its quiet beauty causes us to gaze down upon its still, silent bosom with admiration, then more snow-sheds, which we do not admire so much, are quickly passed. Humboldt, that oasis in the desert, furnished us with a late supper and bad dreams, which the next day's ride over the great plains of Nevada scarcely dispelled. The following evening found us at Salt Lake City, where the truly good and wise pilgrims did, as at Santa Fé and Los Angeles, remain on board their cars for sleep and rest, while the younger and more giddy ones sought "pastures green and fields anew," to their subsequent discomfort.

Morning found us on the alert. We virtually sailed the Salt Lake City over. Camp Douglas, the grave of Brigham Young, where no tears were shed by us, the Tabernacle, where the funeral of the Mormon Burt was being held, and many other points of interest were visited, and then after dining we took the "Silva" ride to the lake itself. How we disported in its saline waters, and the fun we had at each other's expense in the attempts at diving and floating, will serve to mark that visit well in our memory, and cause us to remember with gratitude the knightly courtesy of Sir Silva. [*Applause.*]

The return to our "Pullman homes," the serenade by the Opera House band, the good-byes from friends were all successively made and spoken, and almost ere the echoes had died away we were at Ogden, where the cry was *ice*, ICE, give us more ICE. [*Laughter.*] This was preparatory to plunging through the Devil's Gate, Weber and Echo Canons, whence we emerged upon the fertile plains of Wyoming Territory, over which we rode the succeeding day, thence through Nebraska, over the river at Omaha, across Iowa's grain fields, on to Chicago The elegant meals at the Grand Pacific Hotel, the rides and rambles about the city, all the more enjoyable from being allowed to "go as we pleased," free from the restraint of escort and the superintendence of officious friends, were much appreciated, so much so by a few of our Sir Knights that they concluded to join us later in Montreal, which they did.

From Chicago to Battle Creek for supper, thence to Toronto for breakfast, and the Windsor Hotel, Montreal, for a "day off," were now our destiny, and one which we accomplished in remarkably good time. At Montreal we met dear friends who had come up to greet the pilgrims. How glad we were to see them! They had watched and waited, and now, as they shook our hands, we read in their eyes how anxious they had been for our safety, and how much they had gloried in our successes. God bless true friendship. Mount Royal, Lachine Rapids, Victoria Bridge, the Cathedral of Notre Dame, various churches and convents, were duly visited the next day, and some do say that, notwithstanding they had scanned the great plains of Nevada and Wyoming with powerful field-glasses, they saw no buffalo until they found the *Beef* in Montreal. But all good things, even this speech of mine, must have an end [*Go on, go on*], and in the early evening of that beautiful fall day we left for home; uneventful the ride during the night, but with keen appetites we broke fast at Keene, N. H., on the morning of Sept. 4, and as the clock struck one on that day our train stopped in the Fitchburg Depot, Boston, whence we had departed thirty-one days before, — thirty-one days! the busiest and happiest of my life. Can the memories of that pilgrimage ever die? Eight thousand miles together, in the same cars, without sickness, accident, or cause of regret at having gone; wonderful consummation of an ambitious scheme to give prestige to old Boston Commandery, honor and glory to the Knights Templars of New England, and to cultivate fraternal feelings from farthest East to farthest West.

Our magnificent reception by De Molay Commandery, who are ever ready to do honor to Boston Commandery, the banquet, the welcome home, speeches of our hosts, the solemn service in our asylum as the longest Conclave ever held by any Commandery of Knights Templars was closed in due form, are not, nor ever will they be, effaced from memory's tablet.

With a heart full of joy and gratitude, I renew my welcome to you individually and collectively, — joy at meeting you again under so pleasant auspices, gratitude that our numbers are unbroken by death. Long may it be ere "the silver cord be loosed," "or the golden bowl be broken" by any member of our happy band of pilgrims; but when that time shall come, as come it surely must, we will mourn their loss as that of a brother or a sister, and revere and cherish their memories "till time shall be no more." And now being sated by the feast, we will spend the remainder of the evening in listening to remarks from our *fratres*, and to music from our vocalists and band; but the sweetest music which will reach my ears to-night will be that made by the merry voices of my friends and companions of the California pilgrimage of Boston Commandery, as they rehearse the pleasures of an event toward the accomplishment of which I was permitted to contribute my best endeavors. [*Great applause.*]

The Temple Quartet, which added very much to the pleasure of the evening, then sang, after which Sir Z. H. Thomas, Recorder of Boston Commandery, read the following telegram from Past Grand Master Dean: —

DETROIT, MICH., Oct. 24, 1883.

EMINENT PAST COMMANDER JOHN L. STEVENSON:

To you and the companions of our trip across the continent to the Grand Conclave, pleasant greetings. Though absent, my heart is with you. That your reunion this night will be one of joy and gladness, and that the friendships so happily begun may last with ourselves, is the sincere prayer of your Past Grand Master,

BENJAMIN DEAN.

The following letters expressing regrets were then read by the Recorder: —

BOSTON, Oct. 4, 1883.

JOHN L. STEVENSON,
Eminent Commander of Boston Commandery:

Dear Sir Knight and Brother, — I am sorry for it, but have to inform you that I cannot attend the reunion of Boston Commandery pilgrimage party on the 24th inst. Important business, which cannot be avoided, expedited, or postponed, compels my being at that time many miles from Boston.

Though far away my heart will be with you, and I trust I shall have the pleasure of many times hereafter meeting you and those whom I accompanied to San Francisco.

If we went as pilgrims we returned as palmers.

With sentiments of knightly regard,

I am yours sincerely,

BENJ. DEAN.

GRAND COMMANDERY OF KNIGHTS TEMPLARS AND APPENDANT ORDERS
OF MASSACHUSETTS AND RHODE ISLAND.
OFFICE OF THE GRAND COMMANDER,
LAWRENCE, Oct. 24, 1883.

SIR JOHN L. STEVENSON :

Eminent and dear Sir, — I regret very much that sickness in my family will prevent me from being present this evening at the reunion of the Sir Knights and ladies who participated in the pilgrimage of Boston Commandery to San Francisco.

Please present to them my hearty congratulations upon the happy termination of their pilgrimage, and my sincere wishes that this reunion, filled with so many pleasant memories, may be the forerunner of many similar occasions.

With kindest regards I remain,

Courteously yours,

CALEB SAUNDERS,
Grand Commander.

Letters expressing regret at their inability to be present were read from Sir Samuel C. Lawrence, Grand Master of Masons in

Massachusetts, and from Eminent Sir Edwin Wright, Commander of Boston Commandery.

The Past Eminent Commander then introduced Sir the Rev. Oliver A. Roberts, Prelate during the pilgrimage, who read an original poem, which was heartily received: —

LINES WRITTEN FOR THE RECEPTION OF THE CALIFORNIA PILGRIMS,

AT

HOTEL VENDOME, OCT. 24, 1883.

INTRODUCTION.

All hail! Sir Knights, again we meet,
With grateful hearts each other greet.
Remembering Him who led the way,
Kept ward and watch day after day;
And full of tender love and care,
Grants us this night this joy to share.

The pilgrimage was happy done,
With all its trials, dust, and fun.
Its joys we prize and live them o'er,
As in our eyes, from shore to shore
The mountains rise and waters pour;
The plains outspread midst sand-hills red,
And fields so green with harvests bright,
Are constant seen in memory's light.
But for the joy, and more — return,
To Him our hearts should grateful burn,
Who sees the tiny sparrows fall,
And loves alike both great and small.
To Him we offer first our praise
For kindly care those blessed days,
When journeying o'er our spacious land,
Returning safe, a thankful band.

To Boston Commandery.

Hail! eldest of the Templar clan,
Whose banners wave throughout the land.
Hail thou the chiefest star that shines
Resplendent in the Templar skies!
We hail thee chief with lin'age true,
Reaching far back when all was new,
Before the Revolution's wak'ning gun,
Or fight for liberty begun.
When Boston was a sea-girt town,
Without her present great renown.
The fields outlying then were tilled,
The hill-tops green were then unfilled
With homes and busy marts as now,
And from the gently sloping brow
Where lovers had their oft retreat,
There could be seen no ocean fleet
Steaming across the quiet bay,
Or at their anchors peaceful lay.

St. Andrew's Chapter.

Far back in seventeen sixty-nine,
Maybe before that far-off time,
In Masons' Hall St. Andrew's light
Dispelled the darkness of the night,
And brought to view the Templar rite.
It was before our fatherland
Was heavy pressed by Britain's hand,
Before the day of Concord fight,
Or death of true and valiant Knight,
When Warren fell on Bunker's height;
Before great Washington's command
Of the brave colonial band;
Before that day, in seventy-three,
When Indians made "a mess of tea";
Before Bostonians in the street
Were shot like brutes at soldiers' feet;
Before the boys to General Gage
Their cause declared and boldly waged.

It was quite near the joyous night
When Fort Hill shone with bonfire light,
When bells were rung and cannon fired,
When " Liberty Tree " was gay attired,
When Francis Bernard left this shore,
And trod on freemen's rights no more.
Those trying and eventful days,
St. Andrew's, true to knightly ways,
In Masons' Hall its Conclaves held,
Forming a brave and valiant guild.
The record says that it was here
Four steps were given to Paul Revere.
A Templar 't was who rode by night,
And gave alarm for next day's fight.
Joseph Warren, immortal name,
Deigned to honor this sacred fane.
He here was made a valiant Knight,
And died for liberty and right.

St. Andrew's Hall.

In Masons' Hall
Suppose we call!
We see the Templars meeting. —
A loyal band,
With sword in hand,
Each other knightly greeting.

We meet them there
One evening fair;
Behold their solemn faces!
The Templar forms
Their work adorns,
For well they fill their places.

The work is done,
And talk begun
Within the secret chamber.
Beyond the touch
Of Britain's clutch
They freely plan and ponder.

With ancient rigs
And stylish wigs,
All white with choicest powder,
Knee-buckles bright
And breeches tight,
They talk o'er flip and cider.

The patriots here,
Without a fear,
Have learned of Christian freedom:
Without a boast
They'll meet the host,
And gain their country's ransom.

That altar light,
So warm and bright,
Inspired these loyal leaders.
From thence arose
That band of foes
Who humbled Britain's soldiers.

REORGANIZATION, 1802–1806.

In spring-time, eighteen hundred two,
St. Andrew's Chapter gave to you
The priceless glory of her name,
Her forms, her rituals, and her fame.
Ten Knights the holy work began,
And shaped these orders for your hand.
By them foundations new were laid;
By you the final touches made;
Till Templar work with you so grand
Outvies all other in the land.
The "ten" of eighteen hundred two
Are now an army great and true.
Six hundred names the book contains!

Immortal number! brave six hundred men
Were David's guard around his desert den.
Six hundred shekels of pure gold by weight
King David gave the threshing Jebusite

For Mount Moriah's rocky summit bare,
The site whereon the wise man with great care
Built his grand temple, overlaid with gold,
Six hundred talents' worth, we 're plainly told.
Who can compute the influence wide
Upon the ceaseless, living tide
That since St. Andrew's early time
Has flowed within the Templar line ?
How many souls have been inspired?
The Templar work how oft has fired
The hearts of age with earnest youth,
And hearts of men with deathless truth ?
Rich legacy from time long passed,
Thy worth we know and firmly grasp,
Believing vigor will be thine
When pale in night the lights of time.

Templar Truth.

In all the creeds of creedful earth,
There 's nothing found of Christian worth
That in the Temple's ritual grand
Does not in simplest statement stand.
We learn of God, the Holy One,
Of Jesus Christ, his only Son,
Who taught and suffered, man to free,
Enduring death upon the tree,
Then rose triumphant from the tomb,
Forever scattering nature's gloom,
Rising with majesty sublime,
Beyond the realms of death and time.
As Templar Knights, we know the three
Called Faith and Hope and Charity :
The Faith — that 's witness of the real ;
The Hope — that 's bond of human weal ;
And chiefest of the blessed three,
We preach and practise Charity.
We seek the orphan to befriend :
With widows' needs our aid to blend.
As Templars true we 're always bound
Where'er distress by us is found

To grant relief, supply all need,
The naked clothe, the hungry feed.
For Christian truth on every field
Our plighted swords we'll fearless wield.
The holy Bible, open, bright,
Sends forth its unobstructed light,
With truth illumines all our forms,
From first to last our work adorns.

CALIFORNIA PILGRIMAGE

The phrase "Knights Templars" brings to mind
The Crusades of an earlier time,
When armies, fired with warlike zeal,
Tried in the East the strength of steel,
Till vanquished, when the sacred tomb
Was wrapt again in Arab gloom.
That warlike age has fully passed;
A knightly era dawns at last,
When Templars journey far and near,
But only *peace* — the list'ning hear.
Of all crusades of Templar host
Of which Commanderies can boast,
The grandest, greatest, and the best
Was when the "Bostons" journeyed West,
From cold Atlantic to the shore
Where golden sands their blessings pour;
Then East, across the country's dome
Were knightly welcomed in their home.
Kings travel with "the right of way";
Princes and lords, in ancient day,
Were welcomed with a princely fare,
With lordly welcome, warm and rare.
Thus kingly sped the Pullman train,
And "Welcome!" was the glad refrain
That constant fell on every ear,
From cities, towns, and hamlets near.
Princely the trip from shore to shore,
The grandest lords could ask no more.
On every hand across the land
The joyous, hearty welcomes rose;

The knightly band, with bearing grand,
Made hosts of courteous friends — not foes.
Cities arose with open hand
To greet with joy the pilgrim band ;
The villagers oft gathered near
To give the hast'ning Knights a cheer,
And Indians at dead of night
Gave their wild war-whoop as in fight.
The cow-boys, as we passed their way,
Gave their salute at break of day.
When first we crossed the mountain heights,
More welcomes came from courteous Knights.
The "angel land" its bounties spread ;
Like kings and lords the Knights were fed.
With welcome warm and balmy air,
With luscious fruits and weather fair,
With sad regrets — those not a few —
We bade the "Fairyland" adieu.
On San Francisco's wave-washed shores
The gold State opened all her stores,
With lavish hand poured out her wealth,
And drank to everybody's health.
No tribute could be more complete
Than that was laid at Boston's feet :
Ten days of joy, both full and great,
We spent within the Golden Gate.

Not less a joy, the journey East !
Arrival safe and Templar feast ;
The greeting of new friends and old,
With which, dear friends, my story's told.

After music had been rendered by the orchestra, Sir Leonard M. Averell arose, and with appropriate words, expressively uttered, addressed Past Eminent Commander Stevenson, as follows : —

Past Commander Stevenson: A pleasant duty has been laid upon me, to give utterance to the gratitude felt towards you by the Sir Knights and ladies of Boston and sister Commanderies, who formed the company of pilgrims, that, under your care, and by your wise forethought, travelled this Western Continent from sea to sea, from the granite and isle-girt shores of the Atlantic to the Golden Gate and placid waters of the Pacific, without an accident, without a disappointment, without a disagreement, in comfort, in love, in honor.

It was a pilgrimage that started from either coast at the very tick of time, and reached the opposite shore precisely as the pendulum swung the moment of scheduled arrival; a pilgrimage that for magnitude, for outlay, for miles of travel, for extent of days, for variety and grandeur of scenery, for honorable duty and grateful pleasure, for manifestation of knightly honor and courteous forbearance, has no rival in modern times; across the territory of the mightiest republic of the world; over the avenues and along the fields of the greatest kingdom of earth; from the Athens of intellect and culture, over the lofty Sierras of the West, on the buoyant waters of the Mormon Sea, through the garden of the angels, to and from the Corinth of luxurious life and enterprise.

As in the pilgrimage of old, so we were conducted through gay and strange cities, received the tribute of popular praise; princely favors were showered upon us, and we seemed to have become the cynosure of ladies' eyes; even the loving and fearless bird of American liberty met us at Wallace, perched upon our beauseant banner, and continued to the end of the journey.

Our transit was as various and as replete with stirring and romantic interest as if it had been a pilgrimage from Paris or Marseilles to the ancient city of Acre; or from Rouen or Strasburg to Tyre and even Jerusalem itself. The harems of polygamy were as conspicuous at Salt Lake as ever they existed at Constantinople; more than the waters of the mighty Danube rolled in Mississippi's tides; Judæa's hills were eclipsed by the lofty peaks and solemn canons of Colorado and New Mexico; and I may suggest that the memory of loves lost and left at the gates of the city of St. Francis are more and dearer to these pilgrims than the dead bones of the Holy Sepulchre.

Of one of the pilgrimages of old, the secretary of Saladin declares that he saw the mountain and the plain, the hills and the valley, covered with the dead Sir Knights; he saw their fallen and deserted banners soiled with dust and blood; he saw their famous warriors, gifted with amazing strength, who had just now walked forth amongst the mighty, standing naked with downcast eyes, their proud bearing gone, wretched and miserable. The cities through which they had passed, Sidon, Sapphara, Nazareth, Cæsarea, Jaffa, and Kanah, had all fallen into the hands of their enemies.

How wide, how striking, the contrast from the pilgrimage made under your command! Not only has every brave Knight returned alive, but with strength renewed, with eyes more lustrous, with heart more strong for duty. Nay, even the fair and delicate ladies of our Sir Knights have come back with added bloom and beauty, and some of them with a new-born love, that makes self-sacrifice a joy and benediction.

The banners of the Commandery, planted with rejoicing on the highest peaks of the continent, and borne with pride and triumph through encircling hosts of friends and strangers, are returned without a soil, and, instead of cities lost to the prowess of the enemy, we have gained the honors of civil and knightly applause from Montreal, Wallace, Kansas City, Las Vegas, Santa Fé, Merced, Battle Creek, Los Angeles, and San Francisco.

From the old pilgrimages Commanderies returned to receive the congratulations of their companions and largess of gifts from admiring friends. Companions and friends, animated with like gratitude and desirious to make immortal the happy memories of the pilgrimage over which you have presided, have instructed me to present, as a memorial of their love and respect to you personally, this keeper of the hours and warder of the pilgrimage of life; may the ticking of its swinging pendulum bring to you, through a long and happy life, many pleasant remembrances of this pilgrimage of 1883, and of the Knights and ladies who therein were your companions and friends. For you do know, sir, that

> It is good to feel ourselves beloved of men,
>   To know that all our anxious cares and sighs
> For others' weal are given not in vain,
>   But treasured up in grateful memories;
> How light the toil for those we fondly love,
> How rich the wages grateful spirits prove!

> But when those men are brothers strongly bound
>   By bond indissoluble, sweet and true,
> When gratitude springs out of sacred ground,
>   And prayers are mingled with praises due,
> Ah then, toil is no burden, girts no load,
> We have full recompense for what's bestowed.
>
> 'T is thus with you, my friend, the voice of all
>   Yields willing tribute to your high deserts,
> But from the Craft there comes a stronger call;
>   From that great brotherhood whose chain begirts
> The broad world round, the grateful wages come
> Whose price is honor and whose favor bloom.
>
> Long may you live in bloom and honor, long
>   To show the Christian in the Mason's guise;
> In strength omnipotent may you be strong,
>   In wisdom heavenly may you be wise,
> And when to death's dark portals you shall come,
> May Jesus banish all the fear and gloom.

The address was very cordially received by the assembly. At its conclusion, Sir Henry L. Batchelder arose near the centre of the dining-room and called for three cheers for Past Eminent Commander Stevenson, which were heartily given. The clock of black marble and bronze represents the Parthenon restored, at the base of which, in front, there is the following inscription: —

Presented to Sir John L. Stevenson, Eminent Commander of Boston Commandery Knights Templars, by the Sir Knights under his command during the pilgrimage to San Francisco, Aug. 4 to Sept. 4, 1883.

The companion side statuettes, on pedestals of black marble, represent Jupiter and Neptune, bearing the insignia of their power. The whole was imported by Shreve, Crump & Low, Boston, and cost over three hundred dollars.

Eminent Sir Stevenson replied to the presentation address as follows: —

Sir Knight Averell and Pilgrim Friends: For once in my life, at least, I am at a loss for words with which to fittingly respond to your complimentary and eloquent address in presenting me with this elegant testimonial of your friendship and esteem. If my rebellious lips and faltering tongue would only obey the promptings of my throbbing heart, they would tell you in words of love and pride how dearly I shall prize this gift, coming as it does from you who shared with me the honors, pleasures, and duties of the already historic pilgrimage of Boston Commandery to California. I accept it with sincere thanks, and will ever preserve and cherish it as a souvenir of our mutual and fraternal love, and as expressing your satisfaction with my administration during the brief time I had the honor to be your Commander.

You have been pleased, Sir Knight, to credit me with the honor of originating, organizing, and executing this pilgrimage. I believe to a very large degree you are correct, and yet had it not been for the great assistance rendered me by a few determined Knights and personal friends, the banner of Boston Commandery would not this year have been saluted on the golden shores of the Pacific; and to those faithful few I tender my profound acknowledgments for the faith they had in me and my ability to carry out my favorite scheme of placing our beloved old Commandery on record as making the grandest pilgrimage ever undertaken in America. [*Applause.*]

For two and one half years was I chairman of a committee or committees engaged in forwarding the object which was at last accomplished with such apparent ease and comfort, and during that time I think I am correct in saying there was hardly one associated with me but who sooner or later became discouraged over the sometimes dismal prospects of success and the immensity of the undertaking. For once it might be said the *sword* was mightier than the *pen*, if by *sword* you will recognize the Commander; for the last two or three days, preceding our departure, found our faithful Recorder "used up" by continued and exhaustive application to work in furtherance of our plans, and yet, although weak in body, he never once faltered in his faith of ultimate success. So at last, standing all alone in my office, committee tired out, Recorder exhausted, I issued final instructions for the departure. These being promulgated, the conception and organization were completed, and every detail had received personal attention; every meal ordered and transportation provided from the Atlantic to the Pacific, and from the Golden Gate to the old Bay State again. How faithfully the plans laid out by the committee were executed by me I leave it for you to judge; but permit me here to say that experience had long since taught me that success is more likely to follow him who dares to lead than him who is led, and acting in that belief, I assumed largely the responsibilities attending the movements and comforts of the excursion myself. This brief explanation I make to exonerate myself from any suspicion of self-aggrandizement, and for the accuracy of my position I point you to the grand results. [*Applause.*]

And thus success, smiling on persistence, perched on our banner and rode triumphantly from ocean to ocean. I endeavored in every instance, prior to our departure as well as during the pilgrimage, to discharge the duties of executive officer with justice and impartiality, and the only reward I desired or expected was the approval and commendations of my companions. These I did fondly hope to win. How well I have succeeded in so doing your kind words of praise, uttered authoritatively for those composing the pilgrimage, should suffice the most exalted ambition. And now you add to that which I most highly prized, this valuable work of art. Yet I assure you, Sir Averell and pilgrim friends, that, as wonderful as is its mechanism, and as beautiful as is its design and execution, I will ever assert that the highest prize I won during the California pilgrimage was the love, esteem, and respect of the Sir Knights and ladies who participated therein. [*Continued applause.*]

Another selection by the Temple Quartet followed; after which Sir Knight V. M. C. Silva, of Ogden, Utah, was introduced by the Past Eminent Commander with grateful words to him for the good time of the Boston Sir Knights in Salt Lake City, and Sir Knight Silva made an eloquent response, which was very cordially received.

Another episode then occurred, when Eminent Sir Stevenson, in token of his personal appreciation of, and gratitude for the efficient services of the Recorder of Boston Commandery, Sir Z. H. Thomas, presented him a badge of Boston Commandery, made of gold and set with brilliants. Sir Knight Thomas was completely surprised. He could find no words. The orchestra, thinking it was their turn to have something to do or say, struck up "We won't go Home till Morning," very much to the amusement of the party. Sir Thomas meanwhile gathered his scattered forces and expressed his grateful thanks. He alluded to the many months that the Eminent Commander and himself had been intimately associated in the preparation of the pilgrimage; that no unkind word had passed between them during the time, and he was glad that he had been able to be of any service in the furtherance of the pilgrimage and in supporting the Eminent Commander.

After musical selections, on motion of Sir Knight Charles F. Atwood, it was unanimously voted that those of the committee on the California pilgrimage who went on the trip be constituted a committee, with full powers, to arrange a reunion at such time and place as they may select.

The Past Eminent Commander then called on Rev. Oliver A. Roberts, who made a short speech, complimenting the committee, Recorder, and Eminent Commander for their zeal, self-sacrifice, and perseverance in conceiving, planning, and executing this memorable pilgrimage. The applause which greeted his words was evidence that the pilgrims realized their obligations to these efficient officers.

Sir Knight Hewitt, of Worcester, who had been presented by the occupants of car "Modena" with a Templar badge in gold, representing a banner, was called for, and responded with a recitation. This, with vocal and instrumental music, concluded the exercises in the banquet-hall, after which the party retired to the spacious parlors and congratulated each other on the success, happiness, and sociability attending the first reception by the California pilgrims.

In the parlors of the Vendôme there was displayed an elegant banner, thirty-eight by forty-eight inches, the property of Sir Knight Wilbur F. Miller, of Springfield, who was chorister of the pilgrim party. In the centre of the banner there is a red cross, on which are painted the words, "San Francisco, August, 1883." Surrounding the cross are tastefully arranged one hundred and eight badges of the different Commanderies represented at the Triennial Conclave in San Francisco. Before separating, the occupants of the car "Echo" were called into room No. 161, where Sir Edwin Winsor presented Sir Abijah Thompson, who had charge of that car during the trip, with a beautiful bronze statuette.

FINIS CORONAT OPUS.

I.

"The end crowns all," and writes its doom
On starry skies and summer's bloom.
To seasons all, to year, month, day,
To wondrous works and children's play,
To little things, as tiny leaves,
To great events the wide world grieves,
To all on earth, to low and high,
Comes one sure end, for all things die.

II.

As days flew by, the pilgrim band,
Rejoicing in our glorious land,
O'erwhelmed with pleasures day by day,
Delighted with receptions gay,
Well knew the law to which all bend,
"Sooner or later comes the end."

III.

"The end crowns all." From start to goal,
From first to last, as time has rolled,
This task has prophesied a time
When we would reach its final line.
Hence here, the story of our tour,
Like every swift and mortal hour,
Comes to its end, with one short prayer:
When "pilgrims" end their earthly days,
May endless life call forth their praise.

www.ingramcontent.com/pod-product-compliance
Lightning Source LLC
Chambersburg PA
CBHW050847300426
44111CB00010B/1155